Chas Hocks

H. Sing.   Newberry Velan
37/12   Lithown

                        Jany/63.

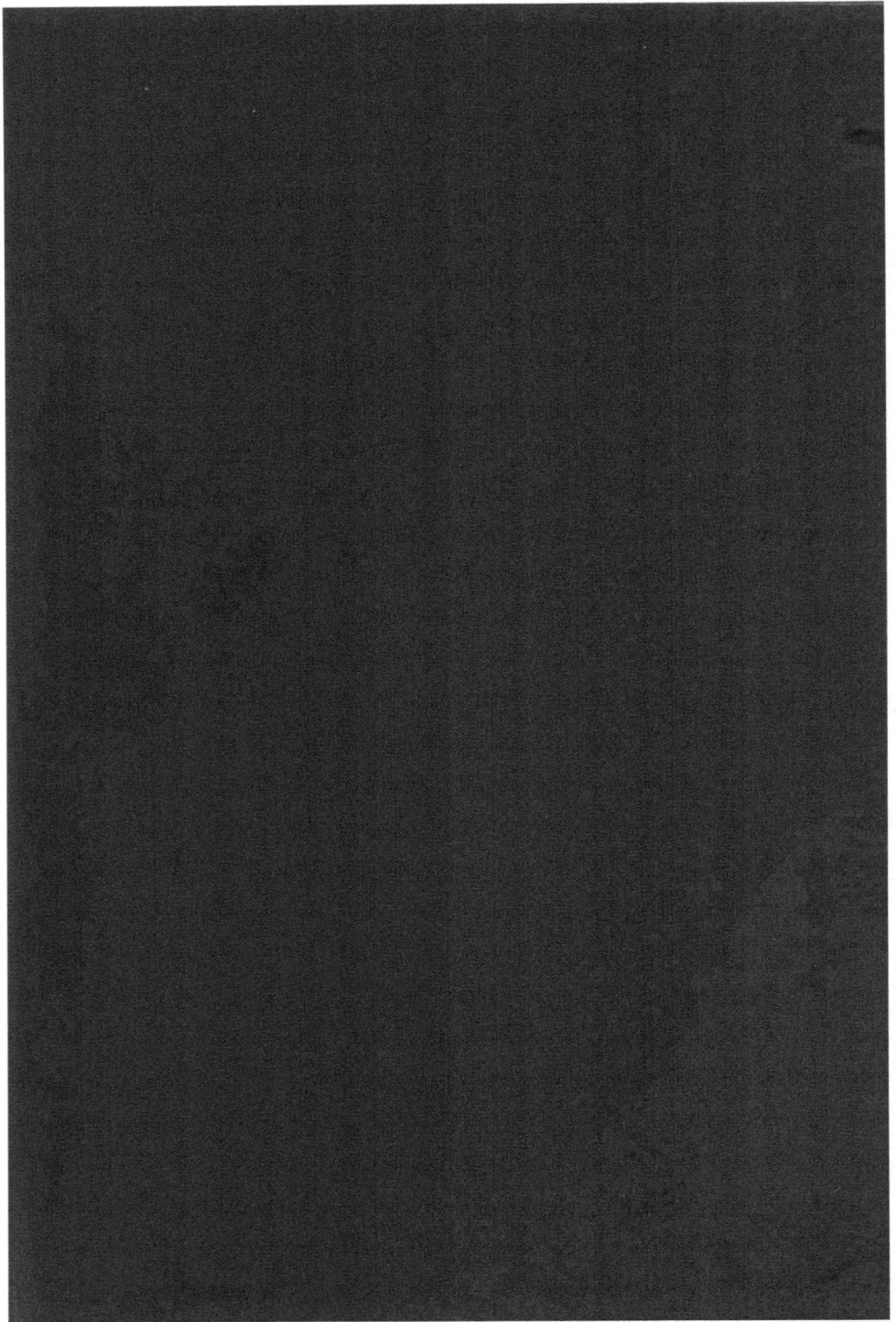

4.º

First Ed

c K

AFRICAN HUNTING

LONDON
PRINTED BY SPOTTISWOODE AND CO.
NEW-STREET SQUARE

AFRICAN HUNTING

FROM NATAL TO THE ZAMBESI

INCLUDING

LAKE NGAMI, THE KALAHARI DESERT, &c.

FROM 1852 TO 1860

BY

WILLIAM CHARLES BALDWIN, Esq., F.R.G.S.

With Illustrations by James Wolf and J. B. Zwecker

LONDON
RICHARD BENTLEY, NEW BURLINGTON STREET
Publisher in Ordinary to Her Majesty
1863

TO MY BROTHER,

THE REV. T. RIGBYE BALDWIN, M.A.

WHOSE GREAT INTEREST IN MY WANDERINGS

WAS THE SOLE INDUCEMENT THAT LED ME TO TAKE NOTES,

THESE ANECDOTES OF HUNTING ADVENTURES

ARE AFFECTIONATELY DEDICATED BY

THE AUTHOR.

CONTENTS

---•◦•---

CHAPTER I.

1852.

EARLY LIFE — LAND IN NATAL — FIRST HUNTING EXPEDITION TO ST. LUCIA BAY 1

CHAPTER II.

1853.

HUNTING EXPEDITION INTO THE ZULU COUNTRY . . . 29

CHAPTER III.

1854.

HUNTING EXPEDITION INTO THE AMATONGA COUNTRY . . 50

CHAPTER IV.

1855.

A HUNTING TRIP INTO THE ZULU COUNTRY 95

CHAPTER V.

1856.

THIRD HUNTING TRIP INTO THE ZULU COUNTRY . . . 112

CHAPTER VI.

1857.

PAGE

THE TRANSVAAL REPUBLIC,— MERICO COUNTRY — THE MACCA-
TEESE, OR BECHUANAS — SECHELE — THE MASARAS — THE BOERS
— MOSILIKATSE 142

CHAPTER VII.

1858.

MACHIN — I AM DESERTED — FIRST VISIT TO LAKE NGAMI —
LECHULATEBE — SECHELE'S DAUGHTER — THE BUSH ON FIRE
— MERICO 231

CHAPTER VIII.

1859.

SICOMO'S — MASARAS — LAKE NGAMI — LOPEPE — RETURN BY VAAL
RIVER — ANECDOTES OF CROSSING THE TUGELA . . . 304

CHAPTER IX.

1860.

RESULT OF A ZEBRA HUNT — REACH MERICO — VISIT SECHELE
— ELEPHANT HUNT — THE BATOKAS — THE ZAMBESI FALLS —
MEET WITH DR. LIVINGSTONE — INTENSE HEAT — ADVENTURE
WITH A LION — AM JOINED BY ENGLISH TRAVELLERS — ACCI-
DENT TO ENGLISHMEN — RETURN TO NATAL 364

LIST OF ILLUSTRATIONS.

———•◦•———

		PAGE
1. An Alligator disappointed	. . . .	10
2. A Boat attacked by Hippopotamus	. . .	19
3. Asleep in a River	. . . . .	27
4. A forced Return	. . . . *To face*	39
5. Knocked from a Hut by a Lioness	. . .	47
6. Shot a Hippopotamus	. . . .	89
7. The Waggon and Oxen race down Hill	. .	97
8. Dead Alligator dragged into Water by Comrades	.	101
9. Shot Rhinoceros — Calf and Dogs fighting	. .	107
10. Inyala, Dogs, and Hyenas	. . . *To face*	118
11. Two Lionesses roaring at me	. . .	119
12. Hide-and-Seek with Buffalo	. . .	123
13. Stalking Koodoos	. . . . .	129
14. Leaped by a Buffalo	. . . *To face*	139
15. A cold Encampment	. . . .	157
16. Giraffe Hunted and Shot	. . . .	172
17. Black Rhinoceros tossing Dog	. . .	196
18. Return to Camp by Moonlight	. . .	197
19. Hunting Baboons	. . . .	209
20. Chased up and down Hill by Elephant	. .	213
21. My Beard admired by Natives	. . .	218
22. Killing Snakes	. . . .	222
23. Giraffe Hunt — Herd of Buffaloes chasing	. . *To face*	223
24. A Giraffe in a Tree	. . . .	242
25. Deserted and alone by Fire	. . .	251
26. Shot Oryx — Dogs wounded	. . .	256
27. Native chased by Buffalo Cow and Calf	. .	258

			PAGE
28.	Elephant chases me	To face	262
29.	Dining with Kaffir Chief . . .	„	266
30.	Travel by Moonlight . . .	.	285
31.	Forest on Fire	.	297
32.	Hyena chased by Torchlight . . .	.	351
33.	Crossing the Tugela — A Ducking . . .	.	358
34.	Zebra Hunt — Fall with Horse . . .	.	365
35.	Chase of three Elands . . .	To face	376
36.	Shot a Gemsbok before Horse's Feet . .	„	383
37.	Horseback — Pass by savage Elephant . .	.	386
38.	Chased by infuriated Buffalo . . .	To face	404
39.	Chase of Ostrich	„	420
40.	Lion Shot	.	442

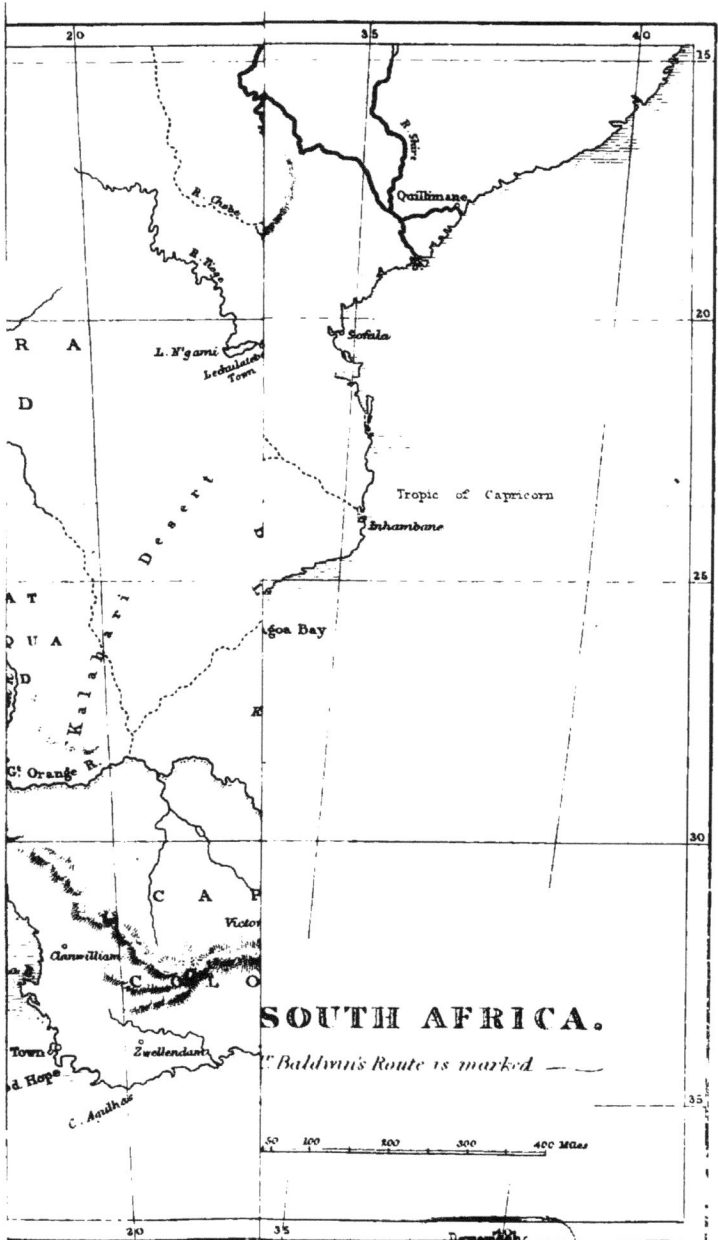

SOUTH AFRICA.

Baldwin's Route is marked — — —

Quillimane

R. Shire

R. Chobe

R. Teoge

R. Ngani

Sofala

L. N'gami

Ledulatebe
Town

Tropic of Capricorn

Inhambane

K a l a h a r i   D e s e r t

R A

D

A T

Q U A

D

G! Orange R.

goa Bay

C   A   P

Victor

Clanwilliam

C   O   L   O

Town of

d Hope

Zwellendam

C. Aguthas

50   100   200   300   400 Miles

AFRICAN HUNTING

FROM NATAL TO THE ZAMBESI.

CHAPTER I.

1852.

EARLY LIFE — LAND IN NATAL — FIRST HUNTING EXPEDITION
TO ST. LUCIA BAY.

WHEN the following pages taken from my journals were written, sometimes in ink, but often in pencil, gunpowder, tea, &c., in Kaffir kraals or wagon bottoms, and chiefly for a brother's eye, I little thought that they would ever come before the public ; and it is only now, at the earnest solicitations of my friends— and almost promises made to many I left behind me in Natal, who noticed the once short trips grow longer and longer, till, in my last, 2,000 miles of an almost unexplored country had been traversed and the Zambesi reached — that I am now induced, with some diffidence, to publish them.

Conscious that in going ten years back I am necessarily travelling over ground already pre-occupied

B

by other sportsmen and travellers, and that the
hospitality of my friends in England, and days with
the Quorn and Mr. Tailby's, combined with my
natural aversion to any set task, have ill fitted me to
redeem the monotony inseparable from a journal, or
the apparent egotism in that of the lonely traveller, I
nevertheless appear before the public, with the hope
that if again I should return to the land of my adop-
tion, beginning my travels where I have now left off,
I may hereafter produce something better worth their
perusal.

I feel that I owe a few words of explanation to
my many friends in Africa as to the reasons why
I went there at all, with a page of my earlier life
which may perhaps be omitted by the general
reader.   The love of sport, dogs, and horses was
innate in me.   From the age of six I had my two
days a week on my pony with the neighbouring
harriers; until, one unfortunate day, an extra achieve-
ment, as I considered it, brought a kindly and well-
meant caution to my father from the worthy squire,
which had the effect of sending me off to school.
There I got on, I suppose, much as others, and on
leaving it, being of a roving turn of mind, I was
placed in the large merchant's office of an ex-M.P.,
with a view of being fitted for going abroad.   No
doubt I did my best (though, to say truth, my boats
and bull-terriers, with our beagles and meetings,
somewhat militated against the duties and discipline
of the office), till at last, upon comparing notes with

the junior partner, we arrived at the same conclusion, viz., that quill-driving was not my particular vocation, nor a three-legged stool the exact amount of range to which I was willing to restrict myself through the sunniest part of life. So I went into Forfarshire to learn farming — very pleasant, but ending in what our transatlantic friends term a difficulty with the master. I changed my location to a West Highland farm, where on thirteen miles square of mountain, flood, moor, and lakes, some two acres of arable land, and two whiskey stills, the fond parent no doubt imagined that his hard-worked son was being duly initiated into all the science and mysteries of light Scotch farming. Be that as it may, what with the game, fish, and vermin, my dogs and the round of trysts with old L——, than whom a better-hearted fellow never ' took his morning,' I was what might be called master of the situation. I look upon those years as among the happiest of my life. But time wore on, and having no earthly prospect of the command of anything like a moor or a stud in the old country, I cast about me for some land of greater liberty (at least of foot), and had engaged a fine young Scotchman to go with me ; but while debating whether Canada or the western prairies of America was to be my destination, two intimate friends, the sons of a neighbouring gentleman, who were going to Natal, advised that colony ; and Gordon Cumming's book, which appeared at that moment, and as I thought in the very nick of time, settled me at once. My preparations were soon made; my little all consisting chiefly of guns, rifles, saddles, 'et id genus omne.' Perhaps the only expensive, and as it proved useless, part of my outfit, was seven deerhounds, purchased from a keeper of Lord Fitzwilliam's, for though Hotspur and Laddie were as good dogs as were ever slipped, they soon grew useless and died. The younger ones, being better acclimatised, did me some good service for a time, but they, too, soon succumbed to the climate, and taught me never again to take out what the country itself can furnish better.

I landed in Natal, December 1851, after a ninety-two days' passage. I was most anxious to be introduced to 'Elephant White,' as he was called, a great hunter; but whether he earned that title from his own elephantine proportions, six feet four inches, or from his prowess with the animal from which he derived his name, I have yet to learn. I believe he had been very successful formerly when elephants were more plentiful, but he had grown idle, and left the hard work to younger hands. This Mr. White was making preparations for a start into the Zulu country, hence my anxiety for an introduction. No such a thing, however, was needed in the Colony as it then was, and my dogs proved sufficient introduction to a brother sportsman. I made, I believe, some ridiculous offer, and joined the party; and such was my keenness for

the sport, that I verily jumped at the proposal to
sleep under one of the wagons, both of which were
crammed full up to the very tent, and one topped
up with a boat, keel uppermost. But I would then
rather have slept in six inches of water than not
have gone at all. This trip consisted chiefly in the
slaughter of sea-cows (as the hippopotamus is
here called), which abounded in St. Lucia Bay, in
the unhealthy season, just as if that God-forgotten
land, as I have sometimes almost thought it, did
not present sufficient drawbacks in itself, or hardships enough to encounter in everyday occurrences,
without seeking out death. But so it was, and if
older heads had only been placed upon the shoulders
of the enterprising and the young, I might not
have had to tell how out of nine hunters who
went out full of vigour and hope, in all the ardour
of enterprise, Gibson and myself alone returned,
enervated and prostrate after months of insensibility
in Kaffir kraals. I would gladly forget, and must
pass by, some of the details of that trip.

Within three weeks from my landing we started—
three wagons, seven white men, and lots of Kaffirs.
The powder ordinances being very strict in those
days, every wagon searched, and none allowed to
leave town or cross the Tugela with more than
ten pounds of powder, we each of us shouldered
our weapon and carried ten pounds of powder on
our backs, done up in a sort of knapsack fashion,
till we had crossed the Tugela, the boundary of

the Colony, seventy miles distant, when we pitched all into the wagons. Near the Umvoti, forty miles from Durban, we each hired a Kaffir to attend upon us individually, it being strictly prohibited to order another man's Kaffir to do anything for you, as they have a great objection to wait on any but their own master, whom they generally attend faithfully, honestly, and willingly. When they understand your wishes, they are most obliging; but most of the rows between black and white originate from their misunderstanding what you wish them to do. Two more white men joined us across the Tugela, Monies, a Scotchman, a capital and experienced hunter, but rash and daring to foolhardiness, and Price, as nice and gentlemanly a man as ever lived, and who was, I believe, a son of Sir Charles Price, the London banker. They both died, poor fellows, of fever, together with two others of the party, M'Queen and Arbuthnot (the latter a fellow-passenger), within two months of our start. We got on very slowly, no one being in any hurry apparently, and as it was the rainy season, the rivers detained us, and the tracks were very heavy. My occupation, and indeed that of all, except the three wagon-drivers, was to shoot game — bucks, ducks, peaus, or anything we could get for the party, and I soon got into White's good graces by my success and perseverance. It was the very thing of all others I had been longing for, and in those days I worked like a horse, and the older hands were very glad to be saved the trouble. Reitbucks were very plentiful, duikers, and farther on, steinbucks; and I could imagine no greater enjoyment than in shooting them, till every bone in my body ached again with sleeping on the wet ground. We had more or less wet every day, and frequently cold soaking rain all night. We tried to make ourselves more comfortable by fencing on the weatherside and cutting a deep trench round between the wheels, as the water came in more from underneath than above, but on wet nights, do what we would, we generally found ourselves in a pool of water in the morning — a lot of Kaffirs at our feet curled up like dormice in their blankets, and generally sleeping through everything, and a host of wet and dirty, muddy, shivering, dreaming dogs on the top of us. The grass, which grew to a tremendous height, was so saturated, that one might just as well walk through a river, so there was no use in putting on dry clothes in the morning. Three were snugly housed in the wagons, and six of us had this fun to endure. Occasionally some of us tried the boat-wagon, but we found it like a cage I have heard of, made by one skilled in the refinement of cruelty, in which there was no possibility of either sitting, standing, or lying; and eventually, I believe, we all gave that up as being, though dry, infinitely worse, for a continuance, than any amount of rain.

On the 7th of January (1852) one of the party killed a sea-cow calf—very good food, tasting something like veal; and I lost myself out buck-shooting on the plains of the Inyesan, but eventually found my way back in the dark, guided by signal-guns fired from the wagons, the plan we always adopted when any of our party were missing after sunset.

On the 12th, while treking leisurely along early, our whole party were put into a great flurry and excitement by seeing a large bull elephant cross some 400 yards ahead, quite unconscious of any danger. We were in so great a hurry unstrapping our guns from the sides of the wagons, that all of us, except White, forgot to take our bandoliers and more bullets. Four of us went on foot after the elephant as hard as we could run. As he was going up wind on the open, he did not hear us till we were within twenty yards, when White shouted, and he immediately turned half round; snap went White's gun; Arbuthnot and myself shot him behind the shoulder, and Ellis also, with a little twaddling weapon fifty to the pound. White meantime capped again, and, just as the elephant appeared hesitating whether to charge or not, gave him a good shot in the middle of the shoulder-blade. With a terrific scream the elephant turned and went off at a great pace, evidently crippled by the last shot. Eventually Ellis, myself, and Fly brought him to bay in some reeds three miles on, and the former, taking advantage of a commanding rock, on the top of which we were comparatively safe, gave him no less than nineteen bullets out of his pea-shooter (most of which we afterwards extracted from the elephant's ear) ere White, whose wind was long since exhausted, at length got up and settled him with the fourth ball. Seeing the spoor of a large troop gone ahead (this old chap bringing up the rear proving that delays are dangerous), we broiled a rasher on the spot for breakfast, hard and tough as a halter, and away on the spoor some nine or ten miles, sending word to the wagons to outspan, and for a relay of powder and bullets; but we never came up with them, and supposed they had taken alarm at hearing the shooting. Got back tired, at night, to a supper of elephant's heart, very tender and good ; and breakfasted on the foot baked in a large hole, very glutinous and not unlike brawn.

14th. —Went out duck-shooting at the mouth of the Umlilas ; it being high tide, the wagons were obliged to wait some hours to cross. Had capital sport ; heaps of wildfowl of all varieties, and very tame, and eventually bagged as many as I could hang round my waist-belt. As the sun was going down, and I saw the wagons ascending the opposite hills, having crossed at the drift some miles higher up, I endeavoured to cross opposite where I then was, though I had previously seen many crocodiles in the river. I got more than two thirds across, and was on a kind of island not deeper than my knees, and before me the stream ran deep and fast, about thirty yards wide. I had my gun and ammunition,

all the ducks, and a heavy pair of shooting-boots,
though the rest of my attire was light enough,
consisting only of shirt and gaiters. Still I thought
I could manage it, and pushed slowly off, making
very short strokes with my arms for fear of losing

my gun, as it was laid across just under my chin,
and I think I might have succeeded, had I not just
at that moment seen the head of a huge crocodile,
above stream, sailing down upon me, leaving a
wake like a steamer behind him. I need hardly
say I struck out legs and arms for my life, utterly
unmindful of my gun, and in a few vigorous strokes
made the opposite bank, breathless and frightened,

with the loss of my gun. The following morning
Arbuthnot, Monies, Ellis, and myself went to try and
recover it, and dived alternately, one firing shots
from the shore, meanwhile, to scare the crocodiles.
As the gun was a very valuable one, before relin-
quishing the search, we made a capital drag, cut
out of the bush like a huge rake, but all to no
purpose, and I was obliged to put up with the
loss.

18th.— The wagons separated, two going to the
King's trading, and the other with five white men
going to St. Lucia Bay sea-cow shooting. Outspanned
at the Inseline (a small river), nearly devoured by
mosquitoes.

I was here initiated in the art of trading with the
natives, and bought an ox for four picks or hoes
which the Kaffirs use for breaking up land·to sow
mealies, and which are worth in the colony 1s. 6d.
each. Reached the Black Umveloose, where we left
the wagon in charge of a Kaffir chief, and sent the
oxen some twenty miles back, the country farther
ahead being very unhealthy for cattle, and indeed,
for human beings too, only we did not know it at
the time. Got out the boat, which was the inno-
cent cause of many a miserable soaking night to
myself and others. The mosquitoes were so dreadful on the river banks, that we lighted cow-dung
fires in every pot we had, and put them inside
the now empty wagon, and all turned into it, and
had the choice of two evils — to be worried by

the mosquitoes, or almost stifled with heat and smoke in the wagon. I believe we all preferred the latter, and, as sleep was altogether out of the question, the general wish of all the party was for daylight, when the mosquitoes vanish. White-leaded and varnished the boat and made a sail, and tried a lot of iron bullets I brought out with me ; however, they did not answer at all, and I eventually threw them all away, as they were much too light and flew high, though they penetrated to a great depth.

24th.— Launched the first boat ever seen in the Black Umvcloose, and tried sleeping in a Kaffir hut, but I believe it was out of the frying-pan into the fire ; heat and mosquitoes intolerable, sour milk and Kaffir beer our fare, without meat of any kind.

25th. — Tried a bath, to refresh us ; three went in with a plunge, keeping, however, close to the bank, whilst the two on shore shouted, threw in big stones, and fired a shot or two to scare the crocodiles. Though numerous, they are very timid, and I don't think there is much cause for fear when the above precautions are taken ; but although the bath refreshed us, none of us could be said to thoroughly enjoy it.

26th.— Having drawn lots who was to accompany Monies in the boat, he put the walkers across the river, on account of its height, and then returned and packed the boat with Gibson, to whose lot it fell to accompany him. Arbuthnot, Price, and myself walked across country with our Kaffirs and a guide some twenty-five miles, where we stayed for the night, and having forgotten to bring any beads or brass wire, I had to tear up my silk pocket handkerchief into lengths about two inches wide, with which the Kaffirs ornament their heads by making a sort of band across the forehead fastened behind, to buy amas, beer, and amobella meal to make porridge. Arrived at our destination about 2 P.M. the following day, and Monies and Gibson turned up about 8 the same evening, having left the boat some twenty miles back, not being able to get on any farther in consequence of the crocodiles having broken the paddles and oars. In drifting fast down the middle of the river, Monies saw an elephant in the reeds, pulled in and shot her dead within fifteen yards, between the ear and the eye, and having axes, they cut out her tusks and her ear and put them in the boat; and continued their journey. The smell of blood most probably made the crocodiles so savage, and although Monies shot five of them, and three sea-cows, they eventually gained the victory, leaving him nothing but the handle of an oar to scull the boat ashore. They put all their belongings on a sandbank and turned the boat over them keel uppermost, and there left her, to make for more inviting quarters.

Went to the bush, and Price, Monies, and Arbuthnot being very handy fellows, made sculls and oars, and started with eight Kaffirs to carry the goods. On the 29th they found all as Monies had left them, and started again on the 30th for St. Lucia Bay. They pulled above twenty miles through a fine country; lots of sea-cows, and wildfowl of every description; and about midday were forced to go ashore, as the wind and sea were so dead ahead that they found they could make no way, and the boat was at times half full of water, so they about sl,ip and ran before the wind, much to their delight, living on geese and water melons (capital things on a hot day); spent a very comfortable night before the fires, without any blankets; and reached their destination at 12 next day, having shot two sea-cows on their way up.

I had employed my time by going out with the Kaffirs. I did not understand a word of their language, but by their signs I came to the conclusion that I was to remain by a small thorn tree, near a corner of the lake full of reeds. Gibson accompanied me. The Kaffirs all left us, and I fell asleep, to be suddenly awaked by Gibson in a great state of alarm bolting up the hill, and calling loudly to me to follow. As soon as my eyes were open, I saw a huge buffalo bull charging right down the hill towards me, pursued by all the Kaffirs. He came at a headlong pace within twenty yards before seeing me, when he hesitated an instant, dashed into the reeds and came broadside past me, within twenty-five yards, at a brisk trot, knee-deep in water, making it fly all over him in a shower of crystal. I fired, and luckily, for it was a bad shot, broke his spine, and down he fell bellowing like a bull-calf; the Kaffirs rushed in pell-mell and drove twenty assegais into him, and finished him, complimenting me, I suppose, much on my prowess, though little credit was due to me, as I must confess to having felt very much alarmed at the suddenness of the whole thing, not having known in the least what I was placed there for.

31*st.*—Off an hour and a half before sunrise to Monies's sea-cows, which had been towed ashore, and on emerging quietly through the bush, and tall, rank, soaking grass, to an open place, I saw some nine or ten crocodiles high and dry, gorged with sea-cow, and fast asleep. One enormous brute, twenty feet long at least, I wanted to shoot, but Monies would not allow it, as he hoped to get more sea-cows, and he feared a shot would frighten them and spoil our chances. I was not half satisfied, and said, ' Well, anyhow let me have the satisfaction of giving him a kick in the ribs ' (I was shod with heavy English shooting-boots) ' by way of a memento,' and was just in the act of raising my foot for the purpose when Monies suddenly drew me forcibly back, saying, ' You fool, he 'll crack your legs off like pipe-stumps with his tail ; ' and that instant he woke up, and I had Monies to thank for saving me a broken bone at least, for I never saw anything like the whirl he gave his tail as he dashed into the water some fifteen yards ahead, and almost immediately floated like a log on the top of the water, taking a cool survey of his morning visitors. Shot my first sea-cow, and we made a lot of sjamboks and whips from his hide,

such as are commonly used in Africa for driving
oxen.   They are very tough and supple when properly dressed and brayed, and punish tremendously.
The sjambok is the threat which the Dutchman invariably holds out to a refractory Kaffir.   We saw a
most amusing chase of a broken-winged golden-goose
by three crocodiles.   He fell pinioned on the water,
and these fellows immediately gave chase, going very
fast, and leaving a wake like a ship behind them.
When very hard pressed the goose dived, to be worse
off than ever, and came up 'quack, quack,' from
abject fear; he managed to flap a bit along the top
of the water and get a start, but they came up with
him again, and he at last took the land.   We were
in a boat watching the fun.   The crocodiles did not
follow him, and the poor thing eventually allowed
me to catch him on land sooner than face his enemies
in the water again.

The sea-cow bacon would not keep, owing to the
damp weather, and we had many hardships to
endure from the incessant rain.   At last, we made
what is called a hartebeest house, of very tall reeds,
stuck close together in a kind of trench dug for
them in bundles, and meeting over head, and they
kept off a great deal of bad weather; still we were
rarely what could be called dry at nights, and spent
three-fourths of almost every day all depths in the
water, and exposed to scorching suns, towing sea-
cows ashore, as we generally provided work for the
day before we breakfasted, for the tusks had to be

cut out, the best of the meat salted, and all the inside fat rendered down. The pots for that purpose were scarcely ever off the fire until the bottoms were burnt out. We were infamously provided with everything, and we used the bladders of the sea-cows to put the lard in—necessity being the mother of invention.

It was no wonder, then, that I was taken ill on the 10th (February), with racking pains in my head, and giddiness and faintness, and was left behind at a Kaffir kraal, with a small bag of rice, and my Kaffir, Inyati (Buffalo), a big six-foot fellow, to attend to me. He was very young, and a magnificent specimen of a savage ; he looked after me like a child, and nothing could exceed his kindness and attention to all my wants, and he risked his life more than once in my service. Monies told the captain of the kraal to give me milk when I required it, in return for which he would give him a blanket. The captain promised to do so, but never brought me a drop, and Inyati used to go into the cattle-kraal in the middle of the night and bring me my tin cup full, holding about a pint, and see that I drank every drop, lest they should find him out, in which case his punishment for stealing would most probably have been death, the only punishment they know of. He would pass the day in scouring the country for wild fruits. I had a medicine-chest with me, and took lots of emetics, ipecacuanha, Dover's powder, calomel, &c., but did myself more harm than good, not knowing the quantity, or anything about it, in fact. I passed a week on my back on a hard cold floor, a Kaffir mat and a blanket being all my covering ; got better, and joined the rest of the party, who had been having great sport, having killed something like twenty sea-cows each. Monies and Arbuthnot, Price and Gibson, did not shoot, or could not hit anything. They told me I looked as if I had been whitewashed. I found things looking much more comfortable — a sort of camp erected on some high land overlooking the bay, and directly opposite where the river St. Luey runs in, drying-houses for meat, &c., and a large hartebeest house to sleep in, which was moderately dry from above, but terribly wet below, after heavy rain ; heard lions and hyenas every night.

As the Kaffirs all round the country were well supplied with meat, they declined any longer to bring us meal, beans, beer and milk, in exchange for flesh ; so, after cutting what we wanted off a sea-cow, we towed her out again into deep water and sunk her. Monies did this on two or three occasions, and the Kaffirs, quite shocked at such a waste of food they are so fond of, ever afterwards brought us small baskets of the different produce of the country as presents.

21st.—Had a very narrow escape of an upset. Monies wounded a calf, and it bellowed out lustily close to the boat ; the cow immediately rushed at the boat, caught it about the stern, and raised it clean up on end, half filling the boat with water. Monies fired at it, and the shot went into its back and through its lungs, and it shortly died. Caught some good barbel, and shot a very fine bull; towed him within one mile of camp, and had to leave him on account of a strong wind and sea running against us.

28th.—Had great sport at the mouth of the Inyelas. Arbuthnot and Monies each shot two, myself four; saw upwards of forty altogether. We sailed down upon them fast, keeping the boat exactly trim, that we might shoot steadily; suddenly lowered the sail (a piece of blue calico) flat, and the sea-cows showed capital heads, being very curious to know what on earth was coming down upon them like that. We shot well that day, and Price managed the boat to admiration; and not the least amusing thing was seeing scores of Kaffirs going in to bring them out. The water at the head of the bay being shallow, they take hold of each other's hands, shouting for their very lives to scare the crocodiles, not unfrequently many of the middle ones swimming short distances, but not loosing their hold of one another for a moment. The crocodiles seemed afraid to attack so large a body, though very far in the lake; the Kaffirs showed great courage, but they never ventured into deep water singly or in small numbers.

On the following day, as it was too rough for sea-cows, we crossed the lake to have a day's shooting in the bush opposite. After lunching on a wildebeest we shot, I left my knife behind, and Monies kindly returned with me to find it, foolishly leaving our guns behind; he walked very fast, and was fifty yards ahead of me, when three lions walked leisurely out of a bush not ten yards in front of him. Monies, having drawn a huge clasp-knife, his only weapon, remained perfectly firm and collected, and eyed the lions for a few seconds, when they made off for the bush, 200 yards away. Waited some hours for the wind to go down, and had hard work to get across. I thought we must have been swamped. The sea-cows were making up the river, and Arbuthnot stunned one with a ball, just touching the brain. We fired alternately, three of us putting sixteen bullets, seven to the pound, in different parts of her head before killing her.

March 5th.—Thunder and rain like a second deluge all night. Got up like drowned rats. I had my first attack of ague, and Gibson, seeing my teeth chattering in my head, and frightful convulsions, could stand it no longer, and bolted very wisely with two Kaffirs back again to the Black Umveloose, where we left the wagon and some surplus stores, and I have no doubt in my own mind saved his life by so doing.

9th.—Edmonstone arrived with a message from White, saying he was not coming, and we must start the Kaffirs off at once with all the sea-cows, ivory, lard, bacon, &c., and all the spoils of the chase, amounting to fifty-five sea-cows, and only one elephant. Started the Kaffirs off on the 11th, heavily laden, a long string of them, and we pulled the boat round again to the mouth.

12th.—Broke up our camp, as usual, with a huge bonfire, and started on foot with thirty Kaffirs carrying; paid them on arrival with brass wire and blue salempore, or calico. I did not arrive till the 15th, dead knocked up, the journey quite overpowering me in my weak state. Inyati, my Kaffir, stalked ahead, carrying everything but my gun, which I was forced to lug along myself; and many a time during the march, being quite exhausted, I was obliged to knock under, and lay down under a shady tree till I had recovered. After calling and shouting in vain for me to come on, he would leave me, and apparently go on his journey. He could not have been carrying less than eighty pounds weight of one thing and another, principally a huge calabash of fat, with which they smear their bodies all over, and value it immensely, and therefore could not possibly render me any assistance; but his going away was only a make-believe, to try and induce me to follow, as the faithful fellow always returned to look me up. I at last, however, reached the wagons completely exhausted, and very, very ill, and shall have a wholesome recollection of that walk as long as I live. Found Gibson and Charley Edmonstone very ill, and joined them. Monies, Gibson, and Price arrived the same night without the boat, not being able to pull up against the stream, or to get her carried by Kaffirs. I was very much worn out from the cold and incessant rain.

On the 16th we started for Natal, and I can give from this date but a very poor account of anything more that occurred, as I must have had many days' insensibility myself. What I do recollect was that Arbuthnot and Monies joined the wagons again on the 20th, after two very hard days' elephant-hunting on foot, during which Arbuthnot killed one. Arbuthnot complained of being very ill, and threw himself down in the hut, from which he never rose, dying the following day of fever and ague. We made the best of our way to Natal to get advice for the rest of the sick, but on reaching our destination poor Price died also, within forty miles of the town. Monies stayed behind to bring out another wagon, having never had an hour's illness, when he suddenly took desperately ill, and died next day. M'Queen reached Durban, where he died in a few days, though he never went into the unhealthy country at all ; Purver, Hammond, and Etty, three elephant-hunters of White's party, also died in the Zulu country about the same time; Gibson, Edmonstone, Charley Edmonstone, and myself eventually, but not for nearly twelve months, got better again. We were all, I think, carried out of the wagons in Durban more dead than alive, and I shall never forget the very great kindness and attention I received from Mr. and Mrs. Tyzack, to whose house I first went on landing in the colony, and where I was now taken. In the course of a few weeks, I was able, by the advice of my physician, to go up to Pieter Maritzburg for change of air, where Mr. Collins, the post-master and a fellow-passenger of mine, most kindly took me into his house, treated me with the utmost attention, and forestalled my every want. It is to Mrs. Collins's nursing and care — and all the little delicacies, so grateful and refreshing to a sick man, which a woman's forethought can alone supply—that I am indebted for my eventual recovery, after a very long illness. On first getting into the scales, on being able, with assistance, to get about a little, I only weighed five stone and eleven pounds; but laid on weight again, shortly after, almost as fast as I must have lost it, and regained strength altogether, on the high lands of the Inanda, about twenty-two miles from Durban and nine from the sea, where I joined White on a 9,600 acre farm of Proudfoot's, built a wattle and dab-house, and existed there, almost alone — I can hardly call it living — for two years or more, I should think, selling cattle to Kaffirs, which White traded in the Zulu country and brought

or sent out to me.   I have sometimes sold forty or
more in one day, and had upwards of 600 on the
place at one time, averaging, anywhere in those days
before the lung sickness, from 10s. to 2l. a head, for
which the Kaffirs in Natal always paid cash.

It was a horrid weary, solitary, monotonous life ;
not often could I prevail upon anyone to come
and stay with me, certainly not unless driven to
it, as was not unfrequently the case, by having no
other home and no money — when they would pay
me a visit till something better turned up.   Certainly I had no great inducement to offer to them to
remain : lean fowls, salt beef and rice, and heavy,
ill-baked bread, was our fare, varied occasionally by
bucks, partridges, and bustards ; tea and coffee our
only beverage.   I must not, however, omit oceans
of milk, most of which the Kaffirs and dogs ran
through, and I won't say but that it might have been
possible to have been very comfortable ; all I can
say is, that the experience I had of it gave me such
a wholesome dread of the like ever again occurring,
that I took to the wandering gypsy-life I have ever
since led.   I was never without two or three horses
and a host of dogs, and, though they assisted very
materially, together with my rifle and shot guns,
to get through the days, yet the long evenings, the
everlasting roar made by my Kaffirs, frequently
continuing half the night, rats squeaking, gnaw-
ing, and scraping in every room, and almost
everything that I brought out being long since

eaten into shreds by white ants, which were fast undermining the posts and walls of our habitation, made me think another Zulu trip would be preferable to remaining alone any longer ; consequently, I shut up the establishment, and went in again the following year.

My nearest neighbours were Mr. Lindley, a missionary from the American Mission Society, a man most deservedly respected and esteemed by all in the colony, his amiable wife and charming family, at whose hospitable house I always felt myself quite at home. I used frequently to ride over on Sundays to Kaffir service, or whenever I could frame an excuse for making a break in my existence, and, after passing an evening with him and his united family, it put me so much in mind of my own home, that I used to feel in a better frame of mind for weeks to come, though the contrast was very great between his cheerful, comfortable house, and happy family, and my own solitary, dismal-looking abode— a deal table and a lot of velt stools and wagon chests the only furniture, and myself the only inhabitant.

One day, at St. Lucia Bay, after partly recovering from my first attack of fever, we went sea-cow shooting, and I was landed on a small island among the reeds, knee deep in water and very warm. After waiting some time for a shot, and feeling very weak and weary, I beat down a big bundle of reeds and sat upon them, my legs dangling in the water, and went fast asleep. Meantime, Arbuthnot and Monies

were shooting and driving sea-cows, which showed
good heads past my hiding-place, and they could
not imagine why I did not shoot, but in the excitement of their own hunting forgot where they had
left me, and poor Monics said they hallooed in vain ;
but he had noticed three or four of the largest
crocodiles swimming backwards and forwards in one
place, and close into the island, and on pulling in
found me fast asleep within fifteen yards of these

pleasant companions, who, no doubt, would soon
have made a meal of me. All the sympathy my
unenviable and dangerous position excited was
being soundly rated for going asleep and not bagging a couple of sea-cows ; but I felt too grateful
for being rescued to be angry in my turn.

Whilst on the subject of crocodiles, I will relate an

anecdote that happened to me on the St. Luey's mouth, where it runs into St. Lucia Bay. I shot a goose, almost full grown, though a flapper, and he was drifting nicely to my feet, when he unaccountably disappeared. Not taking particular notice at the time, I thought he might possibly have partly recovered and dived. Gibson was with me at the time, and, disappointed of our intended roast, as we had not breakfasted, I shot another, and he likewise disappeared in the same place and manner. There being plenty, I shot a third, and, determined not to lose this one, went gradually into the river to meet him, armed with a heavy lancewood loading-rod shod with iron, and had nearly got up to my middle, making a tremendous noise and splashing to scare the crocodiles, when, just as I was stretching out my arm to reach my goose, he suddenly went under water. I had no fears in those days, and did not know the real danger, so I made a grasp and caught the goose by the leg, striking the water as hard as ever I could. In an instant the goose came in halves, the legs, back, and some of the entrails falling to my share, Mr. Crocodile getting the better half, and two or three violent blows on the nose into the bargain. I need hardly say I lost not an instant in getting ashore again, and did not think much at the time (which is often the case) of what a foolish thing it was to do, and what a narrow escape I had had. It is only once in a man's lifetime he does these daredevil sort of things, and it is wonderful how lucky he invariably comes off; but a few more years, and a wider experience, make him as cautious as those whom he once thought timid.   It is equally difficult for youth and age to hit that golden mean, which is no doubt the best way in hunting, as in other things, to attain the main object — bagging your game.

CHAPTER II.

1853.

HUNTING EXPEDITION INTO THE ZULU COUNTRY.

JULY 15*th.*—We started on our Zulu expedition from the Inanda with two wagons, Gibson and myself going on horseback across country. We got out of our way, and fell in with a hospitable Scotchman and his wife. On going up a steep hill, leading two horses, I went to touch up one that was hanging back, when my mare took fright, and, after several plunges, succeeded in kicking me in the stomach and arm, though not very severely. I was able to go in pursuit in a few minutes, and, after more than two hours' hard chasing, succeeded in driving her into a Kaffir kraal. At sunset I reached Fuller's, where the wagons had just arrived.

17*th.*—After sundry ' doctors,' concoctions of rum, eggs, and new milk, we inspanned and got under weigh to the Tongaart. We loaded the wagons with two muids (360 lbs.) of mealies, Edmonstone's traps, and a host of blankets, treked on some eight miles by moonlight, and outspanned for the night.

18*th*.—We were delayed in starting by the oxen having strayed. We treked to the Umslali, saddled up and rode to Maclean's, where we took in a sack of potatoes, and stored our pockets with capsicums. I killed a koran.

19*th*.—Again we commenced the day by losing the oxen, which were not found till after midday. We reached the Umvoti after dark. I made two nose-bags for my horses, and had some good fun trying to make my mare stand on the velt, every attempt being a signal failure. She set my nooses at defiance, and ended by breaking the bridle.

20*th*.—To-day I engaged two Kaffirs, Jack and Jacob; and brought a muid of mealies for the horses. On coming into a mud sluit, down a steep bank, the sudden check of the wagon threw me off the box, under the near wheel, which passed over above my knee. I rolled out of the way of the other wheel, and fortunately escaped without further injury than a very severe bruise. Though I had no bone broken, my thigh swelled very much, and the shaking of the wagon increased the irritation and gave me great pain. It was a wonderful escape, as there were 3,000 pounds weight of picks in the wagon, and nothing but the fact of the ground being very soft where I fell could have saved a broken thigh; the swelling was so rapid that my trousers had to be slit up with a knife in order to get them off, and for the next twelve hours I had two Hottentot women, the wives of the drivers, rubbing in

turpentine and oil, their infallible remedy for bruises.
Their beautifully formed, delicate, diminutive hands,
ancles, wrists, and feet, a marked feature in all
Hottentots, presented a singular contrast to their
repulsive monkey-like faces.

21st.—We got as far as the Umvoti, where we
joined Gassiot's wagon, which had been waiting our
arrival for three weeks; treked on some six miles,
with four wagons and a host of Kaffirs, Hottentots,
men, women, and children of all sorts, colours, and
sizes, who, having got possession of a case of gin
that Gibson had in his wagon, spent the most noisy,
quarrelsome, abusive night I ever witnessed.

On the 22nd we crossed the Tugela, the boundary of the colony, half a mile wide, without
accident, the river being very low, and treked on
about four miles, where we met Mr. Clifton of
Lytham, a lieutenant in the Rifle Brigade, who was
also on a hunting trip, and had been waiting our
arrival some days. He was at a low ebb; a friend
of his, Mr. Fletcher, having just been killed by a
cow-elephant, which they were about to shoot,
when it charged and killed Mr. Fletcher before a
shot had been fired. This was the first they had
seen; rather an unfortunate beginning. Mr. Fletcher
had only been a few days in the colony.

On the 23rd we crossed the Matakoola, and outspanned four miles beyond. The following morning
White, Gibson, Steele, and myself mounted at sunrise, in quest of elands. We fell in with a herd of

about seventeen, and gave chase at a killing pace, very soon overhauling them. Gibson and Steele fired without effect, White giving a bull a shot rather too high up in the shoulder. However, he separated from the herd, and Steele gave him a finisher about a mile off, where he had taken the water and was standing at bay. After a long chase, I brought down the largest bull in the troop, shooting him dead off the pony Billy, being unable to pull up and fire, in consequence of my leg being still very painful. It was his first essay at elands as well as my own, and he proved himself a good one, running very stout and fast. After returning to camp for breakfast, I rode out again with Clifton and twenty Kaffirs to bring the meat home, some five or six miles.

25th.--We treked on to a high hill called the Gun, some ten miles farther; a very cold, raw day, with slight showers. Maclean ran against a bank in going into a sluit, got pitched off the box, and nearly upset the wagon on the top of him. We saw a fine herd of elands, but are keeping them for to-morrow. I made my first attempt at preserving, on the head of a cow-eland I shot yesterday, and found it a long, tedious job. I engaged another Kaffir, Mafuta (Grease) by name, a strong, likely-looking fellow.

26th.--This morning we found that Maclean's after-ox, Basket, had been killed by a lion. We treked on a few miles and then outspanned, with a fine herd of elands in full view. We saddled and went in pursuit, the ground being very heavy and boggy. Clifton and myself tried to head them and bring them to the wagon, but they made exactly the contrary way. After a very hard and long burst, Clifton shot a calf, and about two miles farther I put a ball through the ribs of a fine old bull, but as Billy was dead beat, I did not bag him.

The next day we treked on to the Umlilas, where we waited five hours for the river to go down, and outspanned for the night on the top of the hill on the other side. On the 28th we crossed the Umslatoosi, a large party: five wagons, seventy oxen, fifty men, women, and children, twelve horses, and eleven dogs. The following day, however, this number was considerably reduced by the departure of eleven of the Kaffirs to trade for different members of our party.

On the 30th we crossed the Impangane, a small river, near which we had to remain for several days. I got a good soaking in the bush, looking for guinea-fowl without success. As I had done my leg no good by the walk, I laid down in the wagon, eating cheese and jam, and enjoying Sponge's 'Sporting Tour.' The game here was very scarce and wild; but we were well supplied with milk, amas, tchualla, mealies, Kaffir corn, and all the Kaffir produce, and we had some laughable scenes in our bartering.

We were much amused by the bellows used by

D

two Kaffir smiths, who were trying to mend one of
the wagons which had broken down.   The bellows
consists of a small clay tube or pipe next the
fire, and two cows' horns fastened on two leather
bags, which are kept alternately open and shut.
It requires some knack to work, but when
skilfully handled it makes a really good current
of air, producing a red-hot charcoal fire in a few
minutes.

August 6th.—Notwithstanding a dreadfully stormy
day, high wind and rain, and severe cold, we treked
on a few miles. In the evening a panther seized Hopeful by the throat almost from under the wagon, and
within five yards of the tent where we were eating
our supper in the dark, on account of the wind. We
all sallied out just in time to save the dog, who got
off with a frightful wound in the throat, which
swelled nearly as big as his body.   It was too dark,
however, to shoot the panther.

7th.—Got safely up Panda's stony hill, the worst
I ever saw, it being all that twenty-two oxen could
manage to drag up one wagon ; but the poor things
were labouring under great disadvantage, most of them
having the tongue and clove sickness.   The next day
we came in sight of Nedwingu, Panda's kraal, but
we were still some fifteen miles distant, owing to the
hilliness of the country.   Our progress was very slow,
on account of the illness of the oxen.   On the 10th
we saw a herd of koodoos, and were told by the
Hottentots who brought us wood at night, that there

was a herd of buffaloes near the river Umveloose, and we agreed to wage war on them at sunrise.

Accordingly, we were off at peep of day with seven guns, and after about three-quarters of an hour's hard walking, over frightfully stony ground, came in sight of a herd of about forty buffaloes, but they made off out of shot, hearing the noise we made over the stones. After two hours' hard chase, running and dodging in all directions, five were brought to bag. Steele had a narrow escape; a young bull, with his leg broken and his tail shot off, just hit him on the heel as he dropped his gun and sprang into a thorn-tree. I shot a fine fat young cow at full speed, hard pressed by three dogs, right through the spine and lungs. She fell bellowing after a few yards, almost on the top of the one which had charged Steele, and which I afterwards killed myself. The cow I shot was claimed by Anton, who had given her the first bullet, without the slightest injury; but the rules of the chase are, that the first shot lays claim to the animal, the bullet being the proof. Edmonstone had given the young bull the first shot, and therefore claimed him, so I had my sport for nothing. The Zulus, hearing the shooting, came down like so many vultures; but the lazy blackguards refused to lend a hand to carry the meat back to the camp, and one fellow was caught helping himself to some nice steaks from a leg cut off, and ready to be taken to camp, by our own Kaffirs. White knocked him over with a heavy stone in the ribs, and the rest made themselves scarce for a little

while. They knew, however, that they would ultimately get the lion's share of the meat, as it was
utterly impossible that our party, though twenty
strong at least, could carry the whole of the meat of
six buffaloes, especially on such ground—a tremendously steep, stony hill, some four miles from camp—
and at night they could take all with impunity.
White, however, kept watch till the choicest parts,
the tongues, &c. were secured. We got back about
12 o'clock, and drank a great quantity of tea and
coffee, and breakfasted on buffalo kidneys—a great
luxury—a few quails, and a dikkop (thickhead), the
daintiest bird in the colony, fully equal to woodcock.
The poor dogs, too, came in for their share, and had
as much as ever they could cram into them.

On the afternoon of the 12th we crossed the
Umveloose, and outspanned within a mile of Nedwingu, Panda's kraal, which we rode up to see on
the following morning. It is fully two and a half
miles round, and contains nearly 2,000 huts. We
did not see his sable majesty, but were honoured by
drinking a calabash of tchualla with his prime
minister Likwázi, through whom we sent presents
of beads and blankets to Panda.

The next few days were wet and raw, and all
hands were busy making and repairing velt shoes.
One afternoon we were coming well on a fine herd
of buffaloes sleeping, when a Kaffir hit my unfortunate dog Hopeful with a stone. The dog, who
was more dead than alive from the effects of the

encounter with the panther, roared awfully. The buffaloes started off, and, though we gave chase as hard as we were able, we could never get within shot.

20th.—We were early in the saddle, and took different routes to endeavour to circumvent a herd of buffaloes which were to be seen from the wagon. Edmonstone and myself had just reached our post when a bullet whistled most unpleasantly near us, closely followed by nine buffaloes. I immediately endeavoured to head them back, but the ground was so stony and bushy that I only lamed my pony, and tore my hands to pieces, without doing any good. I frequently got close to them, but before I could dismount they were out of sight in the bushes. Steele's Kaffir broke the leg of a fat young cow. She charged straight at one of White's horses, and the Kaffir who was holding him struck his assegai into her ribs.

On the 22nd, Edmonstone, myself, and three Kaffirs set off to ascend the highest hill in the neighbourhood. After walking hard all day we reached the bottom, where we bought amas, tchualla, meal, &c., with beads : supped sumptuously on a fat peau I killed, and slept in a kraal. The next morning we ascended the hill. It was a long and heavy pull, but we were rewarded by a fine view of the surrounding country, very hilly on all sides, but not well wooded. We got back to the wagons about noon on the following day, rather jaded and footsore.

31st.—We all saddled up early to pay a visit to

Panda. His Majesty, however, was asleep, and his attendants did not dare disturb him. After remaining some time we were ordered to go to the gate and wait there, so we took huff and rode away without seeing him, broke up our camp, made a great bonfire of all the huts the Kaffirs had erected, and once more proceeded on our journey. We had not gone more than two miles when one of Panda's captains came up in a great fury, swearing awfully by the bones of Dingaan, Chàkà, the much-dreaded and cruel, and other renowned warriors of the nation, that if we did not immediately turn back, an impi (regiment 500 strong) would be down upon us and kill us instanter. He was in a great state of excitement, would not hear of our outspanning or delaying our return a moment, said the signal for attack was crossing that watercourse (pointing to a running stream not twenty yards ahead); and as we were entirely in their power, we thought discretion the better part of valour, and did as we were ordered, looking very foolish in both our own and our followers' eyes. Panda had always opposed our wish to go that way, and it was bearding the lion in his den, and most foolish and misjudged on the part of White, to go in direct opposition to his orders. On passing his kraal gates we went through two lines, at least 200 yards long, of magnificent men, armed with assegais, shields, knobkerries, and knives, in close file, waiting only the slightest intimation from His Majesty to annihilate us instantly. It was a

A FORCED RETURN.

nervous moment; I did not half admire it, and all
our Kaffirs were in the utmost alarm : a dead silence
was maintained by everyone ; and poor White was
awfully annoyed and vexed about it. To do him
justice, I believe, if any of us would have stood by
him, he would have infinitely preferred shooting
half a dozen and being spitted himself, to the dis-
grace to white men of having to obey a Kaffir ; but
it was all brought on by his own obstinacy.

Likwázi, the prime minister before mentioned,
came down to us—a fat, good-tempered, jovial fellow
— made the peace, and eventually all was settled
amicably ; but our long-meditated route was peremp-
torily forbidden, and we were obliged to rest satisfied with the shooting Panda thought fit to give us
. in the Slatakula bush, where the old fellow knew
well there were rarely any elephants worth shooting.
He is a wily old savage. On Clifton wishing particularly to see him out of curiosity, though he sent
many presents to him, the only answer he sent
was, ' I have nothing to say to him ; does he think
me a wild beast, that he is so anxious to see me ?
I won't see him.' Nor did he see any of the party
but White and the interpreter.

September 1st. — Treked on our way back again.
Some Kaffir boys told us of a herd of elands.
White, Edmonstone, and myself went in pursuit,
and after a sharp burst round a big hill, White came
upon them. I also ran to get a shot, and we each
of us had two shots at not more than a hundred

yards, every bullet telling into some part of them, but none fell, and we had the mortification of seeing them all go away and make for the hills, where we had no chance of reaching them.

2nd.—We got safely to the bottom of Panda's stony hill, and parted company with Steele. The next day we struck down into a deep valley of the White Umveloose, in quest of large game. After some very hard climbing, we all returned to the wagons with only one eland bull.

5th.— Struck off the road, and made for the Slata-kula bush. As we were obliged to clear a way for the wagons, we made but slow progress.

7th.— The Kaffirs told us there was a large herd of elephants within a few miles. I went in pursuit, accompanied by two Hottentots and two Kaffirs; • supped on a buffalo, which some Zulu Kaffirs had killed, and spent a tolerably comfortable night in the open air, notwithstanding a few showers of rain. At daylight we started again, hunted without any encouragement, and returned to the wagons under the impression that the Kaffirs were humbugs.

After cutting our way through the bush with great difficulty, on the 10th we came in sight of the Black Umveloose, when we saw three rhinoceroses, a herd of elands, and a herd of buffaloes from the wagons. The greater part of the night we were kept awake by lions, tigers, and wolves. Fly, venturing too near, was caught and severely bitten in the throat by a tiger, but escaped with life.

11*th*. — Crossed the Black Umveloose, a very bad drift, and outspanned on some beautiful new grass, which was quite refreshing after all the dry, withered stuff we had been seeing so long. We saw lots of bucks and koodoos. In the afternoon we treked on to a Kaffir kraal, where we got oceans of milk, amas, &c. The Kaffirs told us that the lions had got into the kraal the evening before; we therefore drew up the wagons and made the best barrier we could for the horses, and all slept with our guns at hand. The lions, however, disappointed us.

On the 12th our party broke up, White's two wagons and Gassiot's going on to trade. Maclean and Edmonstone went on with them, while I took up my quarters with Clifton, intending to stay a week or so for shooting. The next day we treked away from the kraal, the Kaffirs stunning us with their noise, and outspanned a few miles off. Leggins and I lost the wagon, having misunderstood where they were to outspan, and were first initiated into the art of making fire with two dry sticks. I saw a buffalo bull cantering leisurely in the direction of Leggins, and hallooed to him to look out. He had seen the bull, and made for a tree as hard as legs could carry him. The old bull snuffed danger in the wind, but could not make it out, and actually stood under the very tree within two feet of Leggins, who was so paralysed with fear that he had not strength to shoot. It was long before he ventured to come down, and then he got off as quickly as he could, thinking that he, and not the buffalo, had had a wonderful escape.

14*th*.— From the top of a hill I saw two herds of what I took for buffaloes, but just as I was going after them I had the mortification of discovering that they were wildebeests. However, I mounted, and seeing two old bull buffaloes standing under a tree, managed to get within twenty-five yards, when five old bulls jumped up. I rolled over the first like a rabbit, shooting him through the lungs. I then heard Clifton firing, and rode in that direction, when we saw a large herd of elands and one fine old bull as blue as a slate. The ground was bad for a horse, being bushy with long grass and full of large stones. I went away, however, at a hand gallop, and keeping below the wind and under the hill, managed to come up with them. I singled out the old bull, and, after some hard riding through the bush, losing my hat and tearing my shirt and hands to pieces, I drove him from the herd, and shortly afterwards, taking advantage of 100 yards of open, tumbled off and gave him a ball high up on his hind leg, but without doing him much injury. He kept along at a swinging pace through the bush; I could not wait to load, for fear of losing sight of him. The ground was frightful, and I thought I never should have come up with him, though Billy carried me marvellously. At the edge of a steep kloof leading into thick bush, where I must inevitably have lost him, the bull suddenly came to bay, and made a stand facing me. I gave him a bullet in the breast, and he rolled down to the bottom of the kloof. I went down to inspect my prize, but all my efforts were unavailing to cut his head off, from the position in which he had fallen, and I was obliged to leave the noble animal for the lions, wolves, jackals, and vultures.

15th. — Started off with a host of Kaffirs of both sexes to see what the lions had left of my eland, but on my way I saw an old bull buffalo making away for some thick bush, quickened my pace, and he crossed me into a kloof; I jumped off and shot at him, as he appeared broadside out of the kloof, and fancied I broke his fore leg. As he went away very lame I gave chase, and came up with him standing under a tree. I was edging off a little to get a good broadside at him, when he charged so suddenly and fiercely, and so fast, that Billy whipped round like a shot, and dashed off at full speed through the trees, sending my gun spinning yards away out of my hand, and a strong branch, catching me across the breast, all but unhorsed me. The enraged brute was for 200 yards within two feet of Billy's tail, and continued the chase for 400 yards. After recovering my gun I followed him into a thick bush and gave him a shot, when he again charged, but fearing to come out of the bush again, retreated, and I lost sight of him. On riding round I saw him again, and he forthwith gave chase, but being on the open, I was all right this time. I therefore allowed him to come close up, but as he would persist in facing me, I was reluctant to spend my last bullet, and it was long ere I got a shot to my liking. At last, however, he gave me a broadside, and I gave him a settler. He was certainly the savagest old monster I ever had the pleasure of seeing.

I had to return to camp seven or eight miles in a woful plight, minus my hat, and my shirt torn to ribbons, exposed to a fearful hot sun, and my whole body blistered and sunburnt, giving me great pain, and my throat and tongue parched up for want of water. I was well greased with eland fat from head to foot, which was a great relief to me, but for several days I could rest in no position from the frightful extent of the sun-burns, than which I know nothing more painful, as every atom of skin peels off. I found my eland nearly eaten up, but I brought his horns back as a trophy.

16*th*.—Went out on foot, as Billy had had two hard days in succession. I saw a buffalo canter away, and then stop in a thick bush. I followed, got a shot, and heard the bullet tell. He was a long way off, and going at full speed. I had another shot without effect, followed on, and next saw him lying at full length. I spoke to the Kaffirs, when the beast immediately jumped up and faced us. The Kaffirs disappeared like smoke. I gave him a shot meant for the breast, but it struck him in the neck and he at once charged. Fortunately, Crafty was between us, and he made a furious onset on her, which gave me time to load again and change my position. The poor brute was evidently severely wounded, and again lay down. I had two more shots at him, but he was so tough that it was not before the fifth shot that he was dead, and then the Kaffirs reappeared.

17*th*.—Clifton lent me a horse, and I rode over to see the other party, having heard that they were at a kraal only a few miles off. Edmonstone had been at a great Kaffir hunt, at which all the natives far and near turned out. They were delighted with their sport. One Kaffir, however, got a bullet through his foot, and as Edmonstone got the credit of it, he was obliged to give a cotton blanket worth 3*s*. by way of compensation. I returned the next day in time for four days of regular deluge, which we spent inside the tent, killing time as best we could with books, &c. I waded entirely through the 'Soldier of Fortune.'

23*rd*.—Breakfasted on chocolate and dry bread, having eaten all our fresh meat during the four days' rain. As the larder was empty we sallied out and had a hard day's work over a great extent of country, returning home well laden, long after sunset, having bagged two cow-buffaloes and a bush-pig.

26*th*.—Fifteen Zulus came down to our camp to-day, and I turned out to shoot them some meat. We travelled a long way without seeing anything, but my perseverance was at length rewarded by the sight of a troop of buffaloes a long way off. We executed a very scientific stalk, and I bowled over a young, tolerably fat bull. We lighted a fire and demolished a good part of him on the spot, the Kaffirs eating alternately a lump of roasted flesh and an equal quantity of the inside raw.

27th.—Pouring rain all day. As the wolves plagued us much, we set a gun at night and shot an old dog-wolf through the head.

29th.—We were waked up suddenly by hearing one of the oxen bellowing and the dogs barking. It was moderately dark, and I seized Clifton's double rifle and rushed out, not knowing where, when I saw the driver perched on the top of a temporary hut, made of grass, about six feet high, roaring lustily for a doppè (cap). I scrambled up just as the poor ox ceased his cries, and heard the lions growling and roaring on the top of him, not more than fourteen yards from where we were, but it was too dark to see them. I fired, however, in the direction of the sound, and just above the body of the ox, which I could distinguish tolerably well, as it was a black one. Diza (the driver) followed my example, and as the lions did not take the least notice, I fired my second barrel, and was just proceeding to load my own gun, which Jack had brought me, when I was aware for a single instant only that the lion was coming, and the same moment I was knocked half a dozen somer-saults backwards off the hut, the brute striking me in the chest with his head. I gathered myself up in a second and made a dash at a fence just behind me, and scrambled through it, gun in hand, but the muzzle was choked with dirt. I then made for the wagon, and got on the box, where I found all the Kaffirs, who could not get inside, sticking like monkeys, and Diza perched on the top. How he got there seemed to me a miracle, as he was alongside me when the brute charged. A minute or two afterwards, one of them marched off a goat, one of five

that were tethered by the foot to the hut which we had so speedily evacuated.

Diza, thinking he had a chance, fired from the top of the wagon, and the recoil knocked him backwards on to the tent, which broke his fall. It was a most ludicrous sight altogether.

After that we were utterly defeated, and the brutes were allowed to eat their meal unmolested, which they continued to do for some time, growling fiercely all the while. The Kaffirs said there were five in all. I fired once again, but without effect; and we all sat shivering with cold, without any clothes on, till near day-break, when our enemies beat a retreat, and I was not sorry to turn in again between the blankets. I was just beginning to get warm again when I was aroused by a double shot, and rushed out on hearing that the driver and after-rider had shot the lion. We went to the spot and found a fine lioness dead, with a bullet through the ribs from the after-rider; a good shot, as she was at least 150 yards off. Another had entered the neck, just behind the head, and travelled all along the spine nearly to the root of the tail. I claimed that shot, and forthwith proceeded to skin her. I cut out the ball: it proved to be my shot out of Clifton's rifle; this accounted for her ferocious onslaught. The after-rider was rather chopfallen at having to give her up to the rightful owner.

Diza got a claw in his thigh, and the gun which he had in his hand was frightfully scratched on the stock : rather sharp practice. A strong-nerved old Kaffir woman lay in the hut the whole time, without a door or anything whatever between her and the lions, and kept as still as a mouse all the while.

30th. — Hearing that White was back again at the Kaffir chief Umbop's, Clifton and I rode off to see the party, some twelve miles off. Clifton gave me a mount on Arab, and we found them well, with the exception of Maclean. Their affairs looked rather badly on the whole: eight oxen had died, several more were very ill, two dogs had been carried off by tigers, there was no game, and consequently not much to eat, and they were out of coffee and sugar. We got six blankets, some brass wire, and black calico, and returned to camp.

I had the remains of the ox dragged to the best spot for getting a shot, if the lions should pay us another visit. They did not keep us waiting long. In less than an hour after dark they came, and immediately began their meal. The night was very dark, and we had nothing but their own growls to guide us in shooting. We three blazed away in succession for a long time. The ox was placed just in front of the wagon, about twenty-five yards off, but they dragged it away considerably farther. Crafty must have had some narrow escapes, for she would not come in, but kept up an incessant row all the time; and, encouraged by the firing, came to very close quarters with them several times. They charged her frequently and savagely, but she showed great pluck. I saw one lion tolerably distinctly once, and fired, when for the first time he uttered a fierce roar, and charged at the wagon. We had, however, a strong fence between the wagon and them, and when the lion lay down about seven yards off for a long time, I felt sure he was wounded. He

E

made off soon afterwards, and I turned in before they all took their departure.

October 1*st.* — Went up to see our last night's work. It was evident that one or more had been severely wounded, but we endeavoured in vain to trace them. I turned out with my two dogs and one Kaffir, Jacob. I was obliged to offer him a rewards of 5*s.* before he would consent to accompany me. We gave the dogs the wind, and hunted down the nearest kloof. I had not got 400 yards from the wagon when I saw that Hopeful winded something, but neither growled nor barked, in spite of all the encouragement I gave him. He was very near the kloof, and came away. At length I mustered courage to go down, and, proceeding a short distance, saw an old lion dead, at the bottom. A large bullet had gone right through his middle, and I was in high spirits at my success.

As I was occupied in skinning the lion, I heard three double shots in succession, and rushed out, gun in hand, expecting a couple of lions at least, when I found Clifton standing over one of the oxen, just breathing its last. The lions the night before had driven it mad, and he had been obliged to shoot it. We had now only ten oxen left, and one so ill that it could hardly travel. However, on the evening of the 2nd, we reached some Kaffir kraals, and the lions again favoured us with their company. On awaking I looked out of the tent, thinking it was a wolf, and that I might get a shot, when I saw one

lion distinctly, and Hopeful and Crafty barking at
him furiously. He at length charged against the
side of the tent, unpegging two of the ropes; so we
struck a light, and kept a candle burning till the
morning. He gave us one fine chance of shooting
him, but Clifton had given strict orders that no one
must fire, lest the lion should come into the tent.

5th. — Outspanned within a mile and a half of
the Umveloose.

6th. — Jack and I started before daylight, to try
and bag a wild goose or two, as there are plenty of
them about the Umveloose, but we had to return to
our quarters with two brace of quail and a blue
heron. I had several long shots at geese, but they
require a heavy dose to bring them down. We got
back to a splendid breakfast of quail, beautifully
cooked by Leggins, while the rest were inspanning.
I followed them shortly on my pony, my Kaffirs
carrying the kettle, saucepans, dishes, and condiments, and overtaking the wagon at the drift, which
we crossed in good style, though not without difficulty, as the river was four feet deep, and the
sand heavy. Seeing two wagons, we outspanned at
a kraal just before sunset, and drew up alongside.
Clifton purchased three oxen from a Zulu trader, and
we passed a jolly evening together, hearing all the
news; among the rest, that England and France were
positively at war with Russia.

10th. — Clifton and I laboured hard to get a
black goose, but there was no getting a shot. I was

up to my waist in water half the day. One ox knocked up, and was left behind.

11th. — Sent two Kaffirs for the ox, which was unable to rise, so they had to leave him. My dog Hopeful also was missing, probably taken by a tiger. Jack and I hunted all round, but could find no trace of him. There was no doubt, however, as to his fate. I had heard Crafty barking furiously in the night, but hearing wolves also, I thought it was they. All hands turned out to hunt the horses, which had strayed, but we soon recovered them.

12th. —We reached the Missionary Station, but found that the missionary himself had been sent for by Umbop, a Kaffir chief, to poison lions ninety or a hundred miles off. His good lady was at home, but we could make nothing of her. She was a Norwegian, and had not the slightest smattering of any other language. Clifton, after trying English and Kaffir in vain, returned to the charge with French, but to no purpose, so we had to give her up.

12th.—Outspanned four miles beyond the Umve-loose. I tried to get a klip-springer among the rocks, but returned unsuccessful, having seen only three. I saw lots of baboons. Mosquitoes for the first time bit and plagued me a good deal in the night. Sent a Kaffir to the bay for letters and news.

15th.—Having been told of a herd of elands, we saddled and went in pursuit, but it came on very wet, and we made for a kraal, without seeing them. The wagon appeared shortly after, and we outspanned a mile from the Inyesan. I cut the head of a koran clean off with a bullet, and found it in the long grass some seven yards from his body.

17th.—Turned out on Billy to look for a buffalo, and came on a herd of about fifteen, which made off at full speed a long way ahead of me. Billy soon overtook them, and I singled out an old bull, and gave him a bullet just as he dashed into the bush near the Inyesan. The herd crossed the river, and appeared on the other side; and I had great difficulty in following them. Eventually I killed a tolerably fat cow, and my Kaffirs told me they had seen the old bull go away with a broken leg. I also shot a pig, after a sharp burst, Crafty bringing him to bay. We brought home as much as three Kaffirs and a pony could carry.

18th.—To-day I gave Billy a rest, and turned out with a half-bred cur to shoot quail; got three brace, as well as a partridge. A honeybird met us, and called us vigorously. We followed, and he took us to a bees' nest, but, owing to the incessant rains, there was but little honey in it. There was, however, a good deal of fun and excitement in following the little fellow.

19th.—Went out in quest of elands, Clifton, his after-rider, and myself, taking different roads. After a long ride, just as I had ascended a very high hill, I saw a large herd, but could not make them out till they began to move. The wind and ground were both

in my favour, and, after some hard work, I came
within about 600 yards of them. They were very
wild and shy, having been much shot at lately, and
they had taken alarm at three Kaffirs who came
along the road, and they were taking themselves off
rapidly.

Crafty dashed into the herd and brought out a
cow straight across a heavy bog. I was luckily on
the right side, so I galloped off as fast as I could,
and, after a long burst, got within fifty yards of her.
Now or never, thought I, as she went like the wind.
I jumped off, fired and missed her. Away she went
at a swinging trot. I looked at my pony: he was
ready for another burst, and I took up the spoor of
the rest of the troop. I soon came upon them crossing a bog, and making in my direction. I managed
to get Billy over the bog with great difficulty, gave
him a minute to recover his wind, mounted, and, as
I had saved half a mile, I was on the middle of
the troop instantly. I shortly drove the old bull
from the troop, and made play. In consequence of the
heavy state of the ground and the distance I had
come, Billy was labouring hard under me, and, I
fancied, rather losing ground. I thought exhausted
nature could hold out no longer, so I pulled up within
fifty yards of my bull, but I was so shaken that I
again missed. Before I had reloaded, however,
Billy had recovered himself, and fretted so much to
be off that I had difficulty in ramming my bullet
home ; and he was again galloping at a break-neck

pace before I was fairly in the saddle. The bull was some quarter of a mile ahead, going at a steady trot, with Crafty at his heels.

I gradually made up the lost ground, saving and nursing my pony to the utmost, and had been riding a long way within fifty yards of him, utterly unable to get an inch nearer, when I saw Clifton and his after-rider meeting him. Clifton turned out of the way, to let me have the whole honour to myself. The bull rushed broadside past him within twenty yards, a sore temptation for a man with a double-barrelled Westley Richards in his hand; but he allowed the bull to pass him unmolested. Billy, on seeing the other horses, made a last spurt and ran right up to the bull, horse and man doing all that nature could. The brute strained every nerve to reach the river, which was within one hundred yards of him, but it was not to be. I jumped off and bowled him over, giving him the ball through his tail, high up and right into his lungs, and he fell dead in a few yards; Billy and I ran down like a mill-stream. I took off saddle and bridle, and the pony was himself again in no time. My prize was a noble brute; his skin measured ten feet, cut off at the neck. The Kaffirs came up in about an hour, and we skinned him. He was in first-rate order, and I returned to camp, after having cut him up and taken out his fat, with the breast across my saddle. The Kaffirs lighted a fire, and stayed there all night feasting.

21*st.*—After a splendid breakfast of marrow-bones
and buffalo tongues, I went out again, my Kaffir
leading Billy.   I was determined not to mount, unless I saw elands or buffaloes.   I took my blanket,
as I intended to stay out all night.   After about
three hours' walk, I saw a large herd of elands, and
got unperceived within 500 yards of them.   I did
not mount till the last moment, when away I went
at the top of Billy's speed.   I was soon in the
middle of the troop, and singled out the largest bull.
Crafty and Billy stuck to him like leeches.   He
bounded and tore away, and made every effort to
regain the troop, but in vain, so he rushed down
hill for the Matakoola river.   I stopped Billy at
the edge of the river among the reeds, and, just as
my bull appeared on the opposite bank, I shot him
dead through the heart.   I had just loaded, and was in
the act of capping, when two cows rushed frantically
by me and up the opposite bank.   I was just in time
to stop the hindermost, shooting her through the
tail and heart ; I found her dead within 100 yards
from where I struck her.   A moment after, two of
Walmsley's Hottentots came tearing up on horseback,
just in time to be too late, and have the satisfaction
of seeing the elands a mile ahead, on the farther
side of the Matakoola.   We cut off the tails of the
two I had killed as trophies, and took the fat and
some of the best of the meat, and hid it under some
stones, carrying with us the breast of one, and four
marrow-bones, and made our way towards the

Matakoola mouth, to try for a sea-cow. It was nearly dark before we arrived. We saw a lot of sea-cows, but they were very shy. I struck two, and think I killed one, but there was no sign of him in the morning, and if he was really dead he must have drifted some distance down the river.

It rained incessantly the whole night, and we were miserably uncomfortable, as we had no shelter whatever, but lay smoking and steaming, and got up as stiff as biscuits the next morning, without a dry rag to put on, some fourteen miles from camp, and the grass in many places up to the waist, and of course soaking wet. To complete the delights of African shooting, it was so murky and foggy that I never could have found my way back alone; but the Kaffirs have a wonderful instinct that way. On reaching the camp, I got a cup of hot coffee and dry clothes, and was soon all right, but sustained a grievous disappointment at receiving no letters from home; the Kaffir we despatched having returned from the bay bringing word that there were none for me, though three mails at least must have arrived.

White and the rest of the party got so far back again all well, but they had had no sport. I rode over to see them in the afternoon, and spent a very pleasant couple of hours with them. I got a sack of mealies for my unhappy pony, which greatly rejoiced me.

23rd.—White and his party treked on, intending

to cross the Tugela as soon as practicable, and get
into the bay, as they were nearly out of the common
necessaries of life.

27*th.*—Met George Shadwell and his party returning, who said they had killed no less than 150
sea-cows and 91 elephants; a most splendid hunt,
two parties, and a whole posse of guns. We eventually reached our different destinations all right,
and separated in Durban, many of us never to meet
again.

This will serve to give the reader some idea of
the sort of life led in a hunting expedition. It is
miserable enough at times, but altogether it is a
roving, careless, wandering life, that has charms
for me. We do just as we like, and wear what is
most convenient. When on foot, a blue and white
shirt and a stout pair of gaiters, with the addition of
a cap and shoes, are all that I burden my body
with.

CHAPTER III.

1854.

HUNTING EXPEDITION INTO THE AMATONGA COUNTRY.

APRIL 10*th.* — Left Natal Bay, and, having only just returned from a trip over the Drakensberg Mountains buying horses, I rode round by the Inanda to get a small outfit of shirts, &c., and found the sole occupants of the place one solitary young cock, which fled at my approach, and a wonderful pig, which always keeps himself in good 'condition, defends himself against all the attacks of wild animals, and has a strong attachment to the place, where he was brought a suckling. I met White by appointment, and was agreeably surprised at seeing Harris on the box of Proudfoot's wagon. He and Maxwell were setting out for a couple of months' shooting. Rode on to the Nonoti, where I remained two days, and, not knowing what to do, had a great washing of clothes at the river.

15*th.* — Started off again on horseback, with three Kaffirs, across the Tugela, intending to stay a few days with Edmonstone's party, who, I heard, were waiting for us at the Matakoola river, about twenty-

four miles ahead. I spent the night at a friend's
encampment, and rode the next day across as
rough and bushy a country as can well be imagined.
Missing my way, I was obliged to sleep in a Kaffir
kraal. At sunrise I was again in the saddle, and
with some difficulty found the encampment, but my
friends had gone. Disappointed of my expected
meal, I had to look out for myself. I came across
the morning spoor of two buffaloes, and followed
them into the reeds, but they broke cover and got
away unseen. Uncommonly hungry, I caught sight
of three elands a long way off, and gave chase without the remotest hope of coming up with them, as
they had a long start, and my horse, Justice, was
wretchedly poor. Mile after mile, however, he just
managed to hold his ground, the elands trotting on
at their leisure. Twice I tried to make a spurt, but
Justice had but one pace. Just, however, as I had
surmounted a hill, having with some difficulty made
the horse gallop, I came on a troop of about thirty
elands. I jumped off and fired at a long distance,
and broke the hind leg of a young bull, who
immediately separated from the herd, and lay down
on a clump of grass. I finished him with a bullet
in his breast. I slept out that night, after a heavy
feed on the eland, of which the Kaffirs reserved for
my special benefit the tongue and a marrow-
bone.

   We came across a troop of about thirty elands the
following day, and tried to stalk them, a Kaffir

leading the horse beside me. They made off, however, a long way, and I fired without effect. I
then endeavoured to mount and give chase, but
could not, for my life, get the bridle over the head of
the horse, who was backing, plunging, and rearing
frightfully, and I had the mortification to see the
herd going far away, hotly pursued by Venture and
Fly, two dogs I bought over the Berg, who succeeded in turning a fine cow out of the herd, and
baiting her well; but I could do nothing with
Justice, he was the veriest brute in the world. I
pocketed my disgust as well as I could, and rode
leisurely to some kraals, to await the arrival of the
wagons, my bullets being exhausted. The Kaffirs
turned up shortly, bringing loads of meat, and
having lost Dusty, the last remaining one of the
breed of Scotch deer-hounds I brought out with
me.

On our return from an unsuccessful buffalo hunt,
on the 22nd, we found Proudfoot and Maxwell
arrived. We had a jolly afternoon, with a little
target practice and athletic feats, and finished up
the evening with singing.

23rd. — Treked on a few miles across the country
over the Inyesan. We saw through the telescope a
troop of about one hundred elands, which we
reserved for Monday's sport. We had a most
exciting run with the dogs after a bush pig, my dog
Venture running gallantly, turning, and, eventually,
with the help of the others, killing him. A better

and richer sample of well-fed pork could not be conceived.   We salted him down for future use.

24th. — All turned out after the elands, four horses, and the rest on foot; but we only bagged one young cow amongst the whole party.   Two or three more, badly wounded, fell into the hands of the Kaffirs.   On our return we found the horse 'Sweep' dead, and were kept awake most of the night by the laughing hyenas and dogs fighting over him.

25th. — Moved our quarters a few miles.   We found a very nice fruit, called by the Kaffirs amabouche, resembling a mangrove in flavour, very luscious and good.   Hunted the strand bush unsuccessfully, bathed in the sea, but had to beware of the ground sharks.   Played whist until a late hour, finished the grog, and wound up by a soaking wet night (from the heavens, I mean).

26th. — As I foresaw a continuance of rain, I set about making a pair of felt shoes, which were to be unrivalled for skill and neatness of workmanship, but the soles took so long softening, that we were unable to finish them.   The rest of the party killed time by draughts, books, and bullet-casting, and wound up with whist, as usual.

27th. — After a sumptuous breakfast on cold pig, three of us and an after-rider started in quest of elands.   On the way, Venture ran a tiger-cat to bay in a tree.   I shook and stoned him out, and the dogs, after a short, quick burst, worried him in good style.   I dragged him to the wagon-road and rode after Proudfoot and Maxwell, who had gone forward. We soon came across two eland cows, dismounted, and fired together at about 200 yards, hitting one hard ; the other was a very long shot with the second barrel of Harris's Westley Richards' rifle. The dogs went away in gallant style, and soon brought them to bay. I was the first to come up with them, on Justice, but could not pull up to shoot. Proudfoot dismounted and knocked over the last with a ball in the neck, firing past me. I gave chase to the other, tumbled off and hit her, but she went away, and Justice also. When I had reloaded, I saw Proudfoot's eland coming up, but did not like to shoot. I threw away my chance till too late, and then missed her. She fell dead, however, shortly after, without another shot.

After having succeeded in catching Justice, by driving him up to the other three horses, we saw a troop of one hundred elands in the distance, and watched their movements for a full hour. As the wind was right against us, we eventually came up with the last of the troop, going away far ahead, having got wind of us. We gave chase: I succeeded in overtaking them, and they turned suddenly, and came in single file past me, within fifty yards. We were a long way from camp, and I knew that if I let go of the bridle I must tramp home. I therefore pulled the bridle over Justice's head and through my arm, and three times the brute pulled back, and jerked the gun from my shoulder. I fired at last, and missed. Proudfoot did the same, and his horse, Blesbok, went off at score, and followed the spoor as accurately as any dog. We got back to the eland just before sunset, and soon stripped her of her skin. The wagon coming up soon after, we quartered her, stuffed her in, and returned to camp.

28th. — White, Harris, and I, hearing that a sea-cow had been seen the day before in a large vley, just below the wagons, went in pursuit, but the cow had decamped, so we returned to the wagons, and I finished my' shoes — a first-rate pair.

The next day we went in pursuit of elands, but were unsuccessful ; we therefore treked on a few miles to some new grass near the Umlilas, and had to go supperless to bed.

30th (Sunday). — A gloomy, wet day. Found it hard to kill time. At noon, we succeeded in getting the kettle to boil, and had a cup of coffee. Found my ink upset, though luckily without doing much damage. Harris and I rather in a strait, our Kaffirs having bolted.

May 1st. — A repetition of yesterday. The tent leaked like a sieve, and Harris and I were as miserable as can be imagined. We cut a drain round the tent, which greatly improved matters. To add to our discomforts, we were short of fire-wood. Our Kaffirs had bolted to the kraals, having been unable to face the inclemency of the weather any longer.

2nd. — Still raining, but with a hope of improvement. Justice was nowhere to be found. Maxwell

at last sighted him with a telescope some three miles
off. Steele and I went after him, and found him
as nearly as possible strangled to death with his
halter, his head and face swollen enormously, and
fearfully thin, having evidently gone without food
for two days, and perishing with cold and rain.
Yet, even when reduced to this strait, the brute
refused to be caught, and though so weak that he
fell twice, and staggered all the way like a drunken
man, he went headlong into a river; fortunately,
however, he succeeded in making the opposite bank.
At length I drove him into a kraal, and caught him.
At sunset I came up with the wagons, which had
treked on four or five miles to better grass, wood,
and water.

4th.—Having seen the spoor of sea-cows, White,
Proudfoot, and Harris went down, taking the tent
and some food, to try and shoot one by moonlight.
Isaac severely wounded a cow, which, however, made
her escape to the river. I did not go, having no
Kaffir to carry my blankets.

After a day employed in re-soling shoes and super-
intending the dyeing of shirts and trowsers, we had
a long tramp on the 6th after reed-bucks, with but
moderate success. Nothing to eat at the wagons,
except a steinbok, which did not go far amongst so
large a party.

7th.—Steele and I started early with four Kaffirs
to bring home a ram I had shot. It was a very
large one, and I had cleaned and stuffed it with

F

grass and hidden it, leaving Fly to guard it from wolves. After breakfasting sumptuously on broiled kidneys, steaks, and mushrooms, which we luckily found near, we loaded the Kaffirs and returned to camp.

8th. — White and Harris left us. Proudfoot, Maxwell, and I, accompanied by a host of Kaffirs, turned out in downright earnest for buffaloes or elands, without breakfast, as there was not a morsel of anything in camp. Proudfoot shot a cow buffalo, and Isaac an old bull. I purchased a dozen pounds of beads from Surtees, and joined White's wagon in the evening, wishing Proudfoot and party good-bye.

Seeing four elands coming down a kloof, straight ·upon us, we dismounted in all haste and crawled to the edge of the kloof, leaving our horses below the hill, out of sight. I ought to have known better than to place such confidence in Justice. I spent the most miserable day I ever recollect, chasing my horse through the most frightful tangled grass and brushwood, up to my armpits, and in many places over my head, through kloofs and valleys. This was at the base of the Umgowie Mountains. It was an hour after sunset before I caught Justice, and when I succeeded in reaching the wagons I was thoroughly fagged. One more such day would have driven me mad. A cup of coffee, however, and a delicious supper of buffalo kidneys, somewhat restored my spirits and temper.

9th. — A day of feasting on tongues, marrow-bones, and all the delicacies of the two buffaloes.

10th. — Harris rejoined us, and we treked on a few miles to a small river, called by the Kaffirs Inkukusa, where we had a delightful bathe. We remained here two days, hunting up the river one day, and down the next; but none of the party burnt powder either day, so we treked on in the afternoon a short distance, to the Umslatoose. We met two traders, who were returning, in consequence of Panda having entirely stopped the trading. He has made the penalty for disobedience to orders certain death, and has commenced by killing about thirty men, and all their wives, children, and relatives. This had so terrified the rest, that no one would come near a trader's wagon. All traders are ordered out of the country, and the reason which Panda alleges for this is that his heart is sore, owing to the sudden death, by dysentery, of two of his chief captains.

13th. — Turned out fully determined to bag something, as an old tough bull-buffalo was all that we had in camp, and he was fast diminishing, under the united powers of half a dozen dogs and as many Kaffirs, and four white men. No one can have an idea of the appetite of the Kaffirs, without actual experience. We had a hard day's work, and never fired a shot.

White and Harris overhauled the stores in the wagon, and found the rice nearly musty, owing to

the wet, and the coffee and sugar almost exhausted.
It was therefore resolved that Harris should return
to the bay with the wagon, for a fresh supply of
provisions and a little lead, and to procure Kaffirs for
himself and me, as it would have been madness to go
into the country so badly provided as we were then.
White and I were in the meantime to go to the
Umgowie Mountains for shooting, and were to spend
the next three weeks under canvas. We crossed the
Umslatoose the next day, and the day after we unloaded the wagon, stowed everything away in the
tent, and Harris and the driver started early for the
bay.

On the 17th, after a soaking wet night — our tent
leaking like a sieve, until the canvas swelled with the
rain — we turned out to hunt, with our usual bad
luck. On our return, we found my Kaffir, whom I
had hired a few days before, and to whom I had
given the name of Goat, had run away. I got a
pound of powder from Mr. Newton, whose wife
made us a very welcome present of a few candles
and needles. We lived for three days on a most
recommendable stew, composed of two sorts of
buck, and wild pig (cured), rice, and pumpkins,
which appeared, warmed up fresh, at every meal.
Our eatables were hung upon a sort of gallows,
erected just before the tent, out of the reach of
our five hungry dogs.

A few days after, the said dogs, taking advantage
of my being absent from the tent for a few minutes

to superintend the baking of some bread, walked off
with a cold goose and a pot of amas — the whole of
our larder, with the exception of two pieces of salt
pig. On my return one day, after an unsuccessful
hunt, I was delighted to find that White had succeeded in buying a goat from the Kaffirs, for four
ostrich feathers.

21*st* (*Sunday*). — Not going out anywhere, I took
the opportunity of putting my three guns into killing
order, considering it no worse to employ myself use-
fully than to pass the time loitering about, whistling,
&c., to kill time.

We remained in the same place a fortnight longer,
chiefly occupied in cutting out felt shoes, dyeing
clothes, and casting bullets, and making other preparations for our hunting expedition on the return of
the wagons. The weather was cold and wet, game
exceedingly scarce, and provisions in camp, consequently, very short. We were reduced at last to
water porridge, rice and pumpkins, with a few occasional ducks and pigeons.

30*th*. — Killed three snakes out of a rotten
tree, all different kinds of tree-snakes. They all
came out of the same hole, while I was cutting
out two bullets.

Had some exciting sport with sea-cows in a
narrow river, with very high reeds on both banks.
To get a shot, I was obliged to climb the trees overhanging the river, and had one or two good chances,
but the villainous black ants fell upon me vigorously,

and in such countless multitudes, biting so severely, that flesh and blood could not possibly hold out another second. I was forced to descend; and an old sea-cow I had been dodging for two hours is indebted to the black ants for her life.

The night before the arrival of the wagons, we went down with our blankets, in the hope of getting a shot at a sea-cow by moonlight; but the moon set before we met with them, and we had to take to our blankets in the long wet grass, without the satisfaction of having secured one.

June 5.— The crack of a whip announced the approach of our long-expected wagon, which had been detained by the river being swollen. Two others came with it, but they brought no letters from the bay, as there had been no mail for two months. Two more wagons joined us the next day, so we celebrated the occasion by setting to work to prepare a first-rate dinner of three courses, for ten, consisting of some buck and buffalo soup; stewed buck and sea-cow, seasoned with lots of onions, pepper, &c.; three sorts of vegetables; and a roast of wild ducks, pigeons, and dikkops. Barter had engaged to provide a dish of fish, but at the second bite he lost all his tackle, and came home discomfited, with one small barbel. Dinner was followed by a bowl of gin punch, with lemons and all other requisites, made in the washing-basin. Three rubbers of whist, and lots of capital songs, finished up the evening.

7th. — All got under weigh, and in about a mile and a half went on our separate ways, two wagons going back to the bay, two to the King's trading, and our own party over the Pongola. Maxwell gave us a good lump of cheese — a great treat in these parts.

8th. — On my return to the wagon, I found some of the party gone up to a kraal to shoot a Kaffir who had threatened to assagai one of Walmsley's Kaffirs, in order to obtain possession of a string of Makanda beads which he wore round his neck. They found, however, that the Kaffirs had decamped in great haste.

11th. — Commenced by shooting my dog Venture, who had lately taken a sulky turn, and would not follow me a yard. Afterwards, I bagged one peau (bustard) and four snipes, and on my return I found White complaining of illness.

12th. — Outspanned at the river Umsindoosie, and as White had made up his mind to return, we unloaded the wagon, and each took our share of provisions, and parted company.

13th. — Francis kindly lent me his old horse, and I and my Kaffir set out, and, after two good soakings, took up my quarters in a kraal, where I found Maclean. We dined together on amas, followed by roast guinea-fowls, in a wretched hut, containing ten Kaffirs, two of whom we employed to hold lighted grass, that we might see to eat. As soon as one straw was nearly consumed, they lighted another by it, so as to keep up a continual light. Each straw burned about a minute.

On the 14th, I came on to the Umveloose. I made up my mind to leave two-thirds of my provisions behind, and go into the country with as little as possible. With this view, I converted an old pair of breeches into bags. These, and half a towel which I spared for the purpose, contained my sugar, coffee, tea, bullets, beads, red kalis, &c. Maclean went off in the afternoon, and I was again left alone.

I was anxious to be off the next day, but as I did not know the way, I was obliged to wait for a friend's wagon. I much feared that my Kaffir would run away, as the Zulus, from some cause or other, had killed all his relations, and he expected that they wished to make an end of him also. His alarm was not unreasonable, as his sister had been impaled only two days before.

With a small frying-pan, which I bought for a few beads from a Kaffir, who did not know its use, a tin cup and plate, pocket-knife and wooden spoon, I managed cooking and feeding pretty well. But the nights of fourteen hours, without books, lights, or anything whatever to do, were indescribably tedious, and the horrid noise which the Kaffirs made, and call singing, only made matters worse.

17th.— Up for once in my life before the Kaffirs, about an hour and a half before sunrise. After a long, tough job in removing the barricade, which is made at the gate to keep out wild beasts, I got out and shot a splendid golden goose, as it was feeding on the mealies within one hundred yards of the kraal. As it is always very cold before the sun rises I turned in again, but was roused by the cries of a child evidently in pain, and was thereupon witness to a new fashion of administering a warm bath. A child of about ten years old was being held down to the ground, while the doctor, with the sole of his foot previously heated on an earthenware pot just off the fire and turned upside down, was pressing the body of the child all over and rubbing it up and down the back, causing it, no doubt, very great pain. The Kaffirs have no feeling in the soles of their feet, the skin being like the hoof of a cow, and fully half an inch thick.

While staying at the kraal, I killed the finest specimen of the eagle tribe I ever saw, and regretted much that I had no arsenical soap to preserve the skin. I saw a great commotion among a troop of guinea fowls across the river, and presently this fellow rose, so gorged that he could only just rise, feathered to the toes with beautiful black and white plumage, and talons fearful to look upon.

The next day I left my goods and chattels in charge of the Nkozi Kazi (the chief's principal wife) at the Black Umveloose, and followed the wagon-track to the Inyelas, about fifteen miles a head, and once again took up my quarters in a kraal.

22nd.— By dint of great persuasion and a promise of thirty strings of Umgazi beads, I got a Zulu to come with me to the Amatonga land, to carry bullets, powder, and other things, as a friend of mine reclaimed a horse which he had lent me, one of his Kaffirs having run away to the bay.

23rd.— As the party I had been waiting for again delayed their starting, I determined not to be delayed another hour ; and, although I did not know an inch of the way, or anything else, I started with two Kaffirs and Fly. Everyone assured me that I should lose myself, but I got on very well over flat country on a good sandy foot-path. A good half of the way I walked bare-footed. I saw wildebeests, quaggas, koodoos, and waterbuck. At sunset I camped out about four miles after crossing the river St. Luey, kindled a large fire, roasted a koran, made some tea, and turned in. It was a bitter night, with a high wind, and I took pity on my Kaffirs and gave them half my blanket, which was a double one. They lay curled up like a ball of worsted at my feet, one of them turning out from time to time to heap fuel on the fire. During the night I heard lions and wolves, but they did not molest us.

24th.—We started early, and had made about twelve miles, when we were overtaken by six or eight Zulus, who begged me to shoot a wildebeest for them, as they were nearly starving. I had an early opportunity of complying with their request, and they lost not an instant in lighting a fire, flaying and cutting up the animal. After a moderate feed they went off with their prize, all staggering under very heavy loads of beef. The paunch they converted into a bag, and scooped up the whole of the clotted blood from the inside of the animal, which had been shot through the lungs, filled the bag with the most nauseous mess you can imagine, fastened up the mouth with two sticks crossed rather ingeniously, and at the first Amatonga kraals took possession of a pot, and boiled bag and all the contents for a glorious repast.

I preferred a mess of Inyouti porridge, a new seed to me, small and not unlike millet, to supping with my morning's friends, and found it very nice, but I greatly missed the new milk so abundant in the Zulu land. The Amatongas have no cattle, lest the possession of them should excite the cupidity of their warlike neighbours, who would soon exterminate the more timid Amatongas.

After about seven hours' sharpish walking through a very thick scrubby country, and apparently very poor land, we came out into a clearance and saw cultivated grounds, the first Amatonga kraals I had ever met with. They much resemble the Zulu huts, but have larger door-ways ; and as the Amatongas have no cattle, there are no fences round their kraals, which are dotted about much more irregularly than those of the Zulus. There was nothing but dense bush and large timber to be seen in any direction.

I was hospitably received by the captain, who allotted me a hut to sleep in. At supper I had the most delicious Bashoo nuts I ever ate. They were roasted in the embers of the fire, and taste exactly like filberts. They grow in pairs in a large husk. The Amatongas' cuisine is decidedly superior to that of the Zulus, but the traveller will nowhere find in their country the rich amas, which is to be had amongst the Zulus.

25th. — Hearing from the Kaffirs that there were inyala in the bush, I sallied out, but without success, until nearly sunset, when, as I was returning home, the Amatongas showed me two inyalas feeding—the first I had ever seen. I succeeded in bagging the stag, a most beautiful dark silver grey buck, with long mane and very long hair like a goat. He is of the bush buck species, but on a much larger scale than the inconka of the colony, with long spiral horns, tanned legs, very long hair on his breast and quarters; a beautiful animal weighing from 250 to 300 pounds, and very fierce when wounded. They inhabit the coast from this to Delagoa Bay, and are numerous; the does are often to be seen in large herds, and are likewise very beautiful, resembling a fallow deer, but of a much darker red, striped and spotted with white; they have no horns, and are half the size of the stag, and nowhere else in Africa have I met with them. I had some trouble in getting him, and must have lost him but for Fly, who brought him to bay several times. I gave him a slanting shot through the shoulder, and out at the neck, and tumbled him over, but he was on his legs again in an instant, and dashed into the bush. When I at last secured him I thought I should never have sufficiently admired him;

but the sun was setting fast, and it was all I could do to get him skinned, and the meat hung up in a tree, before dark. The Amatongas found their way back through the dark in an astonishing manner; they carried the skin, head and horns for me, held back the branches, warned me of stakes or stumps in the path, or took up thorns that lay in my path, and altogether treated me with more courtesy than I had ever before experienced in my life.

27th.— I made an attempt to preserve the skin of my inyala, but, owing to the want of arsenical soap, I failed. The skull and horns were all that I could keep. To-day I paid off my Zulus, and engaged two Amatongas in their place, to carry my things to the next kraals, only a short distance, and arrived early. Got two of the best hunting Amatongas to follow up with me some buffalo spoor which I noticed. I came up with the troop, stalked in upon them, and shot a fine young bull.

28th. — Hired two fresh fellows to carry, and again got under weigh early. After a stiff walk of about four hours, we stopped for breakfast and drank abouti inyouti (Amatonga beer), which is very good, when not too thick. After another stretch of two hours, we halted for the day at a kraal, where I engaged a fine Amatonga to carry my gun, &c., all the time I was in the country. The terms of my engagement were that I should give him the inside fat of an elephant, if I should have the luck to get one. Another Kaffir joined my forces to-day, gratis, and

I gladly enlisted him on those terms. I only wanted
a couple of companions, or some books, to make me
perfectly happy during the fearfully long nights,
when I lay stretched out on my mat, sipping coffee,
and eating roasted nuts and salt, with a fire burning
close to me on the floor. I could easily have concocted a light of some kind or other, if I had had any
use for it. Rats annoyed me considerably during
the night, owing to my having so much flesh in
the hut.

29th. — Off at sunrise, and saw three lions sneaking off from a wildebeest. I was anxious to go after
the former, but the Amatongas would not hear of such
folly and danger, and argued the matter thus :
'What should I do with one, in case I was fortunate enough to kill it?' — instead of the tables
being turned, which they seemed to think the most
probable issue to the attempt ; besides, the lions
were their friends, and provided them constantly
with flesh, and they would take no part in molesting
them. Though strange, it is quite true that the natives throughout are indebted to the lions for many a
dainty repast. Crossed the Umkusi, a beautiful river,
with large trees overhanging and spreading across.
Saw wolves, waterbuck, and several troops of pallah,
and took up my quarters for the night with an Amatonga chief, named Job. The Amatonga brought
all manner of things for sale. I invested in a fowl,
eggs, nuts, some good rice, beer, and a very strong,
neatly-made mat, to carry my blanket and to sleep

A RIVER SCENE.

J. Wolf lith.

Hanhart imp.

on, for a few strings of Umgazi beads, and a red kali,
a piece of curtain binding, about eighteen inches long,
which the Kaffirs are fond of wearing round their
heads. I told the Kaffir to kill and pluck the fowl.
The latter operation he accomplished very completely, but as he had neglected the former, when I
took the fowl in my hand to take out its inside, I
was horrified by its struggling out of my hand, and
running off, as bare as a board !

30*th*.—I paid off my former carriers, and engaged
two others. We toiled a long, weary way through
dense bush all the day. We passed innumerable
vleys, covered with ducks, widgeon, geese, waterrails,
cranes, and divers of all sorts, very tame; but as I
was loaded with ball, I did not molest them. I followed up a herd of impalas, and got a shot at one
more than 200 yards off, and cut both his fore legs
from under him, skinned him, and breakfasted on
him on the spot, and carried away the fore quarters
and the skin with us. I slept in a capital hut, fully
ten feet high in the centre, and neatly finished off.

July 1*st.* — I started early for the Pongola, with
three or four Amatongas. In going through the
bush, I saw a great number of pit-falls, about nine
feet deep, and very narrow at the bottom. They
are made by the natives to entrap all sorts of game.
After walking several miles, the Kaffirs cried out
' Nance inthovu ! ' (see elephant), and I beheld,
about three-quarters of a mile off, a huge monster
flapping his enormous ears, just at the edge of the

bush. I was in great excitement, filled my bandolier with about twenty-four bullets, re-filled two
powder-flasks, took an infinity of caps, and two guns,
which most unfortunately happened to contain but
small charges of powder (three and a half drachms),
as I had not expected elephants, and had no means
of drawing the bullets without firing, which would
have started them instantly. Oh, for a breech-loader !
In this dilemma, I determined on firing at his knee,
if I could not get a side-shot between the ear and
the eye. When all was in readiness, I looked up
again, and saw about fifteen elephants, one apparently with long white teeth, which I set my mind
on securing. I kept well below the wind, and came
within 100 yards of them, when my Amatonga guide
declined proceeding farther. It was rather nervous
work, going up alone, as I saw them breaking
off huge boughs of trees, which crashed all around.
I went up stealthily, however, within thirty yards of
a large cow, but, not liking her teeth, was proceeding with the utmost caution to inspect some of the
others, and endeavour to find the one I had seen at a
distance, with the long white tusks, when, to my
horror and mortification, I heard Fly barking in the
middle of the troop. In a moment they were off,
smashing everything before them, in a great state of
alarm. I ran about six miles after them, through
the bush, and came up with three of them. I gave
one a shot behind the shoulder, but they all made
off, and I saw no more of them ; and, though I

instantly rushed in, a calf and the stern of a retreating old cow was all the chance of a shot I got. In the excitement of the moment, I had forgotten all about the dog, and felt much mortified at the mischief she was the cause of; for I was perfectly cool and collected at these, my first elephants, and should most undoubtedly have got a good shot, even if I had not disabled, and eventually, perhaps, bagged one of the best of them. I never hailed anything with more joy than the Pongola: I was half dead from thirst, never having touched a drop of water all day; and the river was as cold, clear, and beautiful as any I ever saw. It is at this point about 100 yards wide, and its banks on both sides are covered with the wild fig-tree, which grows to an enormous size.

After crossing the Pongola, and sleeping at Moputa's, I was ready to start early on the 5th, but had to wait some time for the return of my Kaffir, Jack. When he arrived, I administered a little wholesome chastisement with a rhinoceros sjambok, and started on a long, heavy walk through deep sand, and finally arrived at a kraal, where I was greeted as usual by a set of noisy curs, which invariably, at the sight of a white man, tumble head-over-heels in all directions, upsetting everything, as frightened as if they had seen an apparition. After the first alarm they bait you unmercifully, and for many minutes it is impossible to hear yourself speak. I don't know that I ever succeeded in making friends

G

with a real Kaffir cur in my life, not even a puppy, and I scarcely ever saw, or knew, or heard of one good for anything ; they do indeed lead the life of a dog. They are well-fed when quite young, but afterwards they are expected to provide for themselves, and are, consequently, wretchedly lean and mangy, but they continue to exist.

After pacifying them a little, driving them to a more respectable distance by sweeping the legs of two from under them with a well-directed hedge-stake, and felling a third with a stone, I ordered food to be cooked for me, and enquired the news, and heard there was great sickness in the country, and that a friend of mine, John Dunn, whom I had hoped to join, had just been carried out of the country by the natives, almost dead. I had, fortunately, met two hunters, Jack and George, the previous day — the latter very sick — and had got a little jalap from him ; and having with me calomel, tartar emetic, and laudanum, took an emetic as a preventative, and continued doing so weekly as long as I remained in the unhealthy country.

6th. — Started early with a hunchbacked dwarf for a guide. He had two of the most extraordinary legs I ever saw — I cannot call them a pair — but with them he managed to give me a great deal of trouble to keep up with him. I saw to-day Guinea fowl of a kind new to me, very like a black cock in plumage, with buff tufts on their heads, and no tails. We crossed the Pongola and reached some large

vleys of water, with lots of wild fowl and large black
geese.   We saw also a few sea-cows, three of which
I struck at long distances.   They were very shy,
having been shot at a good deal.

The Kaffirs brought me in the evening some vile
water porridge, made of inyouti, a small seed grown
by the Kaffirs, which was quite uneatable.   I bought
some twenty fresh eggs, and made a great discovery
in cooking.   I fried this same inyouti porridge in
fat, broke some eight eggs over it, and so concocted
as fine a mess as anyone could wish for; indeed,
it was so good, that I reserved the remains for the
morning.

7*th.* — Off early again after the sea-cows.   On
arriving, I saw only one up, which I had killed the
afternoon before, and which a Kaffir had found out,
and was going in for, but he made off on seeing me.
I soon came on a lot asleep, and, getting pretty near,
I shot the biggest of them.   I soon had some eighty
or a hundred Kaffirs around me, and they hauled
up the cow.   Nothing could be more courteous than
their behaviour while I took what I wanted ; but as
soon as I delivered over the carcase to them, there
ensued an indescribable scene of confusion.   The
Kaffirs rushed at the beast with assegais, knives,
picks, and axes ; hallooing, bellowing, shoving, and
fighting, in a manner that no one would believe
who had not seen them.   Occasionally the captain
ran in, and laid about him with a rhinoceros sjambok
in every direction.   The strongest of the savages got

at the beast, cut off pieces, and hurled them over
their heads to their accomplices outside, who dashed
at them and ran with them, each to a separate heap,
where he deposited his piece, and where no one
meddled with it. In a very short time the whole
cow was disposed of, and not an atom left for
about one hundred adjutants who were stalking
about in hopes of a share of the prey. The same
scene took place at the next, they both being
uncommonly fat, young, tender, and delicious meat.
A man with a thrifty housewife need not starve in
this country, for I killed to-day about five tons of
delicious meat with unlimited fat.

The sun was down before we reached the kraal
again, where I found myself suddenly a great man.
Presents of all sorts were made to me — eggs,
bread, rice, beer, pumpkins, and all the produce of
the land. The bread looks just like roasted potatoes,
but I cannot say much in its favour.

8th. — Spent a quiet day at home, making bell-
tong, and pickling the tongue, &c. of the cow. I
made the captain a handsome present of a choice
piece of the beef, and inspected the kraal. The
natives have the good taste, when making a clearance for their gardens, to spare the gum-trees. They
are very beautiful trees, with dark green leaves
sweeping the ground. Their foliage is so thick, that
no daylight penetrates to the interior. The Amatongas are very industrious, both men and women
working in the gardens — a thing almost unheard-of

among the Zulu men, who would think it degrading, and an occupation only for the women. You seldom meet an Amatonga without his carrying a fire-stick, and big fires are slowly consuming all around the clearance.

9th. — Loth to leave such good quarters, I took a stroll with half-a-dozen Amatongas, to another vley, where I saw lots of sea-cows lying asleep, almost high and dry, with large white birds sitting on their heads, looking just like the hulls of so many vessels, but in unapproachable places. I got a shot at one facing me, and gave her a bullet in the forehead, and was waiting to see if she would rise, when opposite me, over the vley, I saw six elephants. My guide brought me well up to them with wonderful sagacity. A young bull stood between me and the only cow worth shooting; they moved on so quickly on seeing me, that I fired at the bull, and hit him behind the shoulders, laming him a good deal. We chased them about a mile on the open as hard as ever we could run; not much, if anything, to choose between the Amatongas and myself. I was only clad in a long shirt and gaiters, with light felt shoes, and we ran upon pretty even terms, and kept very near the elephants, though never able to get near enough for a broadside. The large cow with a young calf turned and showed fight, whereat the Amatongas fled. Now was my chance, as she stood with her trunk in the air, to have shot her in the chest, but I first aimed at the top of her trunk, then I thought I would wait till she turned, and when she did so, I struck her too high, and I never came up with them again. I returned to the kraal, as the reader may imagine, not in the best of humours.

10th. — Off again : a weary, long walk, through heavy sand. However, I got a good bath about half way, and lots of beer at the different kraals, and at sundown we arrived at the residence of the chief, Umpongal, a man of gigantic stature. He received me well, and gave me the best hut I have ever yet seen, all made of reeds, with the roof beautifully worked. I was honoured by drinking beer out of his private cup, which holds about a gallon, and by a present of a fine fat fowl.

On the 11th, I went to Mathlashlas, and the next day I crossed the Umsutie or Mapoota, a beautiful broad river, very deep, about ninety yards wide, and apparently navigable, emptying itself into Delagoa Bay—with magnificent trees upon its banks, abounding with sea-cows, and swarming with crocodiles. I counted twenty-two at one time, on a small sand-bank in the middle of the river. The stream runs swiftly, and though I walked along its banks for two days, I saw no chance of crossing anywhere without a canoe. The Amatongas lost themselves in the bush, and it was four hours after sunset when we made some kraals, where we put up for the night, and fared rather badly, after a hard day's work, on mealies and cold water. I had no blanket with me, and felt the cold considerably, though we kept up a good fire. I shot badly, and with worse luck, killing nothing, though I had two good chances at buffaloes, four at sea-cows, one at impala, one at a waterbuck ram. Most of these I hit; but hitting and killing large game are two very different things.

13*th*. — We started early on our return, and on the river I got into difficulties with the canoe. As there were no natives at hand, I got into it alone, but could not keep her head up stream. In drifting down at a rapid pace, she shot under the overhanging bough of a tree, and swept me out. I clung to the branch, and got my heels into the boat, and then, with a desperate effort, my whole body ; but I lost my long pole, which, being made of greenwood, sank to the bottom. I had a paddle, however, and brought her to the side, where I clung on to some branches, and awaited assistance. As long as I held on to the trees, there was no danger, except from crocodiles, which were rather numerous there. An Amatonga at last came to my assistance in another canoe, and we fastened them together. I worked the paddle ˙ and he the long pole, and we got across, making one boat fast, and working the other up stream, to the landing-place.

14*th*. — Partook of my last coffee and sugar, with deep regret and many a pang.

The captain made me a present of a small pair of tusks, and tried hard to bargain for one of my guns,

offering me five splendid tusks, worth ten times as
much as the gun.

15*th.* — Roasting hot day.   Took a turn in a different direction, when I swam to a place some twenty-
five yards wide, and laughed heartily at the faces of
many who could not swim being towed across by
their companions, and the convulsive, spasmodic
efforts they made—the most abject fear being de-
picted on every muscle of their countenances. Some
of them were first-rate water-dogs, and brought my
guns and traps over dry, which I could not have
done myself. Oceans of good beer here yesterday :
an old woman brought a basket of sand, laid it on
the floor, made a large hole in the middle, and
placed in it an immense jar of beer, which could not
have held less than nine gallons. Another supply
followed in the evening, in a basket made of grass,
and perfectly watertight.

17*th.* — We mustered a strong party of fifteen,
including the captain of the kraal, and three fellows
to carry beer. We took our blankets with us, and
walked a long way without seeing anything. At last
an old bull buffalo jumped up close to me, and I
gave him a bullet behind the shoulder, which brought
him on his knees ; but he soon recovered himself,
and went off. I sent a second ball after him, to no
purpose. Farther on, I saw a large sea-bull lying
asleep close inland behind some reeds, and proceeded to crawl in on him ; and just as I showed
myself, half way to my waist in water, to my

surprise, instead of endeavouring to make his escape, he charged right at me, at great speed. He stopped for a second about twenty yards off, and I gave him a pill under the ear, which made him spin round and round like a top. I fired two more bullets into his body without effect, missed him

with a third (meant for his head), and began to fear we were to lose him altogether, as he seemed recovering, and was gradually getting farther and farther away into deep water, and giving very poor chances of a shot. The sun was shining so directly on him, that I could not see to shoot a bit; the footing was slippery, and I was half way up to my middle in mud and water, when I got a last chance, and put the ball exactly between the ear and the eye, and

killed him. The sun was fast setting; the Kaffirs
got him nearly ashore, and we lighted three huge
fires (with a cap and powder on the heel-plate of
my gun, giving it a smart blow with a stone),
and fed on him, but he was horribly tough. The
night was awfully foggy, and the dew heavy; and,
when morning came, I had every symptom of
fever. Notwithstanding, I was obliged to walk
twenty-five miles home, with scarcely any shade on
the road. Many a vow I made, during the day,
never to return to the country.

The next day I kept my bed, and my ink being
exhausted, I continued my journal with a compound
of tea and gunpowder. Being very anxious to get
back to the Pongola, where I had some faint hopes
of finding Barter and Moreton, and obtaining a
little quinine, and a fresh supply of provisions — as
I had nothing in the shape of food, and was so weak
that I could no longer eat beans, mealies, and
inyouti — I started, and reached Umpongal's.

21st. — Again got under weigh, trying to make
Utumani's, but, after fighting on for about four hours,
I had to give in. I could not walk five yards
straight, or keep in the path at all. After about two
hours' rest under the shade of a tree, I made some
kraals, where I took up my quarters, and took three
emetics, none having any effect. As a last resort,
thinking it was all up with me, I got a Kaffir to
tickle my throat with long grass, full of little seeds,
pushed far down. This, at last, had the desired

effect, and in the course of a couple of hours I felt better.

22nd. — Reached Utumani's at sunset, utterly done up. Spent a miserable night, never closing my eyes : rats annoyed me beyond all possible endurance — galloping and chasing one another all over my body and face. I roused my Kaffir, struck a light, and took a strong dose of laudanum, and towards morning I got a good sleep.

I was now better, but the ague returned with dreadful punctuality at four every afternoon, and lasted about two hours.

I had managed to make a short journey almost every day, and on the evening of the 24th I reached Moputa's, and was hospitably received by the captain, who sent me heaps of eggs, &c., and I had a good night's rest. A long walk brought me on the next day to the Pongola, where, instead of the quinine which I had been looking forward to, and the luxuries of coffee, sugar, and bread (which last I had not tasted for seven weeks), I found simply nothing. At last, however, I discovered a little rice, which I had left behind me on my last visit, and which was now really welcome. The next day, Tom, the messenger, arrived with a supply of all comfortable things, and raised my spirits considerably.

On the 28th I started early, and long before sunset reached Tagati's, where I stayed the following day with Austin. He left me the next day, after making an exchange of salt for some needles and

thread. Got over this much-dreaded part of the
road, twenty miles across — a dreary sandy flat,
without a tree or a drop of water — and then five or
six miles through the bush, wonderfully, being highly
favoured with a beautiful cool cloudy day, with a
fine lively breeze of wind all the way.

August 2nd. — I offered my hunter some beads,
if he could show me another inyala. We proceeded a long way, through very thick bush ; at last,
I saw the Kaffir's eyes sparkle, and, on emerging
out of the bush to a water-pool, he made frantic
gestures to me to go round another way, which I did
with caution, not knowing in the least what I was to
see. A moment after, I beheld a noble buck inyala
walking leisurely away, having slaked his thirst,
about seventy or eighty yards off. Presently, he
turned half round, and was greeted with a ball
in the shoulder, when he made a tremendous spring
into the air, and dashed headlong into the bush.
The Amatongas ran like lightning, and with wonderful sagacity followed him through thick bush, and
brought him to bay, where my Kaffir, to whom I had
given a second gun, brought him down.

A day or two after, I bid adieu to Tagati, and, on
the 5th, I crossed the Umkusi, and engaged my
Kaffir's two brothers to accompany me to the bay.
On the 8th, I crossed the St. Luey, and on the following day got back to the wagon. As I was still
unwell, and much fatigued, having walked hard for
seven successive days from the Pongola, I deter-

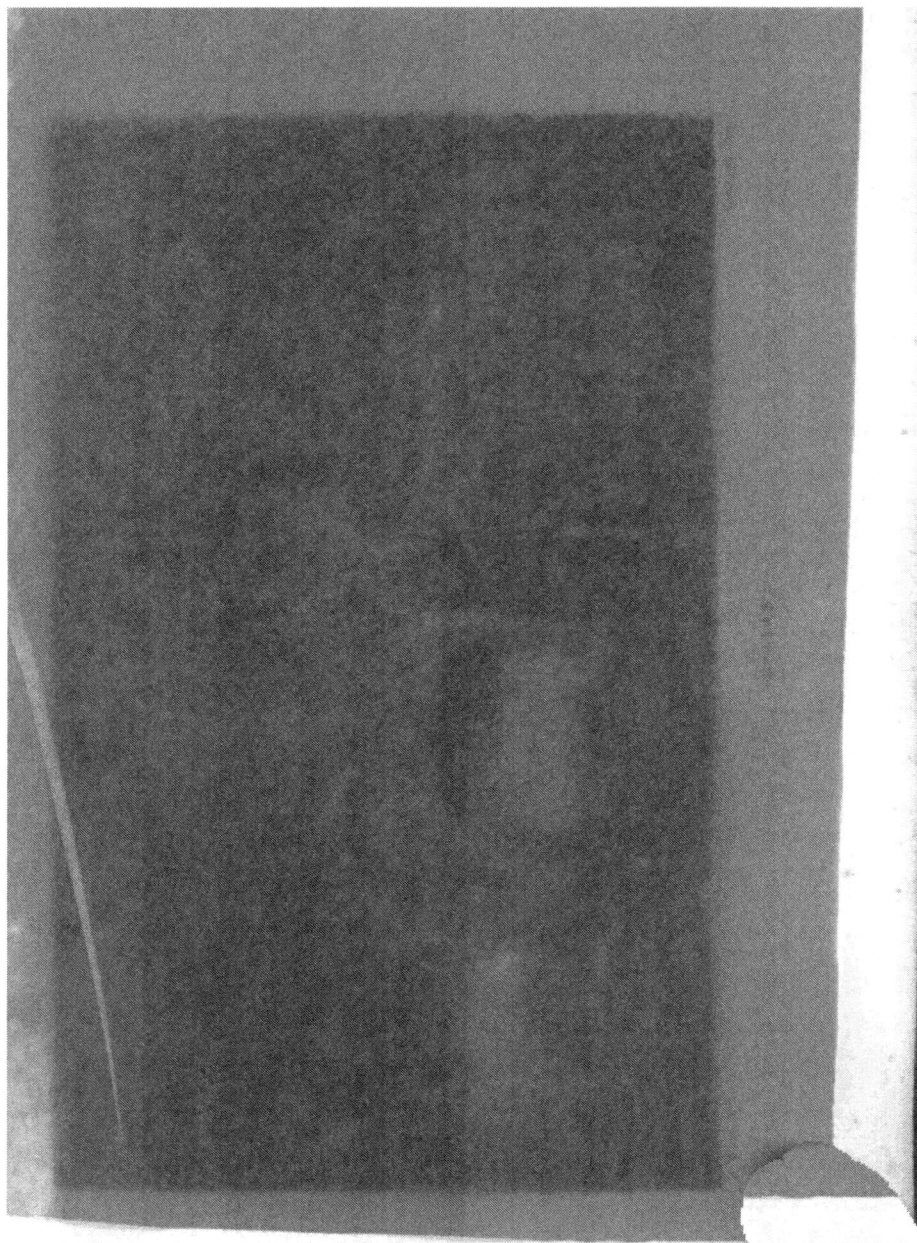

mined to send on two of my men to bring me my pony Billy. It was a walk of about eight days to the bay, and my original Kaffir was in great fear of the Zulus, and begged a shirt of me to disguise him a little, as then, he said, they would know that he was a white man's Kaffir, and would not molest him. I could ill spare it, having only two, but I could not prevail on him to start without.

While waiting for their return, three mounted Dutchmen rode up to me one day, and kindly offered to sell me an old broken-down horse, worth about 6*l*., for 400 dollars (about 30*l*.). I declined their obliging offer, whereat they all rode off again.

13*th*.—Reached Makite's kraal, where I found the ivory of nine elephants, shot by my two hunters, buried in the cattle-kraal, as they had told me ; but, before giving it up, the captain, in whose charge it was left, made my fellows point out where it was buried, to show that we were the rightful owners, which my fellows were luckily able to do, having been told beforehand by the hunters who buried it.

On the 15th, I heard of poor Harris's untimely death. 'Poor fellow ! we had agreed to go together the following year to Mosilikatse's country.

20*th*. — Started my indoda (old man) off to the Umslatoose, to look after Billy and the Kaffir, and bring them on here. Paid a visit to a friend trading at Umlandillas, and, on comparing notes, found I was two days behind-hand in my dates, and can only account for it by supposing I must have been insensible in the Amatonga kraals, across the Pongola, when those days slipped by. Bought sixty-seven head of cattle and six sheep, thirteen shillings a head all round, after several days' bargaining; and had a day's work, sorting, choosing, and branding, out of some four hundred Steele had traded.

26*th*. — No signs of the pony at the appointed place of meeting, so I again started for Durban.

29*th to* 31*st*. — Spent three miserable soaking-wet days, with the choice of being almost suffocated with the smoke of damp wood, or being drenched to the skin. My food all the time consisted of bread and milk, sometimes boiled for a change; which would have been all very well, but I was obliged to put myself on short commons, as my meal was only 2lbs. weight to begin upon, and I made it hold out the three days.

September 1*st*. — Found my messengers, but no horse. They had never crossed the Tugela: the indoda fell into bad hands, got well thrashed, and everything he had taken from him. He tried to give me a long account of his grievances, but I did not understand one word.

9*th*. — Made Durban at last, having got the loan, at the Umslali, forty miles off, of a fearfully fat pack-ox (Monkey), and got a burster off him in jumping a sluit; my rheim broke from his nose, and away he went home again.

CHAPTER IV.

1855.

I HAD been making my head-quarters as usual at Brindle, a farm in the Umvoti district, belonging to Mr. Eastwood, a most intimate friend and neighbour in England, who had been also a fellow-passenger on the voyage out to the colony. We had a great deal of trouble and annoyance in getting Kaffirs, but at last I managed to start on March 31, with only a driver and foreloper, having agreed to give the latter a heifer to go to the Tugela — a most exorbitant price. Our first feat was to upset the wagon, and scatter its contents far and wide. This caused us a delay of a couple of days, during which I succeeded in engaging three Kaffirs. I therefore dismissed my foreloper, and got on as far as Grey Town, where I was again delayed three or four days by incessant rain.

I left Grey Town on April 7, and, after continually sticking in the mud of the worst roads I ever saw, I reached, on the 10th, the house of a

Norwegian missionary named Lawson.   The descent
which we had to make from here rather staggered us,
but Mr. Lawson advised tying up three wheels and
having rheims and Kaffirs to hold up the wagon on
the upper side, as the descent was very slanting as
well as steep.   He followed up his advice practically
by the loan of an old trek tow, which I must confess
to having subsequently appropriated.   With its assistance and two rheim chains we reached the bottom
in safety.   In a similar position two days afterwards we
were not so fortunate.   By dint of screeching, and
flogging the oxen, we had reached the top of a desperate hill.   The descent commenced almost immediately: the foreloper did not warn us in time to stop
the wagon, and put on the drag, and lock the wheels;
so down we went at a frightful pace.   I, not liking
the situation, threw myself on a big thorn-tree, which
we were passing at full speed, and escaped with no
further injury than the ruin of my shirt.   I had just
got clear of my not too comfortable bed, when I heard
the wagon come to a sudden halt.   I ran forward
and beheld ten of the oxen round a tree, and one
of the Kaffirs wringing his hands and dancing in a
frantic manner, roaring out ' mammo mammi, mammi
mammo,' over the foreloper, who was on the ground
covered with blood, and looking as wild as a hawk.
What had happened to him I have never yet been
able to understand.   On closer examination, I found
that the poor fellow's skull was split on the left side,
and it appeared as if the wagon had gone over his

right arm. I gave him some sal-volatile, and, after washing his wounds and cutting his hair away, fixed his head tightly between my knees. The Kaffirs looked on in awe, but when they saw me take out

needle and thread, thimble, &c. to sew up his head, they raised a fearful outcry, in which the wounded man joined: I was therefore obliged to desist from my operation, and content myself with binding up his head as tightly as I could. I made up a nice bed for him in the wagon, but he positively refused to go on. The other two Kaffirs also refused, and wanted to know how many head of cattle I intended

H

paying his father for his being killed in my service.
There is no use arguing with Kaffirs; when they
take a thing into their heads, they are worse than
mules, so I was obliged most reluctantly to leave
the poor fellow behind. I was left in a pretty fix,
with no one but the driver to manage four loose
horses and as many loose oxen, as well as the wagon.
I managed for a few miles, and then had the luck
to pick up a boy to go with us to the Tugela for
half-a-crown. In the evening two Dutchmen stopped
at my wagon, who said the Kaffirs who had left me
wanted gunpowder—a very usual remedy with them
in many cases—and also told me that the Kaffirs
intended to bleed the wounded man between the
shoulders and rub in gunpowder. I fear they must
have killed him amongst them all.

On the 14th I reached the Tugela, where I was
detained a fortnight for want of a proper pass,
signed by a resident magistrate. On May 1st I got
the pass, and crossed the river, which was very high.
In the course of a few days I lost three of my horses
from the lung sickness, and on the 10th my mare
Bessie Bell sickened. I sent her off immediately to
Lewis, requesting him to bleed her, and followed
the next day with a sorry heart, to hear her fate. I
was in time to see her alive. I loosened her halter,
and she followed me about like a dog, looking most
piteously. I could not bear to see her, and thought
of shooting her, but, before I could make up my
mind to do so, her miseries were ended. She was a

mare I valued beyond price for her many good qualities, but chiefly for her attachment to me, and her wonderful powers of endurance. She carried me seventy-five miles in one day with the saddle only once off her back, without showing the slightest symptom of fatigue!

May 14th.—After making various exchanges, such as beads for canvas, powder for cooking utensils, &c., Lewis and myself parted company, intending to meet again in about a month. I tried to find a practicable road to the Umgowie Mountains, as, since the loss of all my horses, my only chance of game was among the mountains and bush. I could find no road, so I followed Lewis's track. In the course of the day I unaccountably lost my dog Fly: I think he must have been bitten by a snake; I had killed a mamba, nine feet long, the day before.

Hearing from the Kaffirs that there were sea-cows in the Umlilas, I outspanned, and waited till the sun was getting low, and went in pursuit. How my heart beat at hearing the well-known blow just round a bend of the river, and, cautiously peering round, saw three, making up the stream! They were very shy, and showed poor heads. I took a round, and got above them unperceived, and made an excellent shot at a very large bull; he only just showed his eye above the water at about fifty yards, and I put a bullet from Burrow (my No. 7) in the very centre. I was loth to fire at so poor a chance, but the river being narrow I thought I must take the first chance, or I might see him no more.

15th.—I found my sea-cow on his back in the middle of a large hole, about forty yards from land, with half a dozen crocodiles round him. I bribed the Zulus, and bullied my Kaffirs, to go in and fasten cords on him to tow him ashore, but in vain ; so after firing a couple of shots, and throwing stones to frighten the crocodiles, I swam in, made the cords fast to him, and made for the shore again as soon as possible, shouting lustily to scare the crocodiles. The ropes had been so carelessly fastened together that they came undone as soon as they were used, and I was obliged to swim in again. It was not a very pleasant position to be rolling about on a sea-cow with crocodiles all round one, and I did not at all relish it. Through bad management I had to go in four times, and once, while swimming from him to shore with a slip-knot round my arm, striking out vigorously, the rheim being too short, checked me suddenly, and sent me a good depth under ; the Kaffirs howled again, making sure the crocodiles had me.

At last, however, after several failures, we got him to land. The next day I brought up the head, which the crocodiles, adjutants, and vultures had picked tolerably clean, and buried it near a kraal, in charge of an old Kaffir, salted the tongue and a tub full of meat, stretched some sjamboks and whip-lashes round the wagon, and in the afternoon started in pursuit of more, but without success.

17*th.*—Off long before sunrise for buffaloes, but, owing to the want of dogs and the stupidity of my man, we were unsuccessful. On our return to the wagon, I shot a crocodile lying high and dry, fast asleep. It was some time before I could make out which was his head and which his tail, and I was nearly shooting at the wrong end. When the bullet struck him, he threw up his head and opened his huge jaws, and I saw that I had broken his

spine. He would, however, have wriggled himself into the river, had I not given him a bullet in the throat and another in the chest, which settled him. I watched him from the opposite bank for a full hour, ready to give him another ball if he showed any sign of life, and when I was satisfied that he was

stone dead, I hastened round by the wagon to get
assistance, and a hatchet, to bring home his head as a
trophy; but, on returning to the river, nothing was
to be seen but pools of blood :·the other crocodiles had
dragged him into the water in the meantime. I was
much disappointed, as it is difficult to get one, except
in the water, where they always sink when shot.

Here is a recipe for an excellent stew : about one
pound and a half of breast of sea-cow well stewed,
cut up small, about three table-spoonfuls of inside fat
rendered down as white as snow, a few red peppers,
salt, a handful of rice, a handful of fine flour, a couple
of pickled walnuts, with a few sprigs of thyme, or
some such herb. The ingredients seem rather miscellaneous ; all I can say is, that I made it by guess, and
put in anything I had; but when it came up, I thought
nothing could improve it. The long nights were
rather dreary with nothing but 'Blaine's Field Sports'
and a few old ' Family Heralds ' to read; but, though
I should like companions in the evening, I should
always prefer to shoot alone.

25th.— I recovered my oxen, which had been lost
for two days previously, and with some labour got
over the rise of the Umlilas.

26th.— A long blank day on the tops of the
Umgowies ;— wearisome up-hill work, and saw
nothing but an eland cow, which was too wary
to let us approach, so we went supperless to bed.

28th.— By the advice of a Dutchman, Joubert by
name, I changed my route, and he accompanied

me back to Nungela's, who was very gracious, and
offered to kill a beast in return for a bottle of grog.
We stayed out nearly the whole night trying for a
sea-cow, but the wind was so capricious that we never
could get near them; and at last they made off,
followed at a killing pace by Joubert, two Kaffirs,
and myself. I strained every nerve, more to beat a
Kaffir, who was flying along with a blanket fastened
round his neck, streaming behind him, than with any
hope of coming up with the sea-cows, who were tearing along ahead at a fierce pace. I was first up,
but the sea-cows had gained the long grass, and we
saw no more of them.

June 3rd.— I went to church, and saw such a
medley as I should have thought mortal would never
have the chance of seeing. The side walls were
built of mud, and, with the help of wooden posts,
supported a zinc roof. To windward, the walls had
fallen in, leaving the building airy and open. From
the beams hung Kaffir ropes, the tent and sides of a
wagon, loads of mealies, old saddles, yokes, skeys,
neckstraps, and all apparatus for wagoning, old hats
and bridles, and part of a splendid tiger-skin. In
the midst of all this and ten times more, rose a
pulpit, the cushions and hangings of which bore
marks of a great deal of service; and in the pulpit a
tall, bushy-whiskered Norwegian missionary, in a
black coat buttoned to the throat and reaching to
the heels, with spectacles of course, held forth. About
thirty Kaffirs, men and women, squatted on a mat on

their hams, huddling close together, two under one
blanket, hunting the borders for ———, and cracking
heaps of them, or taking thorns out of their feet
with wooden pins, unseen by the pastor, who held
forth for more than three hours.

A kinder, more hospitable, better-hearted man,
however, never breathed. He used to summon his
congregation to Divine Service by having a bell sus-
pended round his horse's neck, tinkle-tinkle all the
way he went. Though I must narrate things as I
found them in different parts of Africa, I shall always
entertain the highest opinion of Mr. Schroeder,
and feel grateful to him for much kindness and
hospitality received at his hands on several occasions ;
and, if any man ever succeeds in converting to
Christianity the Zulus, or any part of the nation, he
is as likely a man as any I know, being uncommonly
well read, thoroughly acquainted with the language,
manners, and customs of the nation, and having great
influence with them ; and, though I doubt his making
converts, the Zulus respect and look up to him, and
would on no account injure him.

4th. — I had two chances at buffaloes; gun missed
fire both times first barrel, and, what may probably
never occur again, I killed *dead* with the second on
each occasion an old cow and splendid heifer ; very
fat, delicious meat.

The days passed one so like another, that for a
month I kept no account of them. On July 4, as
we were out buffalo shooting, an old cow buffalo with

a young calf charged me ferociously in the bush, down
a steep hill. I stood my ground, as I had no time to
run away, and gave her a bullet high up in the near
fore shoulder, as she came within about ten yards of
me. I then made a spring on one side, and she crashed
past me, almost grazing my breast. With my second
barrel I rolled her head over heels, not more than
three lengths from me. She soon regained her legs,
turned and made up the hill, trying to get at my
gun-carrier, who was up a tree, just out of her reach.
I was behind another tree close to.her, but she did
not see me, and I kept as still as a mouse. She then
hobbled away down the hill mortally wounded, and
I finished her off with a third ball.

July 22*nd.*—We crossed the Black Umveloose, and
on the following day the Inyoni. At the kraal which
we visited, the Kaffirs were all very inquisitive to know
how I came by the wagon and oxen, as last year,
when I had spent some time there, I had not even a
Kaffir in my service, and I had increased 500 per
cent. evidently in their estimation, as they despise a
poor man as much as they respect a rich one, to whom
they are very fawning and servile.

29*th.*— I got three letters from home and a Natal
newspaper, and by their help and that of my driver,
who recollected the days of the week, I corrected
my reckoning, which had been two days out.

August 1*st.*—We were ploughing our way through
long, heavy wet grass and scrubby thorn trees, when
an old rhinoceros cow got up slowly from behind a

thorn tree, and, after giving me a good stare, advanced
slowly towards me.   I had only my small rifle,
my gun-carrier being about twenty yards behind
with my No. 9.   I beckoned frantically to him to
come on, but he seemed very undecided.   At last,
however, being a plucky little fellow, he came up,
threw the gun at me, case and all, and ran up a tree
like a monkey.   I lost no time in getting the gun
out of the cover, and gave the rhinoceros a ball in
the chest.   She turned round in double quick time,
panting like a porpoise. I followed, but a Kaffir cur
prevented me from getting very near, so she got away.

On climbing the top of the hill I saw two more,
and sent my Kaffir below them, thinking they were
sure to make down hill. I could not get near them,
but just as they were about to make off, I shot one
in the shoulder, but rather too low, and away they
went.   The dogs turned one, and brought him back
not fifteen yards from me at full trot, his head up
and his tail curled over his back, stepping out in
splendid style, with fine high action.   He looked very
much inclined to charge me, but a bullet behind his
shoulders, which dropped him on his knees, made
him alter his course.   I felt convinced that I had
killed him, and followed him.   At last, we saw a brute
lying down in so natural a position that I never
thought he could be dead, and shot him behind the
shoulder, but he had laid down for the last time
some hours before.   It was the one I had shot first.
After cutting out his horns, some sjamboks and his

tongue, and hanging them up in a tree, we went off
for water, and had not gone far when I saw another,
about twenty yards off, looking at me, uneasy, and
apparently trying to screen herself from being
seen. I waited some time till she turned, and
then shot her behind the shoulder, when she immediately came at me, but a ball in the centre of
her forehead stopped her progress, and she fell dead

not ten yards from me: a lucky shot, as I hardly knew
where to fire, and I had not an instant to lose. I
must have been impaled on her very long horn if I
had not been fortunate enough to kill her. She had
a very young calf, squealing most lustily, which
the dogs were fighting with. I got them off, and
wanted very much to take him to the wagon, and
sent off my Kaffirs forthwith for half a dozen fellows

to carry him.   He was like a well-bred Chinese pig,
prick-eared, very fine skinned and fat, and shone as
if he had just been polished with black lead; but
while John and myself had gone to shoot a wilde-
beeste to make something to carry him in, slung
between two poles, the hyenas had killed him, pre-
ferring him to the mother, though I had expressly
cut a great portion of her hide off, that they might
feed, as we were obliged to leave the calf all night to
get water.

13th.— Hard day's bargaining with Mopitas, and I
was forced to pay very dear for four young oxen,
which I was obliged to buy to replace deaths.

14th.—Ascended a very high hill, and spent some
hours at the top in taking a survey of the surrounding country, as broken, rugged, and hilly a country on
every side as can well be imagined, but the view well
repaid my labours.

15th. — Started off again in the direction of the
Pongola, crossed the Umkusi, and pitched my tent
for the night, being unsuccessful in getting any game,
though I worked very hard.   I was the more
astonished at this, as I never travelled over more
promising ground, beautiful short, new, green sweet
grass, with plenty of bush and water.

18th.—Returned to the wagon, killing only one
reed-buck. As I was trying to jump the St. Luey, the
bank broke in with me, and I fell in, over head and
ears. Saw a great number of koodoos and two troops
of elands, buffaloes, and a vast quantity of game, but

did not stop to shoot, as I had lost myself, and was afraid I should not reach the wagon that night, and my Kaffirs had my blanket.

19*th.* — The hottest wind I ever yet felt in the colony. I was in the water half the day, and knew not where to put myself. These hot winds are, however, of rare occurrence.

20*th.*—Just as cold as yesterday was hot, and raining hard; but, fortunately, I have got the loan of 'Martin Chuzzlewit' for a few days. Turned out in the evening, got a steinbuck, koran, and dikkop.

Sept. 19*th.*—Inspanned, and started on my return; two deaths among my oxen, the rest rather fine drawn; have been the most of my time away from the wagon, shooting and spending a few days with Riley, Forbes, &c., and some very wet weather we have had. On the whole, very bad sport; five old bull buffaloes afforded good sport, and took a deal of killing. I had many chances at black rhinoceros, but they are not worth a shot; lost Nettle, by a tiger I suppose; saw five lions at different times, but being alone, did not venture battle, as I did not see one by himself. Almost tumbled over three rhinoceros in the dark, and they hunted me away, following me up a good way, and showing every demonstration of their displeasure, ploughing up the ground, &c.: made a sad mull of two sea-cows, which I took for rhinoceros, the night being very much overcast, and did not venture as near as I might, as it was an open plain. I was not more than twenty-five yards off, but

the wind being very favourable, I might, had I
known they were sea-cows, almost have gone up and
scratched them, and made dead sure of my shot; as
it was, owing to having no white paper on the
muzzle of my gun, I could not aim with any
certainty. Saw several large snakes about the St.
Luey, and one horrid puff adder alarmed me considerably. I was trying to despatch him with an iron
ramrod, when his head and throat swelled to an
enormous size, turning a hideous livid colour, as he
reared himself up, and, with a horrid hiss, pitched
himself at me; but I managed ·to dodge him, and he
disappeared. Got a couple of crocodiles, and caught
a small one, about one foot long, alive—a wicked
little monster; took from one a lot of beautiful fat,
which burns brilliantly ; have got about 350 pounds
of ivory to take down with me, and shall endeavour
to make up my load with twenty-five buffalo hides,
as I hear there is a sale for them.

25th. —After losing the oxen for a couple of days,
and a couple of stick-fasts, got on to the missionaries
without any adventure. Mothlow shot a sea-cow,
and I went down with a whole troop of Kaffirs to
bring up half a wagon-load of speck, hearing she was
a very large cow, and so she proved, but as lean as
a crow. It was an awfully wet night, so I made a
Kaffir kraal, and stayed the night, supping on a
delicious wild duck, amas, tchualla, and coffee, and I
contrived to bake a loaf of bread between two
pieces of a broken Kaffir pot, so that I was truly in

clover. My tent kept very heavy rain off surprisingly, and the soil being very sandy, soaked all
up, and I spent a most comfortable night, when I
had expected, from all appearances, just the reverse.

26th. — Made the wagon again. I got over the
ground, twelve or fourteen miles, barefoot, very well,
to my intense satisfaction; it is an accomplishment I
longed to achieve. Inspanned a young ox, which I
had christened Lanky, after several hours' hard
fighting with him. I never saw so wild a brute; he
roared, and bellowed, and charged all before him in
the most savage, determined manner, and butted
furiously a bull-stag he was coupled with, but a right
good buffalo rheim defied his utmost efforts, and
when everything failed, he lay down, alas! never
more to rise. I thought dragging him a few yards
might have the desired effect, but when we stopped
the wagon, his neck was broken. I cut his throat,
skinned, and cut him up, and have converted the
most of him into bell tongue.

CHAPTER V.

1856.

THIRD HUNTING TRIP INTO THE ZULU COUNTRY.

I LEFT Mr. Eastwood's, on Tuesday, October 7, on a tramping tour into the Zulu country, for the purpose of looking up my hunters, and taking them fresh ammunition. I took six Kaffirs with me, and while detained for four days at the Tugela, we were nearly starved. On going out one morning in search of a buffalo, I left one of my men under a tree, saying he was dying, but on my return with the news that I had shot one, he immediately revived.

I and one of my Kaffirs did not fare so badly. Being unable to shoot anything, as game was wild and wary, and the bush very thick and impenetrable, so that we could not get on without making a noise and scaring the buffaloes, we swam the Tugela at night, and had a good feed of boiled mealies and milk, but were unable to bring anything across for the rest of the party, in consequence of the breadth of the river and the rapidity of the stream.

My old horse Mouba (Sugar) strayed away, owing to the carelessness of the Kaffir in whose charge he was, knee-haltered, with a head-stall on, and a strap attached to it fastened to another very strong padded one, buckled above his knee, which kept his head within one foot of his knee. This plan is usually adopted in the colony, to facilitate catching one's horse without hindering his feeding. We could not track him a bit, owing to the stony ground, and he remained knee-haltered for nearly three months, when he was found by a party of Dutch Boers hunting. I eventually recovered him, with no further injury than a deep scar above his knee, and a ring of white hairs round. The Boers who found him told me that, from the tracks he left, he must have slept and drank every day and night at the same place; he was still knee-haltered, and it was extraordinary that he escaped the lions so long.

On the 20th, we reached the house of Mr. Schroeder, the Norwegian missionary, by whom we were hospitably entertained during several days' bad weather. I thought myself very fortunate to be under his roof, as neither my little tent nor a Kaffir kraal are very agreeable, under such circumstances.

I left Mr. Schroeder's on the 23rd, with a supply of medicines, which he kindly gave me. I tried walking barefoot, but did not get on well. After sleeping at a Kaffir kraal, we continued our journey through a bad broken country, very slippery after the rain. However, I was in very good condition, and stood a long day's unsuccessful hunt after a sea-cow without fatigue. On the 25th, we crossed the Umslatoose,

I

where my biscuits had the misfortune to get a thorough soaking, owing to the carrier getting into a quicksand.

26th (*Sunday*).— Spent the day at the Norwegian Missionary Station, where there was a large muster of Kaffirs at church.   The Norwegians are excellent hands at making up a good dinner out of poor materials, and on this occasion Mrs. Aftebro fully sustained the reputation of her countrywomen.

A fat Muscovy duck, however, when young and tender, is not a bad subject to work on ; the stuffing, made of mealie meal and eggs, is excellent, and a substitute for apple sauce, made of sour dock, is worth knowing of.   They have a queer custom of giving you soup, afterwards, which I declined, but changed my mind on hearing it was sweet, made of arrow-root, preserves, &c.

I left the station the next morning, and had a good bit of shooting, bagging two steinbuck, one peau— a brilliant shot at 140 yards — and two koran.   On reaching the kraal where I had told the Kaffirs to stop, I found them dancing and singing over two more steinbuck which they had killed.

28th.— The Kaffirs were very importunate that I should shoot two reedbucks which they saw close at hand, so I took my gun and knocked one over, and soon afterwards a splendid crest-peau or bustard. We already had more meat than we could carry, and even the dogs turned up their noses at the daintiest morsels ; but the Kaffirs, though heavily laden, could not make up their minds to leave anything behind, so we cleaned and plucked, and made all as light as possible, and the Kaffirs carried off everything, not excepting the huge crested bustard. In the course of the day we crossed the Umsindoosie, and, after some hard walking, reached the Umveloose at sunset.

The next morning we walked about four miles up the river, and, having found a crossing-place, we got safely over, though the river was high. The day was burning hot, and we reached Johnson's wagon in the afternoon. An attack of English cholera laid me up there for several days, and I did not leave till late on November 4. I walked hard and reached the St. Luey, which I found much flooded, at sunset. In the course of the night we heard numbers of lions, but saw nothing of them.

5th.— Went into the bush, where the thick foliage and underwood and the long grass made the travelling bad and the shooting worse. However, I succeeded in bagging two bush buck. Ragman, a six-months' old puppy, behaved remarkably well, sticking to the second, a young doe, for fully two miles through the bush, and finally bringing her to bay at the river. He was dead beat when we found him, but he still held on like a vice. He is a whelp of great promise, bull and greyhound, with a dash of the pointer, the best breed possible, and the best feeder I ever saw, eating huge rashers of any animal just killed, when the sun is at the hottest, at which time very few dogs will feed, however hungry, saving us the trouble of carrying food for him. The natives make their curs carry their own food, by cutting a hole in a huge piece, slipping it over their heads round their necks; and I have frequently met a score of curs ornamented with a necklace of the kind, cut from a hind leg, which part they value least of any, and each weighing half as much as the animal which carries it, and they can neither get it off nor eat it.

6th.—Rain all day. I made two sheaths for knives, and had a shot at a hyena in the evening, but being out of breath with running, I missed him. He was gorged to the verge of bursting.

7th.—Crossed the St. Lucy, one of the best rivers I know of for sport of all kinds, and nearest to the colony; it rises somewhere at the foot of the Ombombo Mountains, and runs through a splendid wooded valley. Lions are very plentiful. One night I was encamped in my small tent, weighing only 10lbs., which I had pitched as usual at the foot of a large tree, easy of ascending in case of need. My old pack ox Dancer was made fast with a rheim through a hole in his nose, and pegged down close to the tent for safety; and two Kaffir boys (the rest of my party having gone back to the wagon for stores) were at a large fire in a small belt of thorns (mimosas) within twelve yards, just opposite the opening of my tent, when I heard the deep low subdued murmurings of a lion gradually nearing us. Old Dancer became very fidgety. There was a lot of meat hanging in the tree — koodoo, waterbuck, &c.— out of reach of the dogs. The lion came on very stealthily

and quietly, the night being very dark, and actually
tried to claw the meat down from the tree close to me.
I was sitting cross-legged, with my double rifle across
my knees, expecting every moment to see his outline
between me and the fire, where my lads were, as I
thought, asleep; the brute actually stumbled over
the tent ropes at the back, which were pegged down
some six yards behind, causing a jar through the
tent. Just at this critical moment something burst
through the opening into my tent, quick as thought,
and fell at my feet, and I was within an ace of shooting my two Kaffir boys, who had been awake all the
time, lying as still as dormice, but could stand it no
longer. I expected every moment the lion would
have sprung on old Dancer, who remained perfectly
passive, but after in vain trying to claw the meat
down again he left us. On getting up in the morning I saw some six or seven different varieties of
game; I hardly knew which kind to hunt, but gave
the koodoos the preference.

8th.—A long, heavy walk, through vleys and
water and foot-paths running down with wet, brought
us to the first Amatonga kraals, the most wretched
habitations imaginable. The poor fellows were all
but starving; they had nothing to live on but wild
figs, Kaffir oranges, and other fruit of the kind.

9th (Sunday).—Another wet and miserable day, my
clothes, blankets, &c. all damp and unwholesome.

10th.—To-day we had a long tramp through the
bush. I wounded an inyala doe, and had a long

chase after her, but eventually lost her. They are
very wild and wary, and it requires the greatest
caution to get a shot at them. Shortly after, I broke
the leg of a buck. Ragman and Juno soon brought
this one to a stand, and it dragged them a long way
through the bush, bleating lustily. The dogs held
on splendidly, and we followed the sound through
the bush. At length I came on Ragman covered
with blood, and was greatly surprised to find he had
left the buck, but, hearing a row in the bush, I went
on, and found three hyenas tearing away, and
bolting skin and flesh at such a rate that in three
minutes more there would not have been a
particle left. Juno had fled in fear and trembling,
and did not appear again for an hour. The hyenas
retreated on my approach, and I was unable to get
a shot at them, though I followed them, growling, a
long way.

I went on afterwards to St. Lucia Bay, which I
found swarming with wild fowl. I knocked over
five geese at once, and shot a crocodile also.

12th.— As we were going out after a sea-cow, the
Amatonga who was leading cried out, 'There is a
dead buck,' and I saw what I took to be an inyala
doe, and went leisurely towards it. My fellows,
however, ran, and when within about thirty yards,
up rose a fine black-maned lion, and slunk into the
bush close by. The Kaffir in advance vanished like
smoke. Ragman ran, and was barking, when out
came two lionesses brilling savagely, at which the

INYALA, DOGS, AND HYENAS.

Kaffirs all fled at the top of their speed. The lionesses eyed me some time at a distance of about thirty yards, and I was casting my eyes round for a

tree, as I expected them to come at me, but they slunk into the bush, and I never saw them again.

I afterwards gave a sea-cow a shot which I thought was fatal, but as he did not rise I went to look for another, and shortly hit one just under the root of the ear (the best shot you can give), and, after plunging and rolling over and over, for about ten minutes, he subsided, and we dragged him out some 200 yards below. The poor Amatongas were delighted, and carried all away but his head and back bone.

13th.—The first fine day we have had for a long

time. I turned out about two hours before sunset, and got a good chance at an inyala, but my gun hung fire, and the second barrel snapped. In coming back I gave one of the Amatongas a prod behind, to call his attention to a kind of wild dog, when he gave a most unearthly howl, and a bound which I never saw equalled, dropping all his assegais, whipping off his moutcha in a twinkling, and entreating me to come away, saying that an inyoka snake had bitten him, and that he should die. It was some time ere I could persuade the fellow otherwise.

14th. — To-day I started my Kaffirs in quest of my other hunters. The rivers had detained them until now, as they are frightened at deep water and very few of them can swim. I mended a gun belonging to one of them, and he went off in high spirits.

We had a long chase after an old bull buffalo, along the river's edge. I put forth all my powers to beat Mahoutcha, a fine Kaffir, who aggravated me by passing me at railway speed. I had the advantage of him, as he had a gun to carry and I none. We passed and re-passed one another about six times, my gun changing hands three times. I was utterly blown, and just about to yield the palm to Mahoutcha, though I was leading, when luckily for my credit the buffalo took the water and vanished into the dense bush on the other side.

I espied water-buck over the river, waded, and got

a long shot at a fine doe, which we eventually bagged after a long chase. We were kept awake in the night by the dogs fighting wolves, and turned out once, thinking we heard buffaloes drinking, but the sound proved to be only running water.

15th. — Off long before daylight down the river after sea-cows. I scrambled into a tree to see over the reeds, and got a shot, and though my gun hung fire, I struck him fairly, hearing the bullet pat. While waiting for it to rise, the rain came on furiously, and continued all day.

Anything more miserable than our situation can hardly be conceived. I made a kind of awning for my Kaffirs out of my large blanket, and they were comparatively snug. The ground was saturated with rain, all my traps wet and unwholesome, and my tent had begun to leak. This kind of life is sufficiently hard in fine weather, but in the drenching rain one gets in Africa it is positively unbearable, and enough to give the most light-hearted fellow a fit of the blues. As I had no cooking utensils of any kind except a kettle, all I could do was to roast my meat on a stick.

16th (Sunday).—I was lying in my little 9lb. tent enjoying Byron's poems, and meaning to have a day of rest, when the Amatongas came in a large body and were most importunate that I should go out to shoot them some meat, as they were very hungry; and there came also a lot of pretty girls to back their entreaties, bringing me small presents of

meal, rice, eggs, and beer. I at length agreed. They
shortly hit off the spoor of two old bull buffaloes
which had fed on an open plain early in the morning.
We spoored them beautifully into a dense thicket,
black as midnight, and so still and silent you might
almost hear a leaf fall at the entrance ; the Amatongas
one and all most politely made way for me to go in,
silently pointing to the spoor. For the first time I
began to take an interest in what I was about, took
my double-barreled gun from the hands of the carrier,
took off my shoes, and stept cautiously and very quietly
along the path, and had proceeded about one hundred
yards, when, just as the path turned, I found myself
face to face with an old bull fast asleep, lying down
within ten yards. I dropped on one knee, cocked
the left hand barrel, holding the trigger back to
prevent the click, and, as soon as I felt the lock catch,
took a steady pot in the centre of the forehead.
Just as I touched the trigger my gun went down and
stopped at half cock. The bull instantly opened his
eyes wide, and was half up when I cocked and fired
the second barrel and hit him. I ran through the
smoke fifteen yards back, and dropping behind a bush
to ascertain the effects of my shot, heard a crash
through the bush. It was the other breaking cover,
and my old friend on his legs, with his nose high
up, snuffing the air for me. He made a dead set,
getting my wind ; and immediately made a desperate
charge right through the middle of my bush, which I
avoided by jumping on one side. He turned im-

mediately, and made another dead set at me.   There
was but half a bush between us, and he stood not ten
yards off, eyeing me furiously, the blood streaming
down his face from a bullet between the eyes, but too
low to be fatal.   A second tremendous charge I

avoided almost literally by the skin of my teeth. All
this time, which seemed to me almost as many hours
as it was in reality minutes, not a Kaffir or even one
of my dogs came to my aid to attract his attention,
though they must both have heard all that was going
on. A third time we stood in close proximity; there
was nothing but the remnants of the trampled bush
between us. I never removed my eye an instant from

his. He backed some four feet and lowered his head
as if about to charge, and we stood for two minutes
or more with some tangled brush-wood not four feet
high and very thin between us. I hardly know
myself how I avoided his last charge; I threw out
both arms and pushed myself from his body, and
away as hard as I could, closely pursued by the bull.
His hot breath was on my neck, and in two strides
more nothing could have saved me ; but at this spot
the path turned to the right, and missing me he went
headlong through a fearfully tangled thicket and
broke into the open not twenty yards a-head and
about seven or eight on my left, carrying half a cart-
load of rubbish on his horns. I threw myself on my
back in the thicket to prevent his seeing me, on
reaching the open. Just as he broke, and when he
was about twenty yards from me going straight away,
I recovered myself, gave him my second barrel, which
I had had no opportunity of firing before, hitting
him high up on the last rib on the off side just in
front of the hip, when he threw up his tail, made a
tremendous bound in the air, and dashed through
bush thorns so dense and close that it was perfectly
wonderful how he managed it, and fell dead in about
200 yards, with the low moaning bellow so gratifying
to a hunter's ears. My trusty Amatongas descended
immediately from the different trees which they had
climbed as soon as the affray commenced, and were
most lavish in their compliments to me. I was
going to rate them soundly for their cowardice, but

I found I had lost the use of my tongue, which I did not fully recover for many hours, and vowed over and over again I would hunt no more on Sunday, knowing it to be Sunday.

I afterwards made some experiments with the buffalo, and found his brain so very narrow that there is every chance of missing it, in which case you do not injure him in the least. My bullet had penetrated between the eyes about two inches below the brain, which it had missed altogether, although close beside it. We cut out the ball just at the top of his head, within an inch of the hole into his brain. In my experiments I had all but killed my best dog, Ragman, in trying if the bullet would penetrate by shooting in the soft place between the horns. At night I sallied out by torchlight, to try to get a shot at some laughing hyenas, who had taken a water-buck skin from the very feet of the Kaffirs, and were laughing in fits over it, utterly heedless of the dogs.

17*th*. — Got under weigh with some difficulty, as we had a large quantity of meat to carry. Killed four impalas, and then went to pitch on a place for our camp, near sunset. After making the necessary arrangements I strolled out to try and fire off my gun, as I wanted to clean it. I saw a hyena prowling along, and killed him so dead, at fully one hundred yards, that I thought he had dropped into a hole the moment I fired.

18*th*. — I was awakened by a white rhinoceros

charging past, with three dogs at his heels, and
Mahoutcha calling out lustily to me; but, unfortunately, I was not loaded, and Mahoutcha's gun
snapped, so the brute got away.

We turned out afterwards to try for a rhinoceros
cow we had seen the day before. We were con-
sulting as to the best means of getting at one, which
we saw standing at some distance under a tree, when
a troop of impalas came charging down, with a fine
old lioness after them. We went, and saw her
lying down, but so flat to the ground, head and all,
that no man could shoot with any certainty; and she
never for a moment took her eyes from us. When
we got up to her, she was lying down flat as a plate
to the ground; but her head might have been on a
pivot, as her watchful eye glared on us all round,
without appearing to move her body, as we decreased
the circle, in the hopes she would stand up and give
us a fair chance of a shot behind the shoulder. I could
not place the smallest dependence on Mahoutcha,
whose face was the colour of boiled liver. As we
walked round the lioness, he described a circle full a
dozen yards larger than I did: I therefore, taking
into consideration that discretion was the better part
of valour, looked for a tree to climb up, near enough
to make tolerably sure of my shot. I was just
getting up one, when the lioness made off: not much
to my credit, certainly; but in case of a charge,
Mahoutcha would have been sure to miss, and then
nothing could have saved us.

In the course of the day, I shot a fine impala, which we hung up in a tree, intending to take him home as we returned; but when we came back, we found nothing but bones left: the vultures had pulled him down, skinned, and finished him.

19th. — I was resting under a tree, when we sighted a white rhinoceros cow. I stalked up to within about twenty yards of her. She was very uneasy, perceiving danger, but not knowing from what quarter to expect it. She made straight for me, at a round trot, and I dropped her with a bullet in the chest. She rose immediately, and I struck her again, but she got away. We were long in tracing her spoor, as the ground was hard and stony, and we never saw her again; but, in following her, we came on an old black bull, which I shot dead behind the shoulder. I pitched the tent near his carcase, intending to have a shot at a tiger at night, but it was too dark to see anything, and the wolves, jackals, and hyenas made such a noise all night as I never wish to hear again. They fought over every mouthful, and chased one another madly, and, though I fired occasionally at random, it had no effect. Frequently some of them tumbled over my tent-ropes, startling me out of a broken slumber. My fellows had strongly advised me not to sleep there, and wisely took themselves off three or four hundred yards; and, could I have found them in the dark, I should have moved my quarters. The wolves and hyenas had made an end of the bull by the morning.

20*th*. — I saw more buffaloes than I had ever seen before in one day. They were galloping in all directions, and at last I accounted for it by there being an immense party of Amaswazis hunting. I shot a fine wildebeest bull, and saw many black rhinoceros, but they do not pay to shoot. We camped in a beautiful place, under a large tree, with rivers running on three sides, and a huge mountain at the back, called Tegwan, which I ascended. On this mountain, a whole tribe were massacred by Charka's people : they scrambled up to the summit, but were all butchered and thrown off. The country is now uninhabited, and the mountain swarms with baboons.

Five black rhinoceros, an old buffalo, and a wild boar, grazed quietly within 300 yards of my tent, but I left them unmolested, as we had more meat than we could use, and the dogs were perfectly useless from obesity. Even the Kaffirs could only touch the morsels which they considered the daintiest.

21*st*. — Had three shots at a white rhinoceros, with remarkably fine horns. I saw a good number, but they were in the open, and though they are stupid things, and easy of approach, if met with alone, they generally keep near quaggas, wildebeests, or buffaloes, who give them the alarm.

22*nd*. — Reached the St. Luey, across a hilly, rough, stony, broken country. After being roasted in the sun, till I thought I must have had brain fever, waiting for a cow koodoo (the sentinel of the

troop) to disappear over the ridge, I came so suddenly, at last, upon the troop, that, though usually
most shy, wary, and difficult of approach, they
seemed now quite stupified, and I got right and left
at two magnificent old bulls, hearing the bullets tell
loudly, like the drawing of corks, both within twenty-
five yards ; but, being too anxious to get both, I

got neither. It was very mortifying, and I felt very
small in my own eyes. I had left my hat far back,
and suffered terribly in consequence — burying my
head in the grass, and twisting it over me, to endeavour to keep off as much scorching sun as possible.
To crown all, I lost the finest horned rhinoceros I
ever beheld. I found him, while endeavouring to
trace the blood-spoor of one of the wounded koodoos, standing half up to his middle in a mud hole,

K

with his tail towards me. I endeavoured to direct his attention to me in various ways. I was within fifteen yards, and had been for many minutes, and could have picked my place to fire twenty times, but, after the last discomfiture, I thought I would make dead sure, when, without a warning of any kind, he suddenly made right off, and I had only a stern shot left me, which is of no manner of use. I had lost my way entirely, and did not get back till three hours after dark, guided by the shouts of the Kaffirs.

The bagging of large shy game on foot is a complete science, and requires no small skill. You must take your bearings, study the wind to a point, and, if seen by the animals, go in an exactly opposite direction, marking well the place, and gradually work round, never stopping to look dead at them, unless well concealed. It is impossible to use too much caution. I have heard an old hunter say, that if he got one good chance in a day, he was perfectly satisfied. The first dawn of day is the best time to commence, and a good telescope an immense assistance.

The crocodiles are the greatest drawback to this country. I got to a lovely hole in the St. Luey, wearied and hot, and a plunge would have been worth any money, but the spoor of a large crocodile which had just gone in warned me, and I was forced to content myself with a shallow place, where the stream ran strong, and where I was safe from them.

We took six bees' nests in this neighbourhood, thanks to the honeybirds, but it was the wrong time of year, and we did not find much in them.

25*th.* — Made a pair of gaiters of impala skin, but was in great straits, as I had lost my sail needle. Shot a bush-buck, and severely wounded a koodoo bull, but lost him, as the dogs were worse than useless, owing to the excessive heat and overfeeding. The heat was so great that the gun-barrels would blister my hands, and the heel-plate was so hot that I could not bear it to my shoulder, through a thick shirt. On one occasion, on stooping down to drink, some blue flint-stones on which I had placed my bare knee raised a blister instantly.

I had sent Mahoutcha to buy some amobella meal of the Kaffirs a day or two previously, and he returned to-day with the intelligence that all the young. and fighting men were gone. Two sons of Panda's were quarrelling who was to succeed him, and a civil war was imminent. I decidedly wished myself out of the country, as the sight of blood makes Kaffirs worse than wild beasts, and when once they have tasted blood, they would think nothing of knocking on the head anything that comes in their way.

28*th.* — I was awakened out of a sound sleep very unpleasantly. It blew a hurricane, and my tent being broadside to the wind, the pegs on the weather-side all gave at once, and were carried to Bagdad by the jerk, and I was left exposed to a downfall of rain, more like a waterspout than anything that could come from the clouds. I roused the Kaffirs, made knives, two ramrods, and assegais supply the place of pegs, and got the tent put to rights.

When I first came to the colony I was four months sleeping out during the rainy season, steaming and soaking four nights out of the seven, and made light of it; but at this time I had suffered too much from ague to be able to stand such work. One morning I sent all the Zulus to the rightabout, and made them go back minus a morsel of beef, for not bringing me milk, &c. This had a wonderfully good effect upon them, for the next morning, ere I was up, they brought me a heap of amasi, beer, and milk.

December 1st.—Moved my camp for better water, and on the 3rd reached my old quarters of last year, where I was very warmly received, and inundated with amasi and milk. On Sunday we were visited by three lions, which kept my fellows awake almost all night, singing and shouting for their lives, and keeping up an incessant clatter with two tin dishes, which the lions are much afraid of.

On the 4th I got back to the place where I had left the wagon, and expected to find Johnson, and pictured to myself a long yarn, as I had been tongue-tied for more than a month. Bread, sugar, and rice, also rose before the eyes of my imagination, but, alas! only those of the imagination. There was no vestige of anything. Johnson had left five days ago, and nothing was to be heard of the Kaffir hunters, to whom I had given twenty days as their utmost limit of time.

So I made two imaginary bets with a little Jew, of the name of Cohen, that, upon resuming my old Burrow, I would, with twenty bullets, bag ten head of large game, including two koodoo cows : 5l. on each event. These were a source of fully as much excitement to me as if I had actually made the bet. I won both events on Tuesday night, with three bullets to spare, and was highly delighted.

8th.—Mahoutcha told me that the impi (army) had killed five white men and all their Kaffirs, and there was no use in waiting any longer for my ivory, as no Amatonga would dream of coming into the Zulu country. He proposed, therefore, that we should go and hide in the reeds of the Umveloose, and come out to a kraal at night, and hear the news.

I made up my mind to move out at once, and forthwith packed up my traps, and took a circuitous route, avoiding the road. I left all my goods and chattels with an old witch-doctor, the captain of the kraal, who strongly advised us not to remain with him any longer, as, although willing, he was utterly unable to protect us. I have never yet (1862) returned to reclaim my property, but, should I ever do so, I shall no doubt get what the rats have left, as Zulus are scrupulously honest. Seeing lots of cattle coming out, we went to a hut to hear the news, and were told the most extravagant yarns, but that no white man would be molested unless he commenced the assault.

The Kaffirs who were on the victorious side told me that the Tugela was red with blood, and that the Inyoni, another river, about eight miles nearer, was so fœtid from the number of dead bodies, that no man could drink the water, and that I should walk over dead bodies all the way between the Matakoola and the Tugela, a distance of fifteen long miles.

As there was every appearance of heavy rain, I feared the rivers would be flooded, and that I might be detained an indefinite time, which would have been horrible, as my stores were all gone, and I had only twenty bullets left. I therefore resolved to cross the river, come what might, sorely against the will of the Kaffirs, who were in dread of their lives, and yet afraid of leaving me. We slept at the Umsindoosie, and were almost eaten up by mosquitoes.

9th. — Started before daylight, being uncommonly anxious to get to the Missionary Station to hear the news. It rained heavily the greater part of the day, but I stuck at it for fully twelve hours, and reached the station shortly after sunset. I found from Mr. Aftebro that the country was nearly depopulated, thousands and thousands of men, women, and children being stabbed or drowned in attempting to cross the Tugela. He calculated that fully one-fourth of the whole Zulu nation must have been destroyed, and told me that 8,000 head of cattle had passed his station alone. The victors lost a great number of people also. It is most extraordinary to hear them talk about the fight ; they appear to think no more of taking human life than an Englishman would of killing a rabbit. One man said he had killed six, another five, nine, or three ; and one great warrior had killed twenty, and then he would count on his fingers so many young men, so many wives, and so many unmarried girls — Zintombis — and laugh and chuckle over it immensely.

Panda, who was alive and well, while his two sons were fighting which should succeed him, had himself killed seven of his brothers !

10th.—The thermometer usually stands at about 93° in the shade, and 135° or 140° in the sun ; some days it has been 104° in the shade.

13th.— A fine cool day, with slight showers. Started at railway speed, stuck at it for sixteen hours and a half, getting over about fifty-five miles, the greatest walking feat I ever performed. I fell fast asleep on the road before my blanket arrived, being quite knocked up in ascending the Matakoola hill to get away from the mosquitoes.

The only Kaffir who stuck to me throughout was Mahoutcha, a splendid fellow, formerly in Elephant White's service, and much attached to him—whether owing to a tremendous piece he took out of the calf of his leg with the wagon-whip when foreloping, and so gaining him proper respect, I cannot say. On one occasion Mahoutcha did his master good service. White had claimed, and outspanned on the spot, an ox which two powerful Boers had in their wagon, so they waylaid and suddenly attacked White at night,

and he fell over the dissel boom.   Taking advantage
of his mishap they fell upon him, and while they were
all struggling together on the ground, White getting
the worst of it, Mahoutcha seized the after-sjambok,
and played into them with such terrible good-will
that they instantly jumped up, and White caught the
nearest on the under jaw, breaking it, and knocking
him backwards over a flight of spiked rails.   The
other fled for his life.

The whole country was entirely depopulated,
hundreds of wagon loads of green mealies and amobella all going to waste.   We passed heaps of Kaffir
traps, pillows, mats, calabashes, pots, sticks, and
baskets, strewed about, evidently dropped in a hurry.

14th (Sunday).— The whole air was tainted with
dead bodies for the last twelve miles, which I walked
against a head wind.   They were lying in every possible attitude along the road, men, women, and
children of all possible sizes and ages ; the warriors
untouched, with their war-dresses on ; but all in a
dreadful state of decomposition.   I was never so glad
of anything in my life as of getting the Tugela
between me and the dead ; as what with the strong
head wind, and the horrible effluvia, it was quite
overpowering, and proved eventually too much for the
stomachs of even my Kaffirs.   For a long time they
endeavoured, by taking widish circles, to avoid
treading on or coming very near the dead, being
very superstitious ; but as we neared the Tugela, the
bodies lay so thick in the road and on each side that

it was impossible to avoid them any longer. The Kaffirs walked very quickly, and never answered once any remark I made, appearing frightened as well as intensely disgusted, and no bribe that could be offered would induce a Kaffir to touch one. I saw many instances of mothers with babies on their backs, with assegais through both, and children of all ages assegaied between the shoulder-blades.

I met a portion of the victorious army returning, carrying branches of trees over Kitchwayo, walking very stately and slowly, teaching him to be a king, as they said.

I was a little nervous as to my reception, but put a bold face on the matter, grounded my gun about forty yards off, and asked ' Is all well?' when they did the same with their assegais, said 'All is well with you,' and we advanced and had a long parley, my fellows treading on my heels. They were very civil, and told me that as I had taken no part in the fight I was free to go and come wherever and whenever I liked, and all the oxen taken from the Englishmen should be sent to a large cattle-station on the Umslatoose, and the owners must come in and claim them, and that those that had been slaughtered for food should be made good. Beer was broached, and, after some heavy pulls, we parted on the most amicable terms.

On arriving at the river, I saw about 150 poor wretches on the banks waiting to come across, as the river was full, and I had great difficulty in getting

the boat to come over for me.   After firing several
salutes in vain, I was obliged to strip, to show that I
was white.

15th.— I got the loan of a horse from Mr. Fynn,
the magistrate, stationed there, and proceeded to the
Umlila, where I had a horse of my own.   All the
way down I received numerous congratulations from
all my acquaintances, and from many strangers, on
having got out safely from among the savages.   It
was the general opinion that all the white men in
the country would be killed ; and Johnson, whom I
left at the missionary station, and myself, constituted
the *all*.

I am tempted to add here a few anecdotes of
adventures in buffalo-hunting, which befel me about
this period : —

One evening in the valley of the Tugela, on returning to my encampment, after a capital day's sport
(three hartebeests, an eland bull and buffalo bull), I
was leading a fine grey mare, packed with the hartebeest skins, when I saw a huge beast before me so
encased in mud that I at first took it for a rhinoceros.
I let go the mare, and ran from behind unperceived
very near, as it was walking slowly.   It proved to be
an enormous old bull buffalo, and the first intimation
he got of my presence was a bullet in the centre of
his big ribs.   How he made the stones fly and clatter
as he rushed down the hill !   I reloaded, went back
to the mare (which remained standing just where I

A LEAP.

left her, as all South African trained shooting-horses
do for half a day or more, if required), and proceeded
in the direction my old friend was making, not
much . expecting, however, to see anything more of
him, and had given him up, as it was fast getting
dark, when I saw the outline of a large beast under
a shady thorn-tree, and had not quite made him out
when he emerged and made at me. I threw a hasty
glance around for a friendly tree, and then at the
chances of getting on the mare's back, but that was
hopeless, as she was loaded with hides ; my arm was
through the bridle rein, the bull mending his pace,
and as I put my gun to my shoulder the mare, alarmed,
jerked back and I fired a snap shot at his breast, not
turning him in the least. The mare reared perpendicularly and fell backwards ; the rein being
through my arm, I also fell between her legs, and the
brute went over us both, knocking the skin from the
mare's eye with a kick from his hind leg, and rattled
along. I found him dead in the morning not 200
yards off, my bullet having struck him in the centre
of the chest.

I saw across the Pongola an immense herd of
buffaloes, and my fellows were most anxious that I
should shoot them a fat cow. I got on a large open
plain between them and their stronghold, the bush
we were then in, and ensconced myself behind a very
small low bush below the wind, with two double
guns, and sent my fellows a long way round, above
wind, to drive them towards me. There must have

been 300, and they came directly for me, at a slow trot, making the earth shake, and raising clouds of dust. I lay as close as a hare in her form on the open plain; nothing but this little shrub, perhaps three feet high and four feet in circumference, until the leaders of the herd were within three lengths, and I saw every probability of being trampled to death. I jumped into the air as high as possible, with a tremendous shout. The whole herd, for a few seconds, appeared panic-stricken, and remained stock still. I selected a sleek, glossy, dumpy cow, and fired, and never raised such a commotion in my existence. I was almost deafened by the rushing noise, and blinded by the dust. I fired, however, my other three barrels into the middle of the dust, but could hardly hear the report; and not until the dust cleared away, some 300 yards, I saw the whole herd going away, and my little pet, Smoke, at their heels. She picked the wounded cow out of the whole herd, stuck to her till she died, a mile ahead, and whilst we were trying to hit off her blood-spoor, came back to us, and trotted on ahead, and took us to the cow, the only one bagged. I relate this to show there is very little danger from a large troop.

A buffalo is a dangerous animal, from being so very quick. One day I had stalked close up to some lying down in long grass, and had cautiously, by taking advantage of every opportunity, got to a forked tree within twenty yards, when I whistled low to alarm them gently, and they slowly rose. I fired at the best cow full in the breast, and sprang, at the same instant, almost into the fork, and was knocked out of it again as quickly with the tremendous charge she made against the trunk, almost splitting her skull, and rolling over dead at the tree-root, shot through the middle of the heart. Another time I and my companion both fired together at an old bull, hitting him hard, and I was chasing him at my best pace, for a second shot, when I became aware of another galloping alongside me, twenty-five yards to my right, on the open. I pulled up immediately, aimed forward, and fired, hitting him in front of the shoulder-blade, and, in all my experience, I never saw one knocked over like that. His legs flew from under him, and he lay sprawling some lengths ahead; there was a low thorn-tree between us, with wide-spreading branches almost sweeping the ground, which I made for. He jumped up instantly and charged, and as I ducked under on the lower side he came smack through, breaking off one of the main limbs on the upper side, and away he went, and I never set eyes on him more. We eventually bagged our first, my companion hitting him in the eye as he came on.

CHAPTER VI.

1857.

THE TRANSVAAL REPUBLIC — MERICO COUNTRY — THE MACCATEESE OR
BECHUANAS — SECHELE — THE MASARAS — THE BOERS — MOSILIKATSE.

MAY 25*th.* — After many unforeseen delays, and
losing our oxen for a week, we at length got away
from Ladysmith, on our excursion into the far interior,
with a heavy wagon, sixteen oxen, and seven salted
horses. This pretty little town derives its name
from Lady Smith, the wife of Sir Harry Smith, formerly governor of the Cape Colony. It stands on
the Klip river, about 150 miles from Durban, with a
splendid view of Nelson's Kop, Job's Berg, and the
range of the Drakensberg Mountains, about eighteen
or twenty miles off, the dividing range between
Natal and the Orange river Free State and Transvaal Republic. The finest view of the colony of Natal
is from the ascent of the Drakensberg, from which
it looks beautiful, well watered and wooded, and like
a large well-kept garden when compared with the
country on the other side, to the west, which is
devoid of a stick of wood, flat, barren, and unprofit-

able, but, notwithstanding, has good farms for horses and sheep.   Harrysmith, just under the Table Mountain, never gets a glimpse of sun till about three hours' high, and is a dreary, cold place in the winter.

As the nights are very cold, with hard frost in the early mornings and high cutting winds, I have the nags blanketed up to the eyes.   Game is very scarce ; a few quaggas and wildebeests, and some shy, wary ostriches, are all we have seen yet ; the grass is as dry as a chip, and the oxen and horses must get poor, as it contains so little nourishment.   Joubert shot a cow wildebeest last night, and, on my return from skinning her an hour after sunset, I thought mine the happiest life in the world : a snug wagon, a roaring fire of dry cow-dung, horses and oxen feeding close round the former, waiting for their mealies, and as tame as barn-door fowls ; three fat ducks hissing and spitting away, just ready for supper ; two lamps burning ; and all around my wagon-home one dreary flat waste, with no wood for days and days.   It is a dull, uninteresting country, but the air is so bracing and healthy that you must be in high spirits, come what will.

Poor Ragman, a faithful and plucky young dog of my own breeding, got a severe prod from the wildebeest last night behind the shoulder, and could scarcely limp home, but he will recover, and I hope the hint will make him more cautious for the future.

June 8th. — We are now within nine hours of Mooi River Town, nothing having happened on the road worth mentioning, except that we stuck fast once yesterday and had to unload, and that Donker, my best ox, is dead, having got at a poisonous kind of grass, called by the Dutch tulp, which has much the same effect upon them as a tremendous blow-out of clover, causing them to swell fearfully : this was the only casualty, but it was nearly being the same with several others.

We have been living well on koran, guinea fowl, wild ducks, springbuck, and blesbuck. I made an exchange with old Luse, a Boer—tea, powder and lead, for bacon and sausages ; and had two glasses of grog with him, as it was a bitter cold day ; and lost two oxen, Quiman and Roman, for two days : they had taken the road home again.

I had a tremendous fall from Jack yesterday, while hunting blesbuck, right into a new burn. I got up as black as a nigger, but my horse was not in fault, as he is blind, and I was pushing him to his utmost speed, when he set his foot in a hole and rolled for yards—by no means an uncommon occurrence. I have had very many such spills ; and on two occasions found my double rifle with the muzzle facing me, and both barrels at full cock. While going at full speed, luck is all you have to trust to, clever though your horse may be ; an old shooting-horse is always on the look-out for holes, having himself a wholesome dread of them. There is frequently such a cloud of dust raised by the immense herds of game you are pursuing that you can see nothing, and, though you can often hear the bullet clap loudly, you must wait till the dust clears away to know what it is—quagga, wildebeest, blesbuck, or springbuck. I have frequently had herds of all these sorts in immense numbers scouring away before me and on all sides, amid such a cloud of stuff raised by their own tearing away that I never knew what I was firing at, my only endeavour being to aim low.¯ I first saw the effects of my two barrels on the dust clearing away ; sometimes a couple of quaggas, and on one occasion three blesbuck, and several times three springbuck, not unfrequently a wildebeest; but most commonly nothing on the spot, though it is very usual for one or more to fall farther on or drop to the rear, being wounded. At these times good dogs are of immense service.

I must mention my success at ducks yesterday, as it may never occur again. I marked six into a small water-hole and stalked well in upon them in the long grass, bagged four with the first barrel and dropped another with the second the instant he rose, and had but just time to load one barrel when the sixth flew round again, and I dropped him, thus bagging the whole lot in less than half a minute. They are large, fat, and delicious, and equal in flavour to any in England. Several hyenas have been following the wagon and frightening the Kaffirs, but the lions have not molested us; they only came to the wagon once, frightening old Graham, one of the horses, almost into fits. He got his back to the wheel, and snorted and blew as if he was choking. I had had them all well

blanketed, and I think the lions could not make them
out. Besides, we had a little moonlight, which makes
the lions less daring than they are on dark nights.
They are boldest when the nights are stormy.

9th. — Caught an armadillo alive, and made his
tail fast with a rheim, and dragged him to the wagon
through the long grass. The Kaffir had to exert all
his strength, as the armadillo held on with his claws
for his very life, and grasped the long grass con-
vulsively, and had rolled himself as large as a
haycock. Brought a letter of introduction from
Dr. Kelly, resident magistrate of Klip river, and
a present of books to Pretorius, President of the
South African Republic. I donned my best attire to
present them, and approached him with a low bow,
as here he is all-powerful. The only remark after
reading it was : — ' What cost is there for the trans-
port ? ' I was quite taken aback ; and this was all that
passed between us. This was almost my first acquaintance with the Transvaal Dutchmen, and I did
not then know their manners and customs. It is
considered polite and the correct thing always to offer
payment, to give them the opportunity of declining,
you of course thanking them then for their kindness ; but I must say that very rarely, if ever, will
they accept payment for food or anything taken
in their own houses, and they are remarkably
hospitable.

I did not anticipate any difficulty from Pretorius
in getting into the interior, as peace had been declared,

the Kaffirs all quiet, and free trade open all over the country. Windy, stormy, very cold weather.

13*th.* — My Kaffir Umgeba gave us the slip, and ran away on Thursday morning after getting the wagon started, and got four hours' start ere we missed him; we immediately saddled up Graham and old Bryan, and went in chase. Anticipating a long ride, I crammed a couple of ducks and some biscuits and salt into a haversack, and put a blanket under my saddle; we rode back to Mooi River Dorp, a good forty miles, never meeting a soul all the way; and never getting the spoor of the Kaffir; gave the horses some forage, and slept a short time in the stable till the moon was high, and started back, the coldest ride I ever had in my life; at last, was obliged to get off and run, to keep alive at all. I was never so anxious for sun-rise in all my life before, and it seemed as if he delayed his rising on purpose. Never a footprint of the wily savage; he fairly beat us, and knocked up our horses, and they can ill afford now to lose any flesh. I saw a man whom I formerly knew, a widower, with seven children, in the most abject circumstances, and had not a scrap on earth to give them; his children are drafted out like hounds among the farmers, one here and one there. He would have me go with him to his place—merely a poll-house, he said, a temporary residence — and I was shocked to find nothing but the bare walls, a miserable bedstead and dry grass to sleep on, the lid of an old box on the floor, half a candle in the neck of a bottle, a few lucifers and a heap of tobacco, and, amid all this wretchedness, this poor fellow (a thorough Irishman) trying to seem happy, and he said he often laughed to himself to think, in case of a fire, what a small sufferer he would be. He almost exists on tobacco, and assures me that he often does not eat for several days together — yet he talks of his father's (the Hon. — —) rent-roll, 12,546*l*. 9*s*. 3*d*. per annum ; but I think he is slightly deranged. That is the second instance only of abject poverty that I have met with in this colony.

Treked on to a Dutchman of the name of Vessell Bartness last night, through a beautiful country of dense thornwood, quite a relief to the eye after the endless plains we have come through. This is truly a sweet spot, a lovely stream meandering through thorn covered with water-cresses, a magnificent orchard, and the oranges and lemon trees covered now, in the middle of winter, with delicious fruit, but I thought to-day I had come nearly to the end of civilisation when I was offered half a farm, 3,000 acres, in exchange for a plough. Joubert shot two springbucks yesterday with one bullet.

14*th* (*Sunday*).— One of the finest days I ever beheld. This is certainly the finest climate in the world, at this season of the year. We have now had six or seven weeks of uninterrupted lovely weather, and every prospect of a long continuance; I took a stroll to-day, and had a beautiful view, and thought of home and friends, and the chances of my ever

returning to England. I was much amused last night
at my Kaffirs trading with the Maccateese for ostrich
feathers; they could not understand one word of each
other's language, and my fellows were trying to make
them believe buttons were money, and would buy of
the white man cows, horse, or gun, and eventually
succeeded in buying a lot of black feathers for ten
buttons. I lost my supper in waiting to see the result. The Maccateese brought heaps of mealie kops
to make a big light lest they should be cheated, and
went through the most frightful gesticulations.

15th.—Bought some meal, oranges, potatoes and
dry peaches, the latter very cheap, 2s. a stable bucketfull; left Younkman behind dead lame in the hip;
outspanned for the night at a Boer's.

16th. — Of course my oxen had been on the land,
my dogs had eaten the frau's soup, and I must
pay damages. I gave some lead, coffee and sugar,
as they were decent people, barring stealing my curb-
chain, which is a great nuisance, as I cannot replace
it. Arrived about mid-day at Joubert's, to whom I
lent four oxen in Natal when he was on his last legs;
received a most hearty welcome, but he has only a
hartebeest house made of reeds, and the good wife
was sorry she had nothing in the world to give
us but flesh, and set us down to a large dish full
of broiled wildebeest—rather poor fare for a weary
traveller, but I had still some biscuits left, and we
made out pretty well. The repast was hardly according to English notions; but I am well used now

to life in a colony, and I received a most hearty
welcome, which is more than half the battle. There
are lots of game here, and a nice thorny country.
I like the place much, and shall probably stay ten
days or more, as the oxen are fairly used up.

17th.—Had a long ramble to-day; shot a fall raebuck
and springbuck, and saw plenty of guinea fowls.
The horses got frightened by a hyena last night and
took themselves off. I heard them galloping, but it was
too dark to follow. I have only recovered four as yet,
but two Jouberts and a Kaffir are now out looking for
the rest. I think they must have taken the road back,
as I have been up to the highest hills and can see
nothing of them. There is a severe frost every night,
and we have a baking-pot full of fire in the house,
and huddle around it in the evenings just as we do
at home — something new for Africa.

When I arrived, my host and his family, who are
capital hunters, were almost out of ammunition. Franz
had killed, *mirabile dictu*, with the same bullet, three
or four hartebeest bulls, the shyest and most difficult
of approach of all the antelope tribe, and very tough
also. He was off at daylight, sparing neither time
nor trouble in stalking till he made sure of his shot,
putting just sufficient powder to drive the bullet
through to the skin on the other side, then cutting it
out and reloading. Each skin was worth to him
about twelve to fifteen shillings when tanned. Poor
fellow! he met with a sad accident shortly after. The
lions killed his horse in the middle of the day, a very

unusual occurrence. He vowed vengeance for the future, and some days afterwards he and his brother John saw three, and they immediately gave chase on foot. Franz overtook and cut off the last, and stood in the path ready to receive her, and as she came on covered her steadily and pulled, when his weapon, a flint, missed fire ; the gun missed fire a second time, when the lioness sprang on him, clawing and biting him frightfully, crippling and disabling him for life. She was grinding away at his thigh when John got up and pluckily shot her dead on his body. I have heard him tell the story in the coolest manner possible, saying he must have shot her through and through if the old gun had not missed, and regretting he had not had a doppi-roer (percussion gun). Another similar instance happened to a Boer at Scoon Spruit, not far distant. The lions frightened the oxen treking in a wagon one very dark night. The Boer jumped off to try and stop them, but the pace being too fast he jumped up on the trap behind while the oxen were going at full gallop. The lion sprang on him, pulled him off, killed and ate him on the road, and his brother, on searching for him in the morning, found the lion still there. He coolly dismounted, and shot him dead on the remains of his brother's body.

27th. — Had a shocking bad cold and headache, a kind of influenza, the last ten days, and have consequently not been doing much. Found the horses two days after losing them, on the road back. Killed yesterday, after a great amount of toil, a bird strange

to me, called here the Namaqua partridge—a dirty-
brown, yellow neck, long tail, forked wings, and
feathered to the toes like a grouse; his head somewhat
resembles a partridge, and he has half a horse-shoe
across his breast; he is plump and fat, but only half
the size of an English bird; his flights are very long
and quick, and he makes a whistling noise not unlike
a golden plover; he is speckled over the back and
wings with a blueish, greyish, yellowish brown, if
the reader can form any idea what a mixture of those
colours would look like.

I shot yesterday a large crested bustard, the fattest
and largest I have ever seen; not being able to weigh
him, we can only guess, but the lowest estimate is
fifty pounds Dutch, fifty-four English. The only
utensil we could hit upon that was big enough to
cook him in was a soap-boiler, which he just fitted,
and in which he was admirably baked and served
at table every day for a week; we rendered down
more than a bottle full of oil from his inside fat,
which is the very best thing you can use for guns.

I made up my mind to-day I could go no farther; the
oxen and horses are too poor, and the winter is very
severe. I must put off for another year, as my oxen
could not possibly trek my wagon through the
heavy sands in their present condition, and the grass
is so dry and so scarce that I fear they will have
enough to do to get through the winter without work.
I feed the horses nightly on Kaffir corn, which I trade
from the natives for beads, knives, copper wire, &c.,

but it is very dear here. I must try and sell my
wagon for oxen, stores, &c., and go back to Natal,
leaving my horses and oxen here in charge of Joubert
until the end of next April, when I must try again.
There is plenty of game here, but none of any value,
except ostriches, which are now in splendid plumage,
but shy and wary to a degree. I have never been able
yet to get a shot at them, though I watched twelve
yesterday for several hours. Wildebeest, quagga,
hartebeest, blesbuck, and springbuck, with a sprinkling
of duikers, and steinbuck, roy and fall raebuck, we see
every day we go out, but they are the only kinds here,
and of little or no value, and are dry eating. Koran,
plenty of guinea-fowl and peaus, with a few partridges,
are all the winged game ; but I have hardly any shot,
and no dogs worth a rap, for small-winged game,
though first-rate for bucks of all sorts. The Boers
have not civilised the natives much, for I saw them
every day getting water in an old ox-horn ; nothing
could well be more primitive, and they dress entirely
in skins, killing numbers of bucks in pit-falls. These
pit-falls resemble a honeycomb, and the Kaffirs muster
in great force and drive the game helter-skelter over
the holes, and they knock one another in ; the holes
are of all shapes, round, oval, oblong, square, and
there are generally about fifty in one pass, and fifteen
or twenty passes in a space of two miles of country.
A strong fence on each side confines the game, which
have thus no opportunity of escape.

July 5th (Sunday).—Had a visit yesterday from

Masau, a Coranna chief, and seven of his followers, all well mounted. He agreed to buy my wagon for twenty-five fat oxen, which I expect to be here to-morrow for inspection ; they drank any amount of coffee, and put in sugar *ad libitum.* I then gave them some oranges, and they carefully preserved the pips — old Masau claims one of my horses, which he says he lent a Dutchman to ride home to his farm four years ago, after buying his wagon ; all his people swear to the horse and to the cropping of his ears, so I fear I must give him up, as I have no doubt he is their horse, for no white man would cut a horse's ears off to bleed him ; but I don't see who is to re-compense me for my loss, for I bought and paid for him.

The reader will perhaps excuse my giving here an account of a night I once passed on the open veldt on the Feight Kop road between the Vaal river and Harrysmith, on returning to Natal from Mooi River Dorp.

The wagons had been quietly treking along over an immense open country without wood for nine days, when one beautiful afternoon I mounted Adrian to shoot a wildebeest, Hopeful, a splendid stag-hound, accompanying me. As far as the eye could reach, the road apparently ran straight, and I took to the right, knowing I must come back to hit the road again, when we could see at once by the spoor whether or not our wagons had passed, and follow on or go back accordingly.

Game took me farther than I intended, and the wagons must have diverged to the left, for I could never cross the track again, and as the sun went down I began to get very uneasy and very chilly, a shirt and trousers being all my attire. Just after sunset jackals first began to make their appearance, and a flac farc (veldt pig) came out of a hole near me; this I shot for supper, and then found I had forgotten my knife, and could not get through his skin. As darkness fast set in, I knee-haltered my horse to feed, and began to try and collect dung for a fire, but could find little or none, and was forced to give up the attempt, and, before it was quite dark, I caught Adrian, drove my iron ramrod deep into the ground with the heel of my boot, and made him fast to that with the rheim, which is invariably round all our horses' necks. I curled myself up for warmth — a saddle-cloth less than two feet square being my only covering. There was a bitter cold white frost, and a dense mist, and, like an idiot, I had got into a valley by a vley of water, the very coldest spot I could have chosen, and the long grass soon began to get reeking wet. I tried every dodge and device to make Adrian lie down, hitting him below the knees with my gun-barrels, making the poor old horse lift one leg up after another, as if he was standing on hot cinders. I next stood and leant against him on the lee side, and then tried lying down again, and tore up a regular hole in the ground with my teeth, and was half choked with soil. A concert was going on

round me of lions, hyenas, and jackals, mingled with
the snorting and stamping of wildebeests, barking of
quaggas, and the occasional rushing away of springbuck or blesbuck into the darkness, as they came
noiselessly towards the water, and first got our wind.
Expecting lions every moment, I put my handkerchief round the lock of my gun, to keep it as dry as
possible, and prevent its missing fire, as everything
was reeking wet, and sat cross-legged, almost between Adrian's fore legs, as I made sure they would
attack him, being proverbially fond of horse-flesh.
After being in this frightful state of suspense an hour
at least, with their low subdued growls on all sides,
as they kept moving round, they left me, Hopeful
now and then giving vent to a low savage growl; but
I kept him near me, as there was a sense of protection in even an animal; and his time and attention
were devoted and fully occupied in licking carefully
two holes in his chest, just previously made by a
wild boar, who carried him bodily away on the
points of his tusks, full fourteen yards. I shot it in
the breast, and it fell on its knees. Hopeful rushed
in at it, when it jumped up, prodded him, and carried
him away this distance, when it fell over dead, most
probably shot through the heart.

I suffered dreadfully from cold, and was getting
worse. I at last hit upon the following device: I
made loose my stirrup-leathers, put one round Hopeful's loins, and buckled it loosely above my knees;
then put the other behind his shoulder, between

his fore legs, bringing it back over his neck ; buckled
it loosely, and slipped my head and my left arm and
shoulder through.   Being a shy brute, as most

of the greyhound breed are, on finding himself fast
he got alarmed, and began to struggle tremendously,
hanching and snapping like a baited fox.   I threw
myself down (he on the top of me), held his black
muzzle fast with my left hand, turned half over,
and, having my right hand free, hammered into
his ribs with my fist till I knocked every particle
of breath out of his body, and half suffocated him
at the same time by keeping his mouth shut. .His
struggles for some time were fearful : he foamed at

the mouth as if he were rabid. I was hardly sure if
I had not killed him, but as I relaxed my grasp on
his muzzle, he gradually came to, when I tightened
the leathers and gave him a repetition of the above,
when inclined to be refractory. At last, my voice
had the desired effect, and he lay on the top of
me all night; and I firmly believe the warmth of
his body was the means of saving my life, as I
was so cold I could do nothing till the sun was
high. It must have been an unusually cold night,
as I saw wildebeests get up so stiff they could
hardly stir for many minutes. When I eventually
got the use of my limbs, I took very violent exercise, to set the blood in circulation ; went to the
highest visible ground, and fired my first shot into
an ant-heap, that I might recover my bullet, and
then, having plenty of powder, fired some tremendous heavy charges with six inches of grass, tightly
hammered down, to make a terrific report, but no
answer ; and knowing I must, by going due east,
come to the sea at last, I took that course, and about
eleven o'clock saw a faint smoke; made for it at
once, and found the remains of a large fire, which
my party had left burning as a guide for me. They
had passed the night there, and gone on ; and after
off-saddling a bit, I followed the spoor, and overtook
them about 4 P.M.

Proudfoot and Schikkerling, my companions, had
been all the morning in quest of me, firing innumerable shots, and the former quite sure I should even-

tually turn up, though I was quite given up by the rest, as the veldt was known to be full of lions.

I was truly thankful to reach the wagons, which was all a matter of chance, as I knew no more where the wagon-track was than Hopeful did ; and I am convinced, even if I could have got food and fire, I should hardly have weathered two more such nights, and I might have gone seven or eight before coming across any habitation.

Wild boars are dangerous things.   A friend of mine, once, on chasing a very large one to ground, made a large fire and smoked him out.   He rushed through smoke and flames, and vented his rage on the horse, goring him terribly. .He eventually recovered, after a deal of time and trouble.   They afford excellent sport, however, with good dogs, with or without a rifle.   Proudfoot and myself, one morning, stuck five before breakfast with large clasp knives.   We had excellent dogs, well up to the sport, holding on like vices, each by an ear.   Frequently, when they make for holes, down which they invariably go tail first, give them a little time, and jump a few times heavily above them, three or four together, and they bolt like rabbits.

I have chased a jackall into a porcupine's hole, and the inmates have at once driven him out, choosing rather to trust his life once more to his heels than have his whole body stuck full of quills — almost as bad a predicament as a fellow-traveller (a wagon-driver) assured me happened to him once.

After outspanning on the same road, during the time the oxen were grazing he strolled out to try to kill a buck. He wounded a steinbuck very badly, and was almost catching him, when he got into a hole. He had a dog with him, but it was chasing spring-buck, so he went head first into the hole himself, and succeeded in reaching the buck, but, in his endea-vours, had got so far that he could not make an effort to get back; his arms were right before him, and his back wedged fast. He struggled so hard that he became insensible, and must have been all but suffocated, when his dog (bull and pointer—I have often seen it) saved his life by going back to the wagon, and attracting the notice of his Kaffirs, who followed the dog to his master's assistance, and dug him out more dead than alive, having been about five hours in this situation.

August 16*th* (*Sunday*). — I have sadly neglected my log for six weeks past, and must now hark back again. Having sold my wagon to a Coranna for thirty oxen, and all my goods and chattels also for oxen, I went to Hartebeest Fontein to buy a cart, to go at once to Graham's Town. I there fell in with Mr. Vermaas, who was just starting into Merico country, and I changed my plans, and agreed to go with him — myself finding powder, lead, coffee, and sugar — and, as we meant shooting giraffes, I laid in a stock of forage for my nags, and bought a new one for four oxen, and started next day for Merico, to meet his son, who had been elephant-hunting, and bring out the ivory. We were seven days in getting to our destination, having gone far out of the way. Swartz and young Vermaas had got back, having had a glorious hunt. They had shot twenty large bulls, besides what they traded from the Kaffirs, and the sight of so much fine ivory determined me at once to lose no time in trying to get among the mighty bulls; and, Swartz going in again shortly, I agreed to go with him, and to find a span of oxen — he to bring out all the ivory I got so far; and I at once started back again for my oxen, horses, guns, &c. I disposed of Graham for seven oxen, and also my double gun, for 141 lbs. of ivory, two very fine teeth, which had, however, only cost Swartz eight pounds of beads and two bullets.

I made the best of my way back to Hartebeest Fontein, and, taking the right road, and travelling day and night, I got there in four days; bought a cart for 15l., and two dogs also — a bull and greyhound, a perfect model, Torey by name, and a well-bred pointer bitch, which I christened Donna, and got back to Joubert's the following day, having been away three weeks. Found all well; one ox dead or lost. John had sold 'The Saxon' for six oxen, which I was very sorry for, as he had had the sickness, and was a quiet shooting pony; but it was my fault.

I left fifty-four oxen in charge of Joubert, and John and myself started, two days after, back again

M

to Merico, with nine oxen and five horses, and
five guns, four dogs, &c., and arrived at Swartz's
in five days. We had the company of an Englishman on the road, Metcalf by name, whom I
met in the Merico country, and I offered to give
him my beads, blankets, knives, &c., to trade
for me on halves ; and, thinking this no doubt too
good an offer to be overlooked, he forthwith hired
a wagon, and turned up at Joubert's the day before we started to come here, so we made fast
the cart behind the wagon, and all came together. I was not sorry to have a wagon to tie
the horses and oxen to at night in the Lion veldt,
instead of my cart ; for, in the event of their
paying us a visit, the beasts would most undoubtedly
have smashed my cart all to pieces ; however, we
had a fine moon, and they did not come near us,
though I saw ten in the day-time.

The Merico country is a beautiful land, and most
fertile and productive ; the crops splendid, and
fruit *ad libitum*. It is warm, and well wooded,
but a little short of water. There are no rivers,
only one or two small streams, and plenty of fountains ; but it is a charming country to live in—
hilly, rather too stony, but with large fertile valleys intervening. The only drawback is the great
scarcity of game, and yet a more likely country
I never saw, and I cannot account for it. My dogs
are looking poor, and, were it not for some lung-
sick oxen, which die very opportunely, I don't

know what they would do. I wrought hard for
them all day yesterday on Darby, whom I left
behind here, a bag of bones, and he carried me
as fresh as a lark over a vast extent of land, but
I never burnt powder. This is the last house in
the Merico country; the Boers have not penetrated
farther, though I consider them first-rate pioneers
in a new land. We are only four days from
Sechele, a very powerful Maccateese chief. Swartz
is now not going to start until the 31st August,
so I have a fortnight to kick my heels about here,
with nothing to do; but I am not sorry for it
on the horses' and oxen's account, for we have
had two days' rain, and the new grass is springing
up fast and green, and there will soon be a marked
improvement in the appearance of the animals.
They have had a hard winter — cold, frosty, and
windy — to contend with, and very little grass.

We were treated most hospitably and kindly by
one and all the Boers in the neighbourhood, and
Swartz kept a capital table, and an almost open
house, there being lots of visitors every day, and
a soupii, or a glass of Cape brandy, for every
one. The flasks were never off the table, and the
day invariably wound up by target-shooting, at
which the Dutch are great adepts. A yokeskey
at 100 yards, or a bottle, was frequently the mark,
and sometimes the crack shots called for Eau de
Cologne flasks, short, squab little things, no higher
than a wine glass, and looking uncommonly small at

100 yards, which were, notwithstanding, frequently
smashed.   Horse-racing was another amusement,
which consisted in letting the bridle loose on the
horse's neck, and going at it hammer and tongs,
legs and arms, and flogging all the way: 1,000
yards the distance.   The Boers are also great musi-
cians, and very fond of dancing, and appear to
live exceedingly happily.   Many of the Dutch
nöes, or young maidens, are very pretty ; and
they are a very moral set of people.   They have
a singular custom of first becoming acquainted.   If
you admire any one in particular, you take the
first opportunity that presents itself of asking her
to upsit.   Should this be accorded, when the old
people and all the rest of the household have
retired, a curtain frequently being all the partition
between the sitting and bed-rooms, the chosen one
again appears, with a candle, short or long, according as she fancies you or otherwise, and remains
as long as that burns, all conversation being carried on in whispers, and the fair one being obliged to
sit very close and talk very low, for fear of disturbing the inmates on the other side of the curtain.
These upsits frequently last far on into the morning, and the happy swain is at great pains to
trim the candle — not let it flicker or flare, or
get into a draft, and so keep it burning as long
as possible, for it is imperative to retire when that
is out.

    I have been present, stretched on the floor, on

a blanket (asleep, apparently, no doubt), when two upsittings have been going on, at opposite corners of a large room, all still as the grave, but the subdued whisperings of the happy pairs.

There is something very charming about the whole proceeding; at all events, it had the effect of banishing all inclination to sleep, and I came to the conclusion that taking an active part for the future would be far more preferable than again being merely a passive spectator.

They are a primitive, hospitable, good-hearted set; marry very young; live to a good old age generally; and very frequently have large families, and most of them are very comfortably off, and take things very easy. Some of the poorer, however, both live and work very hard; but their wants are few, as they are brought up to do everything for themselves. Groceries, prints, and moleskin are all the poorer classes buy, except powder and lead; almost all other requirements they make for themselves. And the upsitting business I consider about the best of their old customs. All matches are then and there clenched, provided you are both of one mind, and brought to a speedy conclusion: no very long engagements, for no purpose whatever. The dower of the bride generally consists in some cows, sheep, and goats; a span of oxen (twelve), and a quiet riding horse — if the bridegroom can furnish about the same, with a wagon. They start life very comfortably, and with every prospect before them of eventually becoming rich in stock, which is money; for they have a good custom likewise, when a child is born, of making over a cow, a ewe, and a goat ewe, which are never parted with, and, by the time he or she is married, they have the increase of this lot to start life with for themselves. They have, however, previously sold more or less to provide themselves with luxuries, a good rifle, riding horse, and wagon for the men — dress, bonnets, and knicknacks for the women; and they buy all the most expensive things that can be procured from the Cape or elsewhere. And a 'kop-spuiling' horse, a brute that is always tossing his head, being sharply bitted and curbed for the purpose, is indispensable for a dandy young Boer in his courting days, and eagerly enquired for.

September 1st. — I have been doing all sorts of things the last fortnight, endeavouring to expedite our departure — tent and sail-maker, painter, shoe-maker, doctor, &c., by turns; and we have still a good week's work before us, partly owing to the sickness of a baby, which I have been expecting to die every day.

The wild dogs got amongst my oxen the other night, biting three (one severely), and killing one. It was a pitch dark, cold, rainy night; and last night the wolves killed one of Swartz's, and bit two more.

I sold Jack for six yellow inoculated oxen, as he was too blind to do any good in the bush, though in all other respects unexceptionable. I have now only four horses left.

Breakfasted on a buttered ostrich egg this morning : it was excellent, but five of us could not quite manage it. Traded half a dozen large leather sacks from the Maccateese for beads, very cheap ; they will hold two muids apiece, and are beautifully braided and sewn. I am very anxious to be off ; I have shot next to nothing here, for the best of all reasons — there is nothing, except a small troop of impala, very shy. I got one — a 200 yards shot at least. One wagon we have been painting up to sell to Mosilikatse, and have taken extra pains. It comprises nearly all the gaudy colours of the rainbow : whether Dutch taste, or in order to take the eye of the savage, I know not.

I wrote a long letter home a week ago, which will not go, however, for probably two months, if it ever reaches its destination. There is no post, and no opportunity of sending to any post town. They are at least a century behind the rest of the civilised world here, but appear to live very happily and contented.

10th. — Still here, but we have got all ready for a start on Monday, the 14th. The baby is dead and buried. Jack nearly frightened his purchaser to death, and he returned him, which I am not sorry for. Swartz bought eleven goats and sheep from the Maccateese, and, having no one to herd them, they made back ; and yesterday the Kaffirs brought two wretched lean skeletons, half eaten, being all that the wolves and wild dogs had left out of the flock. They were out only one night.

My Kaffir, Matakit, upset the kettle of boiling water over his bare foot the other day, and took about as much notice of it as I should have done with a strong shooting-boot on. They have regular hides, not skin at all.

I was amused at seeing four Dutch women — two old and two young — sharpening their knives on the door-step, preparatory to cutting the throat of a huge goat, which they did, and then skinned and cut him up in a masterly style, without showing the slightest feeling whatever, though they had a good fight ere they could throw him : altogether, too manly an exhibition to heighten my opinion of them. A German missionary has outspanned here on his way to Natal, just giving me time to write a line home.

15*th*. — At last, made a start with three wagons, nine horses, and forty-two oxen. Lots of salutes firing on both sides. Got only to Moiloi's, and laid in a store of Kaffir corn.

16*th*. — Passed through a beautiful country, along a well-wooded valley. Came to Mr. Edwards's old station, which is well situated, and has a fine garden, but the buildings, which are very large and substantial, are all going to ruins. A great deal of pains have been taken here ; the chapel is now converted into a dwelling-house for Kaffirs, curs, &c. I saw half-a-dozen of the latter stretched before the remains of a huge log-fire in the middle of the floor. Kleinboy, Gordon Cumming's old after-rider, joined us this morning. He is an amusing little dog.

17*th.* — On getting up in the morning, found all the neck-straps from three wagons, and the trenches, eaten by the starved curs before mentioned, which gave occasion for a scrimmage between Swartz and their owner, a Hottentot. We sent for a skin to mend damages, and the Tottie was impudent; words soon came to blows, and the Tottie covered his retreat manfully, keeping his head well up, and warding off the blows like a master hand, and putting one in occasionally, straight from the shoulder. It was all made up over a bottle of grog, ten minutes afterwards, and, when all repairs were completed, we treked again.

Saw tsessebes for the first time, and had a long burst after them on horseback, but did not get a shot. Jack sprained his fetlock badly, but I reduced the inflammation by cold water bandages and opening the place.

18*th.* — Had a long ride in quest of giraffes; saw spoor only. Bacon lagged behind, very sick. John bled him in the mouth, and left a Kaffir behind to bring him slowly on. I overtook him on the road, and found him nearly bled to death, and had great difficulty in taking up the vein; he fell several times from exhaustion. I eventually succeeded with horse-hair, twisted with a small stick, and made fast on his upper jaw, under his upper lip, but not

until I had broken off two needles in the roof of his
mouth.   He had been ailing long, and I bled him
copiously ten days ago, all to no purpose, for he died
soon after we went to bed.   He was a cream colour,
with black points.   The horse-sickness is very bad in
this country.

19th. — Not a bit of meat at the wagons.   John
and Swartz started early on horseback for a koodoo,
tsessebe, or giraffe.   I went on with the wagons,
and they came up where we outspanned, having
killed nothing.

I took a cup of coffee and a biscuit, and again
saddled up for a giraffe.   I rode old Bryan, a tall,
narrow-built, ewe-necked, remarkably long blue-
skimmel horse, resembling very much in appearance
the animal we went to hunt, but with a great depth
of shoulder and breadth of chest, and good girth, and
some capital points about him, though an ungainly,
ugly brute, and very heavy in hand, with no mouth
whatever.   We shortly met six Kaffirs, who told us
they had seen fresh spoor of a troop of giraffes, and
turned back to show us.   We followed the spoor
some four miles, through thorns, and very stony and
bad travelling, ascending the different heights to try
to see them, but always following the spoor as fast
as the Kaffirs could keep up.   I saw them first, full
500 yards off, seven or eight of them, and, on
whistling for Swartz, they immediately took right
away, with a tremendous start.   We made good
play, at a swinging gallop, right through bush and

stones, and, after a long burst, I came within twenty
yards of them, when Bryan stopped in fear and
trembling of the huge unwieldy brutes. I plied
him sharply with the spurs, and got him once more
under weigh, keeping above the wind, as the giraffes
have a strong effluvium, which frightens horses unused
to them. We came out on the open, Swartz forty or
fifty yards in advance of me, and as far behind the
giraffes. The sight of the other horse gave Bryan
confidence, and he bounded away in good style, and
was alongside instantly, when they again dashed into
thick bush; here Swartz turned out a cow, the very
one I had set my mind on, and I at once took after
a large bull. Now he bounded away with his tail
screwed round like a corkscrew, and going in one
bound as far as I went in three. Bryan crashed
through everything, and I tore my hands, arms, and
shirt to pieces.

At length I got nearly alongside him, and fired,
hitting him high in the neck, and taking no effect
whatever on him. Here I got a pull on Bryan and
managed to re-load, still going on at a smart gallop,
and once more got alongside, and, in trying to pull
up to dismount, he went bang into a bush, which
brought him up short, and he had to back out, the
giraffe meanwhile getting 100 yards in advance. I
soon made up the lost ground, and headed him,
endeavouring to turn him, but he slewed round
like a vessel in full sail, bearing down almost on
the top of me, with his huge fore legs as high in

the air as the horse's back. I had lots of chances
to dismount, but had no command of my nag, his
mouth was dead ; but there was not a sign of flagging
about him. I steered him close alongside on the
near side, held out my gun in one hand, within two

yards of the giraffe's shoulder, and fired. The gun
shot over my head, and nearly broke my middle
finger, and down came the giraffe, with a tremendous
crash, with his shoulder smashed to atoms. I must
have had a desperately heavy charge of powder in,
as I loaded at random.

Bryan was as still as a post instantly, and I lost not
a moment in off-saddling him, ere I inspected my first

giraffe, and then put the saddle-cloth over my bare head, as the sun was intensely hot.

I must have had nearly five miles through hack-thorns and stones of all sizes, as straight as the crow flies. I followed him about twenty yards in the rear for a mile at least, the stones rattling past my head occasionally. Whenever the ground favoured, and I made a spurt, he did the same, appearing to have no end of bottom, and Bryan, though he has a long swinging gallop and strained every nerve, could not come up with him for a long time.

Swartz killed his cow about a mile back, with one shot in the stern, about one hundred yards off. John had nothing at all to say to it, being badly mounted, and the giraffes going straight away. Cut off his mane and tail as a trophy, and the tongue and marrow-bone for immediate use; and Swartz and John coming up, we went to his giraffe, which was the fattest for meat. The Kaffirs were there, and I offered them some beads to find my hat.

20th (Sunday).—We don't travel to-day. I de-spatched all the Kaffirs and dogs for meat early this morning, as it was late when we got back last night. The Kaffirs have just brought my hat, having fol-lowed the spoor from the dead giraffe. Supped on his heart and marrowbone: the meat is really tender and good.

21st. — Treked to Kolobeng, and saw the remains of Dr. Livingstone's house, which the Boers pillaged

when they sent a command out against Sechele. On
saddling Darby, I perceived a swelling above the
eyes — a sure sign of the horse-sickness. Bled him
copiously, and rode Croppy instead. Shot two roybucks, and outspanned for the night, without reaching water.

22nd. — Saddled up Bryan early, and we all went
to try for a giraffe : soon lost one another, in chase
of tsessebes. On reaching the road, I saw fresh
wagon-spoor, and rode on to Sechele's, and was
well treated by two German missionaries, who have
lately come. Mr. Schroeder was one, whom I
slightly knew in Natal. Lost Ragman and Smouse :
the latter found the wagons ; the former, I fear, I
shall see no more.

23rd. — The wagons arrived, and we soon had a
visit from Sechele, a fine, intelligent-looking Kaffir,
and well dressed, but having too good an opinion of
himself. He said I must go back again, he would
not have strangers coming into his country to hunt ;
and, besides, I had not treated him with proper respect, in not first going to see him. I managed to
explain to him, at last, satisfactorily, the reasons
why and wherefore I had not done so, which were,
that on riding up to some women working in a
garden to ask the way, they fled precipitately,
throwing everything down, and shrieking for aid.
Then I must make him a present, to show I was
well-disposed towards him ; and, when this was done,
he shook hands, and we were friends.

Darby very bad: I bled and blistered him severely, but all to no purpose; he died in the night, putting me sadly about, as I depended solely on him. He was as good a bit of stuff as ever was put together. The Kaffirs bring all sorts of things to the wagons to trade, but charge very high, and principally want powder, and lead, and caps. They reckon the Kaffirs here to amount to 20,000; and Sechele himself lives on the top of a huge berg, with kraals all around in every direction. They are an independent lot of Kaffirs, and have no end of guns. Some fellows from Phillipolis have been here the last week, putting them in order for his people.

Old Reffler, a Hottentot driver, took himself home again this morning, without giving any reason, or even saying he was going.

24*th.* — Spent a lazy day at the wagons, the weather being very hot. Some fine karosses came, but all wanted guns or powder in exchange, and took them away again. Tried to buy a horse from the Bastards for a gun, but they were going in to hunt, and could not miss one. Lots of ostrich feathers and eggs — the former very dear, and most of the latter bad.

25*th.*—Left Sechele and had a long trek, leaving the main road in order to obtain water, through gardens most of the way, the Kaffir women having done an immensity of work.

26*th.*—Came on to a place called Kapong, where we await the arrival of Sechele, who is going with

us on Monday afternoon. This is the last water we
shall see for three days. The poor oxen and horses I
pity sadly, as the former must trek three wagons
day and night, and a great part of the road lies
through heavy sand. The country here is very flat,
through bush all the way, but sandy and heavy, and
the sun very hot and game scarce. I have not fired
a shot the last two days, but we are going to have a
little target-shooting, to keep our hands in. I was
amused at Sechele the other night coming to the
wagon with his body-guard, carrying a drawn sword.

27th (Sunday).—Had a glorious thunderstorm,
worth worlds to us, as we shall now probably get
water on the road. We were all busy converting
ostrich eggs and bullocks' horns and bladders into
water utensils.

28th.—Sechele came on horseback with sixty
followers, bringing all sorts of things to the wagon
on pack bulls and oxen. He had changed his mind
and would go no farther; he and Swartz were bargaining all the afternoon for the wagon we had been
taking such extra pains with for Mosilikatse. Sechele
ultimately bought it for 800 lbs. ivory, about 250l., as
they must all be large bull teeth. Had some target-
shooting in the afternoon, and Sechele said his heart
was sore at being beaten; he had a beautiful double-
barreled rifle. I bought Luister (Listen) from Swartz,
—a vicious horse, sore backed, thick fetlock joints, lots
of splints, and a determined kicker—for two magnificent teeth weighing 154 lbs., and worth 50l. at least;

the animal in any other part of the colony would be dear at 12*l*., but here he is worth the money, as he is thoroughly salted and won't die, and a most enduring brute. He is used to being under saddle every day, and an unexceptionable horse at elephants. I think I shall lose no more now by sickness, as they show no signs as yet, and have all had the sickness below ; but Jack and Croppy are worth nothing, the former nearly blind and a bolter, the other purblind, deadly stupid, lame and stiff as a post. Sechele very anxious to sell me a horse for a gun, but he is a shuffling little weed and the risk is too great to run, as, if it came to the hearing of the Boers, they would probably confiscate some of my property, or inflict a heavy penalty.

29th.—Parted company with Sechele, he going back again. Sent Medcalfe two oxen, which almost got him into difficulties ; treked far on into the night, and made the oxen fast.

30th.—Inspanned very early, and made good play —highly favoured by the cool and cloudy weather— through this rightly-named *thirst* land. Got a little water for the horses in the afternoon, in a deep cleft in the rocks — a most unlikely place to look for it. The Kaffirs had previously been making holes, and drinking stuff as thick as mud. Every kind of utensil was put in use, and I thought bladders the very best, being so light to carry and holding a good quantity. The road uncommonly heavy deep sand, bushy country all the way, camel thorns principally,

N

with large open patches. I got a long shot at an
ostrich, but he was going like the wind. Treked
far on into the night, and made the oxen fast, as
their throats were too parched up to eat.

October 1st.—Got to some wells, called Batlanarmi,
where we found a good supply of water in a deep
hole. I enjoyed a good wash immensely this morning,
as a damp cloth is all we have had for two days.
Drew out the water in buckets for the horses, and
then made a circular hole and poured away, having
lots of hands, and passing the bucket from one to the
other quickly, till we had about nine inches deep, and
then brought the oxen six a time to drink, Kleinboy
sitting on his hams with a sjambok to prevent them
from trampling it all into mud ; by this means they
all got a tolerable supply. The ladder by which we
descended to the well was a tall camel thorn-tree
with the branches lopped off, leaving about two feet
to stand on. The Masaras stood on it, and we passed
the zinc bucket from hand to hand.

When the sun had gone down a little, inspanned
again ; Swartz, John, Kleinboy, and myself, going on
horseback for a giraffe. We soon saw seven going
away leisurely, and cantered after them, trying to
bring them near the wagons. I kept in the rear,
with old Bryan pulling hard, when, unfortunately, the
curb broke and he shot ahead, and I was alongside a
large cow in 300 yards. My gun missed fire, and I
had great difficulty in putting on another cap, having
very little command of my nag. As I was again

nearing the giraffe, he took me at full speed into the middle of a dense hack-thorn tree, which tore me to pieces and sent my gun flying over my head backwards, and it was all that I could do to keep my seat. Bryan swerved and got through, and I soon turned him, dismounted, and rode back for my gun, picked it up, and kept on at a good round gallop in the direction I saw my giraffe last, and was not long in catching sight of her. I had a very long gallop through thick thorns all the way, waiting in vain for an opening to put on the steam. I at length pushed Bryan close up, firing from the saddle, and giving the giraffe the ball in the stern, about three inches too low. The blood streamed in a torrent, but she kept on at a good pace, I contenting myself with just keeping her in sight, and she was going the right road while I reloaded. I then galloped alongside, jumped off a little ahead, and as she came broadside past me, shot her through the heart, and she fell dead in ten yards. I off-saddled and knee-haltered Bryan, and Kaffirs and dogs were up in five minutes, Bryan serving me a pretty trick by running away to the wagons. Tired and half dead from thirst as I was, I had to follow him on foot, and then lead him back a good two miles for the saddle and bridle; not in the best of humours with him, as I was very badly scratched. On returning, or rather following the wagon-spoor, which was ahead, I met a Kaffir, who told me that John had broken his arm, and on reaching the wagons found the news, alas! too true. The account

he gives of the accident is as follows:— On pulling
up Luister short to jump off to shoot his giraffe, as
his body was bent to dismount, Luister reared straight
up in the air and then plunged and kicked violently,
finishing by taking a bound to the left.   John came
off and heard the bone of his left fore arm crack like
a cap.   Luckily Swartz and Kleinboy were close at
hand, and immediately pulled up and set his arm,
and when I returned he was properly splintered and
bandaged up, with his arm in a sling, and drinking a
cup of coffee.   Medcalfe made the splints with the
back of a book and part of the lid of a tea-chest.

2nd.—Inspanned early and treked far to a vley,
the horses and dogs winding the water full a mile
and a half off, and setting off briskly with their heads
up in the air.   Kvelt fell with Swartz, unfortunately
breaking the stock of the double-barrel he bought
from me.   I had the Kaffirs at work at each
of my legs to-day, and extracted forty-two thorns.
I need hardly say I suffer great pain, as my
hands festered, and ached, and throbbed to such
a degree that I got no sleep, and I did not lessen the
pain to-day by applying blue stone.   The hack-
thorns, or vaac um bechi—a most appropriate name
given them by the Boers, signifying ' wait a little,'—
are the most fearful things to get through I ever
came across.   They have low square tops, strong
and very dense, with short stubby sharp thorns, set
on both ways, and no garment of any quality can
stand against them, and the more desperate your

struggles the faster you get ; neither horse, dog, ox, Kaffir, nor Christian will knowingly face them a second time, except by using great care and caution. They are most virulent and poisonous in their nature. My right knee and elbow are perfectly stiff.

A lot of Maccalacas Kaffirs came for water ; they are poor wretches, called dogs by the Maccateese, and are not allowed to eat anything they kill but just the intestines ; they must take all the meat to Sechele. They had nothing to carry water in but ostrich eggs and the intestines of large animals tied fast at one end, and they scooped up the water in tortoise-shells ; they had the eggs slung to their backs in a skin or a kind of network, and each of them carried from twelve to eighteen. This place is called Lopepes vley. No spoor of any game coming to drink, and seeing ducks which took right away, I judge there must be another vley near at hand.

3rd. — About eight o'clock the Kaffirs that were herding the oxen came to say there were three black rhinoceros. We up-saddled and went in pursuit, following the spoor not far, however, when we saw them, and they at once went straight off. I was about twenty yards in the rear, Swartz going at a smart gallop, Bryan star-gazing, and pulling hard, when down he came, a tremendous bang, right on the flint-stones, or rather rocks, breaking both knees and grazing his shoulder badly. Luckily, or rather unluckily, my gun entirely broke the force of my fall, and I was not hurt in the least, but the gun got

an ugly bend, and a crack you might put a sixpence
in half round the barrel, and about nine inches below
the muzzle, and split the stock down the middle, and
I was entirely thrown out.

Swartz chased them far; jumped off and killed
the cow and a large calf right and left, and they lay
within 150 yards of one another.

Inspanned in the afternoon, and I stopped behind
to have a swim. Just before sunset I saw giraffes
from the wagon, and Swartz and Kleinboy were
soon in the saddle, and the former killed a fat cow,
after a very long stern chase. It was full moon, and
it was about an hour and a half high, when we saw
a fire some three hundred yards from the road, and
found Swartz and giraffes there. Outspanned for a
few hours, and the Kaffirs put nearly the whole of
the giraffes in the wagons, as we shall not get game
again for three or four days, being now near
Sicomo's.

4th. — Inspanned about three o'clock, and got to
a large vley of good water, called Sangarni, about
eleven A.M.; scorching hot; the wagons very, very
heavy. I had to outspan one of my oxen, which
had nearly pulled his eyes out.

To give an idea of the stomachs of the Dutch women, one proposed they should have a marrow-bone
between them; the other objected, saying she could
eat a whole one! The proposer thought she could
too, and forthwith they had the two largest broiled
— nearly a yard long each, without exaggeration —

and that without salt, or condiments of any kind whatever, and in the middle of a regular roasting hot day. The cow was very fat, and the bones full of marrow.

The Kaffirs are happy dogs. One bushman Kaffir, after working two years for two heifers, took gladly our escort to his kraal. He left his heifers in charge of another Kaffir, while he went to a giraffe I had shot for meat, and, on returning, his heifers were gone. He followed the spoor far, and early next morning he saw lion-spoor also, on the track of his heifers. His hopes were faint, and a little farther he found their remains, and rejoined us the following day, and, laughing from mouth to ear, said, ' The lion had eaten them up ; ' and they do not appear to have cost him a second thought.

I bent my gun straight again, made her fast to a tree, and fired her with a long string. I then put in nine drachms of fine powder, and fired her again in like manner : to my joy and surprise, I could see no enlargement whatever of the crack, and think I shall continue shooting with her, as she is my favourite gun. It is more than a crack : I could put a three-penny piece right through into the barrel, and cannot make up my mind whether it is dangerous or not to shoot with now. I fired four bullets from the shoulder at a target, and she appeared to shoot as well as ever.

5th. — Got early to Sicomo's, a wild, queer place. The Kaffirs all live on the top of a high berg, having no access but up a gorge, between two stony mountains ; a dry watercourse, which, in any other country, would be a roaring torrent. Sicomo was hunting, and we did not see him. Though there are several thousand Kaffirs living on the berg, a stranger passing through the country would think it uninhabited, but in the evenings and early mornings, on going to and from their work in the gardens, the whole pass is one continued line of people, and constant hum of voices. Traded a lot of feathers, two karosses, and about forty pounds of ivory ; the Kaffirs much more civil than I expected to find them.

6th. — Parted company with Medcalfe, and treked away, he remaining behind. Though our course lies directly forward, it will take us about two days to round the precipitous rocky mountain. Outspanned at sunset, and got water in a dry watercourse, after scraping about three feet deep : cool and delicious, as we have had two burning days, with hot winds, which completely prostrated me. We had, however, lots of Kaffir beer, which is a little acid, and very refreshing. Stayed behind the wagons, to try and exchange Jack for another horse, and, though I risked my neck in galloping him among the stones, as he is almost blind, I could not swap.

8th.—Although I walked ahead of the wagons all day I saw nothing. Swartz wounded a quagga, and a few minutes after the shot I heard the dogs had something at bay, and on running a few hundred

yards in the direction, saw the Kaffirs squatting on
their hams behind the trees. I thought it was a
wounded buffalo, but I saw, to my surprise, an un-
wounded cow giraffe. I gave Swartz a ball, and
we fired together a running shot, both hitting her
too high, but she stood again 200 yards ahead, and
I being first loaded and first up, shot her through
the heart, dead.

9th.—Yesterday our direction lay right through a
large mountain, and the path was horribly stony, and
we had to cut our way with axes through a great
part, but the weather was luckily cold, and I could
not keep warm, walking hard, with two coats on.
Saddled up early for a giraffe or eland, but it was so
cold we had to off-saddle and light a fire, which I
did with a cap, two stones, a bit of rag, and powder.
We waited for the wagons, breakfasted, and again
started, when we soon saw three lions ; gave chase to
the lioness, and she ran hard through the bush a good
distance, when she lay down. Donna, who is always
in the way, went up and started her again, and, as she
was nearing the thick bush, Swartz, fearful of losing
her, jumped off, fired and missed her. I galloped on,
and she came to bay, lying under a bush facing me
twenty-five yards off. Swartz came up, and when
reloaded, I fired from Bryan's back, my arms aching
so with holding my horse that I missed also. With
a fierce growl she changed her position to a big bush,
some twelve yards off. When I was reloaded, Swartz
fired from his horse with better success, hitting her

on the point of the shoulder and disabling her. She
champed the branches of the tree in impotent rage
and fury, and I went up and finished her off. She
was a fine old lioness, very large and fat. We
skinned her, and Swartz took the skin to the wagon.
I took the skull, though, but for my infamous bad
shot, I should have had the honour of killing her.
I saw yesterday, for the first time, a harrisbuck,
or potoquaine, but he was far off, and on the
side of a most precipitous mountain. Hearing
our wagons thundering down the dry stony ravine,
he was taking himself majestically off, out of harm's
way. He appeared to me to be of a glossy jet
black, and I ran hard to get a better look at him,
but he had disappeared, or rather I got deeper and
deeper into the kloof, and the bushes, trees, and
rubbish intercepted my view.

10th. — Had an easy victory over an immense old
giraffe bull. Not having a measure, I am afraid to
say what height he stood; but from his fetlock to
his knee, and from his knee to the point of the
shoulder, were both over four feet. His tongue,
which I slung to my belt above my hips, hung below
my ankle. I saw him standing alone, and, knowing
he would take up wind, kept 150 yards below; and,
after an easy gallop of about a mile, he came directly
across me, within 15 yards, at a tearing pace. Bryan,
being on his best behaviour, pulled up short; and I
gave him a bullet in the stern, about 100 yards off,
which soon caused him to slacken his pace; and the

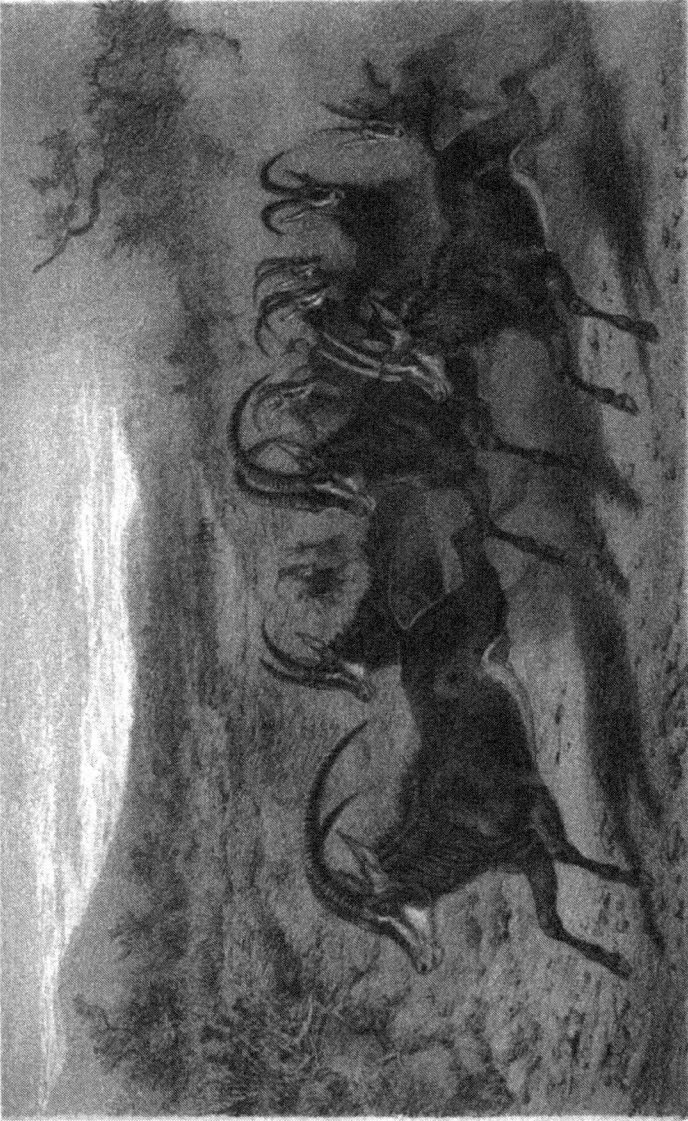

J Wolf lith.

Hanhart, Imp

ground being good, after in vain trying to drive him towards the wagons, I finished him with another shot behind the shoulder. I have had my gun cut down by the gunsmith. She is now ridiculously short, and very dangerous, but uncommonly handy on horseback, and she carries as well as before. I counted six species, and it rains still; but in two or two days . . .

. . . .
. . . .
. . . .
. . . .

. . . the stirrup, and one buckle of a stirrup-leather, which we found a good half-mile from the wagons. This is most unfortunate, as no amount of money can replace the loss here. If I could only recover the old saddle-tree, I could easily get someone to make it answer the purpose again; but as good saddles in these parts are nearly impossible, in the least . . . . are very hard to get, even, notwithstanding all the care that can be taken.

11th.—Found the cork out of the bottle, and the last drop of ink spilled, and had to continue my journal with a mixture of gunpowder and water.

. . . no elephants yet. I saw two wagons just outside . . . . or I was mistaken, that is the wagons, apparently making for my . . . .

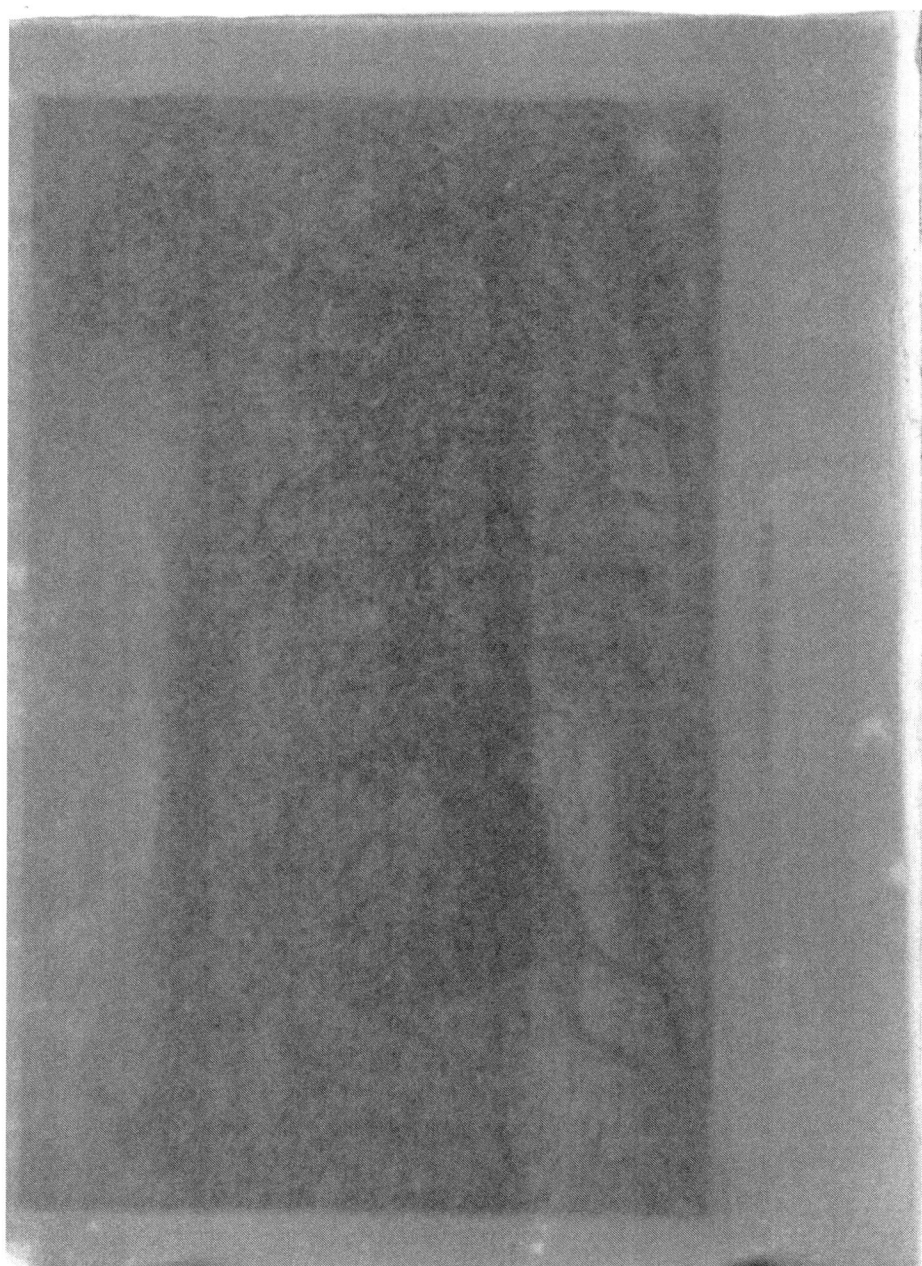

ground being good, after in vain trying to drive him towards the wagons, I finished him with another shot behind the shoulder. I have had my gun cut down by the Bastards. She is now ridiculously short—barely 18 inches—but uncommonly handy on horseback, and she appears to shoot as well as before. I bagged 11 pigeons and 4 ducks with her in two discharges.

11th (Sunday).— Kleinboy last night carelessly left out my saddle, which I had lent to Swartz. Though it was not two yards from the wagons, and there were lots of dogs and Kaffirs sleeping out, the wolves took it bodily away; and though we turned out the last man in search, as yet we have only found the girths, stirrups, and one buckle of a stirrup-leather, which we found a good half-mile from the wagons. This is most unfortunate, as no amount of money can replace the loss here. If I could only recover the old saddle-tree, I could patch it up somehow or other to answer the desired purpose; but a good saddle in this country is quite indispensable, as the horses' backs are very liable to get sore, notwithstanding all the care that can be taken.

13th. — Found the cork out of the bottle, and the last drop of ink spilled, and had to continue my journal with a mixture of gunpowder and water.

15th.— No elephants yet. I saw this morning three beautiful harrisbucks, as I was strolling on in front of the wagons, unfortunately without my gun.

The days are cruelly hot. It is quite impossible to travel in the middle of the day; both man and beast are quite prostrate. I shall hunt no more in the summer, as the exposure to the fierce heat, the burning sands, and the hot sultry winds, dries you up like an old mummy, takes all the sap out of your body, and adds about ten years to your appearance. We are eaten up with flies; and the wagon affords but slight protection from the sun, which is so powerful, that a side of bacon, by no means fat, and protected by two thick canvas sails, melts away. My hands are still very sore from the hack-thorns, and I cannot get them well. Rode my new purchase, Luister, to-day, for the first time, but found nothing. John's arm still pains him a good deal. He had a Kaffir doctoring him yesterday, cutting numerous small niches all over the arm, and rubbing in some preparation of leaves and roots; but I place no faith whatever in his skill, and should be sorry to undergo the pain.

18*th* (*Sunday*). — Three giraffes, three white rhinoceros, one black ditto, and one eland bull, must be added to the list of slaughter — three rhinoceros and one giraffe being my share of the spoil. I killed the black rhinoceros and the eland also; but, not giving them the first ball, they do not count to me. We had a glorious hunt after a large troop of giraffes, Swartz, Kleinboy, and myself each singling out one, and each bringing to bay in a masterly manner. I rolled my cow over dead with one bullet; Kleinboy did the same about two miles ahead. Swartz could not go the pace, and fired 200 yards off, giving his giraffe a good shot, however, and making her what he calls 'swack.' It is a good plan, if you are sure of your shot; but at such a distance I cannot make good work.

Yesterday Swartz and myself, being badly mounted, had a long chase after two white rhinoceros cows. I eventually finished them both, though they cost us nine bullets. On jumping off to fire, Jack ran away, and I had a long chase on foot ere I recovered him. Swartz's nag, old Croppy, is dead lame on one foot, but a sjambok vigorously applied had a wonderful effect on him. Rode Luister in the afternoon, and shot a very large bull, with a fine horn, breaking his shoulder the second shot, as he came swinging broadside past me, not more than 20 yards off. I shot well yesterday, hitting nine running shots with ball, from 50 to 70 yards off, all good shots. Killed some Namaqua partridges and two different kinds of bush partridge, totally different from any I ever before saw, the plumage underneath resembling a grouse, with very handsome bills. I regret much my inability to skin them properly.

Our course lies nearly north, verging east and west for water; and we have Masaras, who go ahead of the wagons, to point out the way from one vley to another. This is, without exception, the driest, flattest, most desolate-looking country I ever saw; and the Masaras have burned the last blade of grass.

There is so much sameness in the country, that I dare not leave the wagons in the bush, for fear of losing myself. We find one another by firing guns and lighting immense fires. It is anything but a comfortable feeling when you are lost, as you have not an idea where you are likely to get water, and the ground is so dry and baked with the sun that the wagons hardly leave any visible spoor. We all agreed that we would not willingly set foot in this land again. We are twenty in all at the wagons, black and white, including two women and their children. Bryan is sick, and two oxen also. Jack was lost last night, and we were debating whether the lions had taken him or not, when, to my great joy, the Tottie discovered him. The Kaffirs found ten ostrich eggs yesterday, which were very good. I breakfasted this morning on rhinoceros hump, baked in a hole in the ground, in the skin — tender, juicy, fat, glutinous, and good.

Wherever there is a little muddy spring, which takes half a day to fill a small hole, you will find some poor wretches of starving Masaras close in the neighbourhood; how they support life at all is a mystery to me, in this barren, worthless desert. The Masaras have no cattle or gardens; indeed, I don't suppose anything would grow. Half a dozen stunted goats, and a few curs that can hardly hold together from famine, constitute their all.

22nd.— No elephants yet, and the Kaffirs will not tell us where they are; I think they are afraid of

Mosilikatse. Swartz and myself have killed four buffaloes, two rhinoceros, and one eland, wishing to lay in a good stock of dry meat before we come to elephants. We must shoot no more then, for fear of frightening them, as there is no knowing, when once alarmed, when they will stop again. There is no waste in the great quantity of meat we have killed, as the poor Masaras light great fires by each animal, and eat and dry the last morsel. A whole batch of them moved their quarters to the three rhinoceros I shot, which all lay pretty near together. The rest of the party are asleep as I sit scribbling. We outspan to let the oxen and horses feed and drink, before we go to bed, which we always do as soon as it is dark, for we must be up by the morning star, and have a cup of coffee and a biscuit before we trek. The Kaffirs make a kraal for the oxen every night, as we are afraid of lions.

Yesterday morning we saw a large troop of nearly 200 buffaloes. We lost no time in saddling up Luister and Ludovick, each bent upon shooting a fat cow. Old Wolf got their wind; and being the most disobedient cur in the world, there was nothing for it but to go after him, and we had a grand hunt, the buffaloes tearing along through and over everything, causing stones and branches to fly in every direction, their heavy gallop making the very earth shake. I was above the wind, and got no dust; Swartz being below, was half blinded. One old bull chased Swartz away from the troop. I rode to

the head of them, and could not make up my mind
which to fire at, as they were so intermixed. At
length I saw a round shining dumpy short cow,
apparently very fat, and was determined to have
her, and pushed Luister close alongside. She could
not get into the herd, they were so wedged together.
I fired from the saddle within two yards of her, giving
Luister at the same time a chuck on the off rein, and
a savage dig with the near persuader, to prevent his
being run over by those behind. She kept on with
the herd ; and I, not being able to load at the gallop,
the bush being too thick, unpardonably lost sight of
her. I heard Smouse and Wolf barking at one, and
on galloping in the direction, saw they had succeeded
in turning out an old cow, and were baiting her in
good style. I galloped to their assistance, and after
a short chase, getting close to her stern, jumped off
just as she went into the bed of a dry river — the
Sassy — and shot her dead right through the heart,
and out just behind the shoulder on the other side,
as she was ascending the opposite bank. On returning in the direction where I last heard the firing,
I found Swartz and the Kaffirs exulting over a cow
and young heifer, which they had murdered among
them in about twelve shots, as all hands at the wagon
had a round at them. I said I had lost a fine cow,
which I was sure could not go far, and must go and
look for her, and, singularly, I found her lying dead
not 100 yards from the other two, shot right through
the heart. We loaded up an immense quantity of

beef, as she was, as I thought, in prime order. The Kaffirs take the paunch, and after being well scraped, cleaned, and greased of course, they wear it as a handkerchief round their heads.

23rd.— Ascended a high mountain this morning, and had a capital view of the surrounding country— one immense wooded flat as far as the eye can discern in every direction, with mountains thinly interspersed all over, just like so many artificial grottoes on a gentleman's pleasure-ground. They are round stony hills for the most part, wooded to the summit, and of every conceivable shape and size, decidedly pretty; but there is no water, and the country bears such a parched appearance the very sight makes your tongue cleave to the roof of your mouth. We had been looking forward for several days to the delightful baths we should have on reaching the Sassy, but we found it completely dried up, and had to get spades to work to dig a large hole in the sand in the middle of the bed of the river, when (as is always the case) cool water immediately rose, but only in small quantities, barely enough for oxen and horses. We are now only, I am told, two days from Mosilikatse's kraals; and I hear from the Kaffirs that the Rev. Robert Moffat, from Kuruman, is there—a clever, intelligent man, and better acquainted with the Kaffirs than any man in Africa. The sun here is most oppressive, and there is frequently no air stirring at night; but we have no mosquitoes.

The Maccateese have almost frightened my two

o

Kaffirs to death, by telling them Mosilikatse will most certainly kill them both, as they are Zulus, and spies of Panda's; and I cannot convince them to the contrary.

As near as I can judge of our whereabouts, we are about twelve days from the coast — say 250 miles, more or less — and in about the same degree of latitude as Inhambane, a Portuguese settlement between Delagoa Bay and Sofala. This is what I glean from the Kaffirs; but I may be considerably out of my reckoning. The Bushmen Kaffirs say there are no elephants at all in this locality; they have just returned from a two days' search, and saw no fresh spoors at all; but they cannot be believed — that is one comfort.

I will never again come with Boers; they are hardly one remove from the Kaffirs, have no information whatever on any subject but wagons and oxen, never read a book of any sort or description in their lives, are perfectly ignorant of what every child in England knows, and ask the most ridiculous questions,—spending their spare time in drinking coffee and smoking. How they get through life is a mystery. You can learn nothing whatever from them. Long yarns of their hunting exploits, repeated till you know them by heart, are all you get from them. They are very superstitious, too; nearly as much so as Hottentots. There is one of the latter now by the wagon — a dirty little brute, who, when I expostulated with him on never washing, said he would wait till he got back to the house, where he knew the water had no snakes, blind worms, or crocodiles. The Boers are nearly as bad; they excused themselves for not swimming in the river by saying that a man had once been killed by a crocodile.

25th (Sunday).—We are outspanned at length by some beautiful water, and are awaiting the arrival of some of Mosilikatse's people, as messengers were sent three days ago, saying we were here. We left a Maccateese kraal yesterday, very much against the wish of the captain, who would send no one with us to show the road, and endeavoured to deter us by saying we should find no water, no elephants, and the Blood Kaffirs, or Carl (naked) Kaffirs, Mosilikatse's people, would certainly turn us back. They told us all manner of lies, and contradicted themselves over and over again, by which means we found them out. The Maccateese are called likewise Bechuanas, Bequinas, and Basutos.

I may mention at once that we were kept two months by this river, as Mosilikatse got it into his sagacious head that we were spies; and a large commando was following us, and detained us to see if such was the case, while he sent scouring parties all round his dominions. One party came across some Saltpansberg Boers hunters north of Limpopo, in Mosilikatse's country, without his permission, who, immediately on perceiving the Matabele, altered their course south-west again, though previously they were coming north-east. On this being reported at head-

quarters, we had messages, and a letter from Mr.
Moffat, enquiring if we knew them.   This made
Mosilikatse still more suspicious; as white men were
coming into his country from two different sides, he
thought it was a plot, and quite expected to be
attacked, in which case he comforted himself with
the assurance that he would make sure of us in the
first place, and we should pay the penalty of spies
and traitors.

As we were enjoying a swim yesterday near
sunset, we heard a double shot from the wagon, and
immediately a black rhinoceros cow came tearing
past us, baited by all the dogs, who soon brought
her to bay, when nine shots were fired by six men,
who all, according to their own statement, hit her
behind the shoulder; but when she yielded up the

ghost, only four bullets were to be found in her, and one of those behind, in the stern.   She gave old Smouse a tremendous toss.   He cannot weigh less than 100lbs., and I thought every bone in his body must be broken ; but he is no worse.   He looked uncommonly sheepish, however, after his fall, and was only a spectator, declining to renew the combat.

29th. — I shot my first tsessebe on Tuesday, and last night had the extreme satisfaction of killing my

first harrisbuck.   He is a truly noble animal.   I have preserved the head and skin to the best of my power, having nothing but salt to cure it with, and the long-looked-for rain coming on ere it was properly dry. It was sundown when I shot him, and far from the wagons ; but I was determined to skin him, and John lent a good hand.   So we soon had him well

packed on Croppy, and rode back for the wagons,
luckily having a little moon and the dry bed of a
river to guide us by. John first saw them — four
bulls, in company with a lot of quaggas. He beckoned to me, and we gave chase. I rode hard, and
wide of them, John directly in their wake; and as
they stopped to look back at him, I jumped off. He
fired and missed; and as they bounded from his shot
I hit the last through the hind quarters, and dropped
him, to my intense joy. We had a capital lunch
from some wild fruit, about three times the size of
an orange, called a clapper. It has a hard shell outside, which you must batter against a tree to crack
or break.

I find that we are considerably farther north
than I thought — somewhere about the same latitude
as Sofala, I think — but can gain no information
from the Kaffirs, who won't say how far it is from
the sea or the Portuguese settlement, or give us
any information at all, either through fear or ig-
norance. We are all in good health, only a little
impatient to see elephants.

Nov. 1st (Sunday).—I have just 'boned' part of an
old quill I saw in a Kaffir's ear for ornament. I am
writing my journal with vinegar and gunpowder, but
it is poor stuff.

We are anxiously waiting the return of the messengers sent to Mosilikatse, and are at present kept
in a kind of quarantine. A son of Impugan (fly),
Mosilikatse's chief captain, with some twenty follow-

ers, is at the wagons, and we may go no farther till we get leave from head-quarters. We have had some thunder storms, which have been of vast benefit to the country. Game very scarce. On Friday I shot a tsessebe, and yesterday mounted on Luister, who has had no work for a long time, and is fat and fresh. I again fell in with a single roan antelope, and cannot deny myself the pleasure of giving a full account of the chase from first to last, as it will long live in my remembrance.

I saw him first coming along at a swinging gallop, evidently startled by something, and endeavoured to cut him off, galloping hard and keeping a tree between us. I got within 100 yards, jumped off, and missed him like a man going broadside past me ; swallowed my disgust as well as I could, reloaded, and gave chase. A stern chase is always a long one, and at the end of about three miles I could not perceive I had gained a yard on him. The bush getting thicker, I rode 100 yards wide of him, hoping I might gain ground on him unperceived, and as he burst once more into the open I had bettered my position fully 100 yards, which he perceived and put on the steam once more, and I was just pulling up in despair when I saw his mouth open and heard his breath coming thick and fast on the wind. He was evidently much blown, but my good nag had likewise nearly all the puff taken out of him. The ground being frightfully stony, he had to change his legs, alter his stride, and hop about like peas on a

platter ; still I had faint hopes, if I was favoured by
the ground, I might get a long shot at him. I nursed
my nag to the best of my judgment, rowelling him
well, but holding him fast by the head, and endeavouring still to keep a spurt in him whenever the
ground favoured ; and in this manner I maintained
my distance, about 200 yards behind the antelope,
which I now perceived to be shortening his stroke as
he was nearing the steep bank of a dry river.   Now
or never!   I lifted and shook Luister for my life,
and he put on a capital spurt, and, as he is an admirably-trained shooting horse, I could rely on his
pulling up in ten yards, and I never checked him till
within twenty yards of the bank.   The magnificent
old buck seemed to know, by instinct, that this was
the crisis of his fate, and tore away on the opposite
bank harder than ever, making the stones clatter and
fly behind him.   In the twinkling of an eye I stood
alongside my nag, steadied myself, gave one deep-
drawn breath, planted my left foot firmly in front,
raised my gun, and fired the moment I got the ivory
sight to bear upon him, making an admirable shot
right through the top of his tail, breaking his
spine and piercing the lungs, killing him dead 120
yards off.   I skinned him with care, bringing the
skin to the wagon, head and all complete, which I
hope some day to see at Leyland Vicarage.   I never
suffered more than I did in skinning him with a
dull knife, in a burning sun, amidst thousands of
black ants ; and his skin was tough as shoe leather.

I have now only two or three more varieties to kill, to have shot every buck I know in Africa.

5th.—Had a glorious day on Jack. He carried me well up to a troop of roan antelopes, when my gun, unfortunately, missed fire. Saw a splendid old bull harrisbuck, but lost sight of him in trying to get below the wind, and never saw him again. Rode far, climbing to the top of the hills; at length, saw about twenty-two harrisbucks; got below the wind and within 300 yards, when they took the alarm. I had a very long chase of five miles, at least. The ground being so bad, and my horse blind, I could only go steadily; at length, got them at advantage, and put Jack's powers to the test. He galloped strong and well, and as they were thundering down a pass between two mountains, through a dry ravine, I got within three lengths of the hindmost buck. The pace was tremendous. One magnificent old bull I had set my heart on, and was close to him. Jack drew up short just on the brink of the ravine, and, in my hurry to jump off, I got my foot fast in the stirrup. I had my back to the bucks, and when I had extricated my foot I had lost my bull. I fired at a large black-and-tan cow, and either missed her altogether or gave her a bad shot. In the middle of the chase I almost jumped into an ostrich nest, but I could not think about eggs then. On returning to the wagons, I heard Bryan was very sick; he had treked away from the wagons, and we lost him, though I followed the spoor till dark. I luckily heard from two Kaffirs that they had seen a horse's spoor, on the path going back, at the first break of day. Inyous and myself started in the direction the Kaffirs told us, and, thinking it not improbable we might be away three or four days, I put a cap, box of salt, and a dry eland's tongue in my pocket, and Inyous carried two pounds of beads. On finding the spoor eighteen hours gone, I pressed two Kaffirs from a kraal near by into the service. It was fine work, at times, tracking him out. We had many checks, and all spread out and made our casts in a most systematic style, your humble servant hitting off the spoor three times, but Inyous and one Bush-man Kaffir did the most of the hunting. Once, I had all but given him up, on flinty, rocky ground; we cast around in every direction for an hour and a-half to no purpose, and we followed the spoor for more than 300 yards on our hands and knees, the faintest imaginable track being all we had to guide us—a small stone displaced, or a blade of grass cut off; so we kept on till we again got to sandy ground, when we took up the running four miles an hour, and about mid-day we found him. I need not say how rejoiced I was to see him again.

I must say that to-day's work beat anything I ever saw with Kaffirs. Bloodhounds could not have done better. We followed the trail for six hours through old grass a yard high, and through the midst of lots of quagga spoor. I once called the Kaffirs to a quagga spoor, but they recognised it immediately,

and made me ashamed of myself. They took
quantities of snuff, as being good for the eyes and
clearing the intellects. I tried it, and verily believe
I benefited by it. We had messengers to-day from
Impugan, bringing capital beer, and all wearing
white feathers in their hair, a sign that they are
friendly to us and bring us good news. We expect
positively messengers from Mosilikatse to-morrow.
We sent him many presents, mine consisting of a
large, handsome, double, very bright scarlet blanket,
beads of different varieties, and an immense German
boar-hound, very handsome, shaggy and rough,
called Smouse, who, however, bit the Kaffirs, got
away, and was never more heard of, unfortunately, as
I think Mosilikatse would have accepted and appre-
ciated him. All the rest of the presents, however,
he sent back with the message, ' What was he to do
with them? — they were not things he could eat, he
was not a woman to adorn himself with ornaments,
and he would not allow any of his tribe to wear a
blanket ; they were of no manner of use to defend
himself and his people against their enemies, and we
must take them back and send him a horse, guns,
and ammunition.'

We were kept all the time, however, well supplied
with beer, and had several presents of sheep, goats,
and oxen for slaughter; and at last all our doubts
were set at rest by a present of a snow-white
heifer, which was meant to show that his heart was
white towards us and we had nothing to fear. Had

it been a red one, John told me, who thoroughly understands the language and customs of the Matabele, all our Kaffirs would have fled, as that colour is symbolical of blood.

6th.—Poor Jack is dead. I don't know when I was so sorry for anything; he knew my voice and used to obey me like a dog, and would come to me when I called him. He was only sick about twelve hours, so quick in its effects is the fatal horse sickness.

7th.—Moved our quarters to a cooler place under a huge rock, with some shady trees about ; hunted all day, found a herd of blue wildebeests, and rushed down upon them savagely, having had no flesh for three days. We gave them four bullets instantly, every one telling, and, when the dust cleared away, one was down and two others wounded, which John and Swartz finished. I rode hard after the troop and made a good shot at the last, breaking his back 200 yards off, thus bagging four in less than as many minutes. I killed a tsessebe, also going at his utmost speed, 216 measured yards off, and made an execrable shot at a roan antelope. I saw a remarkable goose on my way back to the wagons; had a cup of tea, fired off the bullet, put in a charge of shot, and went in pursuit of my goose, which I bagged.

We had to send messengers again to Mosilikatse, and shall be detained another six or seven days. I sadly feel the want of books, as I have nothing in the world to do, and the days are by far too hot and enervating to do work of any kind.

8th (Sunday). --Pet and John fishing; they take admirably, but we have only crooked pins for hooks, and cannot catch many. What we do manage are sweet and good, and a treat to us.

Collins's arrival from Mosilikatse gave new life to us all, and at length I have been able to get at something approaching the truth relative to Mosilikatse's whereabouts. Collins thinks it about 140 miles from this, ENE., nearly the same latitude as Sofala, about twelve days on foot from the coast, and about five days from the Zambesi, a large river, navigable for nearly 200 miles. Its mouth is near Quillemaine. Mosilikatse had treated Collins well in every respect, and he was in high spirits, and talked largely of what he would do.

Swartz, always alive to his own interests, offered him the use of Kleinboy to shoot on halves. I proffered John or myself, but he wanted no assistance to fill his wagon in a fortnight with the finest ivory the country could produce; eventually, he took John Joubert, who was a capital interpreter. He had talked over Mosilikatse by some means or other, and eventually got for himself the much-desired leave to hunt. He was attended by twenty Kaffirs, and in the sole charge of one of his principal chief's sons, invested with full authority to procure for him whatever he required in the shape of meat or drink, food and corn for his horses, &c., which were carried with him wherever he went, and, for the time, he was all powerful, and left us poor fellows envying him bitterly. No man ever took the field under more inviting auspices.

The whole sport of this mighty hunter was one bull, the hind leg of which he broke by a fluke in about ten shots, fired from behind, about 150 yards off, and eventually brought to bay. The Kaffirs' accounts, which are always to be most implicitly relied on, were most humorous. The first elephant showed fight, trumpeted, charged, screamed, and chased him out of the bush, and gave him altogether a caution and a lesson to have more respect for the patriarchs of the forest. He set down his discomfiture entirely to his horse's bad behaviour, and next day tried his other, which was equally bad; at all events, the same result ensued, and the following day he was fain to take himself out of the hunting-ground altogether, thus verifying Mosilikatse's prophecy, that he would show him a veldt that he would guarantee he would be quite as anxious to get out of as he was now to go in.

I have heard from the natives that on the Guia (Tobacco) river, north of Mosilikatse and near the Zambesi, it is not safe to cross the veldt day or night, from the number of elephants, many of which are very savage, and keep the country all to themselves.

9th.—Shot a large eland bull on Luister, and lost myself at night, an ostrich having taken me out of my line of country. I suffered very much from thirst, not being able to obtain one drop of water for more than eighteen hours, though I scraped my finger nails off in making large holes in the dry spruits, but not one drop came. I had little or no sleep, and my tongue was so dry and swollen that I positively could not speak.

10th.—At the first dawn of day I went again in search of water, and soon found some muddy, putrid stuff, which, however, was nectar to me ; saddled up and rode back in the direction I came last night, climbing all the hills until, at last, I recognised one, when I off-saddled my weary jade, and got back to the wagons about mid-day. They had fired innumerable shots and lighted large fires on the tops of the bergs, but I had gone very far astray.

Bought a horse (Veichman), a dark chestnut, for six oxen, but he is at present a mere apology of a nag, being skin and bone, sore backed, and his hoofs worn completely through. As all our horses are unshod, I made him shoes of eland hide of a novel fashion, being laced tightly round his fetlocks with raw hide to keep them on ; they saved his poor hoofs immensely on the stony ground, and had the desired effect, for he soon got well again. I need hardly say, however, that I never ventured to hunt him with his mufflers on. His former owner ought decidedly to have been tried under Martin's Act; but Collins said there was not a blade of grass for six days, consequently he was obliged to press on. Bryan has been almost dead for three days, and is a perfect shadow. These are the two animals on which I must face a savage old wounded bull elephant.

11*th*.—Collins left us this morning, and John got leave from old Impugan to go with him just at the last moment. His preparations were soon made, and he took Croppy and Luister; both animals in pretty fair order. I promised him those two nags long since, when I was comparatively rich in horse-flesh, and would not break my word, though it put me to great straits to part with them. I get one half of all he kills.

Sent away four 'Blackwood's Magazines,' which I almost knew by heart, and begged something in the shape of print in exchange from two Englishmen at Collins's wagon. I am wearied to death; I have no horse to ride, and game is not come-at-able on foot, even if one could muster sufficient resolution to undergo the burning heat of the sun. When the sun is nearly set, I bend my steps to a hole about half-a-mile off, and splash about and make the best of three feet water, but there are so many fish, crabs, and leeches, one cannot keep still a minute.

12*th*.—Had a long, hot, weary walk; saw literally nothing. We shall be compelled to kill an ox to-night, but it is the first since we left the house, two months ago. I am doing all I can to get a little flesh on my two bare-boned nags, and stuffing them with Kaffir corn, as the grass is so dry and so scarce they cannot get half enough, although, at this season of the year, it is knee deep in Natal. I have travelled far and wide in every direction into the old colony, up the coast to Delagoa Bay, through the

Free State and the Transvaal Republic, but Natal is
the garden of South Africa, Merico country a good
second.

Whilst living alone at the Luanda, to kill time, I
used to hunt baboons with some powerful deerhounds.
Great numbers of these baboons lived on an overhanging crantz, and came some distance from their
stronghold early in the morning to the Kaffir mealie
gardens. Often I have seen a young one run into
by Hopeful or Crafty, when the old males have

instantly come to the rescue, beaten off the dogs and
carried the young one off in safety, barking savagely.
One day a tremendous fellow marched past the house.
I immediately looed the dogs on, and had a good chase
for a couple of miles; being hard pressed, he endeavoured to climb a tree, when the dogs hauled him

down ; he got his back to the tree, fought manfully, keeping all at bay until I got up, when they rushed in and worried him, some of them getting tremendous bites in the encounter.

One day, when hartebeest-hunting at Bushman's River on horseback, I came on a panther in a valley, and he immediately crouched. I sent my companion for P., an old experienced hunter, whilst I kept watch, as we were both quite green at this kind of game. On going towards him with all the dogs, he jumped up in full view of the pack, with 150 yards start, over a bare country, and we had a splendid run at a great pace. On the dogs almost reaching him he turned the tables on them with a vengeance, charging them with such right good will as to scatter them to the winds. They returned, however, to the pursuit, and eventually brought him to bay among some rocks half way up, where he got his back against an overhanging one, and kept all the pack at a respectable distance.

The pace had been too good for P., or the swamps, bogs, and holes not to his liking, as he was some time in coming up. He did so, however, at last, and, after giving me some good advice as to what I must do in case of a charge, we dismounted and advanced together to the foot, when, dropping on one knee, P. fired, striking him in the centre of the chest and killing him on the spot. The dogs rushed in manfully then, and we skinned him very carefully, I thinking all the time what care he was taking of it for me,

and being so much obliged. After reaching the
wagon, he cured and preserved it beautifully, and
my gratitude knew no bounds; but eventually, when
he left it in the charge of a friend of his to take particular care of *for him*, I began to feel a little uncomfortable and uneasy as to its future destination, and
said, 'Do you consider that skin yours?' 'Why,
what can you possibly have to do with it? You did
not even shoot.' I need hardly say that this happened
on my first introduction to the colony, before I had
got initiated; for, according to all the rules of the
chase, I ought to have had the first shot, when, if I
had missed, he then might have laid claim to him.

Hottentots are fond of dealing in the marvellous.
Kleinboy and Raffeta told me that they were once
near the Great Lake, but fully half-a-mile from the
water, and found a crocodile, twelve feet long, wedged
fast into the fork of a tree, not quite dead, some
nine feet from the ground. They accounted for it
by saying the elephant had carried him and put him
there, that they were constantly in the practice of
plaguing and biting the legs and trunks of the elephants—when drinking and bathing, they go a long
way into the lake for that purpose—and this was the
way the sagacious animal had served him out. If
the story is true (which I don't myself doubt), I can
see no other way of accounting for it.

I was once witness to the effectual though cruel
plan the Dutch have of teaching their dogs to face
hyenas. They catch the hyenas alive in traps built

of logs, having two entrances, with sliding trap doors, supported by a peg stuck loosely into the ground through a piece of meat in the middle of the floor of the house. A young kid is generally the attraction, railed off, so that the brute cannot get at him.

On the occasion I speak of, two were taken in one house together. On finding themselves imprisoned they made the most appalling row, and fought savagely all night. One was shot; the other, after some dodging through the logs, was caught by the tail, his legs slit just above the hocks, and a strong iron chain passed through and hooked. He broke almost every tooth short off upon this chain, in his furious efforts to bite it through; and when he had done this, the trap door was opened, and out he flew among some eight or ten powerful boar-hounds ready to receive him. A tremendous row and scuffle ensued, and the poor brute, owing to his teeth being broken by his previous efforts to gnaw the chain, eventually succumbed.

Hunting on foot once in the Entumeni Bush, I had a very narrow escape from an old bull elephant which I had wounded. He gave chase, and I took up the hill; the ground was very wet and slippery — heaps of dead leaves, no heels to my veldt shoes, which were made of blesbuck skin, and, from being thoroughly saturated with wet, had stretched to nearly double the original size; consequently I went, as they say, two steps backwards to one forwards, was constantly down, and quite exhausted in the strenuous

efforts I made to get on. Seeing no disposition, on
my pursuer's part, to give up the chase, I changed
my tactics, got above a tree, on which I leaned a
couple of seconds to recover my wind partly — a
very critical moment, as the brute was not more
than four of his own lengths from me—jumped then
some ten yards at right angles, and turned down the

hill at full speed, the monster screaming and trumpeting in full career after me at a tremendous pace.
He must have been over me in a few strides more,
when I sprang to the right, and down he went in his
mad career, crashing and carrying all before him,
utterly unable to stop if he had wished, as the hill

was very steep, and he was under full sail : a tremendous relief to my mind, as it was my last resort.
I did not hazard another encounter, but mentally
resolved, for the future, to try another country, where
I could have the all-powerful assistance of a good
horse in emergencies of the like kind, and have carried
out the resolution then and there made ever since.

23rd. — I have been doing nothing the last ten
days but wait impatiently the report from Mosilikatse, which has come at last, and we are just where
we were, as far as hunting is concerned.

Swartz has gone himself to see this imperious
potentate ; but, as he did not send for him, I don't
think Mosilikatse will see him. Bryan is dead, and
two more oxen. We got leave from old Impugan
to move a few miles nearer the game ; but he is
nearly as imperious as his master. Mosilikatse sent
orders, that if he got guns and ammunition from us,
then they were to bring *me* up to head-quarters ;
and Swartz, thinking I was going, made me a very
kind offer to this effect, that if I got hunting for
him, then I should have Kvelt (strength), an old
used-up brute, with a hammer head and Roman nose,
for 200 lbs. ivory, 60*l.*, as he was sorry for me, and
wanted to help me. In case we had got leave from
Mosilikatse, the horse would have been worth double
the money, as he ought, in good hands, to have paid
for himself in a couple of days, and I could have
done nothing without him.

I went out on Saturday, early before breakfast,

with one of my Kaffirs and Donna. A tremendous
thunderstorm came on, with torrents of cold drenching rain. I had on nothing but a very light pair of
canvas 'ducks' and a wretched thin shirt. I took no
notice of the way we came, as I relied solely on my
Kaffir; but when I told him to make haste back to
the wagons, he was lost. We wandered about backwards and forwards as hard as we could go, to
keep the blood in circulation, till sunset, when, in
trying to find an overhanging rock to sleep under,
to give us some little protection, I luckily came on
an old shed, which we at once set to work to
thatch and make water-tight. After great difficulty,
as everything was soaking wet, we succeeded in
lighting a fire, and passed the night not so badly.
The morning was dull and misty, and we could see
no distance, and had no idea of our whereabouts.
We walked hard and silently from one hill to another, climbing the tallest trees; and the Kaffir puzzled
me to death by being sure the sun rose in the west.
Of course he knew nothing about east or west, but
he pointed in the latter direction. It is a dreadful
country to be lost in, consisting chiefly of thick
bush. After descending a mountain, you can see
nothing; and, unless you take great care, you cannot
walk in the direction you intend, as you must twist
and twine about to get through the bush. Then,
if your thoughts wander for an instant, you will
assuredly go wrong. At mid-day I lay under a rock
to rest, when, in spite of myself, most unpleasant

thoughts came crowding thick and fast upon me, as
there are many instances of white men being totally
lost in this endless, almost uninhabited land. If
you stray into the thirst land, as there is great
danger of doing, you will assuredly die of thirst, if
not of famine. Though I had fasted full forty
hours, I did not feel the slightest hunger. I tightened my belt, and drank lots of water. I could
have shot game, but was chary of my bullets,
keeping them most religiously, in case things came
to the worst.

My poor Kaffir's fortitude quite gave way with the
numerous disappointments. I never spoke a harsh
word to him, though he took me in an exactly contrary direction to what I believed to be right. He was
very positive for a long time, and then his confidence
entirely forsook him, and he sobbed as if his heart
would break. At length we got on a Kaffir path,
and very old tracks of cattle, and determined to continue that as our only chance. To our intense joy
we saw, before long, the fresh footprints of a Kaffir,
and resolved to follow that to the world's end, in
faint hope that it might lead us to his kraal. My
disappointment was great indeed, when we at length,
about two hours before sunset, came to a large kraal,
but found it uninhabited. We followed on, and next
came to a pitfall, where there were evident signs of
game lately being captured. I shall never forget the
start of joy that Matakit gave when I said I saw
cattle, and pointed to some black things in the dis-

tance. He thought they were goats; but when we came up they were only burnt stumps. Our countenances fell; still we kept on rapidly and silently for about an hour, when suddenly Matakit said, 'There's a dog!' but, alas! it was only a creature of his imagination. Still we had the footprints to go by, traceable enough after the heavy rain. At last his quick ear caught the sound of a voice, and this time he was not mistaken, and we soon came to a large Maccateese kraal, but so hidden among the rocks that you might easily pass without seeing a human being; and the glimpse I got of a little child gave me, I don't scruple to say, the greatest delight I ever in my life experienced, as I had not heard the Kaffir's call, and thought it only existed in poor Matakit's brain. Matakit testified the most unfeigned delight, talking so fast and thick that the Kaffirs could not understand a word. We found that we were about four hours' hard walking on foot from the wagons.

It is, verily, the queerest place I ever saw in my life, just as Walter Scott describes Ben Venue; and every overhanging klip or fissure in a rock gave shelter to a lot of goats. I was kindly treated by the Kaffirs, who gave me a hut, and brought me lots of green leaves to lie on, and gave me some boiled corn; and we got back to the wagons about midday. Impugan was exceedingly angry, and said I must always come to him in future, and he would send men with me. I got a good fright, and never

felt hunger, though without anything but a little
boiled corn for sixty-six hours!

No one living in crowded England can realise the
almost endless extent of country; all bush, without
rivers, or anything to guide your eye but the
sun.

Of course we did not find the wagons without a
guide. I was the first white man most of these
Kaffirs had ever seen, and they all came to gaze at

me, and my beard of six months' growth astonished
them marvellously. They would not believe it was
really growing there until they had pulled at it.

I envied Donna; she kept on ranging, head up
and tail going all the time, utterly unconscious

of the fix we were in, and made her points, and appeared to enjoy herself marvellously, poor thing!

26th. — Swartz returned this morning. Just as I foretold, Mosilikatse would not see him, and sent messengers in great wrath to turn him back, take his horse and guns from him, and see him back to the wagons. This was some distance from his kraals. He takes him for a spy from the Boers, coming in under false pretences, merely to see his country and strength. I am afraid Swartz has now lost the chance we might have had of obtaining hunting. We shall hear to-morrow, and I expect it will be a peremptory order to leave the country. I am regaling myself on most excellent Kaffir beer; it is really a treat.

I got a note from John some nine days ago, saying he had lost all his bullets on the path, and wishing me to send him more. This morning the bullets were brought here by a Kaffir, who had picked them up two days from here. Their high sense of honesty is wonderful; for there is nothing, perhaps, that they more desire than powder and lead, and this find was a godsend; yet the Kaffir brought them back. There are some excellent traits in their character; but, as they are perfect heathens, it is as much through fear as any better feeling.

I have made a pair of shoes, mended others, and done my best to kill time, and have received four books in exchange for mine, but am very chary of them, reading only a little at a time, and then doing something else to spin them out to the uttermost. Fresh elephant spoor was seen this morning. I went at once to see if Veichman was fresh enough to follow, but his feet are quite worn through.

December 1*st*. — I never was so tired in my life. Swartz has sold the wagons to Mosilikatse for twenty teeth; and we may wait here another ten days before they arrive. After that, he says he will give us permission to hunt, but it comes too late to be of any service to me, as my last horse is dead; and I hear to-day that John has gone back to the house with Viljoen, taking my two horses with him. If this is true, it will be the greatest ' sell ' that ever happened to any poor mortal in this world. I wrote and despatched a long yarn to Moffat three days ago, and I wished to send a messenger to John to-day; but, though I bribed Impugan with a very handsome sheep-skin kaross, he would not give me a Kaffir to show mine the way.

3*rd*. — A great quantity of rain has fallen the last week, and I am quite tired of it. Heard to-day, positively, that John has gone back ten days ago. Never was poor mortal so miserably duped as I am. After coming seven months' journey to hunt, now, when we at last get leave, I have no horse, though I gave 50*l.* for a brute not worth 15*l.*, and this country is so open that it is almost impossible to kill elephants on foot ; and so flat, too, and the trees so small, that a wounded elephant must catch you.

7th.—Tired as a dog of doing nothing; no word of the Kaffirs yet. I expect the heavy rains have swollen the river, and they are not able to cross. Were it not for a small volume of Byron's poems, which I now know most of by heart, I could not kill the time.

8th.—Played quoits with the washers of the wheels, and got through the time with the putting-stone, &c. The messengers and ivory for the wagon returned this afternoon, and, after no end of bargaining, the sale was concluded for twenty bull teeth, and seven more for seven oxen, about 1,300 lbs. altogether— a good sale. We must send another report to Mosilikatse, and then he will say positively if he will give us leave to hunt or not. I suppose he thinks we are all Jobs; after detaining us two months he has completely humbugged us, and got all he wanted from us, as now the season is too late, the weather too hot, and the bush by far too thick to do any good. The wily old fox completely got the best of us; his next message, if we had waited, would most probably have been that, now the corn was sown, no rain would fall as long as elephant-hunters were in his country—consequently, no harvest—and we must therefore go home; and possibly inviting us to come again the following year (only about three months' journey), to receive the same treatment.

9th.—Inspanned and left, to my great joy, having six Kaffirs in attendance to see us clear out of Mosilikatse's country. Swartz killed a snake in the wagon over nine feet long — a mamba, the most

venomous of all— and yesterday, walking with only
a shirt and gaiters, I very nearly trod on one about
twelve feet long ; he escaped knobkerries and
assegais, and beat four of us, and eventually gained
a hole, into which he disappeared like magic. We

hit him several times, but he was so flat to the ground
we could not hurt him, but only made him savage.
The wagon stuck fast, and we had to off-load. The
dissel-boom was sprung, and the hind axle also,
almost leaving us in a fix. We hope it will hold
together till we get to the game, as here there is
nothing, and we have nothing to eat ; and the Kaffirs
will not sell buck or sheep, as they want us to leave
the country.

18th.—We have been making good play towards
home the last few days, having given up all hope of

A GIRAFFE HUNT.

obtaining elephants. Yesterday the wagon broke
down, and we are hard at work putting in a new
axle; the wagon is so heavy that we must all walk,
and it is downright hard work, from the first dawn
of day till sunset, outspanning twice to let the oxen
drink, and swallowing hastily some refreshment for
the inner man. We saw a quantity of game yesterday, and killed four rhinoceros and two giraffes, and
altogether had the finest sport since leaving the
house. An immense herd of buffaloes, 100 at least,
took away right in front of the giraffe I had driven
out of the herd, and we soon passed them, as the
pace was killing; the giraffe then turned to the left,
and the whole troop were not more than fifty yards
behind me, coming along at a tearing pace. I did
not much like my position, as, in case of a fall, I
should have been pounded to mince-meat by the
dense mass; however, the speed at which we went
soon left the buffaloes far behind, and I got my giraffe.
Swartz, coming up on Ludovick, gave her a finisher,
for my bullet was rather far back. I rolled over a
large cow rhinoceros, going at her best speed in fine
style, with one shot, breaking her back—a thing one
can seldom accomplish.

21*st.*—We found a flaw in the wood, not, however,
until the first axle was nearly complete, and had to
seek another, and all our work to do over again.
We had lots of rain, and I took a wrinkle out of
Galton's 'Art of Travel,' and made myself a tent,
gipsey fashion, two blankets fastened together with

wooden pegs thrown over. I cut drains all round, and slept warm and dry as a toast, though the rain was very heavy and of long continuance. Swartz shot three buffaloes out of one troop, though the ground was very heavy, and the buffaloes had a tremendous start. My horse Veichman has been fortunate enough to get through the sickness, by plentiful bleeding, just in the nick of time, and careful treatment, having a stable made for him every wet night. However, he could not go the pace, and I did not like to push him in his present feeble condition, so I had nothing to say to them. We have been varying our diet with guinea fowl, ostrich eggs, and sucking pigs — a pleasant change, this hot weather, from continual flesh meat. Our meal has run very short, and we have bread only once in two or three days, as a treat. The roof of my mouth is quite sore with masticating so much tough flesh.

Yesterday a troop of about seventy giraffes came swinging past the wagons; the Kaffirs and dogs yelled loud, and there was a general rush for guns. They all turned short to the left and put on the steam. I was the only one that got my gun in time, but, ere I could get her out of the case, they were at least 400 yards off. I fired at the head of the nearest cow, and we all heard the bullet clap loudly, but as we could see no alteration in her gait, we took no further notice, and the whole herd were lost in the bushes. About two hours before sunset, Hendrick, Sechele's son-in-law, sang out, ' Sur, sur, sur—surs a

camel is dode.' The Kaffir who was herding the
oxen had found her about a mile off. We started
immediately; she was a fine old cow, and very fat.
I had shot her right through the jugular vein, and
she had bled to death. The giraffes galloped right
through the oxen, alarming the latter very much,
and they all took away in different directions. We
turned out in quest of them, and it was many hours
ere we recovered them all. The ground being soft
with the rain, we were able to follow the spoor. I
cannot easily imagine a greater fix than to lose the
oxen in this country.

I expect the axle will be finished to-day. I am
afraid to go out to hunt, for fear of losing myself.
We have nothing whatever to guide the eye by—
no hill, rock, stream, or mountain—all is one dense,
wooded flat; the wagon-spoor is the only thing, and
having twice lost myself, I have no wish to run a
third risk.

I will give the reader a description of old Ia, our
Hottentot maid :—She is one of Pharaoh's lean kine,
unusually tall, straight as a kitchen poker; long,
lean, scraggy neck; the smallest little pig eyes in the
world; no nose, but two huge nostrils; high cheek
bones, sunken cheeks, wide mouth, very thick lips,
just the colour of the mulberry juice, low forehead, and small head. I believe she has about the
eighth of an inch long of wool on the latter, but, as
it is always swathed in a handkerchief, I am not certain. She is, I believe, somewhere between fifty and

sixty, and you seldom see her without a short, black
pipe in her mouth. She wears ear-rings, necklace,
and armlets, and the gaudiest-coloured shawl and
handkerchief. She is of a yellowish copper colour;
her breast as flat as a deal board, and, altogether,
about as plain, not to say downright ugly, as nature
could possibly make her; but, with all these perfec-
tions, she has, in common with all her race, the most
perfect, delicately-formed, and smallest hands and feet
in the world. This description is not one whit over-
drawn; in fact, I have not done half justice to her
eyes. I believe she can see as far as anyone, though
I will defy anyone to tell what she sees with, as her
eyes are only just discernible — not a sign of a brow or
lash near them, — slightly bloodshot and watery from
exposure to the fierce sun. She would quite charm
the heart of a lady friend of mine at first sight, and
she need not be under the least alarm of taking any
number of such into her service. Though she had
twice the number of growing lads, I would willingly
go bail for the morality of all.

24th.—What we have gone through the last two
days entirely beggars all description. On Tuesday
night we found the vley, where we fully expected
water, dried up, and not one drop to cool our parched
mouths, though we had walked all day under a broiling sun. The Kaffirs had all their bladders and calabashes full of fat, which they prize greatly, and will
drag along with them through every difficulty. Inspanned two hours before sunrise, not expecting

to get water till afternoon. I took only a bit of dry
toast, and had nothing on but a shirt and gaiters,
a silk handkerchief inside my hat, a splendid
pair of thick-ribbed woollen Highland socks, made
by Nancy herself, which I prize greatly—nothing
could be finer for the burning sands—and a pair
of shoes of my own make. I would guarantee
three such days would convert the greatest lump of
obesity into a genteel figure, if it did not kill him.
The poor dogs I pitied most sincerely; one old
stager, Wolf, never showed his nose from underneath the wagon; the others showed their sagacity
by galloping along some distance ahead, and throwing themselves down under a shady tree till we were
far ahead, and then making play again. I did the
same. About three o'clock in the afternoon Kleinboy could stand it no longer, and caught a horse, to
go in search of water; Swartz, myself, and Sechele's
son-in-law doing the same. After riding three hours,
at last we found the vley we were in search of,
owing to the sagacity of Swartz, who showed great
perseverance in following a rhinoceros spoor. There
was not one drop of water in the vley, nothing but
baked clay. On riding round I came on the fresh
spoor of a Kaffir, and we followed it some 200 yards,
when it brought us to a deep hole in the ground
where he had drunk. There were about two inches
of water in it; we drank, and then, with the spade we
brought, enlarged and deepened the hole and fired
signal-guns for the wagons, and, by the time the

Kaffirs came straggling up, we had a sufficiency for
their wants. Their eyes were starting out of their
heads, and their look so wild as almost to frighten
us, but there was not one drop for the poor oxen
and horses; it required all we could do to keep them
from trampling the hole in; their throats were so dry
that the oxen could not low nor the horses neigh,
the loose oxen went half mad and joined a troop of
wildebeests, and I lost one of mine altogether. On
Thursday, luckily a cool day, we inspanned long
before day-dawn, and got to a fountain about mid-
day, when the poor things all got their fill.

I was revolving in my mind on Monday what
little reminder I could send 'the *General*,' a nick-
name for a brother of mine, when the thought
struck me that his ingenuity might turn a couple
of rhinoceros horns to good account, as they can
be straightened by steam and turned in a lathe,
and they take a brilliant polish; snuff-boxes, knobkerries, riding-canes, gun-stocks, &c., are made here
from them. I soon put my thoughts into execution
by ordering Veichman and a couple of slaves to
attend me. The former is a nervous, timid, skittish
chestnut, and has by no means the making of a good
shooting horse, but it was Hobson's choice with me.
I found a young bull, a bad short-horn, and let him
go, and shortly after two cows, the best of which I
bagged in four shots. Veichman was in fear and
trembling of the unwieldy brutes, but the spurs,
vigorously applied, had the desired effect. The horns

were not so good as I could wish, but the best that chance afforded me.

Christmas Day.—What a contrast to the many merry ones spent in dear old England amongst my own family and friends! The comparison makes me melancholy. Here I am in the deserts of South Africa, having been toiling from the first dawn of day under a broiling sun until sunset, and I am pretty considerably fagged. A bit of rhinoceros, cold, and so fat as to make the strongest stomach bilious, and a small portion of half-baked dough, have been our fare—not exactly our English notions of a Christmas feast; but these are among the hardships of a hunter's life, and we have, at times, pleasures that abundantly compensate; and, to look upon it in the light of a philosopher, it is all for the best, for, had we the 'heavy wet' and 'feeds' of England, we should be in but poor trim and wind for the toil of the chase. I must own, however, I should like to drink my friends' health and 'a happy Christmas' in a good tankard of home-brewed, followed by a bottle of old port. Don't mention a mince pie; I have entirely forgotten the taste since I left home to wander amongst the denizens of the forest. I will, however, drink to the health of absent friends in a cup of coffee, the strongest beverage the wagon affords.

We made all possible despatch from this place, travelling day and night, as the moon was at the full, and the sun did not quite bake us alive, snatching two or three hours' sleep when and wherever

opportunity offered.   Kleinboy lost himself once for
half a night, and, on his return, made me roar with an
account of his mishaps.   Two jackals baited him all
the time, endeavouring by their horrid cries to bring
the lion to him, and he did nothing but run all the
time at his best pace.   He fell into holes and bushes
over and over again, and he was so bruised and stiff
as to be hardly able to walk.   We got back to
Swartz's, without further mishap, about January 6,
1858.   After remaining there three or four days, I
started for Maquazi with a cart and four oxen, and
from thence I went to Bloemfontein, one of the
principal towns of the Orange River Free State, with
a troop of fifty-five oxen, all of which, with one
exception, arrived there safely.

CHAPTER VII.

1858.

MACHIN — I AM DESERTED — FIRST VISIT TO LAKE NGAMI — LECHULATEBE — SECHELE'S DAUGHTER — THE BUSH ON FIRE — MERICO.

I SOLD all my oxen well in Bloemfontein (flower fountain), and invested the proceeds in a wagon, stores, horses, and dogs, and, with great difficulty, powder, lead, tin, caps, and flints, having found two friends to stand security for me that I would not barter any part of these latter articles to Kaffirs. I eventually got a permit from the President, Boshoff, to convey it from the Government stores into the interior, and this had the effect of satisfying field-cornets and other officers until I crossed the Vaal River, the boundary between Orange River Free State and the Transvaal Republic. These states were, unfortunately, at war with each other. I had not left the boundary far behind me when I was asked by a field-cornet what I had in my wagon, and where my permit was. I showed him Boshoff's with the most perfect confidence and innocence in the world, but it availed me little, for, as soon as the field-cornet had made it out, he spat upon it, trampled it under foot, and treated it with every indignity. I was then told I was a prisoner, and must be taken to Mooi River to Mynheer Pretorius the following morning; and I set off accordingly, on horseback, accompanied by three Boers; my wagon, oxen, horses, and servants remaining behind. We arrived the day following, about three o'clock, when I was taken to the cantour, and this charge of smuggling was brought against me. On my way I met a Natal friend of mine, and asked him to go with me to act as my interpreter, but the Sandrost (magistrate) ordered him out without hearing a word, and expended a great amount of breath in reading the laws to me in high Dutch, not one word of which I could comprehend.

He gave me to understand that the charge was most serious; that there was no doubt I was in Boshoff's service, employed to smuggle this powder to the Kaffirs beyond, in order that they might make war on the Transvaal country from the other side; that it was the greatest crime I could be guilty of, and that hanging was too good for me.

Through the intercession of many friends I was at last released, and my wagon was sent for and brought up before the door of the cantour and thoroughly overhauled, and it ended in all my ammunition being confiscated to the Government, but I was allowed 20 lbs. of powder out of 150 lbs., and 100 lbs. of lead out of 500 lbs., with caps and flints to match, with which I was forced to content myself and go on my journey. My three or four guns I

was allowed to keep, a memorandum being taken
of them.

My old friend Franz Joubert, meaning to do me
a friendly action, came out of Maquazi, two days'
distance on horseback, to tell the Sandrost he was
quite certain I was the last man in the world to sell
powder to the Kaffirs, and that when I had been
staying with him previously I had refused positively to let the Kaffirs have a grain at any price;
but I let him have two sacks at cost price; and on
producing witnesses to prove this, which ought to
have gone far towards re-establishing my blemished
character, the Sandrost immediately brought another
charge against me of selling powder without a
license, for which there was a heavy penalty. However, after a couple of days, this charge was eventually quashed, and I was allowed to proceed on my
journey, after being detained about ten days, and
taken a long way out of my road.

I joined Swartz in Merico, and went with him to
Letloche, about fourteen days' trek, where our
routes separated, he trying Mosilikatse again, and I
taking the route to the Great Lakes.

Letloche.—April 17*th.*—I am now left entirely to my
own devices in the deserts of South Africa, with three
Kaffirs, two Hottentots, a driver and after rider, a
wagon, eighteen oxen, a cow and calf, five horses and
seven dogs, with guns, powder and lead, beads,
wire, and supplies of tea, coffee, meal, &c., for a

twelvemonth, at least; add to these a dozen of
brandy and a cask of good Cape Madeira. I have
not much to wish for that I know of, as there is a
goodly supply of eland and giraffe bell-tong hanging up to dry. I am now twenty-one days from
Swartz's house, in Merico, and have thus far had
far more company than was desirable; eleven wagons,
including two of Sechele's, which we parted company
with three days ago, he going to Machin, a new
Kaffir chief, who has succeeded Sicomo. The latter
has had to retire, as he was not the rightful chief.

It is a great change to find myself entirely alone
after the row and racket of inspanning eleven wagons
daily, but it is my own doing, and from my own
choice. I hear to-day that Swartz must turn back
immediately to Machin, or take the consequences; in
case of refusal, he, his wife and children, are all to be
killed then and there. This is the beginning of the
new chief's reign; he is talking very largely, and has
succeeded in frightening my Hottentots pretty considerably, and they come to me with long faces to
know what I will do. My answer is, ' Inspan at
once, and get through his country as quick as possible.' A full complement of elands and giraffes have
fallen to our rifles, and a lion killed one of Sechele's
oxen one pitch dark night, and escaped unhurt. I
saw a small troop of five elands from the wagon,
and, I grieve to say, we killed them all; but, as some
excuse for such wholesale butchery, I may say that
with our own and Sechele's retinue there were about

150 Kaffirs to provide for, and not a particle was wasted.

19th.—I bought yesterday for beads about 600 lbs. of Kaffir corn, and the wagon is very heavy. The poor oxen are much to be pitied, having to drag it through deep, heavy sand, under a broiling sun, without one drop of water to cool their throats for two days. We must trek most of the night, too, as in the heat of the day they cannot move. A drop of cold, clear, sparkling water would be the greatest luxury that could be set before me just now ; what we do get is stagnant, muddy stuff from pits made by the Kaffirs, which they carefully fence round with hack thorns to keep the game from drinking them dry. Two stately giraffes walked yesterday parallel with the wagon, not more than 400 yards off, for nearly half an hour, and we did not molest them, as we had a superabundance of flesh for men and dogs.

Elephants are, indeed, hard to come at now. I am very much farther to the north and west than Gordon Cumming ever went, and have only seen one spoor, and expect that I shall not be fairly amongst them for another three weeks. This has been almost the driest season ever known, and travelling in this thirst land is no easy matter ; you must undergo great hardships, and much anxiety for your poor live stock. If possible, I wish this year to get to Sebituane's, on the Chobe River, NW. from Mosilikatse's, and far north by east from Lake Ngami, if I can

penetrate so far, but I have sad misgivings about my
wagon, which is twenty-seven years old and very
shaky and rickety, but perhaps, with the aid of green
hides and rhinoceros skin, she may hold together.
There are hardships enough in travelling in the thirst
land, without the anxiety of fearing lest your old
wagon should leave you in the desert far from any
human assistance. I believe I have almost every
other requisite for exploring the continent—health,
strength, a constitution well inured to the climate,
a constant supply of good spirits, a knack of gaining
the good will of the Kaffirs, natives, and Hottentots,
who will go anywhere and do anything for me, as I
always lend a hand at anything, and study their comforts as well as my own. I have no ties of kindred
or friends here to make me wish myself amongst
them. I never weary with vain regrets, but always
make myself happy, and endeavour to make the best
of everything, and interest myself in the journey
throughout. I have now got a two-grooved rifle,
made by Witton, the most perfect weapon I ever
handled. It shoots perfectly true with any charge
of powder, and with a conical ball and six drachms
of fine powder I have never seen its force equalled;
but the recoil will, I fear, twist me out of the saddle.
If I live for another year I trust to be able to
start with not less than three well-appointed wagons,
oxen, horses, guns, ammunition, and stores to match,
and then, if health is permitted me, I can go wherever my restless fancy and my love of excitement

and adventure may lead me, and if the Kaffirs don't
turn me back, or, worse still, make an end of me,
it will be a hard matter if I don't make a good
hunt. I entertain no fears whatever of the Kaffirs,
who are the means of keeping nearly all the Boers
from penetrating so far. I never listen to their
threats, or the most likely exaggerated stories I hear
from my own people of them. Now for a cup of
tea.

23rd.—I have been resting the last three days, to
recruit my oxen, at a place called Nkowani, but have
not been idle myself. We got the first water at
Mahaccan, where there are pits six or seven feet
deep in the limestone rock. The water is not very
bad to the taste, but smells abominably, and I make
it a rule to drink as little as possible except in the
shape of tea or coffee, or else with a small dash of
brandy, and so avoid dysentery. I had a very long
chase after a giraffe yesterday. I was very badly
mounted on Manelle, a short, punchy cob, without
any speed about him, but I eventually tired out
the giraffe, and bagged at the fifth shot. I had been
firing in despair at about 500 yards, and at length
succeeded in hitting her through the buttock. I am
ashamed to say my spurs were so clogged with
old Manelle's hair as to be of no further service in
the chase. My after-rider, mounted on Final, brought
the giraffe round to me, when Manelle declined to
budge another step, and I gave the giraffe the bullet
in the right place. On off-saddling Manelle, I found,

to my disgust, that he was not the least blown, and
he ate and rolled instantly, nothing in the world being
amiss with him.

To-day I mounted Broon, a big, powerful, sixteen
hands' horse, of a different stamp altogether, and
bagged a fine cow giraffe, the first shot, after a chase
of about 1,000 yards, the pace being tremendous.
John, an excellent rider, and by no means badly
mounted, could not live the pace, and was thrown
very far out. Giraffe hunting is very fine sport,
but they are shy and wild here, and it is seldom
you can come within 500 or 600 yards of them
before they are away, but they do not put on the
steam until you get within about sixty, when they
screw their tails and tear away at a tremendous pace.
They are all neck and legs, having very short backs,
but a fat cow is really delicious eating.

I struck yesterday, twice in succession, with a
single ball, a yokeskey, a bit of wood 12 inches long
by $1\frac{3}{4}$ inches broad, which I had stuck into the
ground 120 yards off. My Hottentots were in ecsta-
cies, applauding me most highly, and prognosticating
all manner of success to me. I was obliged to bring
out the brandy, and they managed to get rather more
than was good for them, but a Tottie, half-seas over,
is the most amusing fellow in the world; they are all
first-rate mimics, and John, who was formerly in the
Cape Corps, and servant to Sir Harry Smith, made me
cry with laughing at his anecdotes of the Governor.

The weather at this season of the year, and a little

later on, is one series of uninterrupted blue skies. The air is so clear that the moon is visible the whole day, and the nights are delicious, just cold enough to hug your blanket close and sleep sound as a top; while the horses, oxen, dogs, cow and calf lie in a circle around the wagon, where they come of their own accord from custom and for safety.

28th.—I have had weary work of it the last four days. The weather has been awfully hot, and the clouds of sand raised by the tramping of fourteen oxen, and driven against me by a head wind, all but smothered me alive in the wagon, and has made me as black as a chimney-sweep. I don't think I shall get the grit out of my mouth for a week, as every particle of food is full of sand. There is no game or water. The country is utterly worthless, and will, I have no doubt, remain in peaceable possession of Kaffirs as long as the world lasts. It is an almost endless flat, with rank grass, thorns, brambles and worthless scrub-brush, and it reminds me of being on the line in a calm day. I must own yesterday I was quite down-hearted. After riding for several hours in front with the horses, in search of water, with a damp handkerchief around my mouth to prevent thirst, we at length came to a pit with about three inches of mud and water, but it was such stuff that the very oxen, after being eighteen hours in the yoke, would not taste it; and, in spite of our utmost efforts, trampled the little there was into mud. The Kaffirs throw in the most virulent 'wait-a-while'

thorn branches into these pits, to prevent the oxen
from trampling. Two black dogs stayed behind,
not being able to hold out any longer, but they
came on during the night. The fawn and light-
coloured dogs do not appear to suffer so much from
the sun. I thought this fierce heat portended something, and last night, to my intense joy, we had a
desperate thunder-storm, which has given us water
and freshened up everything marvellously. I bought
a fat goat and recovered my usual good spirits, but
the horses and oxen have fallen off very much. Our
difficulties are now partly over. I hope in five days
more to reach the River Beauclekky, which runs out
of Lake Ngami, NE. I have not seen a drop of
running water for twenty-eight days, although treking north-west full twenty days out of the twenty-
eight, and averaging, one day with another, nights
inclusive, ten hours per diem, at a rate of at least two
miles an hour, as when we trek at night the oxen
move merrily along, and a man must step merrily
along on foot to keep up.

I am much disappointed both in the country and
the game. There is no variety whatever here; only
eland, giraffe, and blue wildebeest, with a sprinkling
of duikers, steinbuck and springbuck, the kinds
that are the least dependent on water, and even
these are few and far between. The country will
not bear a moment's comparison with Mosilikatse's,
and it is my first and last visit in this direction. I
have been uncommonly lucky, so far, with my live

stock ; as yet, I have only lost one horse, of course
my best, but I have no reason to complain.

May 8th.—We got to the river Chapeau, or Beauclekky, five days ago ; at first sight, it appeared an immense bay in every direction as far as the eye could
discern, covered with flamingoes and pelicans. I rode
in on horseback to endeavour to shoot one of the
former, which have most beautiful plumage, but the
bottom was muddy and the horse all but stuck fast,
and the birds stalked and swam out of rifle range. The
Kaffirs told us there were two lions, with young ones,
in the reeds, and we must make all the oxen, &c., fast,
and keep a good watch, as they were very savage ;
we took all due precautions, but neither heard nor
saw anything of them. Treked on to Chapeau, a
Masara Captain's, but he was very sick, and we got
nothing from him, and heard that all the elephants
had treked away from the river since the last rains.
The Kaffirs had a weir across the river, and about
fifty funnel-shaped baskets, set about a yard apart,
facing down stream, in which they caught an immense quantity of fish, barbel and bream, in beautiful
condition, and very good eating. I bought a lot of
picked ones for a mere song, and salted them down,
and enjoyed them not a little. I have shot six
camelopards the last few days, having been very
successful in finding them ; and my two horses —
Broon and Luister—carrying me uncommonly well.
I had a hard stern chase after one, right away from
the wagon, up the wind. After the first shot I

headed her, and by keeping wide away from her,
and shouting lustily, I succeeded in driving her right
to the wagon, and I rolled her over within 150 yards,
in the midst of all the seven dogs. It was a grand
sight, and she was in fine condition. We outspanned at once, and finding water near at hand, in
a vley, made a night of it, and laid in a good stock
of flesh. We were all in high spirits, had an
enormous fire, and huge marrowbones roasting all
round it. It always surprises me that the Kaffirs
do not get sick, the quantity of marrow, fat, and

grease they consume is marvellous ; they have
stomachs like a hyena, nothing comes amiss to them

or disagrees with them. I had more or less sport
with the rest of the camelopards; one, shot through
the heart, went headlong at a tearing pace into a
mapane tree with three forks, about twelve feet from
the ground, where it remained wedged fast and died
standing.

A Kaffir brought an old musket to be mended,
and, in botching away at the lock, I succeeded in
breaking it in two places beyond my skill to mend.
Although I tried to explain to him that it was acci-
dental, and that I was doing all I could to assist him
without any compensation, and had worked unremittingly at it for near two days, and that it was
useless to him when he brought it, and consequently
it was no worse now, he would listen to nothing: I
had broken his gun, and I must give him another, and
being a great man, brother to Chapeau, the Captain,
and having a strong force at command, I was forced
to submit, take his old useless musket and give him
one three times the value. There is no arguing
with a Kaffir; he said that Wilson, a white man,
did the same, that is, broke his gun in endeavouring
to mend it, and instantly went to the wagon and
gave him a new one. I do not doubt that he did
so, as he had a lot of muskets. In the Kaffirs' eyes
a gun is a gun; they will give no more for a fifty
guinea one than a new musket worth about 15s. I
luckily happened to have one I had given 3l. for,
otherwise I must have given him one worth 25l.

A party of Bamangwatos followed the wagon

yesterday, well armed with assegais, axes, bows and arrows, and two guns, saying that. I must not hunt in their country until I first paid them for leave to do so ; and that if I did not do so, and persisted in hunting, they would bring a command against me and kill us all. My fellows talked very big, especially Auguste—a large powerful Kaffir, a Bequina, or Bechuana, one of Sechele's—saying that if they wanted to fight they must come on ; we were quite ready for them at any moment, having plenty of guns and powder. I said nothing, but let things take their course, and merely ordered the wagon to go on, and left the Bamangwatos to do whatever they thought best. At night, I served out plenty of powder and bullets, a watch was kept, and every man had his gun handy. My fellows talk largely, but what they would do in case of an actual skirmish I don't know. I don't place much confidence in one of them, nor do I fear the Kaffirs, unless they can catch me unprepared—and I and my gun are constant companions.

This river appears of immense breadth, nor do I see any possible way of crossing it, as I do not know where the stream runs to, and, as far as the eye can reach, there is nothing to be seen but reeds so tall and thick that it is impossible to force your way through them. There is safe harbour here for all the game and wild animals in South Africa. I never saw anything like it, and my Hottentots say it is the same all the way to Lake Ngami, about thirteen days from here in a wagon. It is not far, but the sand is so heavy that the oxen can only take slow and short stages. We have plenty of good water now, but the frightful annoyance from mosquitoes at night counter-balances this advantage. I know of no country in the world that can compare with Africa for brilliant sport, but it must be confessed that this part of it is a sandy desert, only fit to keep a few miserable goats in existence. There is not a bite of grass now except along the edge of the reeds, but, then, it is winter. Although the sun is overpowering in the day, it is very cold in the early mornings and at nights; and it requires a considerable amount of courage to get from under the blankets before sunrise.

I found yesterday the fresh spoor of a troop of elephants, some very large bulls and cows, intermixed, and tracked them to the water. Last night, all the dogs were made fast, and small fires only allowed, as we were by far too near the spoor with the wagon; but, luckily, the wind was right, and John and I went this morning, as soon as it was light enough to see, to find out whether the elephants had drunk last night, but they had not been. I wait quiet to-day in hopes they may come to-night; if not, I shall take the old spoor and go in quest of them to-morrow, for if they don't come to-night they must find water somewhere else, as they must drink every second night at the longest. There is plenty of buffalo, giraffe, and rhinoceros spoor, but this is not what I want. The elephants are wary, and very hard indeed to come at, as they are now so much sought for, and every savage knows the value of the ivory. I have tried fishing to-day, as I dare not fire a shot for fear of frightening the elephants, who cannot be far away, but the water was too clear and the sun too bright to do any good.

18th. — No success as yet with the elephants, partly owing to the laziness of the Kaffirs, but partly, also, if the truth must be told, to my own impatience, obstinacy, and self-will. I hunted them five days successively, the Kaffirs, in the first instance, taking me to a brack or salt vley, two days out of my road, where there was not a sign of an elephant having been for the last six months. They did this, I have no doubt, under the orders of the Bamang-watos. I was in a desperate way, and on getting back to the wagon I found that the elephants had drunk again at the river. This time I did not wait for the Kaffirs, but took the spoor myself, and eventually lost them in the densest hack-thorns I ever saw. It would have been impossible to have done much good with them, even had I found them there; the poor horses scarcely had the saddles off their backs for the five days.

I shot a fine specimen of the gemsbok or oryx, a cow, one of the kinds I had not yet got, and was well pleased; and I also drove a fine old eland bull to the wagon, not without great difficulty, as the mapani trees were so uncommonly thick that I could not see more than twenty yards before me. We lost him once, and kept galloping on like two fools, each thinking the other saw him, for 500 or 600 yards at least, when John called out, 'Varloup he sur.' We instantly turned, and took up the spoor, following it a good hour and a half, silently and surely. I heard a clatter among the stones, and almost flew to the spot, when I caught a glimpse of my old friend going like the wind. After a mad burst through the mapanis, I came up with him and gave him another pill in the stern, and after that we had no trouble with him.

24th.—I saw on the 17th leches, for the first time, and I was so anxious to get one that I worked hard all day, mostly on my hands and knees, but without success. My driver told me (not without reason) that he was a man who could shoot a leche ram. Singularly enough, the does are comparatively tame ; and I had several chances at them, but would not fire. I was at it again early the next morning ; and, to my immense gratification, I rolled over a fine ram the first shot, at full 300 yards, skinned him with care, and preserved his head and horns in my best style, and was highly elated. Since then, however, I have shot three more fine old rams, and the novelty and excitement of killing a new specimen have worn away.

On the same day that I bagged my first leche I bought, for the identical old musket before mentioned, that I was forced to take in exchange, and which I had managed to patch up with an old nail

and the sinews of a buck, to act, a little Masara boy—
a waddling infant, certainly not more than two years
old, but with an intelligent countenance, and not yet
starved — whom I named Leche ; and he is a fine
quick little fellow. I am now quite fond of him. A
gang of Bamangwatos returning to Sicomo's, from
hunting jackals, lynxes, wild cats, and skins of all
kinds, had picked up this poor little urchin. They
remained all night by my wagon, and the one who
called himself owner brought him to me. My interpreter told me that if I did not take him they were
just as likely to leave him as not, if they got tired of
carrying him across the desert ; and knowing the
fate in store for him, even if they got him home —
the slave of a Bamangwato, who live from hand to
mouth themselves — I took compassion on him, and
rescued him from their hands.

Yesterday, Whitsunday, will long live in my memory, as one of the most miserable of my life. On
getting up, later than usual, as it was Sunday, and I
did not intend to trek, I was struck by an ominous
silence in my followers, which boded no good ; and
as I was drinking my morning cup of coffee, Raffler,
the driver, acting as spokesman for the party, told
me he intended seeking a path to the house, and I
then saw they had all ready for a move. Never for
a moment thinking he was in earnest, I said, ' Very
well — he could do as he liked ;' when five instantly
rose, and gave me back, with great parade, powder, bullets, and caps, and made many apologies

for the loss of one or two of the latter; then the
driver gave me over rheims, straps, and whip, and
asked for their wages. I told them I should not
pay them a halfpenny more than they had already
got, and I was only vexed that I had let them have
anything before it was due, at which they appeared
quite satisfied. They then wished good-bye to
Matakit and Inyous, and started off. The two latter
remained with me, speechless, and all but crying,
telling me that we should inevitably be lost the first
day, and the Masaras and Makubas would assuredly
kill us. Finding the fix I was in — just two months
from the house, in the middle of a bush, of which I
was perfectly ignorant, and having the vivid remembrance of that desperate thirst-land, which must be
still worse now (this and a little later on being the
driest season) — I resolved, after a stubborn conflict
with my pride, to follow the runaways, to enquire
the cause of their grievances, and offer any redress
in my power. Acting on this good impulse, I told
Matakit, who started with a heavy heart to do my
bidding, to bring the horses. They were nowhere
to be found. It instantly rushed to my mind that
the blackguards, five in number, had taken them,
and I told Inyous to go with me at once to try and
find the spoor; and knowing the cunning of the
wretches, and that they would drive them a long
way wide of the path, we dispersed ourselves (as an
Irishman would say), and at last Inyous hit off the
spoor of both men and horses. We followed a long

way, till we found they had caught and mounted the
horses, all of which were perfectly quiet and gentle.
It then struck me that two men on foot going in
pursuit of five mounted men was only a fool's errand,
and we were never likely to come up with them.   I
stopped and indulged in a reverie for a few minutes,
when it struck me nobody was at the wagon, and we
should lose twenty oxen as well.   I called to Inyous
to turn back to the wagon.   No answer.   I then
roared and yelled again, till the woods resounded
with his name.   No response.   I then fired off at an
old stump an elephant shot, that made me reel again.
Not a breath in reply.   I then at once saw that it
was a made-up plot among them all, and that I was
entirely deserted.

I made my way back to the wagon as fast as I
could travel, when I found only poor little Leche,
who had cried himself to sleep under a tree ; the
oxen had strayed away.   After comforting the little
fellow as well as I could, I had to start on the oxen's
spoor ; and by the time I had recovered them, made
the kraal fast, brought wood and water for the night,
washed out the greasy pots and dishes (everything
the Kaffirs had left being in the same state of greasy
filth), I found I had no sinecure.   I discovered that
there is a very great difference between ordering a
thing and doing it oneself.   I boiled a kettle of tea,
and a saucepan of sago for Leche and myself, and was
all this time too busy to give way or have time for
thought ; but when I had put the little fellow to

bed, and sat all alone before the fire, I realised my situation—all alone in the desert, with a wagon and twenty oxen, not a soul that I knew of within reach, and I was wholly ignorant of the Maccateese language. I cursed my own pride and folly over and over again,

in not acceding to anything my Kaffirs wished, rather than be left in this frightful predicament, for I was utterly helpless. The night I passed was horrible — fourteen hours of darkness, for the days were now at the shortest; I do not wish my worst enemy to spend such a one. I hoped against hope that Matakit and Inyous might return, though I could not blame the poor lads, as I knew that scoundrel, Raffler, had frightened them out of their senses, by saying that we were sure to be killed. When I got a few minutes' restless, uneasy sleep, it was only to wake

again to a sense of my utter loneliness and desolation
— that I must leave all I had in the desert, run all
risks, and endeavour to reach Lake Ngami on foot.

The only chance of doing so, that I knew, was by
following the course of the river, which would have
been a difficult and arduous task; and then I could
not bear the thought of leaving Leche to die of
hunger and thirst in the desert. If you could only
have seen the little waddling brat come, armed with
a stick twice as long as himself, to help me kraal the
oxen, and the way he toddled along to make the calf
.fast, without my ever telling him! it brought the
tears into my eyes in spite of myself. He slept at
my feet, and, poor little fellow! he also felt a sense
of loneliness, and knew something was wrong, as he
kept starting up and feeling for my feet, touching
them with the greatest gentleness, and then lying
down again. Thus we passed the night. Two or
three times I was alarmed at hearing footsteps, and
started up with my gun; but it was only the dogs
walking among the dead leaves. I was up half a
dozen times to mend the fire. At break of day I
went to fetch wood and water, and comfort myself
with a cup of coffee, and give Leche his breakfast,
and make the oxen loose. Hearing Kaffirs' voices
over the river, I went to hail them, and fired, as the
surest way of bringing them, for they can scent blood
as far off as a hyena, and are always on the qui vive
when they hear a shot. It was not long ere I heard
a canoe cracking through the reeds, and three Kaffirs

in it; but, alas! I had only four words in my voca-
bulary—'beads,' 'go,' 'good morning,' and 'wagon.'
The two former and latter had the desired effect, and
they came to the wagon, but left again as wise as
they came, as we could not understand one another,
even by signs.   When I tried to explain to them
that I wanted to go to Lechulatebe, the captain
living on Lake Ngami, a very decided shake of the
head, and their villanous 'ngaw,' like a spoiled child,
was all I got.   I left them in utter despair.

Things never come to the worst but they mend;
and in hunting my oxen, which had wandered very
far up the river, I came across a party of Bamangwatos — men, women, girls, boys, dogs, and pack-
oxen — exulting over the carcase of a roybuck.   I
shook hands with the greatest delight with these fellows, who understood a slight smattering of Dutch,
and who asked me for meat.   Not five minutes after
I left them, having made a promise that they would
come to the wagon, the dogs bayed an old eland bull
in the thick bush, and I shot him dead ere he knew
danger was at hand, to the inexpressible joy of these
Bamangwatos.

Though all hopes of shooting elephants were at an
end, I positively jumped for joy when they told me
they were going direct to Mangwato's, and would
gladly assist me to the utmost of their power, if I
would give them a little powder and lead, and a
heifer to the foreloper and cattle vachter.   My
mind was at ease again, and I gave them the whole

eland. My intention was to have gone on foot to
Lake Ngami, to try and get assistance from Wilson,
an Englishman living there, and then to kill time till
I got some opportunity of going to Walvish Bay.

I was planning all this in my mind, making myself
happy with buffalo tongue, when who should come
up to the wagon, jaded, wearied, and foot-sore, but
Inyous. I sprang up, and could have hugged him.
He and Matakit had followed the spoor far on into
the night ; and by a sort of instinct where to find
the runaways (for they could not see), they came up
with them, and induced them to return ; and they
have just arrived with the horses, looking like grey-
hounds. I at first took a high line, and told them
that bringing the horses back was the best day's
work they ever did in their lives, as I would have
hunted them far and wide, and they should have
spent a good part of their days working on the
roads in chains. But they coolly told me they were
under Sechele's government, and did not care a fig
for the Boers and their laws ; and I at once saw the
truth of it, and that I should most likely have had
no redress. If I had come up with them on the
horses, I should certainly have shot one or more of
them, and should, in my turn, have been shot likewise, as they were armed. I was soon obliged to
lower my tone, and come down a peg. They said
all they wanted was their wages for two months, and
that, as I had not the means to pay, they had helped
themselves ; and, on their threatening to leave me

again, I said that, if they returned to their duty
peacefully and orderly, I would never say anything
about the horse-stealing business. They said that
the cause of their deserting was my hastiness, and
not following their advice, and speaking to them in
English, which they could not understand, and they
thought I was swearing at them ; but I think it is
the fault of the old wagon, which was, when we
outspanned, almost tumbling to pieces from the
drought. The iron pins that fastened on the tires to
the filleys had dropped out of one wheel, and I
replaced them by wooden pegs, and ordered them
to put the wheels into the river for twenty-four
hours, to swell and tighten. The last of the grog
was broached, and both master and servants promised to try and get on better together for the
future.

I had a visit in the course of the morning from
five villains, who made me feel anything but comfortable. As soon as I saw them, I put the guns,
copper, and beads, and things that would excite
their cupidity, out of their sight, and made some
pretext of carrying a gun with me wherever I went.
There was whispering and moving round me that I
did not like ; and they seemed at one time to make
a kind of general movement to cut me off from my
guns in front of the wagon ; but I had taken the
precaution of removing the caps, though the guns
were loaded, so that they were useless in their
hands. I jumped in at the back of the wagon, and

carelessly took down one, played with the lock, and
put on a cap, and they wished me good morning.
I did not like their movements or appearance; but
perhaps I do them injustice, and their evil thoughts
only existed in my excited imagination.

27th. — We were unfortunate enough to run over
Lou, about the most promising young dog I ever
had; he was killed on the spot; and yesterday,
two more, Bull and Falk, got severe prods from an
old oryx bull, which I ran down on Broon by fair

speed across an immense flat, distancing all the dogs,
though they had a good start of me, and were fresh
and hungry, and the day was cool; but old Broon

proved himself, yesterday, to be an honest, stout, fast horse, with great endurance. The old oryx had fully 1,000 yards start, took straight away up the wind, galloping low to the ground, fast and strong, and in beautiful form. When I neared him he turned, dodged, and twisted from side to side, with amazing quickness, but Broon was with him at every move. Broon ran like a first-rate greyhound; I shot the oryx from the horse's back; and, being myself very much distressed, neglected to finish him; and when the dogs came up, he gored poor Bull, and caught Falk just above the eye, prostrating them both.

I had a swim in the river, in spite of the crocodiles, which are very numerous: it is nervous work, however, and I was too much afraid to enjoy it, but felt much refreshed. We have been making our way all the morning through heavy sand and hackthorns, which the oxen are with difficulty made to face. I am now going to Lake Ngami direct; I wish much I had a pocket compass and a good telescope; the latter I left behind on my way. I see the river Beauclekky runs south-east from the Great Lake, and not north, as I had before imagined.

Auguste wounded a cow buffalo yesterday, which charged him, together with a big calf or heifer; he scrambled up a low tree, tearing his legs badly; and while the heifer and cow were below, licking his feet, he reloaded and shot them both. Luckily, he had managed to throw his gun up before him, or he

s

might have been kept there for a couple of days or more; he is quite proud of his feat.

29th. — Yesterday afternoon we outspanned close to the river, within a few hundred yards of where elephants had drunk the previous night, and we made all ready for a hunt this morning; and I was awakened at dawn by hearing loud cries from the Masaras, over the river, that the elephants had drunk there in the night. We swam the horses over with the aid of a canoe. The river is about 300 yards across, but the bottom is good, and the stream is not strong. The water is deliciously cold and clear — a great treat in this desert land.

We took up the spoor on the opposite side of three bulls, not, however, until the bones had been cast, and the witch doctor or prophet had foretold that we should find them, and that I should shoot a fat bull, with one long and one short tusk. I followed silently in the rear of the spoorers, through a thick thorny bush. I had a presentiment that we were near them, and took my gun from the Kaffir's hands ; and not three minutes after I saw, from the gesticulations of the Masaras, they had seen them. The dogs were slipped, and all was quiet for some time, when I heard Turk give mouth, followed immediately by the trumpeting of a bull. I made the best of my way in the direction, when I was turned by Raffler's voice shouting, ' Come here, Natoo,' and made for him. I heard a shot behind me, turned at once, and caught sight of the retreating monster. The bush being uncommonly dense, I was fearful of losing him, and fired, striking him in the thick of the thigh, and he took up a position in a thicket, trumpeting and charging the dogs in all directions, making a loud crashing. Unfortunately, the cap was driven into the nipple at the first shot, and I lost some time in trying to get it out, and broke the point of my knife, but I eventually succeeded with a strong needle, which I had in my hat. There were five men with guns, but no one had ventured into the bush to give him a shot ; and the Kaffirs, no doubt, thought me afraid likewise ; but when I was sure of my gun I rode in on Broon, taking care to have a clear passage for a speedy exit. When within about twenty-five yards, he threw up his trunk and came direct towards me. The horse stood steady as old Time, and I gave him a conical ball, five to the pound, backed by six drachms of fine powder, on the point of the shoulder-blade. Flesh and blood could not stand before such a driver; and, staggering and stumbling forwards a few yards, he pitched right on his head within fifteen yards of me; then my brave followers immediately rushed in and gave him a volley as he lay on his broadside, and it was all over with him. I was surprised to see that poor Bull, whom we had left behind on the sick list, had followed us. He had had to swim the river, and was now tearing away manfully at the elephant.

Though the other elephants could not have been far off, all hunting was over for that day, as the sight of so much fat meat was irresistible to the half-starved Masaras; and nothing I could offer would induce them to take up the spoor of the other bulls, so they will live to fight another day.

The scoundrels, when they ran away, rode Luister, my second-best horse, two whole days without a saddle, and have given him a sore back, so that he will be utterly useless for the next month, and even then it is doubtful if he will be able to carry a saddle. What with sun, sand, and flies, it is very hard to heal a back when it is once sore.

June 6th (Sunday). — I have not much to log up.

Last week was a hard and unprofitable time. On Monday we crossed the river at dawn of day; not, however, until I had paid a bag of powder and a bar of lead for the use of two old canoes, which, however, were indispensable to us. We took up the spoor of a large herd of elephants, and followed it unremittingly till within two hours of sunset, straight away from the river, to a thick grove of mapani trees, the leaves of which very much resemble the beech, and are even now, in the depth of winter, green and luxuriant. Here we found a large herd of fifty or sixty, all cows and calves. They were feeding, but on seeing us they disappeared like magic; and, when the dogs got among them, they spread in all directions. I looked in vain for a bull, and then chased and shot a cow, within fifteen yards, behind the shoulder. I stopped to load, however, and lost her in the mapani trees; and, night coming on, we gave her up. I shot, also, an old bull buffalo, and we made our encampment for the night by his carcase; and the Masaras and Makubas, though well wearied, made a night of it, that is, did not stop eating until morning; consequently, only two that we sent for water were able to work the next day.

On the Tuesday morning we found a troop of eleven or twelve bull elephants in a thick hackthorn bush on the banks of the river. As they crashed away, I rode hard in their rear, shouting lustily, and singled out the largest bull. I rode close under his stern, and he cleared a path for me.

He turned to see who had the audacity to ride so near, for the horse's nose touched him, when I gave him a bullet behind the shoulder, and cleared out of his path. In reloading I lost him, and, cantering on his spoor, he very nearly caught me, as he had stopped and turned round just where the path turned suddenly and sharply to the right, and I was almost under his very trunk ere I saw him. He was lying in wait, and made a terrific charge, trumpeting furiously ; the horse was round like a top, and away I went, with both rowels deep in his flanks, as I threw myself on his neck. It was a very near shave ; his trunk was over the horse's hind quarters. I went through bush that, in cool blood, I should have pronounced impenetrable, but did not come off scathless ; my poor hands are shockingly torn, and my trousers, from the knee, literally in shreds, though made of goatskin. After giving the elephant two more bullets I lost him. The dogs were frightened to death, and would not leave the horse's heels.

I shortly came across another troop of bulls, which took against the wind, leaving such a dust behind them, that I was half smothered. I rode, at last, a little wide of them, on the weather side, and was able to get a view of their teeth, and I rode out one with beautiful long teeth. He very soon lessened his speed, turned, and, before I was aware, charged me. I could not turn in time, and, therefore, fired right between his eyes. The shot struck him about an inch above the left eye, and brought him on one

CHASED BY AN ELEPHANT.

knee, and I was able to get out of his way. He
then took up a position in the bush, and I loaded
and gave him two more bullets in the head, one in
the centre of his forehead. He kept backing farther
and farther into the bush, with his two enormous
ears erected like fans, and, as I was thinking the last
shot must tell on him, he made the longest and most
furious charge I ever saw ; he fairly hunted me,
while I was half loaded, clear away. I rode in a
circle to endeavour to dodge him, and at length succeeded. He stopped at fault, and I began to reload.
I had none but conical balls, and the gun was foul.
I could not get one down. That dastardly cur,
John, never came near me all this time. I sought
in vain for a stone, and at length, in despair, took up
a thick branch, and what with hammering the ramrod, and driving it against the trunk of a tree, I at
length got the bullet home ; but my elephant had
made good use of his time and got clear away, and
I returned to the wagons in rags, with the loss of a
spur, and not a little discomfited, but it was madness
to attack them in their stronghold. I also lost a
fine old bull in a most foolish manner. After
following his spoor several hours from the river,
where he had been to drink, I saw him about 600
yards off, and in riding to get at him from below the
wind I lost sight of him. He had taken the alarm
by the horse snorting or treading on a dead bough,
and I never saw him more. Sechele's daughter, the
wife of a trader named Wilson, met us to-day, on

her way back to her father's, with one whity-brown little boy. He has deserted her, or she him; the latter I believe to be the truth. She is a very good-looking girl. I gave her some tea, meal, and salt, as I was sorry for the poor thing. She is going in a canoe as far as the river goes, but how she will get across the desert I cannot conceive. She has a strong party of Sechele's men with her, and plenty of cows, oxen, sheep, and goats. It is a bad business; it will be the means of giving Englishmen a bad name, and Sechele will probably stop our coming in future.

Hottentots are necessary evils, as they know the language of the natives and the line of country; but they are lazy, useless dogs, receiving high wages and doing nothing, wanting to be masters, and making the trek very unpleasant; but I am entirely dependent on them at present, and they know it. John left me on the veldt to-day, to find my own way to the wagon. I had, luckily, taken particular notice of the course we had come, SW.; therefore, of course, I must ride NE. to return. I made a good deal too much to the east, as I had only the sun to guide me, but managed to come across the wagon-spoor, where I found my gentleman coolly drinking coffee and smoking, declaring that he never heard me fire or shout, and thought I had ridden back. He has a bad countenance, is a shocking thief, and the biggest cur and loudest talker I ever came across.

Lechulatebe's State, Lake Ngami.—15th.—We arrived here on Friday, the 11th, not until I had received several messages from the Captain to make haste and be the first wagon at his State; since which time we have been haggling and wrangling about the price of two horses, till my interpreter and I were utterly exhausted, the former drinking half my cask of sherry to keep his throat moist, till to-day I gave in and let the Captain have them for thirteen teeth of ivory, and a saddle and bridle into the bargain. I only gave 9*l.* for one nag, and the ivory I got for him is worth at least 60*l.*, so that it was worth a little patience.

I have just returned from seeing the Great Lake, the nearest point of which is about two hours and a half on horseback from here. The country all around appears to be a perfect flat, very unhealthy and uninteresting, with a lot of rubbishy reeds at this end, but it is wooded to the banks on the other side, and most of the way round. I gather from the natives that it is a three days' ride round the lake, but that the tsetse render it impossible for horses. The natives are afraid to cross in their frail canoes, as when a wind rises the water is very rough. Three canoes were swamped not long since, and their crews drowned. Not far from the southern point, the road the wagons take to Walvish Bay, there is a high ridge of rocks, Lechulatebe's stronghold, in case of an attack from Sebituane. These Kaffirs are always at war, cattle being the prime object. I could only get a very bad view of one end of the lake, but I must confess that I was disappointed in it. The chief went with me, and, by the aid of an interpreter, gave me all the information he could, and was very kind and obliging. He is not a bad fellow at heart, I think, but a dreadful beggar and very covetous. He appears to have no idea of being refused anything he fancies, gives you nothing in return, wants your things on his own terms, and asks outrageous prices for his. He is young, active, an elephant-hunter himself, a good shot, and possesses guns made by Wilkinson, Nock, and Manton. On our return I swam the river, which is here about 300 yards wide, and he invited me to dinner. We dined in the open air, and were attended by the prettiest girls in the kraal, who knelt before us and held the dishes from which we ate. They wear no clothing but a skin round their loins; their legs, arms, necks, and waists are ornamented with beads of every variety, and ivory, brass, and copper bracelets. Finer made girls than some of the well-fed Kaffirs, I suppose, are not to be found. They have small hands and feet, beautifully-rounded arms, delicate wrists and ankles; their eyes and teeth are unsurpassable, and they are lithe and supple as a willow wand.

They say perfect happiness does not exist in this world, but I should say a Kaffir chief comes nearer to it than any other mortal; his slightest wish is law, he knows no contradiction, has the power of life and death in his hands at any moment, can take any quantity of wives and put them away at any moment, he is waited upon like an infant, and every

DINING WITH A KAFFIR CHIEF.

wish, whim, and caprice is indulged to the fullest extent; and he has ivory, feathers, and karosses brought
to him from all quarters, which he can barter with the
traders for every article of luxury. Our dinner consisted of roasted giraffe, swimming in fat and grease.
The intestines are the daintiest morsels, and, putting prejudice on one side, I assure you the English
never make use of the really best part of the animal.
I always do in Rome as Rome does, eat (if I can)
whatever is set before me, and shut my eyes if I feel
qualmish. Nothing approaches the parts most re-
lished by the natives in richness of flavour, and racy,
gamey taste. The Kaffirs know well the best parts of
every animal, and laugh at our throwing them away.
But enough; I enjoyed my dinner. We washed all
down with a bumper of sherry, and then adjourned
to the wagon to drink tea. Perhaps a person with a
delicate stomach might have found fault with the
means used to fasten on the lids of the different
dishes; but the native plan is an excellent one, as
everything is kept warm, and nothing can boil over
or escape. Everything was scrupulously clean; and
jackals' tails waved in abundance by the many slaves
in attendance kept away the flies.

I afterwards exchanged my hat with the Captain
for a pair of leather crackers, but had to give beads,
knife, fork, and spoon into the bargain. The rascal
had no conscience, and after plaguing me till I promised to give him some tea for the second time—for
I had sent him about a pound on my arrival,—he

immediately despatched a messenger for an immense earthenware jar, which would hold at least two chests, and was highly indignant at the pigmy appearance of the tea I put in it. He then plagued me for meal, and when I offered to exchange with him for corn, provided he gave me two measures for one, he declared there was none in the State; he lies like a trooper, and only laughs when you find him out. He appears to be very good-tempered, however; but all Kaffirs have great self-command, and they rarely, if ever, come to blows.

I discharged John for refusing to obey me, and the day after Lechulatebe gave him a wife; he will give me one, also, if I like to remain here, but I must not take her away. Powder and lead he has in abundance.

18th.—Inspanned and started home, earlier than I had intended, in consequence of one of my oxen being sick. Lechulatebe, fearing lung sickness, would not allow them to remain. I was disappointed in an elephant hunt, owing to a man dying most inopportunely in the State. Lechulatebe would not let me go, unless I took one of my own people with me; he said that in case any accident happened he should get the credit of having ordered his people to kill me. To-day I measured two trees called mowane; one was twenty-seven and the other twenty-eight yards round the bole. At about six feet from the ground they spread into four immense stems, all bending outwards, and leaving in the middle a spacious apartment, exactly one foot between each stem, where they branched from the main bole, widening upwards, and at eighteen or twenty feet from the ground the circumference of the tree must have been forty yards at least. I should live in one of these if I stayed in this part. I took another youngster, a Masara, out of pity. He was almost at death's door from starvation, beating, and shameful usage. Mutla (Thorn) is his name. He is a shocking object, and makes me shudder; he is almost a living skeleton, hollow-eyed and hollow-jawed.

20th (Sunday).—We have had a long-continued run of the loveliest weather that ever poor mortal was blessed with, and I am very well. I wish I could say the same of poor Mutla; from the barbarous treatment he has received it is a great chance if he pulls through. His head is half battered in and his whole body is one mass of scars and wounds, and his skin, from starvation, and eating roots and reeds and anything he could find to support life, is in a bad state. We smear him with grease and gunpowder in lieu of sulphur, and, to eradicate the disease, I added a little mercurial ointment, and would have added a few drops of turpentine, if I had had any; however, he is young, and with care I hope he will get round. Before he came into my possession he had had the charge of a flock of goats and some kids, which he had to look after all day and bring home at night, and one of the latter was missing one day; it was eventually proved that the poor starving wretch had killed and eaten it, and the enraged owner flogged and maltreated the boy within an ace of taking his life, as Lechulatebe had done to another boy a little while before. The other little fellow, Leche, is as fat as a porpoise, oily and shining, and very like a young sea-cow calf. I never saw a pig lay on fat so quick; but he does nothing but eat, drink, and sleep, and can hardly waddle. If you lay him on his back, he is like a cast sheep, and cannot help himself. He would have drowned yesterday in a foot and a half of water if we had not rescued him. To-day is the third day we have been without flesh meat of any kind or sort; the game is entirely exterminated, guns, pit-falls, and poisoned arrows have done their work, and last year's drought and famine had left the natives nothing to live on but the spoils of the chase. The pit-falls which they make are about eight feet deep with a bank in the middle, so that whatever game falls into one of them falls across the bank, and cannot touch the ground on either side.

The river is very full, and still rising rapidly, overspreading its banks far and wide, and driving us back to cut a path through the bush, which is so thick that our tent is smashed, and two strong canvas sails are torn into shreds. The lynch-pins, from constant contact with trees and stumps, are knocked into all shapes, and it is a work of time and smiting with axe and hammer to take the wheels off to smear. And yet not a drop of rain has fallen for months, and the river is the only water ; every vley in the country is dried up. I cannot in any way account for it — it is one of Nature's freaks.

I am of Barnum's opinion, that it is not so hard to make money, even here, where it is so scarce, as to keep it when made. The old wagon still holds together miraculously, by the aid of false lears, rheims, and greenhide, and I verily believe will see Natal yet with a few repairs, as the wood is well seasoned. Four days ahead lie the remains of an old wagon tumbled to pieces, with one good wheel, which I shall exchange with my worst, and other-wise fit her out as well as my tools will allow me. I think I have some 700 lbs. of ivory on the wagon, and she is loaded up to the roof with skins and rubbish of the Kaffirs, which must be thrown away, if I can only get ivory. Dubabe is the name of the Makuba chief living at the head of the Great Lake. This place offers no great inducement to come here again, unless from Walvish Bay, as the Kaffirs have got plenty of all they require.

22nd.—This morning I came across a swarm of Kaffirs in great glee, having caught a bull elephant in a pit-fall. They make these very well, and cover them over neatly with reeds, then a layer of grass, and then sprinkle them with sand and earth, so that they are very difficult to detect, and the elephant, sagacious as he is, falls a victim. This country is done for the sportsman ; there are too many Kaffirs, Bushmen, and Masaras, all hunters, and the pit-falls

do very great execution; they are well supplied
with guns, powder, and lead from Walvish Bay, and
they watch the different drinking-places of the animals every moonlight night, and buffalos, rhinoceros,
&c., must succumb. It is only with great toil, daily
labour, and by traversing immense ranges, that, in my
legitimate mode of sporting, I can keep my people
going in flesh, and we have been hard set since we
have left the Great Lake, and have made great
inroads into the meal. My coffee-mill is smashed to
atoms, and we have to crush or pound the best way
we can. We manage with a stamp block, like a
pestle and mortar, as there are no stones in this land.
The sugar has been long since finished—nine fellows,
who all took a sly taste when opportunity offered,
soon made an end of it; it is impossible to keep it,
and we must drink coffee and tea, 'carle' (as the Dutch
say), naked; the former is rather insipid, the latter
I manage well enough. Three of my people who
are married are most anxious to get home, talk about
nothing else, and would drive the oxen to a stand-
still if I did not interfere. This is a great annoyance
to me, and I don't know how to remedy the evil.
Sechele's people receive so much for the journey,
long or short, time makes no difference to them; it
is a bad plan, and I will make different arrangements another time. Everyone but myself has something to look forward to at the end of the trek—
wives, fathers, mothers, brothers, sisters, friends, or
relatives.

The Hottentots and Kaffirs, being used to go with Dutchmen, who are all married before they are out of their teens, and ride like the wind to get back to their fraus and kinders, cannot understand that, as I have no home to return to, all places are alike to me, and that I have nothing to gain by pushing on. As they have nothing to gain by remaining, of course we don't hit it off well, and it riles me to hear them everlastingly talking of getting home.

The only thing I see for me to do, as I cannot get people with the same feelings, or rather in the same situation as I am, is to go to Mosilikatse and live there altogether for one or two years. I shall be well treated, and have the best hunting South Africa can produce. I shall only be following out Albert Smith's theory, who says that the colonies are only refuges for destitute social suicides.

The Kaffirs, though they always get plenty, are too selfish to give me a morsel, when I run short of game, even if the trees all around were perfectly red with meat. They don't refuse point blank, but make excuses, saying, 'The master of the elephant is not there,' 'it is not theirs,' &c., and put you off as well as they can. The best of them are an ungrateful race of heathens. As they sit on their hams with a huge piece of meat in one hand, and a six-feet long assegai in the other, cutting and slicing away, they are in perfect happiness and contentment, envying no man living, as long as the flesh lasts. They have nothing, and, consequently, have no cares,

T

and when they have plenty of food are supremely happy.

26*th.*—I have got on very slowly the last four days. Broon, my favourite horse, was taken sick on Wednesday and died on Thursday, in spite of all the remedies I knew of—profuse bleeding, blistering, and powerful emetics. This is the first instance in my experience of the horse sickness in the middle of winter; it is a sad loss to me, and nothing can replace him here. I had been nursing him up for the elephants on my return. He died hard indeed, poor fellow! and at his final death-struggle I could not repress a tear; he was my best friend, and I never had the same affection for any animal. I could not but admire the symmetry of his form after the breath had left his body. He was a powerful horse with great endurance; he played with the swiftest giraffe, and was more than a match for any game I ever chased. At his swiftest speed I could guide and check him with a pack-thread; he was a noble animal, all that a man could desire in a horse: docile and gentle, at the same time full of fire and courage, and would face fire or water, or the most virulent hack-thorns, and turn his head from nothing his rider had the courage to put him at when in pursuit of game. I killed with him twenty-seven head of large game, and never had a fall through all the holes, pit-falls, and fallen timber with which the bush abounds. I have now lost all heart for the hunt, and care not how soon the trek comes to an end. My

other nag, Fleur, is a regular brute, very timid,
swerves at everything, will not face thorns at all, and,
as he always carries his head as high as his short
neck will allow him, he stumbles over every stump
and into every hole he comes across, keeps changing
his legs continually when pressed into a gallop, and
always appears to be going very much against his
will; and it is very hard work to keep your seat on
him at all, as he makes a succession of buck-jumps
over or into every scrubby bush, consequently makes
no way; and his only redeeming point is that he is
a very fast walker and an excellent roadster, being
uncommonly easy in his paces when on a beaten
path. Manelle, my other nag, is an incorrigible
slug, and, if you ply the sjambok severely, bolts into a
thicket, there stops and kicks as long as you thrash.
The reader will ask why I buy such brutes? My
answer is—They are salted, have come through the
sickness, and are guaranteed by their former owners
not to die; a good salted horse is worth from 40$l.$ to
75$l.$, and is not always to be had, even at that price.

I worked hard at the old wagon for a whole day
with great success, and, with taking the best parts
of the other old one and the one good wheel, I
have patched up mine into a very respectable, ser-
viceable-looking vehicle, and she cannot now be
drawing under 2,000 lbs. weight. We, however,
stuck fast all last night in a mud-hole, had to unload
to the last thing, and trek her out backwards, which
we succeeded in doing to-day, after great breakage

of skeys and two yokes, rheims and straps. We must remain where we are over to-morrow, to repair damages for a fresh start. In the pursuit of a giraffe, yesterday, I lost all my bullets and caps, and after giving her one bullet in the stern, and making sure of her, much to my mortification I had to let her go. The weight of the bullets and hack-thorns, together, had burst the pocket open.

July 11*th (Sunday)*.—I have neglected the log for some time, having been very ill indeed for about ten days from my old enemy—bilious fever and ague. I am better now, thank God, but very weak, and unfit for any work. Thanks to my medicine-chest, I had calomel, colocynth, emetics, quinine, &c., all at hand, and, by judicious use of one and all, having had plenty of experience how to deal with the complaint, I pulled through for the fourth time. My people had given me up entirely, not being used to see a man, with his teeth chattering in his head like a magpie, sitting swathed in blankets before a roaring fire in a broiling sun, and being icy cold. This stage is followed by violent perspirations, attended with excruciating headaches and pains all over the body. I suffered much more this time than ever I did in any former attack. I had no rest at nights, until I took twenty-five drops of laudanum. The coarseness of the fare set before me quite turned my stomach, I could not face it, and nothing what-ever passed my lips but weak tea for seven days; then I swallowed a little pheasant broth, and so gradually

came to. How I longed for soda water, or black
currant tea, and all the little delicacies a man
fancies when he is ill! I tried to make gruel, meal
being all I had; the rice is finished, and everything
else except bread and meat, varied, as they say in
Australia, by meat and bread; the latter, however,
is only coarse meal and water, as I have no sieve to
sift the bran, and though all goes down with a relish
when I am in good order, I found it a very different
thing when ill. One of my Kaffirs, Inyous, was most
attentive to me the whole time, sitting up half the
night chafing my feet and hands, and I frequently,
when in some of my worst fits of ague, saw him in
tears. He evidently thought it was all up with me.
The Kaffirs, one and all, accused Raffler—a Hottentot
—of having given me poison in my coffee, and there
was a great row, Auguste swearing if I died he
would shoot Raffler, and the latter saying he would
leave the wagon forthwith. I had great difficulty in
procuring order once more amongst them, and now
the matter is to come before Sechele. The day previous to my being taken ill they had refused to go
out with me elephant-hunting, in consequence of the
badness of my horse, saying I should assuredly be
killed, and then Sechele would blame them for it.
Raffler and Auguste have also been ill, the latter
really; the former always thinks himself so, and is
bled, cupped, cut, and doctored at every Kaffir state.
He has the most depraved stomach I ever saw; he
always bothers me for medicine, and smacks his lips

over castor oil, and evidently enjoys it, as well as rhubarb and ipecacuanha. In fact, I have tried him with all the most nauseous drugs mixed up in any manner to make them still more disgusting to the taste, and to get rid of him I once gave him a large spoonful of mustard in a pint of warm water, which he sipped off like coffee! I then told him to follow it up by plenty of warm water, and I believe it had no effect whatever on him; he will drink a cupful of strong vinegar at a time if he can get it, and nothing disagrees with him.

I was so much better as to be able to take the field again two days ago, and shot a buffalo, two quaggas, springbok, &c., and once again replenished the larder. The river is still very full, and the face of the country entirely altered. We have to take a fresh course, our old track being under water in most places. This, I fancy, must be a very unhealthy part of the world in the summer months. As the present is the most healthy season, there is generally little fear of fever and ague; but my constitution is much shattered, one fit after another has told upon me, and an attack, instead of leaving one free for a time, only makes one more liable to another. I am afraid I must give up this life and remain altogether in Natal, in the Upper Division, where it is perfectly healthy, and I shall be entirely removed from any fear of more attacks. I have heard Dr. Livingstone has had something of the same kind ten different times.

17th.—I have been better and worse this week—on

the whole, very unwell ; in a great measure, through my own fault. I was excited in the chase of a broken-legged leche ram, which I struck at an incredible distance ; he instantly took the water, and I swam five rivers in pursuit, having on a pair of goat-skin trousers, which struck me icy cold after the old ram was bagged, and I rode all day in them looking for the wagon, which I eventually found in a pit-fall, having fallen into one when going through some water ; they had to offload everything, but eventually righted without any mischance. The Cape wagons are wonderfully suited to the country, and will bear any amount of knocking about, and the oxen's gear is so simple that we can, at any time or place, repair all damages.

I suffered very severely for my rashness. I just got to the wagon and beneath the blankets in time to lessen the severity of the attack, but I felt certain that if I had not found the wagon and had had to bivouac in the open, I could not possibly have got through the night, but must have died, there being no wood to make a fire, and a cold, cutting, windy night. I bought a goat, but it goes no way among ten hungry Kaffirs. I have, however, paid off two, as I found my establishment too expensive, and the more rascals I have the less work I get out of them. Yesterday I succeeded in killing two fine, very fat cow giraffes, each with a single bullet, after a very long, hard chase, in which, for three-fourths of the way, I had only dust to guide me through thick

mapani trees, the whole chase, without one solitary
open place. I and my horse were both beaten to a
stand-still, and I hardly know which of us took the
longest time to recover. We went blundering,
stumbling on the last 1,000 yards, all but down half-
a-dozen times, as I could not afford him the slightest
assistance, until, when I saw the trees were becoming
thinner and the leaves almost all gone, I scrambled
off instinctively, utterly exhausted, gave the gun
a little elevation, and rolled over the fattest cow
in the troop, with her long neck broken in two
places. I had previously jumped off and shot at a
large, well-grown heifer. I heard the cool ' clap,'
but, as she bounded away at a tremendous pace, I
was not aware I had killed her. The Kaffirs, who
followed the horses' spoor, saw the blood spoor, and
found her, not 200 yards off, shot dead through the
body, a little too far back. I lay on the broad of my
back fully two hours, I think, before my after-rider
ferreted me out, and his eyes sparkled when he saw
more than an inch deep of fat in a slit I had made
along her loins. We at once proceeded to skin and
cut her up, and we took the direction of the wagons
with both nags well loaded with delicious meat, and
three niggers staggering after us with as much as ever
they could totter under. I despatched four more
immediately on arriving at the wagon, as there were
still some three hours' sun, for we had gone out early
to hunt, and I grudged leaving the meat on the velt.
I gave the other giraffe entire to the poor, half-

starved Masaras. Bad news awaited my return.
Leche's former owners were at the wagon, in a strong
force, bringing back the old musket, broken, as I felt
sure would be the case after a few shots, and insisting
upon another gun, or his being returned. After a
long talk, in vain, I was obliged to give him up—most
reluctantly, however, as I had become quite fond of
him, and I knew the poor little urchin's fate. There
is nothing but starvation and ill treatment staring
him in the face, but I can do nothing alone amidst
hordes of savages; besides, I must allow that they
are this time decidedly in the right, and brought
back the last thing I gave in exchange most punc-
tiliously. They offered to take another gun, but I
have only two left, both valuable weapons.

We bade a long good-bye to-day to the beautiful
river Beauclekky. I shall, most probably, never
again see it, as I am greatly disappointed in the
country altogether, from the great scarcity and wild-
ness of the game, and the varieties, which constitute,
in my estimation, the greatest charm in shooting,
being few. Since leaving Natal this time, however,
I have shot six varieties new to me, which is in
itself worth the whole time, expense, and distance,
in my opinion. I am always on the look-out for a
new kind of buck, and make every possible enquiry
from the natives, and examine every kaross they draw.
Every man has his hobby, and this is mine, and I
have no one here to please but myself; and, barring
the coast sickness, which is a little hard to bear, I

could not pass my time more to my own liking.
Certain kinds of bucks are only to be found in certain localities : thus the inyala is only to be met
with in the strand bush along the coast, where
it is very unhealthy; then in the deserts other
varieties, independent of water, are to be got.
The harrisbuck and roan antelope are not to
be found on the Great Lake route, where,
again, it is the only place the leche is to be found.
At the end of this book the reader will find a list of
the names, in English and Kaffir, of all the different
bucks I have myself seen and shot; and the nakong
is the only one of whose existence I am aware that
I have not shot.   He is only to be met with among
the reeds close to the water's edge, I believe, but
have never seen him.   There are other varieties, no
doubt, spread over the continent, but I have never
heard of them, even indirectly.

Poor Leche was borne away this morning, poor
little animal, making the most determined resistance
in his power, as far as shrieks and kicks went.   I
have grown very fond of children—black ones, for
choice, I do think — as one never hears them cry, and
they are as patient as Job, never ask for any food,
and are very quick in learning ; and, where a white
one would not leave his mother's apron, the black
youngsters fetch wood and water, make a fire, and
cook their own food, run about, show no fear, and
lend a hand at everything, and sleep on the ground,
rolled up like a ball, in a sheepskin, before the fire :

I am speaking of brats between two and three years old. It was a sore sight for me to see my little manikin borne away; I could not have been fonder of one of my own. His large black diamond eyes, with their long lashes, used to twinkle like stars; and his little teeth, white and even as snow-flakes, were exposed in a double row as he saw me coming to the wagon well loaded with meat behind the horse, and he used to clap his little hands with delight, and scream and dance again. He was a sad little ogre, and I am afraid it was more for love of the meat than of me, as, when I returned empty-handed, there were none of these demonstrations of joy.

19th. — We are now once again fairly in this much-dreaded thirst land, where the villainous salt water has the same effect as Epsom salts. If we are fortunate, we hope, with the aid of spades, to obtain a sufficiency of this stuff to keep man and beast in life, every second day, until we come to the Bamangwatos, when I am going to take a different course to the Merico, by a river called Notowani, which runs into the Limpopo one day below the point where we join it. The grass is very scarce and dry, and all my oxen and horses are in very low condition, two or three of the former almost knocked up.

I must not omit to mention the ant-heaps in this land, which are very extraordinary. They average, one with another, from ten to fifteen, or even twenty feet in height. They are conical, very broad at the base, and tapering off beautifully. There is an eternal sameness across this vast desert, and hardly a head of game ; but, luckily, we have a goodly supply of giraffe, and I am driving two fat goats along for slaughter, whenever the former comes to an end. Eight Kaffirs make fearful inroads into it, boiling, and broiling, and baking on every possible opportunity ; that is, whenever we have a fire. I am decidedly better, but very weak, always feeling a great incli-nation to lie down, and the least exertion entirely prostrates me. I sit in the wagon propped up with pillows and skins, but my appetite is fast returning. I have engaged two Maccalacas Kaffirs, smart, able fellows, to go down to Natal with me, and am well provided with good Kaffirs, which is a great thing in treking.

31st.—*Caballa.*—We are now within three days of Machin, the chief of the Bamangwatos, but our difficulties are not yet over, as I hear to-day we shall find no water along the whole road. This is the worst season of the year to cross the Kalahari desert, for not a drop of rain has fallen for many months. I have not, however, been treking all the time. I have, somehow, lost two days during my illness, as I know by comparing the age of the moon with an almanack which I have with me. We have found water five times since Saturday the 17th, and I remained a day each time to refresh the oxen. Once the water was only sufficient for two horses and eleven oxen. Pioneers, with spades, went out a day

in front, to open the dry bed of a sand river, and
old pits that sometimes had water, but though they
dug down to solid rock they never got anything more
than a muddy puddle, half an inch deep. The
weather has been cool, with a nice wind, and we
made great way in the moonlight nights, treking all

night. I had the satisfaction of once finding water
myself. We were in great need of it, and I was
riding due east across the desert to water the horses,
if possible, for, even if they are not at work, horses
suffer much from want of water. I saw two black
objects in the far distance, which I took to be
ostriches, but, cantering sharply in the direction, I
found they were two Masara women, who, having a
heap of egg-shells in a net-work slung on their
backs, I saw at once were going for water. I made

them show me the way, and I found a small pit in
the solid rock, about eight yards in circumference,
and about nine inches of tolerably good water. I
immediately sent my after-rider to the wagon, to tell
my people to bring the oxen and water-vats. Twelve
oxen drank it as dry as a board, and eight poor
beasts had to go without. It was a long way from
the wagon, and though I started at sunrise it was
sunset before the oxen got back ; we inspanned those
that had drunk and treked all night, the next day
and next night, and half the following day, when we
arrived at Nkowani, where we found abundance.
Three days after leaving the river Beauclekky, I
came across the Bechuanas—Wilson's wife, Sechele's
daughter. Wearied and foot-sore, unused to walking,
she was dead-beat and unable to proceed. I acted
the part of the good Samaritan, and gave her and her
brat a seat in the wagon all the way to Sechele's.
The child annoys me greatly ; he is about twelve
months old, a sickly, pale yellow, having powerful
lungs, and an everlasting squaller. I don't much like
such baggage, and she is attended with a retinue of
Sechele's people, who, though they have bucks,
sheep, and oxen, will kill none, but live on me.
However, I can't help it, and have meal enough to
see me to Merico. Some hard-hearted brutes, Mangwatos, one night left behind them a little Masara boy,
who was entirely knocked up, to die of hunger in
the desert, or, more likely, become food for the
wolves and jackals. I heard of it the next morning,

and, after rating them soundly for their cruelty and want of feeling in leaving him — at which they only laughed, saying he was only a Masara (a dog) and of no consequence whatever — I volunteered to go back and look for him, provided that, if I found him, I was to have him. To this they would not listen, and so I bought him for ten rings of copper, provided I found him, and rode back on the spoor to where we came from. I searched lots of bushes and holloaed lustily, and all but knocked up my poor horse to no purpose, for we could not gain the slightest trace of him.

Over-exertion in search of food and water, and anxiety of mind, brought on a return of fever and ague, and I have been three days very sick, having had no sleep, as it was necessary to trek at nights, and the rolling, jolting, and straining of the old wagon rendered sleep impossible. Yesterday we remained here, and to-day I took the field, though weak as a cat, and shot the finest bull eland out of a large troop, heavier than the fattest ox, and we brought to the wagon a goodly supply of meat— enough to last me to Natal—but I expect these hungry blacks will see the end of it in a week, at farthest. All this time we have had sufficient water for ourselves, being well supplied with utensils—an auker which holds nine gallons, a large water-vat, an immense ox-horn, three or four calabashes, and half a dozen giraffe bladders ; besides which the Kaffirs carry the paunch of a goat, buck, or sheep, and cook and eat the bag when the water is done.

Pet Jacobs, an old elephant hunter, and a good fellow
in every way, was here where I am now standing a
fortnight ago, when the lions killed two of his horses,
and the other two, in their fright, galloped away.   I
do not know whether he has found them again. This
is a heavy loss to him, as they were all salted horses,
and worth at least 200*l.*, and the poor fellow has
been obliged to turn back.

August 2nd.—I think this is the right date, but I
have quite lost my reckoning, and it may or may not
be so.

We left Caballa yesterday, my twenty head of
cattle having drunk all dry, and not got enough,
poor things ; and we treked on to Letloche, where,
three months ago, I enjoyed a swim in at least nine
feet of water, but now it is only one deep mud-hole,
with a little drop of water trickling through.   We
made a drain from the spring through the mud to
the only practicable place for the oxen to drink, and,
seeing lots of quagga-spoor, I stuck a white flag on a
staff into the mud to scare them away, if they came.
It had not, however, the desired effect, as the brutes
came and drank more than half the water that had
run into our reservoir.   I was vexed with myself
that I did not sleep among the rocks and shoot them,
but I am too unwell to risk sleeping out in the open
air, and I was dead knocked up with a two hours'
chase after a troop of giraffes.   I broke the leg of
a fine heifer at the second shot, but wishing to lay
in a good stock of meat, as I knew it was my last

chance, I did not stop, but re-loaded at the gallop, thinking that my after-rider was sure to find her. After a long, stern chase, I again came up with the troop, and shot a cow above the tail, and never in all my experience did I see anything go like her. At the occasional glimpses I got of her through the trees I saw she was bathed in blood, but she kept on, and I could not gain an inch on her. At last, horse and man being utterly exhausted, I tumbled off, gave her a long shot in a clear, open place, and missed her. She had led me directly from the wagon into the mountains, among the klips, boulders, and stones—ground that giraffes, when hard pressed, always make for, as they have great advantage over a horse on such ground. Leading my horse round, I turned to take a last look at her, when, to my astonishment, she was standing; I re-mounted, mustered a canter, by dint of great persuasion, and, on nearing her, she again went away at her long, awkward, swinging gallop; but this was her last effort, she could only hold on about 100 yards, and then stood, and I saw she was mine—so I rode alongside, letting her walk along to a shady tree, where I dropped her dead with a bullet through the heart. My after-rider was thrown out entirely, and never saw anything of my first broken-legged one, and, there being no water, we could not stop to go on the spoor, and I lost her.

I am now outspanned in a valley, my people digging at a sand-hole in hopes that water will rise by morning. The little there was in the hole we transferred most carefully to the anker. I hope to get to the Bamangwato State to-morrow. I hear Sechele is there, having just returned from Mosil-ikatse ; the latter gave him, I am told, forty oxen, forty sheep, forty goats, and lots of ivory.

6th. — I found Sechele, as I expected, at the Bamangwato State ; and, instead of receiving thanks from him for the safe convoy of his daughter, he merely pointed to her and said, ' That is my child, whom an Englishman, your countryman, has thrown away. I thought the English were my friends ; but now I see they are just the same as the Boers, and wish to make me dead ; and as they have treated me so will I treat them.' He told me that I must pay his man, whom I had engaged for two heifers, there and then ; and that, as I had no heifers, I must give him two bags of powder and two bars of lead, and do it at once, as he was going to inspan and trek to his State. I did so ; and then he ordered his people to drive my horse Fleur to his horses, and he should take him also, and let me see the way the Bechuanas acted when they were wronged. I could do nothing but submit, which I did, with a very bad grace. My driver and his driver told me that the moment Sechele was gone the Mangwatos would unload my wagon and take everything, as I had gone through Machin's country without first asking his leave ; and they begged me to inspan and go with Sechele. The road I had intended to

go was stopped, in consequence of the Saltpansberg
Boers having taken the guns from four of Sechele's hunters, and beaten them about the head.
Sechele told me I must not go that road, or his
people would assuredly kill me, taking me for a
Boer, as they do not venture to the wagon in the
daytime, but murder you in your sleep.   In this
pleasant state of things, therefore, with the certainty
of being robbed of everything if I stopped, and
murdered if I went Notowani's road, I was obliged
to take advantage of Sechele's escort.   I found that
all these rows are owing to the war going on between
Moshesh and the Free State Boers.   Mahura — a
powerful chief near Kuruman, on this side the Vaal
River — the Bastards, Griquas, Corannas, Bakatlas,
and a number of other tribes, have, I hear, all joined
Moshesh's standard ; and the latter sent messengers
to Sechele and the Bamangwatos for their assistance
in driving out the Boers, of whom they have already
killed eighty.   Sechele tells me he has sworn solemnly
before God that he will fight no more unless he is
first attacked, and therefore refuses help.   I hear
that Scoonman's men (Boers), in the Saltpansberg
district, surrounded a Kaffir State on the top of a
mountain, inaccessible, or thought by the natives to
be so, from all but one side, which was strongly
barricaded and guarded, and scaled it at night by
the help of rheims.   The Kaffirs in the morning
were panic-stricken, on seeing the Boers on the top
of the berg, and great numbers threw themselves

off. The Boers then slaughtered 1,000 men, 30 women, and 10 children, without meeting any resistance.

But to return to myself and Sechele. For two days I took no notice of him, outspanning far off, and avoiding him on every occasion. The third day he came to the wagon. I did not salute him in any way, or offer him a seat, or take any notice, but maintained a dignified silence ; and he asked me what my thoughts were. I told him I had thought he was my friend, and for friendship's sake I had brought his daughter out of the desert, and treated her in every respect as I would my sister ; and, instead of receiving his thanks, he had taken my horse, and left me and my people to die of hunger in the desert ; that one of my people had already left me on that account ; and I asked him whether this was acting a friendly part. After a long rigmarole about his reasons for taking the horse, he said that, as I took it so much to heart, if I gave him a gun instead, he would return the horse.

His ground for claiming the horse was this : When I asked him on the road for two people to go with me, he asked a horse in payment; but I would not listen to such an exorbitant demand, and told him so, and then he said he hoped God would take care of me, as I was determined to go without people. Our roads separated ; and the following day a Bechuana came to my wagon, and I engaged him for two heifers. However, though Sechele's claim was unjust, I was

in his power; so, after wrangling, and arguing the
point, till the interpreter left us to fight our own
battle, ultimately I had to give him old Burrow
(worth 10*l.*) instead of my nag (worth 30*l.*). I congratulated myself on getting off on these terms, as, I
must confess, I did not expect ever to cross Fleur
again. The Bamangwatos followed my wagon a
long way, saying I must not go away — Machin was
coming to trade with me, and wanted also to see
me; and at last they said, if I did not stop, I should
never more come in the country again; the path
was stopped for me, and they would trade nothing,
but take what I had from me. I was more than
half inclined to stop; but my driver, who knows
the Kaffirs well, was very anxious to push on and
join Sechele's wagons, which were a little ahead;
and I had received such ominous warnings from
Puller and other Bechuanas, who lent a hand to
inspan, and were evidently most anxious to get me
away, that I let Raffler have his own way, and get
away from the State as fast as I could. Sechele
told me he was my friend, and the friend of all the
English; and if the Mangwatos had taken all my
goods and chattels, he would have turned back and
demanded restoration; and if they had refused, he
would have gone to war; but I did not know how
much of this to believe. From the fact of his mentioning the thing at all, I am led to think that the
Mangwatos had some such intention, which I should
not have believed, had he said nothing about it.

Puller told me that he overheard them saying what they would do when Sechele had gone; but I am always slow to believe such stories, as I have been among the Kaffirs of every tribe and nation for the last seven years, and have never been actually molested by them.

Lopèpès Vley. — Last night the lions paid us a visit, frightening Sechele's oxen out of the kraal, and killing two within ten yards of one another, but a good way off from the wagons. I and twenty Bechuanas, all with guns, had a long unsuccessful hunt after them this morning, following the spoor to within forty yards of some very dense reeds; and I feel sure they are safely housed there now. Sechele and his men fired two volleys among the reeds; but I told him it was only powder and lead thrown away. I bought about 100 lbs. of ivory from Sechele, on pretty good terms, as I can make about 200 per cent. profit on it. This will help to pay my losses, or his exorbitant demands. We intend to remain here three days, to refresh the oxen, as the road from here is very heavy, and we shall find no water for three days.

8th (Sunday). — I am now all anxiety to get to Sechele's State, hearing that the German missionaries, who went down for their wives, and by whom I sent two letters, have returned, and I am longing to receive a batch of home news. It is now eighteen months since I heard a word, even indirectly, from my friends. As soon as I reach Kapong, four hard, heavy days ahead, I shall leave the wagon, and ride on, as I can no longer control my impatience.

Sechele makes a great show of being very religious, saying a long grace before and after meat on every occasion ; and he has been holding forth to his people and singing half the day. He will not allow a shot to be fired or any work to be done, and certainly sets a most praiseworthy example himself. He is most anxious to get home, but will not travel on Sunday on any account. I cannot tell whether he is sincere, or only does so through fear of Moffat, a Scotch missionary, who has all the Kaffirs under his finger and thumb, and can do just what he likes with them. He has been living very long amongst them, educates the different chiefs' children, and has thoroughly gained their confidence.

11th. — On the 9th, the hind axle of Sechele's wagon broke, but luckily not till we got to Batlanarmi, where there was a little water at the bottom of two deep holes, which we got at by means of a ladder formed of a tree with several branches. We lowered in the tree, on every branch of which was a Masara, who handed up the water in a large iron can, and we cut a drain running into a sort of dam, and by this means most of our oxen got a small portion ; we brought them two at a time, and my poor oxen had to go without till the following morning, as it was owing to Sechele's forethought that there was any water at all. He had despatched messengers to the Masaras three days previously, to open and clean out the pits. He came to me, saying he was as ignorant as a stone what to do about the wagon, that I must repair it for him, and prove if I was really his friend. It was no use my telling him I could not, for the Kaffirs believe all white men can do anything. I therefore made the best of it, cut down a branch of a camel thorn-tree; and having a saw, axe, adze, and augurs, put a bold face on the matter, and put in a false axle, which will run to the State at all events. A man never knows what he can do till he is tried. When I left England, if a man had brought me a broken-down wagon to put a new axletree in, I should as soon have thought of flying as making the attempt. Sechele looked on the whole time, and proposed the most ridiculous plans of making the axle secure. Amongst others, he hit upon what he and his people were unanimous in considering an excellent one, and they were highly displeased I would not act upon their suggestion: this was, to screw the augur through the false axle deep into the old one, and there let it remain.

We have just had a very narrow escape of being burnt up; our road lay through thick mapani trees, with tall white grass, thick and dry as a deal board, on each side. Some one had set the grass on fire in fifty places behind us and below the wind. A stiff breeze was bringing it to us at a tremendous pace, and we were enveloped in dense smoke. I saw at length, some distance away, the red flames

breaking through, and soon heard the roaring and
crashing of the fire. There was an opening in
the bush 200 yards ahead, and I slipped a box of
matches in my pocket, and ran for my life there,
setting fire to the grass in a dozen places under the

wind, which instantly roared and tore away magni-
ficently; and the wagons, whipping on through the
smoke, had only just reached my friendly burn,
when the fierce flames came tearing up, crossed the
road instantly and burnt themselves out at the tail
of the wagons, for want of fuel. The ground, however, was so hot that I burnt the soles of my shoes
badly, and the poor oxen in the yoke kept shifting
their feet incessantly. Meantime, we were all working like demons, throwing sand on the hot embers

to enable the poor oxen to stand. It was a critical moment, and I don't know when I have felt so nervous as I did then; for, in case anything had taken fire, we had hardly a drop of water to extinguish it.

The road is frightfully heavy, and this is the third day that most of my oxen have not tasted water; only eight got any at Batlanarmi; and though we treked most of last night, in spite of the darkness, I do not expect to reach any until to-morrow, and we must ride all night to-night. Mutla has gone mad, from sun and thirst together, and run away into the bush. Matakit brought him back, struggling frantically, and I have been obliged to make him fast. I hope it is only a sun stroke, and he will come round, his poor head being half battered in in a dozen places by savage, barbarous treatment. I suppose his brains have only a slight covering of skull, and Kaffirs wear no hats or covering for their heads. I have been obliged to load up, for the second time, Sechele's daughter, child, goods and chattels, and half an eland bull killed yesterday. We left Sechele's other wagon behind last night, a perfect wreck; every spoke is out of one wheel, and past my skill to repair. He never asked me to try, his good sense telling him that it was all but an impossibility.

14th.—*Sechele's State.*—We arrived here yesterday; found a large arrival of German missionaries from Natal, no less than six; they are active, energetic fellows, all tradesmen and good workmen, and have in the space of six weeks, with wretched materials to work on, built themselves not only a good substantial house with five large rooms, but really a tasteful, elegant building, with a wide verandah on three sides. They are clever, learned, well-informed men also, and pass every spare moment in hard study, in acquiring the Bechuana language, which is no easy task, as they have only the New Testament, translated by Moffat, to assist them. They are happy, hospitable fellows, and make most excellent colonists, being able to turn their hands to anything in the world. I found two letters awaiting me from Natal, but none from England, so that I must curb my impatience a little longer.

Bad news from Merico; two more of my horses are dead, which I thought were salted, and had sold with a guarantee for 22*l*. 10*s*. each, which I must now refund. I have not heard the fate of two more I left behind, also sold guaranteed. The Kaffirs tell me that the war with Moshesh is over, the Boers having made peace. According to their version, Moshesh had by far the best of it; and I hear Mahura and Pretorius had a little target practice at one another for a few hours, when the Boers retired worsted, but they will tell a very different tale.

18th. — *Hasfowl Kop*, or *Vulture Head.* — Left Sechele's on Monday, the 15th, he presenting me with three panther skins, a mean present after all his promises and all that I had given him ; but it is the character of the Kaffirs to get as much as

possible from you, and give as little as they can in
return.   My new false axle ran well to the State,
over a frightfully stony road, with a heavy freight.
I have shot nothing ; two hard unsuccessful days,
and my people are very hungry.   To-day, by
way of change, I came across a hole in the bed of
a river, with only about two and a half feet deep
of mud and water in it; but it was crowded with
barbel.   My fellows went in and speared fifteen
in five minutes, averaging each from 2 lbs. to 3 lbs.
weight, and some 4 lbs. or 5 lbs. ; but they were not
in good condition, and their flesh was soft.   However, we ate them with great gusto ; if so minded,
we could have killed at least a hundred.

A honey-bird took my Masara to-day almost into
a lion's mouth ; he was within five yards ere he saw
him crouched down ready to spring.   According
to his own statement, he showed good presence of
mind, shouting at once to the lion to ' look there —
look there !' pointing in an opposite direction, upon
which the lion stood up and did as he was com-
manded, when the Masara made an expeditious retreat.   Living the life the Kaffirs do, entirely in the
open air from their infancy, and never having a hut
of any sort or description, such occasional encounters,
I fancy, are not unfrequent.   I have been but very
poorly the last three or four days.   I am totally
prostrated in strength, unfit for anything, the least
exertion bringing on profuse perspiration, and I am
suffering much from indigestion.   I fear I shall not

shake off the effects of this last attack till I can enjoy a few swims in the lovely bay of Natal.

23rd. — Merico Country. — I arrived here on Friday night, and found all the Boers in Laagaar, with all their beasts, sheep, goats, horses, dogs, ducks, geese, fowls, pigeons, monkeys, cats, calves, and children without number. There is hardly a blade of grass to be seen in any direction — a pretty state of things for my jaded hungry oxen. I therefore lost no time in seeking a better neighbourhood, and Dederick Knitse allowed my oxen to run on his farm, which is about an hour on horseback from the Laagaar; and here I now am, and intend to remain for eight or ten days to recruit my oxen a little, and repair the old wagon, which has held together so far marvellously. More bad news: my other two horses were also dead, and I must refund 150 dollars (11*l.* 5*s.*), which is not easily done. I find everything uncommonly scarce and dear, almost a famine in the land; meal, mealies, slaughter oxen or cows, and milch cows, are not to be had for money; consequently, my Kaffirs have a hard time of it; game there is none; and I spent yesterday (Sunday) in the Laagaar. The men are wearied to death from ennui, and pass their time in round loping, drinking brandy and coffee to a frightful amount, swearing and quarreling. One day amongst men of my own colour, although I had been five months without seeing a white man, was quite enough for me; but little real good feeling exists between an Englishman and the Transvaal Boers, and still less their fraus, who are very bitter against the English. However, there are some good fellows ; and I must say that one and all have shown me the greatest hospitality, notwithstanding the scarcity of the times. An Irishman has just been informed against by one of his own country-men for selling powder, guns, and lead to the Kaffirs, which is the greatest crime a man can be guilty of, in a Dutchman's eyes. It seems the two Patlanders, to keep their hands in, I suppose, had had a scrimmage on the path, and the worsted one had taken this mean revenge of informing against the other.

I brought over the field-cornet this morning to inspect my wagon, and see that the number of guns tallied with what I took in. After asking many inqui-sitive questions, and rigorously cross-examining my Kaffirs and Hottentots, he is satisfied, and has given me a pass to Pretorius, certifying that all is correct.

31st. — I am now on my way to Mooi River Dorp, where I intend again to rest my oxen for a few days, ere setting out for Natal ; but I have managed, by swopping and buying, to get nine fresh ones, which will wonderfully assist my worn-out span.

Two bucks' heads that I prized very highly (harrisbuck and roan antelope), which I shot last year in Mosilikatse's country, and left in charge of a Boer, have disappeared. He tells me the wolves went into the house and took them away, and his story is corroborated by another Boer ; but I have strong suspicions it was two-legged wolves.

The scarcity here is so great that there are hundreds of Kaffirs who must die of hunger ere this year's corn is fit for harvest. The poor creatures would only be too glad to work for their food, but they cannot obtain it, as every Boer has on his place as many as he can possibly provide for.

CHAPTER VIII.

1859.

SICOMO'S — MASARAS — LAKE NGAMI — LOPEPE — RETURN BY
VAAL RIVER — ANECDOTES OF CROSSING THE TUGELA.

MAY 15*th*, 1859.—I pass over the last eight months
of my life, during which I have been down to Natal,
and completely fitted myself out for another hunt in
the far interior. I am now outspanned near Sechele's
—three wagons, forty-seven oxen, five cows, five
calves, eight horses, six dogs, thirteen servants (Hottentots, Kaffirs, and Bastards), and two companions.
I am now ten weeks from Natal, and, so far, everything has gone favourably, and looks well and
healthy. Two oxen have been lost through the
Kaffirs' carelessness, and six good horses have fallen
victims to the South African scourge, inflammation
in the lungs ; a few dogs have been run over and
killed, the wagons upset a couple of times or so,
and a few minor casualties, the natural concomitants of wagon-travelling, have happened, which I
pass over without more comment. The game has
been scarce, and unusually wild and shy on the
trek ; and the gunpowder not very straight ; and

the natural consequence is, that very little has, as yet, fallen to our rifles. We have always thus far, however, had a sufficiency of animal food to supply our own wants, and those of our four-footed companions. The grass is good, and yet, with but little work, the nags are in very low condition.

I left sixteen oxen behind yesterday, in charge of Cos Lindsey, Sechele's brother. I was well treated by that chief, and he not only threw no obstacle in my way, but he offered me any assistance in his power. I brought him up from Natal a large iron bedstead, with mattress and pillows, as a present; and all looks favourable for a good hunt. The Boers treated me well also, but tried to deter me from going in by false representations, rumours of war with Mosilikatse, Machin, &c., and saying it was unsafe to think of venturing in; but the missionaries at Sechele's say I have nothing to fear, and that it was only a ruse of the Boers, to endeavour to dissuade me from penetrating farther. My outfit has been a very expensive one, but this year all my appointments are good, and worth any day what I gave for them. The outlay altogether is very heavy, owing to the distance of the elephants, the size of our party (sixteen, all of whom I have to feed), and the presents I have to make on the road. But I fully expect to make a good return on my outlay, if the horses will only be so obliging as to live for a few months. A friend of mine has lost both his horses, and no amount of money can replace them here. I

have sold an old screw to Sechele for nine very large
powerful trek-oxen, worth 50*l.*   We have charming
weather, good food, plenty of exercise and employ-
ment, lots of change of scene, and are all in rude
health. We had a delightful rain two days ago, which
freshened up everything ; and although to-morrow
night we must bid adieu to water for two whole
days and nights, travelling three parts of the time,
still I do not anticipate any great hardship for the
oxen, as the country is good, the weather cool, and
the wagons not very heavy. To-morrow (Monday) I
hope to get a giraffe or an eland, and lay in a good
stock of flesh before reaching the thirst-land, as we
cannot work the horses there, on account of the
want of water.

The wagons are, to all appearance, as good as the
day they left Natal, and I have put a new buik-plank
and lear-booms on my old one, and freighted her
with meal and mealies for the horses and Kaffirs, and
she will, I think, hold for another journey. The far-
famed Kleinboy, of Gordon Cumming renown, forms
one of my retinue.   He is a most amusing dog,
though incorrigibly lazy ; of no use, except as an
after-rider, though he talks largely of his hunting
exploits, and wants me to pay him so much for
an elephant's head, instead of by the month, which I
have agreed to do.   I have another old Bastard —
Raffeta — a really good elephant-hunter, I believe.
My old Kaffirs, Matakitakit and Inyous, and Fanga
also, are still with me, and I value them highly, and

can trust them entirely. Ingunya, alias Mickey, a
sad lazy, independent dog; Sconyan, a refugee, a
worthless, quarrelsome hound; and Incomo, a really
good, useful, handy fellow, who followed my fortunes
from the Lake last year, compose my lot of Kaffirs.
Old Tebè, a horse-tenter, a willing, trustworthy old
slave, joined forces yesterday; and Dirk Raffler, an
excellent driver, but otherwise utterly useless. Alington and Woodcock each have a slave: these, with a
couple of hangers-on, who do nothing, compose our
troop of attendants.

27th. — Sicomo's State. — Nothing particular to
record, with the exception of the death of three
horses — Mowba, Klinkfoot, and Little Fanny. I
grieved much for the last; she was never beaten
in Natal at any pace, and her last exploit, the day
before her death, was being in at the death of a
fine cow gemsbok, or oryx, the fastest antelope in
the country. We have bagged three giraffes, two
gemsbok, three elands, and a fair lot of roybuck,
since leaving Sechele's, where the lung-sickness broke
out amongst my oxen. I immediately shot the first
one which fell sick, and inoculated all the rest, and
we have had no more deaths at present.

I have made Sicomo some presents, and expect
him down at the wagons immediately. He throws
no difficulty whatever in my path, is much pleased
that I came to see him, and says he will be my
friend, and render me every assistance. I had hoped
to get a horse from him, but am disappointed in this

respect. The Bamangwatos are great beggars, and ask for everything for nothing, and have as yet brought nothing down to trade, which does not suit my book at all.

We got through the thirst-land admirably, the weather being pleasantly cool. We made good play at nights. I never felt the want of water so little. The Masaras took us a good deal out of our way, and excited our hopes by saying that a large troop of elephants drank every night at a fountain not far distant. We bent our way there, and saw only old spoor; they had left with the last rains.

My stud is now reduced to three — a woful falling off. I left Natal with seven, and purchased, at tremendous prices, four in Mooi River Dorp, three of which I still have, and the fourth I have sold. All my Natal nags are dead; one ox is dead, and two are lost. These are at present the extent of my losses, with the exception of two sheep; but I have shot or traded nothing, so far, that will help to compensate me for them.

We are all still in good health, but very anxious to get among the elephants, as the season is getting on fast. I have preserved the gemsbok heads, and they are now drying in the sun on the top of the wagon. They are good specimens of a rare and handsome antelope, fleet as the wind, enduring as the giraffe, and shy as the ostrich.

It is intensely hot to-day, and my writing-desk is a

cask of wine, standing on its end. It is harvest-time here, and the gorge is alive with women going and returning with heavy baskets of corn, millet, pumpkins, and water-melons.

June 2nd.—Letloche.—We stayed at the Bamangwato State four days and a half. Traded a little ivory, twelve karosses, fourteen sheep and goats, and a few ostrich feathers. Heard that Mosilikatse's commando was on its way to assist Machin against Sicomo, and that they were coming in two bodies. Sicomo advised us to trek away as fast as possible; that he was quite ready to receive them, and had his spies out in every direction, and. a regular patrol kept. I exchanged three cows and a calf for four oxen; one was very wild and savage, and detained us a whole day, running away, and charging furiously at everyone who attempted to turn it. I was mounted on old President (so named from having been bought from Pretorius, the President of the Transvaal and Free-State Republics), who had the heels of the brute, and avoided nimbly and well several savage charges. We ultimately got the ox tied up to the wagon-wheel, and all thrashed him, and inspanned him next morning, and he treks well.

Last night, while I was absent enjoying a delicious bathe in the fountain, the Kaffirs, in extracting some tobacco from under my cartel, managed to discharge my rifle in the wagon. The bullet went through four double-blankets, a kaross, the cartel, a double chest of tea, glanced along a pick, through a barrel

of wine, and finally lodged in the upper lear-boom of
the wagon.   The kaross is badly burned with the
powder.   The wonder to me is that the rifle did not
burst, as it was lying on the bed, and the muzzle
must have been blocked up with blankets.

To-day we had a difference of opinion as to the
road to take ; my Hottentots all wanted to go
towards the Lake, but the Kaffirs were frightened to
death at the thoughts of going to Mosilikatse.
Incomo has gone back again, and has given me
his heifer for some beads and copper ; he has been a
real good Kaffir to me, and I paid him well.

I took the middle line bearing towards Sebituane's,
or rather Sekeletu's ; the Hottentots sulked considerably, but made no decided objection. I hear another
commando of Mosilikatse's is coming in in the direction I am now going. I would rather not meet them,
though I do not think they would molest me, but all
my people would bolt.   The horses that are left are
fresh and well ; game is very scarce ; lots of rain has
fallen, there is plenty of water, and the grass still
green, plentiful, and nutritious.   The oxen are in
good working order, pull together admirably, and
stick at nothing.

12th (Sunday). — The poor oxen have had a very
hard time of it the last ten days, through heavy
sand and bush, without any running water ; the
little water we have been able to get for them has
been ladled out of wells and poured into limestone
basins ; and on one occasion we had to draw every

drop of water from an extraordinary natural well, some thirty-five feet down to the water. Since leaving Letloche, we have got water at Nkowani and Mahaccan, a Maccalacas post, under Sicomo, Kasir chief, and at Ramaqua—green, slimy stuff. There was, however, delicious water at Massouey, a fountain pure as crystal, where we first saw the Great Salt-pan, and a magnificent piece of scenery exactly resembling the sea coast; it was difficult to imagine oneself so far in the interior. We measured a tree called Cream of Tartar, sixty-one feet round the bole; but there are many very much larger.

A troop of half-starved Maccalacas followed us, and we shot three giraffes for them. Six of them volunteered to go on to show us the waters, but they lost themselves yesterday, and took us in a regular circle; we at length got to some brackish salt stuff, near the Great Salt-pan. We left the Great Lake road some days ago, and have carved out a route for ourselves. The country is very dry here; scrubby mapani trees, and a great scarcity of game, which I attribute to the want of water, and dryness of the grass. We came to some new burns the other day, where the grass was green and sweet, and found a great variety of game, but, after missing some gemsbok, we contented ourselves with bringing two elands to the wagons. No sign as yet of elephants; they are a weary way off, to be sure, but I hope this week to make the acquaintance of one or two. I am sorry to say the people about Mangwatos were

great thieves. We miss now many things that
cannot be replaced, amongst others my bullet-ladle,
the loss of which puts me out a good deal. I have
converted an old iron spoon into a sort of ladle, and
it serves for a makeshift. The tumbler of one of my
guns is also broken, and my large nipple-screw and
small hand-vice are stolen. I hear the sickness is this
year very severe; in fact, at the Lake they think it
is going to sweep them all off the face of the earth.
I was in sad tribulation about Gyp and Juno the
other day. They lost themselves in the thirst-land,
as they remained by a wildebeest I had shot, but
they made their way by wonderful instinct back to
the wagon during the night.

I have twenty-five or twenty-six mouths to feed
every day, and the wagons get most perceptibly
lighter; the stores vanish like wild-fire. I never see my
imp of a cook but something is ' cadan ' (no more) ; it
is fearful work, and I get but little out of the ruffians
to compensate for it. We have so far had more
than a sufficiency of everything, but, owing to the
extravagance of the Hottentots, who have no thought
for the future, I foresee hard times coming, and must
take my share in the scarcity. Coffee and tea without milk or sugar, meat, mutton and game of all sorts
without bread or bread-stuff, not even rice, mealies,
or Kaffir corn, is the fare I have to look forward to,
and I cannot prevent it ; but we shall not starve
altogether as long as powder and lead hold out, and
one nag is capable of exertion. I have no thought

of returning till I have got a goodly lot of teeth together.

I am sorry now that I was induced to change my route, as Kleinboy told me Swartz lost twenty-four oxen last year, after crossing the river Guia, by a small poisonous bush, with which all the country is covered, and which the oxen eat voraciously; but whether the rascal lies or not I cannot say. We have been bearing too much to the west the last few days to please me, but, immediately on crossing this vast pan, which I hope to do in two days, I shall hold north towards the country of Sekeletu.

29th. — Since writing up the journal last, we have been coming NW. and lately NE. We were at one time all but done for want of water. We had pressed into the service a Masara woman, to show us the water, necessity having no law; and, though she stepped out in good style before the wagons for hours and hours without intermission, she at last, at the end of the third day, acknowledged she was lost. She said she only recollected to have been at the fountain once before, and that was when she was a child. She was delighted with a present of beads and a handkerchief, and last not least in her estima-tion, as much dried meat as she could stagger under. In this emergency I saddled up to try and capture another. We are obliged to go about it very cautiously; no shots fired, no whip cracking, for fear of alarming any chance straggler. When first sighted the men generally run, and the women hide

until they fancy you have seen them, when they
leave everything they may have and run as game as
a fox, doubling, turning, and twisting until our
admirably-trained horses' noses are alongside their
ears over their shoulders, when they first give in and
supplicate for their lives ; but on finding they are not
going to be hurt they generally follow readily through
fear, which, however, soon wears off on better acquaintance.   On arriving at camp they are set down
to lots of flesh, and they soon make themselves at
home, and rarely attempt running away again.   We
succeeded in getting another Masara to supply the
woman's place; he brought us somewhere near a
fountain, but having only been there once before, he
also got astray in his reckoning, and on the afternoon
of the fourth day said he was totally at a loss where
the fountain lay.   Boy and Raffcta saddled up to go in
quest : I had had a severe kick on the calf of the leg
in the morning from an ox, which disabled me from
riding or walking.   To our great joy, Boy found the
fountain very cleverly several miles farther off, and
after refreshing himself and his steed he brought us
the joyful tidings, and though it was quite dark before
we arrived, his instinct took us straight to the place.
It was impossible that the oxen could have held out
much longer ; a few were quite exhausted.   It proved
to be delicious water, and more than enough of it
for all; here we stayed three days, to refresh the oxen,
and look up Masaras or Bushmen to show us the way
to more water, being determined not to leave our

lovely fountain till we had some idea of the direction in which we were likely to find more. One morning, just before daylight, we heard a lion coming slowly to the water with his low, subdued kind of murmuring, and, ere I could get ready, Kleinboy and January, the foremost at every game, good and bad, had sneaked down with their guns to wish him good morning. They found him drinking, and missed him with three barrels, and I was just in time to see him scouring across the open. We had a long ride the following day in quest of Masaras, and at length Boy's sharp eyes spied a kraal a long way off, and we galloped our utmost to surround and cut off the retreat of the inmates, and nearly frightened to death an old man and a parcel of children ; the able-bodied men were hunting. We shot them three springbuck and two quaggas, and we found plenty of splendid water, and returned to the wagon pleased with our success, as we could not have moved without guides, and the Masaras fly like chaff before the wind from the sound of a gun, the crack of a whip, or any appearance of a white man.

I am now going to give you a short description of a day's sport amongst the elephants, which we came to at last, going hungry and very cold for two days and nights, as a sort of preliminary.

We started early to a vley to see if the elephants had drunk, and took up the spoor of the day previous. As they had not been that night, the Bushmen, eight in number, followed it beautifully until about 1 A.M., when they got on spoor only a few hours old ; the scent freshened wonderfully, and the Bushmen hunted to perfection, their captain taking the lead throughout, and being infinitely the best man I ever saw. At last, the pace increased to a run, and we took our guns from the hands of the carriers, the spoor leading us out of the bush to the open veldt. Here we had a short check. At length, the captain took up the running again at a killing pace, stopped suddenly, and pointed the elephants out to us. They almost immediately took the alarm, five cows and two calves, and crashed away. We rode between them and the bush to keep them in the open, and my horse and boys being much alarmed ; we came alongside and fired, Boy first, from a long way behind, at the largest cow, which he missed. I waited long for a favourable opportunity, and at about forty yards off, as they stopped and turned, wanting to make the bush, I bagged a brace of cows right and left, both falling to the shot like rabbits. One fell stone dead ; the other, with her shoulder smashed, got up, went about fifty yards, and died. Seeing she was mine, I left her, and dropped a third dead with the first bullet. Alington shot one dead also between the ear and eye, and they lay touching one another ; the last, a small worthless cow, took half a dozen bullets to give her her quietus. Seeing spoor of much larger elephants, Boy and Raffeta followed it, and I soon heard firing in their direction. I galloped off, heard a crack in the mapani trees, and saw two cows and a large bull,

and a great cow without teeth, keeping always
outside, carrying her head high, and as wicked and
savage as she could well be. The bush was very
good, a moderate breeze of wind, which I kept always
below, but I had great difficulty in getting the bull out
from the company of the 'carl kop' (naked head).
At last I went right at him, shouting lustily, and he
bore away by himself, and I shot him dead in two
bullets, both in the right place, at very short distances. I heard Raffeta close at hand hallooing for
help; he had a large cow at bay, and his bullet was
fast. I disabled her the first shot, breaking her
shoulder-blade. Boy still kept firing, and at length
he made his appearance with a bull's tail in his belt.
Thus we bagged eight in about half an hour. A few
clumps of giraffe, a troop of tsessebe or buffalo,
or a white rhinoceros occasionally crossing our path,
with a small lot of gemsbok and a few quaggas, we
did not deem worthy of notice. After losing ourselves, and a very unpleasant ride in the hack-thorns
in the dark, tearing ourselves considerably, we got
back to the wagons again after midnight. Alington
unfortunately burst his gun, lost his hat, pocket-
handkerchief, and ramrod; Raffeta also lost his hat,
but it was very exciting work.

I hear that Swartz is only two days from here,
and that there are a lot of Mosilikatse's Kaffirs with
him, to prevent his hunting in Mosilikatse's country.
Perhaps he will serve me the same. I am anxious
to be off, and am only waiting for the teeth, which

I expect to-night, having despatched yesterday about two dozen Kaffirs with axes to cut them out. Elephants are very scarce this year, and bad to find, or else I doubt not but we should give a pretty good account of them; my oxen are still fresh and well, only poor old Freeman must be left behind to die, as he is utterly exhausted from age and poor condition. All the party are in good health and spirits, and looking forward to having good sport about the Guia river.

July 3rd.—We have heard so many contradictory reports lately that I have been quite at a loss what to do. The Masaras say that Swartz's wagons, and two others just arrived, are in charge of Mosilikatse's people, who will not give them leave to hunt at any price; and he is only waiting for the first rains to send them back to Merico. What foundation there is for these reports I cannot say, but it is certain that there are very few elephants here this year, and I have resolved to go in search of them elsewhere, and began to retrace my spoor yesterday, after having ridden to every vley and ascertained that the elephants had changed their quarters. The want of water presents an insuperable barrier to our further progress due north. The bush is also very thick, and the sand-hills very heavy. I am now going due west for two or three days, where the Masaras tell me that we shall fall in with more salt pans and large vleys of water where elephants drink, and there is a chance of getting, at all events, one battue at them.

I have been rewarded for the great precautions I took to get well-seasoned wood for my wagons in Natal, for they hold together admirably. The wagons built at Natal are not usually considered good, as the climate there is so moist that wood never becomes thoroughly seasoned, and in the dry air of the interior they are very apt to fall to pieces ; even an old sea-soned gun-stock will shrink, and the fittings become too large. A whole troop of Maccalacas, and who are now loaded to the ground with meat, intend taking themselves back to-morrow, and have been endea-vouring to persuade the Masaras not to show us any more water. The latter are starving with hunger, and are only too glad of the chance of going with us, so that good comes out of evil. I watched by the fountain last night to try and shoot a rhinoceros for them, but it was so intensely cold I could not endure it. Several hyenas came very close, and looked in at me within six or seven yards. I was sorely tempted to shoot, and should have done so, but my gun was in the holster. A lot of quaggas and zebras came from below wind and galloped off, much alarmed ; the old patriarch, however, was not so easily fright-ened, and came to make himself sure of the danger, when I put a bullet through him at about sixty yards, killing him on the spot. I then made for the wagons as fast as legs could carry me, fairly starved out. The Masaras went down to keep off the wolves, jackals, and hyenas, taking plenty of fire with them. This morning I had the mortification to hear that two white rhinoceros came immediately after I had left.

Not being able to take the latitude and longitude, I do not know where we are, but, judging from the inquiries I have made as to the distance from other places, I should say we were about 19° S. and 25° E.

9th.—No elephants yet. The Masaras will not tell us where to find them, or show us the water, or anything, having been threatened by Sicomo, their master, with death if they give the least assistance to any hunters. We are now outspanned by a stone fountain, and have had a regular morning's quarrying with picks and heavy stones, hurled with all our might to break up the rocks under which the spring is, and we have succeeded so well that I think most of the oxen will be able to get a little, which will be of inestimable service to them, as the country is very heavy, and the grass dry; we have a long day's trek without a drop before us, and the weather in the day-time is intensely hot.

Denny, a remarkably fine mare, has fallen into a hopo or pit-fall of the Kaffirs, and got staked. We got her out immediately, extracted the stake, and I sewed up the wound, made and buckled a circingle very tightly round the body, and kept up a constant fomentation to reduce the inflammation, all to no purpose; she died in great agony a few hours afterwards; her groans, poor thing, were heartrending. I gave 45 guineas for her two months ago; but, luckily thinking her too big, exchanged her with Alington for the hunt, so that, though the loss ultimately falls on me, it has not inconvenienced me much, for the present. The country is almost devoid of game of any value, zebras and blue wildebeests being the only varieties. I shot an old bull giraffe three days ago, about the last of his race in these parts.

Kleinboy and old Tebè each found a tooth yesterday near an old Kaffir State, where we outspanned; one in a tree, the other buried. The former is a very fine one, about 70 lbs. or more, and in excellent preservation, having only been killed very lately. We have come to some Masaras to-day, who, though old in years, never saw sheep before, and expressed great wonder at their tameness; one old woman followed them about for more than an hour. There is not one of my party, unfortunately, who can understand them, so that we can glean no intelligence or information of them. We have two Masaras who have undertaken to show us elephants for a consideration, which is to be forthcoming when their part of the agreement is fulfilled, and we are now on our way to the vley at which they say they drink, and were never yet hunted; but now I am in fear and tribulation of falling in with the tsetse, which will kill all our horses and oxen, and leave us in a pretty fix.

17th.—It may be the 24th for what I know, but it is Sunday; our timekeeper, Woodcock, is asleep, having been watching by the fountain all night with the utmost patience, but nothing came except wolves, and quaggas, and Masaras. All is as usual, but we have been fortunate enough to find elephants once more, and, considering the fearful hack-thorn bush

Y

in which we found them, and a mistake in not having the dogs fast, we gave a pretty fair account of them — three bulls, mine a very large one, with teeth at least 70 lbs. each. We treked three days to the fountain at which they were said to drink, outspanned below the wind, at least 1,000 yards off, and kept all quiet, and to our joy they came, and we heard them screaming and drinking for a long time.

We had a hasty cup of coffee at daybreak, and took the spoor from the water and followed it for about three hours through dense hack-thorns. The ground was very hard, and the spoorers were often thrown out. At last, I heard old Gyp far ahead, fighting with one. We took our guns from the Masaras and made the best of our way thither. Gyp brought him right back to the men on foot, and they gave him four barrels as he went broadside past; I then got alongside and gave him two good shots, both vital, when he stood at bay and we finished him with a volley. I then heard another shot ahead, and made what speed I could in that direction, when I shortly came on a fine old bull, with long heavy teeth, coming from the shot. I struck him just behind the shoulder, when he immediately charged at a tremendous pace. I had to ride hard always below wind, and seek the best path I could, and very small time was allowed me for consideration. He kept up the chase fully 500 yards. I rode in a half circle, and at length he stopped suddenly, greatly to my satisfaction, and immediately

crashed through the thickest of the bush in an opposite direction. Fearful of losing him, I dashed
after him, though I had no time to reload. When
he found this was the case, he turned, elevating his
enormous fanlike ears, and I expected every moment
another desperate charge, as I was not more than
thirty-five yards from him. My horse behaved well,
and I reloaded, when he again made off. I followed,
and gave him two more good shots ; I would not fire
till he gave me a good chance, and I saw he was
mine, as the blood flowed from his trunk,· and all
charging was taken out of him ; still it took me some
nine more bullets to finish him. Alington came up
shortly and helped me. Raffeta killed a young bull
in six shots. Boy never saw one at all, and was in a
great taking about the dogs not having been made
fast, as he said, 'Who knows what beautiful teeth they
drove away ?' I shot a fine cow roan antelope the
other night, watching a fountain — a most agreeable
surprise, as in the uncertain light I took it to be a
blue wildebeest. We are within a few hours of the
river Tamalakarni, which runs from Sebituane's into
the Zouga, two days east of the Great Lake, and I
think we are at about an equal distance from the Lake
and from Sebituane's, somewhere about Mababe. I
hear ·that farther on, at Tamalakarni, we shall find
leches and nakong, the only buck in Africa I have not
shot, and whose acquaintance I long to make.

19th.—Our poor horses had the saddles on their
backs the whole of yesterday, from before sunrise

till sunset. We rode a weary way, and I had given
up all hopes of elephants, when January hit off
the fresh spoor of two old bulls in the middle of
very dense bush, followed it up fast and well, and
in ten minutes he gave signs that he saw them. I
made all speed towards him, when I saw a large bull
standing under a tree with ears erected ; just then a
Kaffir gave him a shot, grazing his trunk, and, as he
turned to make off, I was ready, and gave him an excellent shot through the lungs. He bore away very
fast, and the bush was so thick that it was as much
as I could do to keep him in sight ; he had gone
about 400 yards, when he stood, just as I was about
to fire again. I perceived him staggering, and my
second bullet took him in the very act of falling.
His teeth were very good, 70 lbs. each. The rest of
the party rode hard, but never saw his companion,
though we found his spoor shortly after, but he got
away free. I wanted to reach the river, but the Masaras said it was too far, and they should die of thirst
before they came there, and so, very unwillingly, we
rode back to the wagons, as we had our blankets,
salt, and all prepared for our bivouacking.

22nd.—I am all alone at the wagon, the rest of
the party being dispersed in every direction, some
trying to get and hold the spoor of my horse, Beadsman, which has strayed away with a brute of
Sicomo's, and has not since been heard of; some
seeking elephant spoor ; three are gone to draw
water some ten miles in a sledge which I made

yesterday, as the elephants stand so far off
from the water that it is impossible to get back
the same day, and the want of water plays more
mischief with the horses than several days under the
saddle. I have therefore come on with one wagon
ten miles nearer to their standing-place, and left the
other two, and all the oxen, at the old place near the
stone fountain. It is now the depth of winter, and
the grass is as dry as old tinder, without the slightest
nourishment in it. As a natural consequence, the oxen
are as lean as rakes, and, worst of all, the mealies
and Kaffir corn are finished, and no more is to be
had at any price, so that we cannot long hold out
under these circumstances. I grieve much for the
poor willing horses, thirteen or fourteen hours under
the saddle, at foot's pace, in a broiling sun three-
fourths of the time, then tied up to the wagon without
food, and stinted in their allowance of water, which
we have to draw ten miles, at least, half the way
through hack-thorns over a stony ground. These
are amongst the hardships we must undergo to get
elephants ; they are dearly paid for, and we cannot
even indulge in the luxury of a good wash, after a
fearful day's toil and dust.

We set off, a strong muster, two days ago, to hunt
part of the forest in which the elephants stand, and
had not gone 300 yards from the wagon when
January hit off the fresh spoor of an old bull,
followed it ten times better than the best blood-
hound over all kinds of country, hard and soft, lots of

open plains, and dense 'vac um bechis,' at a rattling
pace, without an instant's check, hour after hour, expecting every minute to come on him, and cantering
on to the rises, hoping to see him in the open before
us.   At length, January picked up another bull, and
they joined company, still holding right away.   At
last we saw them far ahead, two old bulls; they
almost immediately got our wind and took right
away. We should never have seen them, only, luckily,
the bush was thin.   It was a headlong race who
should get them, and Raffeta and myself had the
honour, my horse having the heels of all, very closely
followed by old President, who is the gamest old
horse I ever possessed.   We each took one, and
Alington and I slew mine quickly, and then we went
to the assistance of Raffeta and Boy, who had done
little towards giving theirs his quietus.   The horses
would not stand, and the elephant ran so hard
that we were some time in settling him.   The top of
my powder-flask came off, and the powder was all
loose in my pocket, and I loaded haphazard by
the handful of fine powder.   I gave him the final
shot, with, I should say, about twelve drachms of
powder, and down came the elephant with a desperate crash, his near shoulder-blade smashed to
atoms.   The excitement was so great that I did not
feel the gun recoil in the least, though afterwards
I found my fore finger half broken and my right
cheek covered with blood.   My bull charged constantly, and I kept galloping round in small circles,

letting him come very near when he looked inclined
to give up the chase; thus, with faint hopes of eventually catching me, he exhausted himself, and fell an
easy prey. This cannot always be done, however,
but the bush in which we got them was very light,
and well adapted for the fun. Both elephants had
very fine teeth, 250 lbs., at least, in all. Now came
the tug of war, getting back again. I lent Woodcock
my horse, and, feeling in high spirits and good condition, took to walking for eight or ten miles, when
Alington gave him a lift; the footmen were dead beat,
Raffler knocked up, and fell down dizzy and done.
Woodcock struggled on manfully to within 1,000
yards of the wagon, when Alington again lent him his
horse. January, one of Pharaoh's lean kine, was out
and out the freshest man of the party. We straggled
back by ones and twos soon after dark, but should
never have found the wagons had it not been for the
wonderful instinct of January, who is the finest hand
at a spoor I ever heard or even read of. On reaching the wagons we fired signal-shots to bring up the
stragglers.

Yesterday, when I walked to the wagons and made
the sledge, I heard seven bulls had drunk the evening
we left. We saw a troop of giraffes and a few ostriches
and elands, but there is no other game in these forests.
I saw four rhinoceros drinking at the fountain the
other night, but, fearful of disturbing any elephants,
would not shoot. We have lived on elephants' hearts
lately, which are really good, but I begin to long once

more for a fat giraffe, or some more curried guinea-fowls — a little lighter food, this warm weather, than the mighty monarchs of the forest.

31st (Sunday). — Nothing but disappointment to log up. First and foremost, we entirely mistook our whereabouts : after a hard day's trek through dense bush, at length the long wished-for river dawned on our sight ; it certainly was most refreshing and beautiful, but it proved to be the wrong one — my old friend the Zouga once more, which I foreswore last year for ever, on account of the great scarcity of game, the quantity of hunters, Kaffirs, and last, not least, the sickness. It was a sore disappointment to me, and here we have been a week. We have not been idle, however, as I have painted two wagons, which had suffered much from the drought, and Raffler has put two new axletrees into the old one, and we have had a busy time of it.

I never saw anything like the number of pheasants here ; thirty brace would be a bad day's sport for one gun, but our shot will not allow of more than enough for our daily wants. The wolves and tigers have been annoying us, the former eating up neck-straps and the oxen's gear. Last night, hearing tigers, I set a gun for them within fifty yards of the fire, and had only just supped when bang it went. I ordered the dogs to be loosed, and we had a most exciting chase in the dark, the Kaffirs carrying lighted sticks, and setting fire to the grass as we went on. Gyp, my old favourite, soon brought the brute to bay, and we hastened to her assistance, thinking it was certainly a tiger, but it turned out to be a hyena, and, with the help of torches to see by, we shot him ; his face was shattered with shot about the upper jaw, nose, and eyes. I am going to send one wagon to the Lake, as it is so near, and shall hunt along the Tamalakarni as far as Mababe, if there is any sign of elephants, and my present intention is, as soon as the rains come so as to make the road practicable, to trek across to Mosilikatse and try to obtain leave from him to hunt next year. I am now convinced his is the only country worth a man's while to come in so far.

August 5th (Friday). — On Tuesday we followed the fresh spoor of a large herd of elephants for nine good hours, and at length most reluctantly, on my part, gave them up. We had only two hours' sun left, and they still going away into thirst-land; the sun was burning, and we had not a drop of water except what the Kaffirs carried, which they drank out themselves, the last of them being dead knocked up. We had a fearful ride back again on jaded, hungry, and thirsty horses, in a bitter cold night, and we made the wagon about 10 P.M. Kleinboy brought us back straight as an arrow, and we had a little moon to help us. Since then I have been completely bewildered with the most contradictory reports ever heard, one man asserting most positively that tsetse abounded a day a-head, that it was certain death to horse, dog, and ox, to go even for a single night, and that, farther on, the Tamalarke, or rather Tamalakarni, was pure tsetse: he had come far out of his way to warn us for the last time, and now the fault must rest on our own heads. In this dilemma I had almost decided to trek back at once, as the man spoke so fairly and so freely that I believed very word.

He had hardly gone, when two Masaras came, proving conclusively that there were elephants a-head, saying that both bulls and cows had drunk that night about four hours higher up the river, that it was quite untrue about the fly, that they knew their standing-place, and that we should certainly find them not later than 1 or 2 P.M. if we started at daylight. I lost no time, inspanned one wagon, and reached the Masara State a little after dusk, and yesterday we took the spoor from the water. We were off at daylight, found them, bagged four, and one white rhinoceros, and got back to the wagons, horses all dead beat. I shot the rhinoceros through and through, a thing that I have once heard of, but never saw done before.

The same day, I fell in with another large cow without teeth, which charged me most desperately and kept up the chase for an incredible distance in the open, at a pace that on my jaded nag was anything but pleasant. I then made for the bush, but could not throw her out, or get rid of her in any way. At last, I lost all patience and gave her a bullet, which made her scream again, and turn and blow in every direction; at last, she took herself off. I was never so glad to see

the back of anything in my life, as it was very dangerous work on account of the number of holes, and the
exhausted state of poor Beadsman. Kleinboy and
I shortly after came across three more, and got very
near before they were aware, but a cow stood
between us and the only one worth shooting, and we
had a long chase ere we got a shot. My second
barrel staggered him, and in fifty yards he fell, rising
again, however, directly; but thinking Boy would
now not have much trouble with him, and Beadsman
being quite done, I left him to finish him. I heard
so many shots, that I thought he must have found
another troop, but on comparing notes at night over
our camp fire, I learned they were all at this same one,
which got away after all. So ended a fairish day's sport.

Lechulatebe sent messengers desiring me to
come up, or send him tea, coffee, sugar, powder,
lead, and a horse, saying there had been no
wagons there for a long time, and his State had
been burned down and all his stores destroyed.
I shall send to-morrow in boats what he asks for,
except the powder, and my people have instructions
to get as much out of him as possible; but he is a
niggardly dog, and is accustomed to buy things cheap
that come from Walvish Bay.

9th. — I am left all alone at the wagons, the
rest of the party having gone, some in boats and
some on foot, to Lechulatebe's, at Lake Ngami. I
have made a last effort to buy corn from him for
our poor exhausted nags, and am afraid that I shall

have but a dull time of it during their absence, as
there is no game whatever here of any sort.   I
was obliged to kill an ox last week ; and were it not
for my little pet Juno, I should often come short of
both breakfast and dinner — the only two meals we
ever indulge in.   I have just returned from a long
ramble amongst the thorns after the smaller bustard,
which we call here bush koran.   They are most delicious birds, from three to five pounds weight, and real
game in their habits.   The grass is quite white, and
so dry that it crumbles into dust in your hand, and the
ground is all cracked with the intense heat of the sun,
so that you would say there could not be a particle
of scent ; still Juno footed up three bustards to admiration to-day.   They are very difficult birds to put
up ; they run like landrails, but, Juno once on the
spoor, no dodge or device whatever avails them, turn
and twist as they like ; she never requires either
checking or encouraging, but is as near perfection as
possible. I bagged all.   These bustards will often run
more than half a mile.   I have shot large ones
weighing over fifty-four pounds ; and a medium size
also, from fifteen to thirty pounds ; geese, ducks, and
every description of water-fowl, guinea-fowls, partridges, pheasants, snipe, and dikkop—a bird about
the size and plumage of a curlew, with a short bill,
also excellent eating.   We can always get one sort or
another, so that our bill of fare presents a tolerable
variety, and anything much better than guinea-fowl,
roast or curried, and buffalo tongue, it would not be

easy to imagine. The word ' sar ' sets Juno off like
a greyhound, and she rushes headlong into the
middle of them, while I run and fire at any distance to break them. When this is accomplished, Juno
returns and stands them one after another as steady
as old Time, and I can go on killing till a Kaffir can
carry no more.

10th.— I saw a troop of old bull buffaloes in thin
hack-thorns, where there was no shelter in case of a
charge. I took a circle, however, and came at them
from below the wind, two only standing, and eight
lying; they were very bare ; I got within eighty yards,
and one bull stood well and I took a steady pot,
hearing the bullet clap beautifully, but it was
Alington's rifle, and, to judge from the report and
recoil, must have had only half a charge in. They
all tore away, and I should have given him up, had
not Juno taken the blood-spoor, and I heard her
baying him 300 or 400 yards a-head, and when I
got up he was just expiring, the bullet in the exact
place and right direction. This will save one nag a
hard day's work, as otherwise I must have gone to
shoot an eland or giraffe, for I have to support daily
eighteen hungry men. I could, had I been so
disposed, have killed four or five brace of pheasants,
thus making rather a good morning's work of it. I
have nothing to amuse myself with but a pile of
Illustrated News, the latest bearing date 1856, but
most of them 1854.

13th. — I never saw such a country as this is for

losses ; you cannot reckon on anything, and live stock
is most precarious property. I lost two valuable
oxen yesterday in pit-falls, both breaking their necks
as they were going to the river to drink; if it had
happened to a Boer, he would have taken two Masara
children in their stead, as we had told the Masaras to
open all their pit-falls and traps during our stay, and
they had neglected to do so. Old Tebè has been
fortunate enough to buy nearly two sacks of Kaffir
corn, so that in case of more elephants we shall still
get a little more work out of our used-up nags.

I went out this morning to solve a riddle which
has been puzzling me all night. Two Makubas
punted me several miles up the river last night by
moonlight, to lie in wait for a rhinoceros as he came to
drink, and, while doing so, we heard game splashing
and drinking below us ; the Makubas said it was
elephants, and we punted noiselessly and swiftly down
to them. Just as the boat glided by a fallen tree lying
in the water, I was ready, and had a snap shot at two
things as they dashed madly out. I could distinctly
see something very white about their heads, which I
took for teeth, but in point of size, speed, and all
other respects, they were much more like buffaloes.
The bush was very dense to the water's edge, and as
it was bitterly cold I took a paddle and we went
right merrily back, assisted by a strong stream. This
morning, however, I could find no signs of any blood-
spoor from last night's shot, so I took up the spoor
of buffaloes from the water some three or four miles,

and at last I saw an old bull buffalo 200 yards ahead, and crept in on him, when I saw three more, and Gyp, who had got their wind, going right on to them. I saw not an instant was to be lost, and ran towards them, when away they went a good 100 yards a-head of me. I drew up, took the outsider, and saw him instantly give to the bullet and fall into the rear, and Gyp brought him to bay in 500 yards in a nasty very open place. Now I knew I must kill him, or he would do the same good office for me; and whilst his attention was taken up with Gyp, I commenced a cautious stalk, but he saved me a good deal of unnecessary trouble by falling dead before I had gone fifty yards, the ball just below his hip, and driven right forwards through the lungs. This fellow solved the riddle: it was an old bull, without a hair on any part of his head or face, consequently, he was a blueish-white colour, as lean as an old crow, and about as good eating, I should say. I got back to a first-rate curried bustard, and feel happy and content with myself and all mankind.

Sept. 24.—*Great Namesa.*—Since logging up last, great changes have taken place in the establishment. I have been up to the Great Lake, sold one wagon, beads, copper, tea, sugar, coffee, soap, and clothes, and with the proceeds have nearly loaded up a second wagon with some splendid teeth. Two more deaths have occurred amongst the stock; the rest, notwith-standing the drought, have improved considerably in condition.

All my Kaffirs that I brought from Natal have bolted, together with two others of Alington's and Wood- cock's. The merits of the case are as follows : the road was frightfully heavy, and wagons were loaded up to the roof with Kaffir traps, utterly valueless rubbish, which it is almost impossible to get rid of, as one or other Kaffir is sure to pick it up, and stow it away somewhere snug. To remedy this, I gave them the use of a pack-ox and saddle to carry all their traps. The third day, unknown to me, the unfeeling ruffians let the poor brute graze about for half a day in a broiling sun without unloading him. I was very angry, and told one, Mick, who had nothing in the world to do (for I had too many hands), that he must carry his own things himself. The next day I found all their traps, old tents, and sacks that I had thrown away long before, stowed in the wagon, so I resolved to make a general clearance, and, being close to the river, hurled buck and sheepskins, tents, sacks, rubbish, and two of their blankets, into the river. They immediately came to me in a body and said they were going to leave me, and off they started ; and their two companions followed them after dusk, the immaculate Umlenzi, Woodcock's servant, who was supposed to be unable to do wrong, walking off with his master's double-barrelled gun. The five Totties and old Tebè stuck to me, and I am put to very little inconvenience so far : in fact, at present, it is rather a relief than otherwise to be rid of them. The weather has threatened rain, and some must have fallen in front, I think, as there is not a sign of an elephant left along the river ; and I fear we shall find no more now. Nothing but food has been shot since I last wrote—some score or more, I think. My share has been five buffaloes, an eland, two steinbuck, and a quagga.

My two little Masara boys, well matched in every way, sharp, handy little fellows, I have christened Ngami and Meercat, and, so far from having at all the character of slavery, it is an act of positive Christian charity to barter one when brought to the wagon, as they are poor little emaciated things, just getting enough roots, reeds, and unwholesome food, to keep skin and bone together. They are consequently all head and stomach, lantern-jawed, hollow-eyed, gaunt and famished, and all look prematurely old ; but the clear water of the Zouga, and wholesome diet, though it is flesh, without a change for months and months, work a miracle in their appearance. Their appetite is tremendous, and I have had to check the young dogs on two or three occasions from eating pieces of old shoe leather, worn-out rheims, and giraffe hide.

Ngami, so called after the Lake, was a present to me from Lechulatebe, the chief. I asked him what present he was going to make me in return for the many he had received. He told me he had nothing. I said in joke, ' Won't you give me a Masara ? ' to which he replied, ' Oh yes, I will send you one down, if that is all you want.' Shortly after, Ngami made

z

his appearance; he was starved and wretched, and understood none of us, but appeared vastly pleased with his change of quarters, and made himself quite at home directly. An uncle of the chief's told me he had just such another, that I might have for some beads, so I sent for him also, as a companion for Ngami. A regular Bushman this was, and I christened him Meercat, from his resemblance to the animal, a kind of ocelot. He was as fine a little fellow as ever I saw when I last saw him at the house of a German missionary in Merico, Mr. Zimmerman, in whose care I left them both.

In my ramblings over the deserts I have been witness to frightful scenes of misery among the Masaras, or wandering Bushmen. Once, I remember, I came across a very old emaciated woman, leading two little boys by the hand, about, I should guess, four and five years of age, subsisting on roots, berries, land tortoises, bitter melons, and anything they could find, without a vestige of clothing or habitation of any sort. I told my fellows to bring them to the wagon, but she would not come, and I never saw or heard more of them. There is little doubt as to their fate: nothing but starvation awaited them.

Sept. 30.— My Kaffirs have all returned to their duty, and expressed great contrition for their conduct. Raffeta's* three girls have run away, and no more has

* Raffeta was a Bastard, a head man in his own tribe, an experienced elephant-hunter in these parts, who accompanied me to hunt and shoot on halves. He had lots of friends, as

been heard of them. My two urchins, mere brats of five and six years old, came home by themselves, some fifteen miles, at least. I had quite given them up, as they were with the three girls, and congratulated myself on my good fortune, which I attribute to the good treatment the youngsters have always received from me, as I have become very fond of them, and they have acquitted themselves admirably lately in retrieving ducks.

I have had a return of my old complaint, fever and ague, and been quite prostrated for the last six days with racking headaches, pains in the back and limbs, loss of appetite, great nausea, profuse perspirations, and all the usual concomitants, but having the most approved remedies at hand, I am now already very much better, and hope to take the field again in a few days.

We continue to keep up amongst us a constant supply of flesh meat, springbuck, buffalo, quagga, and leche, not forgetting to mention two fine cock ostriches. I pottered round with Juno and killed a heap of ducks and a few guinea-fowls, and the Kaffirs kill a fair share of pheasants with their knobkerries. The weather constantly threatens rain, and is very hot. An old bull buffalo caused me a little alarm to-day. I was sauntering along the

he was a good gunsmith, and very handy at doing odd jobs, and they made him presents of all kinds of things, and amongst others the three Masara girls above mentioned. I mention this circumstance, as, on my return to the colony, I was accused by one of the local newspapers of slave dealing.

z 2

bank of the river, when I suddenly saw him lying
asleep in a thicket close before me.   Gyp and Juno,
who were at my heels, immediately got his wind,
and rushed into him.   He sprang up, stood at bay
for some time, then made a charge at the dogs,
passed me, and went back to his own thicket.   I had
nothing but a small shot-gun, and shouted lustily to
scare him ; the dogs fought him manfully, but he
would not budge.   I had no shelter of any kind, and
at length, after two minutes' consideration, much to
my relief, he trotted off with the dogs in attendance,
looking back at me, poor things, as if to ask my
reason for not shooting him.

*Oct. 3rd.—Kerea.—*We are now within a few
hours of Chapeau; the weather is hot beyond all
endurance, and the flies torment us sadly, succeeded
at sunset by innumerable mosquitoes.   Last night, I
could not bear a rag over me, and the mosquitoes
drove me raving mad, and will do the same to-night.
The weather threatens rain, but it won't come, which
makes it so fearfully close and sultry.   I have lost
England, one of my after-oxen, in a pit-fall, and shall,
I fear, feel the want of him very much.   One wagon
has stuck fast in soft places twice the last two days,
and it was all that twenty oxen could do to drag her
out.

*5th.—*The monotony of our journey was most
agreeably broken yesterday by meeting a party
of English, amongst whom were Mr. Palgrave and
Mr. and Mrs. Thompson, who had come up from

the Cape on a wedding-tour ; but as the wagons were
going different ways, and drivers will not keep the
oxen standing in the yoke and in the sun longer than
can be avoided, very little time was allowed for ex-
changing news.   Alington, however, got a handsome
supply of tobacco from Mr. Thompson, which was.
almost worth its weight in gold to him.   They were
on their way to the Great Lake, and from thence to
Walvish Bay.   I had unfortunately gone out hunting
early, and the only one of the party whom I saw was
Dr. Holden, a Lancashire man, from Burnley.

What his object is I do not know ; he has two
white servant-men, and travels with every comfort.
It is his intention to reach the Zambesi, if possible,
and then trek down and join Moffat in Mosilikatse's
country.   He will find his journey a difficult one ; he
appears to be but little of a sportsman, and a knowledge of horseflesh and oxflesh, especially the latter, is
indispensable to success in an arduous undertaking
such as the one he proposes.   We spent a very
pleasant evening together yesterday, and look forward to doing the same this evening.   At daylight
to-morrow I must again inspan, and say good-bye,
never to meet again, in all probability.

12th.—Bachukuru.—We are well over a good
120 miles of our journey, having been highly
favoured by moonlight nights, and, since leaving the
river, cool evenings and mornings, and we cannot be
too thankful for having seen the last of the mosquitoes.   We reached the first water at Nekohotsa,

brackish, and in very small quantity; then, two hard days and nights on to Lotlokarni, where we found a sufficiency, and also enjoyed the society of two English missionaries, Mr. Helmore and his family, and Mr. and Mrs. Price, who are proceeding to Sekeletu's, on the Chobè, and from thence, probably, to the Zambesi. Here we had a hard day's work at the old wagon, which sadly needed repair.

I killed one giraffe, just after leaving the river, Dr. Holden accompanying me, and two giraffe cows on Saturday. Mr. Helmore sent his wagon to bring one back that I gave him. I found him a very nice man, and I reluctantly accepted some preserved vegetables from him — the treat, after bread and beef alone for eight months, was too great to resist. This morning we made Matchevi, a small fountain in the desert, where we had delicious rain, but unfortunately it did not last long. We are now at Bachukuru, where we have at last succeeded in giving all the oxen water, every drop having to be drawn in a bucket, and poured into a stone basin, and two oxen brought at a time; it just held out, and not a drop to spare.

I missed having an excellent right-and-left shot at wild dogs this morning, owing to my after-rider being a long way behindhand with my gun. They were great big fellows, and trotted away as coolly as possible. Another ox, Charlie, has died of lung sickness, and three more that I left at Sechele's, making thirteen lost in all.

Another week will, I expect, see us at Sicomo's,

when our difficulties will be in a great measure over ;
a week more to Sechele's, where the fresh oxen I left
behind — thirteen of which, I hear, are still there all
right—will be of immense assistance to us in getting
to Mooi River Dorp.   The roads here are frightfully
heavy ; fourteen good oxen, pulling all together admirably, can only just move on at the rate of barely
two miles an hour.

16*th.—Caballa.*—Weary work : forty-eight hours
without one drop of water, and the heaviest sand it
is possible to conceive.   The oxen fell in the yoke
from sheer exhaustion, but all contrived eventually to
get here, with the exception of two ; one is dead, and
the other has just now made his appearance.   The
oxen were half mad from thirst, and there is not a
drop of water here.   I had to outspan them and
send them on to Letloche, a fountain twelve or fifteen
miles ahead, and, after drinking their fill, they must
come back again to trek the wagons.   I never saw
such a sight as this place ; there are twelve or fifteen
holes here, and by every one sit several Maccalacas
Kaffirs, watching and ladling out with tortoise-shells
the last drop of sand and water, as soon as ever it
rises half an inch.   I reached here with the horses
late last night, and they got abundance of water ; the
worst part of our journey is now over, and I think,
by resting a few days at Letloche, we may reach
Sechele's, without help.   We overtook, at Nkowani,
four wagons belonging to Boers, the far-famed old
hunters, John Viljoen and Pet Jacobs ; they had had

a glorious hunt, had killed ninety-three elephants, and had ridden forward to Merico. They are hunters of great experience, and know where elephants are to be found. They came across them in great numbers, and got some splendid bulls, considerably north of my farthest point, where I was prevented from going by the positive assurance of all the Kaffirs, that I should not find a drop of water. The most mortifying part of it is that I was in the right direction, had surmounted almost all difficulties, and was within three or four days, at most, from their stronghold. They tell me that it is a splendid open country, with plenty of stone fountains, and that the elephants have never before been fired at, and are perfectly tame and in great numbers. I have no cause to complain, however; I must have nearly 5,000 lbs. of ivory in the two wagons, and some splendid teeth. I killed two eland cows yesterday, close to the wagon-road, after a long, very fast chevy; they both fell from exhaustion, without a shot, when I gave them a pill to prevent their rising.

I am myself better and worse, sometimes able to take field, and at others sick, weak, and helpless; altogether in a poor way. Some of us are obliged to be out constantly, as we have such an immense party to feed; we have been treking all night, the last three or four nights, and have done wonders. I have been too generous with my stores. The Boers had left all their drivers without coffee, tea, sugar, or meal, and I told them they might come and take a share with my fellows as long as the stores held out, and a few days have made an alarming diminution in their amount.

19th.—Letloche.—We had hard work to get here, but we have found abundance of water, and I intend remaining three days to refresh the worn-out oxen. One poor thing, Spearman, was unable to reach the water, and we were forced to leave him ; he came on in the night of his own accord, when a lion waylaid him and made a meal of him. He got off scathless, as I was still at Caballa, waiting the return of the oxen sent forward to drink. My horses, too, are completely knocked up, so we can shoot nothing, and I was never so badly off for food before in my life. My two favourite goats, that have followed like dogs for 1,500 miles at least, were condemned two nights ago, and one was butchered on the spot ; the other has run away, but I expect to see him brought back every minute, to share the same fate.

25th.—Massouey.—I left Sicomo's on the 22nd, where I could obtain nothing whatever in the shape of food from him or his people, though we were all terribly hungry. A German missionary, lately settled there, sent me a sheep and about half a bucketfull of meal ; but there was nothing in the State, all were crying out on account of hunger. The corn is not yet in the ground. Everything is parched up from drought ; there is no grass, and I never saw so little water in fountains where I have always before found abundance. I do not believe a drop of rain has fallen for the last ten months, but, from the threatening state of the weather, we expect it every day now. My favourite cow, Nelly, a splendid milker, died yesterday of lung sickness. Not being able to shoot or buy anything, I was forced to kill an ox on Sunday, as my Masara boys were positively crying for hunger. The day after, I killed two giraffes, and Kleinboy one; and we might, had the roads and wagons not been so frightfully heavy, have laid in a stock of dried meat that would take us to Sechele's. I hope to arrive there in about eight days, and do not care how soon, as we are entirely out of all the necessaries of life.

Nov. 1st.—Lopèpè.—We have at length had four successive days of glorious rain, putting our minds quite at ease as far as water is concerned; but the cure is nearly as bad as the disease, as the bitter cold, always the case when rain falls, has killed two oxen outright, and the survivors are a spectacle. I have been here a week, and in bed four days of it, the change of weather bringing on a violent return of fever and ague. I tried to trek to-day, but found the roads in such a dreadful state that I was obliged to give it up. Stores have long since been at an end, and we are entirely dependent on our guns for our daily sustenance. I killed three giraffes out of a troop. It was very hard work, and I will never attempt it again; my horse fell heavily with me once, which gave him, poor fellow, a good two or three miles additional gallop. Alington and Woodcock have brought three impalas or roybucks to the wagon, so that, so far, our larder has never been empty.

I sent on two Kaffirs a week ago to Sechele's, to bring the oxen I left in his brother's charge, and expect their return in a couple of days.

My Hottentots, without giving me a moment's warning of their intention, all left me at night, at Massouey,˙for no reason, that I know of, but that food was at an end. It is a little harder work for us now, but I do not in the least despair of driving the wagons to Merico. I have purchased two oxen in place of the dead and done up, and, though unbroken, they now trek admirably. This rain will be of inestimable benefit to the whole country, and a plentiful harvest will, I hope and think, be the result. In case of a dry season, the Kaffirs have no resource but to seek a precarious existence in the bush, and many hundreds die of positive starvation.

When food was so dreadfully scarce, Mr. Schroeder, one of the missionaries at Sechele's, brought meal from Merico and made bread, giving each of the baptized Kaffirs a small loaf on Monday morning; they then went into the bush, and contrived with roots, berries, wild fruits, land tortoises, frogs, &c., nothing earthly coming amiss, to eke out a precarious existence, with the aid of the loaf, till the following Monday, when, if they contrived to exist, they got another. There is one poor woman following my wagons now from Mosilikatse's country, saying it is

her only chance of getting food, and she cares
nothing as to where she goes, and tries, poor thing,
to make herself useful in a small way, by lighting
fires and bringing wood.

I have had twenty Kaffirs from Sicomo's, but eight
of them have to-day turned back, as I could not
attempt, when out of the hunting-ground, any longer
to feed so many.   There is, of necessity, great waste
in the food ; the large game is killed so far from the
wagons that it is impossible to bring half the meat,
and the vultures pounce down on it immediately
it is left ; and then the wagons are so heavy, and the
oxen so utterly worn out, that I will not load them
with more than sufficient for the day, letting each
day take care of itself. The Kaffirs eat like ogres,
but at a pinch they can easily go three days without
food.

I once saw a clever mischievous Kaffir lad, named
April, hide inside an elephant we had shot that day.
He caught two vultures by the legs, as they were
tearing away at the carcase, pulled the first inside,
tied his legs, and shoved him forward into the vacant
place where the Masaras had taken out the elephant's
heart, and then proceeded to capture his mate.

The Kaffirs are very fond. of all sorts of small birds
to eat, and, when they succeed in capturing young
ones just fledged, they generally pitch them on the
fire alive.   I was once outspanned near some dense
reeds, on the Zouga, into which thousands of small
reed birds came and went, in the evenings and morn-

ings, in great numbers. The first flight or two was the signal for everyone to turn out armed with sticks and kerries, in throwing which the Kaffirs are very expert, and I have seen five or six cut down with one stick, and some good bags made. There is also a kind of social crosbeak which build large communities of overhanging nests, like purses, on tall trees. On outspanning for the night near these, my fellows, soon after sunset, tied a fire-stick to the end of the very long whip-stick ; the nests being dry as tinder caught fire at once, and the poor inmates fell down in numbers, half roasted. A couple of minutes' more fire was all they required, and they were considered a dainty, being very fat.

5th (Sunday). — I am now within one hard day of Sechele's, having got on by slow and easy stages so far, though we were disappointed in finding the water we expected. I met the oxen I sent for yesterday, but there are only nine instead of eighteen, and they are all as thin as whipping-posts ; most of the remainder are dead from starvation.

I do not know what my Kaffirs would do, were it not for the opportune deaths of divers oxen, which, though so lean that they can scarcely hold together, still manage to support life in the bipeds.

The days are so insufferably hot, we can do nothing but turn day into night, and do all our treking at night. A man that leads this life richly deserves every penny he makes, though the lazy, well-fed Boers, who never leave home, are jealous and envious of our heavy loads of teeth, and the lots of money they bring us in the market.

17th.— I rested the oxen six days at Sechele's, where grass and water were plentiful and good, and even so short a space of time has improved them much, and I am now at Lobatse, well on my way to Merico, where I expect to arrive to-morrow night. The old wagon has plagued me sadly ; she comes on creaking and groaning like a ship in a storm. I bought a muid of meal (180 lbs.) from a Boer whom I found trading oxen at Sechele's, which lasted my ravenous retinue just eight days, and they are now crying out again from hunger : this is without taking into account three sheep, as well as fifteen or twenty gallons of amasi (thick sour milk), a very useful article, as it will make either cheese or butter.

The German missionaries treated us most hospitably. We lived at their table the whole time we stayed at Sechele's, and we thoroughly enjoyed the treat of a few French beans and potatoes, and excellent bread. Sechele has had great losses amongst his cattle, and I got nothing out of him but two young oxen that he never used. He complained much of his poverty, and I believe he has but very little, and most of his people hungry.

A hyena came last night, and took a fine heavy fat goat, which was tied by the leg to the wheel of the wagon I was sleeping in. Five Kaffirs were sleeping under the wagon, and two horses were tied to the hind wheel. There was instantly a regular

hue and cry after him with assegais, fire-sticks, knobkerries, and a most unearthly yelling of dogs and
Kaffirs.   They were guided by the cries of the poor
goat for some time, but no sooner did they get
there than 'bar-baar, baar-bar,' somewhere else,
and the strong ravenous brute at length got clear

away with his prey.   At length, the sounds ceased,
the dogs were all afraid, the night was very dark,
the Kaffirs had no longer anything to guide them,
and the chase had to be abandoned.   I grudged the
brute his dainty fare, for he had taken by far the
best of the three.   I should hardly have believed it

possible he was able to carry away at such a pace so large and heavy an animal; 70 lbs. live weight, I should say.

Three of my Kaffirs are prostrated with ague, and there was a great row two nights ago, some of them accusing another of witchcraft, or poisoning the food. The next day, however, the accused was taken ill, so I have heard no more.

30th.—I am well away now from Merico ; come so far, scathless, through the Boers. I have been detained longer than I expected, partly by heavy rains, and partly from violent fever.

The Merico Boers are most hospitable, and one and all treated me well, but I was too busy to go and visit any but those that lay on my path. My poor old wagon has come to an end at last. The roads were so fearfully stony that she broke down. After a couple of days spent in attempts at mending her, I met a trader with a wagon nearly empty, having disposed of most of his goods, and, after a great deal of hard bargaining, agreed to give him 50l. in exchange for his, and we each off-loaded there and then. Alington and Woodcock have bought horses and have ridden forward to Mooi River, being long ago heartily tired of the wagons.

I have had my rifle carefully loaded and am going to risk treking through the Lion Velt by moonlight to-night for four or five hours, which is what the Boers never do.

Dec. 11th. — I am now outspanned before the

Vaal River, four days on my road to Natal from
Mooi River Dorp. I found there ivory at a very low
price, in consequence of the rumoured war, or some
other reason ; but I was obliged to sell part of my
stock there. I got 5s. 6d. per lb. for 1,000 lbs., and
only 3s. 6d. for 500 lbs. more ; but what with feathers,
at 7l. 10s. per lb., and a few karosses and rhinoceros horns, I sold to the tune of about 430l., a
trifle more or less, and have still a wagon-load of the
finest ivory left, which I am taking to Natal, and all
the best of the karosses. I have become a trans-
port-rider, and am taking in one wagon 3,000 lbs.
of wool and ivory down to Natal, for which I am to
receive, however, only 9s. per 100 lbs.

The first of my difficulties is the Vaal River, which
is now full and may detain me here a week or more,
and we have lots of rain every day, and I hear all
the rivers ahead are also full, and I may be six weeks
on the road.

I picked up two German tradesmen, a mason and
a blacksmith, who begged to be allowed to go with
my wagons to Natal ; the latter carried a gun, and,
not liking the look of it, I said he must fire it off
before putting it into the wagon ; he did so, and it
burst all to pieces, tearing three great holes through
his hat, one in the middle of his temple, and burning
and blackening both his eyes, of course prostrating
him and deluging him in blood, and it was some
time ere we could pursuade him that he was not
killed outright. We washed him well, and doctored

and bandaged him up the best way we could, and he is now not much the worse. I have, in all, now sixty oxen, worth a good sum of money, as I could make four or five spans of as good and well-matched oxen as ever stepped before a tail, and I am now becoming a little *ox*-proud, and take great interest in them.

I had myself two narrow escapes at different times in crossing the Tugela. I was just recovering from fever, when some of the party proposed a swim, and we went down ; just before going in, I felt as if I was about to have an attack of ague, but I foolishly persisted. I had reached within twenty-five yards of the opposite bank, when I got into some back water and a strong stream, and could not make any more headway, and was getting very weak and exhausted. My companion, who had landed, called to me to go back, but I was much too exhausted to make the attempt. I was gradually getting farther off the bank, the back water and stream running round a bend, and should certainly not have made a landing, when a powerful Kaffir, who had previously challenged me to a race across the river, the head man of a blacksmith, came up, put his hand under my shoulder-blade, and forced me through the stream with the greatest apparent ease. He did not know that I was in such a fix as I really was, and a couple of pounds of tobacco delighted him immensely.

I was crossing once, on horseback, when the river

was very low, about up to the girths. I was leaning back rifle in hand, my feet foolishly in the stirrups, on each side of his neck, when the horse fell over some big stones. The stream immediately turned him over on his back, and, on regaining his legs, my left foot had got fast in the stirrup, my head and shoulders were under water, and I could just scrape the bottom with my hands as the sluggish Kaffir horse continued quietly walking on, and I was fast drowning, when I succeeded in grasping him firmly above the knee with my right hand, raising myself with my utmost strength, throwing my left arm up trying to grasp something. Most fortunately, the horse had a very long mane, and I succeeded in catching hold of it: I thus contrived to keep my head just above water, until, deliberately walking on at the same pace, he landed.   I had imbibed a great quantity of water, and was very sick and ill with a horrid dizziness in my head, and singing in my ears for some time after.   I lost my rifle, but after a long search succeeded, with my companion's assistance, in recovering it.

I have never crossed a river since then with my feet in the stirrups, nor ever will.   My foot had turned round in the stirrup, and my instep was a good deal hurt.   My horse was, fortunately, very quiet, as almost all Kaffir animals are.

The Tugela is one of the most serious obstacles to travellers, and I have had many adventures on different drifts.   I was once returning from Overberg

with a covered spring cart (which I had made long
enough to sleep in) drawn by four, six, or eight oxen,
with a small troop of horses I had been buying. I
had fastened eight of the quietest to the wheels, four
on each side, as it was a very dark stormy night,
with a heavy rain, and I feared they might trek
back again. The rest were grazing near, when
those attached to the cart got frightened and pulled
back, the cart began to move, and this alarmed them
more, and with a sudden jerk they pulled it over on
the top of themselves broadside; when a frightful
scene ensued, all pulling different ways, and
struggling madly in the dark; it was a hazardous
thing to go near them. At last, we contrived to
cut them all adrift, and they galloped off into the
darkness. We righted the wagon again, but it
was broken to pieces. At daylight we started in
pursuit of the horses, and being a wet, cold, very
misty morning, we were more than half a day in
hunting them up; eventually, we found them under
the lee side of a large overhanging rock. We
inspanned and reached the Tugela, to find it flooded.
Fearful of losing my horses altogether if we had
another night of it, as there are many Bushmen (all
horse-stealers) in the neighbourhood, I determined
on getting them on the right side of the Tugela, and
succeeded in swimming them over among the loose
oxen in safety. The cart was a still more serious business. I had selected eight of my best water-oxen, and
after a long argument with my three lads, and hearing

what they had to say for and against the attempt, the
convincing argument at last being, if we did not get
over, we should have no supper, they agreed to make
trial. Acting on their good impulse, I inspanned
at once, every spare rheim being knotted together
to make as long a fore-tow as possible ; and the cart
being very light, for fear the force of the stream
should upset it, I put in some very large, heavy
stones for ballast, and Matakitakit on his hams
inside to keep them in their places. I fastened the
remnant of the sail down fore and aft, having
previously lashed all fast to the axle-tree to prevent
everything from going asunder, and having taken the
precaution to strip, and fasten money, promissory notes,
&c., round my neck in a small bag, I mounted the
box, whip in hand. Mick and Inyous took the tow,
and got some twenty yards ahead of the oxen, which
were standing in the water, as deep as they could
get without swimming. It was pretty good ground
going in, when I shouted ' Trek !' and away we went.
The stream carried the leaders down very fast, and
the oxen were gaining on the lads, the cart float-
ing beautifully, and I thought all would go well,
and was chuckling with inward satisfaction. When
the front oxen had reached the boys, I shouted,
' Let go the tow, and get out of the road ;' they got
confused, stuck fast, and pulled the oxen round in
the middle of the stream, and just as the leading
oxen's heads were within two feet of my knees,
sailing down with the full force of the current,

seeing an upset inevitable, I took a header down
stream as far as ever I could go, out of harm's way,
and turned on my back to see the result. The cart
had disappeared; Mick and Inyous, seated on the
backs of two middle oxen, were going round in a
frightful state of confusion, and there was not a

vestige of Matakitakit, who was fastened inside the
cart, and I feared that, the cart being turned bottom
upwards, all the heavy stones must be on his head.
I tried to make up to render assistance, but the
stream was too strong, when, to my intense delight,
up came Matakitakit about twenty yards behind. He
gave himself a shake and a blow or two, and, though

he had previously declared he could not swim a yard, he struck out, Kaffir fashion, as well as any of us. The oxen got partly right, and we all got over eventually, one ox only being drowned. I lost everything that was in the cart, except my two guns, which I had lashed very securely to the sides.

There is great difficulty, at first, in getting these Overberg horses to face water, as they have never seen a river, and I was once nearly all day fighting with them at the Volga, and should never have succeeded had it not been for some Dutchmen with a large troop of oxen. I got the horses amongst them and got them down to the bank, when about five fine powerful fellows wielded their tremendous whips, with handles eighteen or twenty feet long, and lashes in proportion, with such a deafening crack, that the hair flew in a cloud from the back of any unfortunate animal they chanced to light on, with such terrible good will, force, and effect, that it seemed a scramble which could be in first, and so out of harm's way. They all landed safely, and did not stop galloping till they got through Harrysmith.

I found the best way of driving was to have a big bagful of stones round my waist and pelt them, as many a loiterer will not let you get quite near enough to thong him, and, if you press them too hard, they run clear off. It was very hard work for one man, and I knocked up three riding-horses.

Another time, Claas, my after-rider, half Bushman half Griqua, the very smartest fellow and most

unmitigated scoundrel and best mimic I ever knew,
volunteered to take two horses across. He was dressed
in leather, and mounted without divesting himself of
anything ; the mare he was riding swam very fast and
outpaced the other ; in pulling him along, Claas
checked the mare in the middle of the river, and she
fell backwards over him, and he sank. The spectators
on both sides were very much alarmed, and began
to make all sorts of surmises at his not appearing
again, amongst others, that he must have received
a severe kick on his head ; when at length, full
forty yards below in the middle of the river, that imp
of darkness just showed his black head like a dog-
otter, took off a kind of skull cap and waved it a time
or two as a signal of distress, and then went down
again, and kept on this game, coming to the surface
sometimes with a struggle and a gurgle, and throwing his arms wildly about as if he was drowning, as
far as the bend of the river, full 400 yards below
where he first landed. I never saw so finished an
actor in my life, or such a water-dog, and he was
equally good at everything else.

He and his mate David were a pretty pair. I was
once going to the Hantam district, to buy horses,
and took them to help me drive them home. On
reaching Bloemfontein, David commenced by getting
married ; I did not see his bride, and he did not
leave me owing to this, as he said he could come
some other time and take her down.

I bought a lot of horses about forty miles farther

on, and with the assistance of some Bushmen, well
mounted, excellent riders, and very light weights,
we succeeded in reaching Bloemfontein at night,
put them in a stone kraal, and at dawn of day found
they had all broken out. David and I saddled up
immediately, and overtook some of the last stragglers
within a mile of where we had brought them from.
Holme's Bushmen, seeing them coming, had prevented them from again joining the troop, or we
should have had another day's hard work in driving
them out.

We herded them all day, and kraaled them at
night, and started off again the following morning,
and reached Bloemfontein and again drove them
into the kraal, when I gave David most positive
orders not to leave them till I had had something to
eat, and then I would come and watch, but I had
not been long at the inn, when I heard David's
voice in the kitchen. I asked him whom he had
left with the horses, when he said he must have
something to eat as well as I; whereupon I
knocked him down, and on his getting up again,
still inclined to be saucy, I gave him another with
such right good will, that he went backwards through
a reed door down about six or seven steps. He made
off at the top of his speed, exclaiming ' Alaminta,
my boss is mull' (Almighty, my master is mad); and
I never set eyes on him again.

I immediately went to the kraal; every horse

was gone, but luckily they were very hungry, so I recovered them all on the outskirts of the town, feeding. I got them in again with help, fetched my blanket and saddle and watched them all night, not being able to find Claas. In the morning that worthy appeared, and I sent him out with the horses to feed, and lent him a good mare, that he might be able to turn them if they got their heads towards home, and ran away.

In a couple of hours I went to look for him and them, and found the latter scattered about, and the fellow off with my mare, saddle, and bridle. In this dilemma I gave them all in the charge of the master of the skit kraal (the pound), who was answerable, and went to the Field Cornet, and we saddled up and went in pursuit. In case of capture, I was to take the law into my own hands, tie him up and thrash him till I was perfectly satisfied, or could not hit another blow, after which he was to be dealt with in any manner the Landrost thought fit; but I knew the wily rascal was not going to be caught, and I have never heard tidings of him from that day to this.

I then started with a big lump of a Maccateese, who rode so badly and fell off so often, that I had to do all the driving myself; he, however, watched them three nights till we got down to Sand River, when they broke out of a kraal and I lost them for three days. I found them among the Vittebergen

Mountains, and hearing nothing of my Maccateese, who had gone back on the road to look for them, I started alone, and eventually I succeeded in getting all safely to the top of the Drakensberg, where I left them in charge of Mr. King at Nelson's Kop.

.

CHAPTER IX.

1860.

RESULT OF A ZEBRA HUNT — REACH MERICO — VISIT SECHELE
— ELEPHANT HUNT — THE BATOKAS — THE ZAMBESI FALLS —
MEET WITH DR. LIVINGSTONE — INTENSE HEAT — ADVENTURE
WITH A LION — AM JOINED BY ENGLISH TRAVELLERS — ACCI-
DENT TO ENGLISHMEN — RETURN TO NATAL.

APRIL 17*th.*— *Scoon Spruit.*— I am now about 450 miles from Natal, and have got on so far very well, on the whole. I have been detained here three days in getting three muids of wheat ground. The mill was made in the year one, to judge from appearances, and it has gone wrong twice since I have been here, and delayed me not a little.

I went out this morning to try and get a zebra, as my dogs were very hungry. I soon found a troop, and was nearing them at every stride, on my horse Midnight, and was within twenty-five yards of a fat mare I had singled out, when down came my horse in a hole. I picked myself up at a distance of sixteen yards from the hole where the horse fell. The old horse rolled over me twice or thrice, my right foot sticking in the stirrup, but I managed to get stirrup, leather and all, away, just before he regained his feet and was off. It was some time before I could stand up, when I found my gun lying four or five yards away, with the muzzle towards me. I found myself bruised all over the lower part of my body, and the loose bullets and knife that I carried crushed with the weight of the horse into my ribs,

causing me excruciating pain, but I have no serious injuries, and hope to be able to ride again in a few days. An excellent omelette for breakfast, with a very fair amount of pontac, has already righted me considerably, but for the first ten minutes I thought I was nearly done for.

My after-rider came up in all haste on seeing the horse come back to the wagons, and brought a bottle of water. I handed him the gun, and told him to shoot a zebra, as my dogs were famishing. He

has just killed one, and I have sent six oxen to bring
it bodily to the wagons. So far, I have been living
well on koran, wild ducks, and partridges, having
recovered my invaluable little Juno, whom I left
behind last year with a broken leg. She is all
right now, and is invaluable to me. She retrieves
everything in or out of water. I am well off for
dogs this year; another old stager, Ponto, is nearly as
good; and I have Gyp, Painter, Wolf, and Captain,
for large game, five horses, six Kaffirs, and one Tottie,
and have every comfort in my wagons.

I had some difficulty in getting a permit for 100 lbs.
of gunpowder and 500 lbs. of lead, but eventually
succeeded, so that I am now all right, and have
ample ammunition to go wherever my wandering
fancy may lead me. If I can only find a sufficiency
of water, I hope to reach the Zambesi this year.

19th.— I am still desperately sore and stiff, but
nothing but bruises. A goodly array of game is
hanging to the sides of my two wagons, including
springbuck, blesbuck, quagga, and wildebeest, and
both Kaffirs and hounds are sleek and fat. A Boer's
wagon just in front of mine came across six lions
yesterday, and my driver Boccas saw two to-day,
very large, male and female, but did not shoot. I
cannot take the saddle again for a week, but manage
to pot my game by walking on ahead of the wagons,
and rolled over a wildebeest long ere sunrise this
morning. We inspan just as the morning star rises,
and it is very cold till the sun is well up.

*26th.—Lobatse.—*Reached Merico on the 21st, and found my oxen all in prime condition. Meercat and Ngami, my two youngsters, also show signs of good caring for. I left all my jaded oxen behind in the charge of a German missionary, Zimmerman by name ; he is a good Samaritan, and took every possible care of the last batch. Four more are dead of lung sickness, and three others will follow their steps shortly, I fear.

I laid in a great store of mealies, pumpkins, corn and meal, tobacco, dry peaches, potatoes, and onions, all in barter for rice, tea, coffee, and sugar, and made a sheep into sausages. There was a great harvest this year in Merico, and I found plenty of everything.

When I arrived at the frontier, commandants, field cornets, and all officers appertaining to the administration of Boer government, had gone to a public sale of sheep, cattle, and land, some eighty or a hundred miles off, a very rich Boer having most opportunely for me departed this life, and I was annoyed by no one, and might, as it happened, have had a wagon load of powder and lead ; but my 100 lbs., for which I have a permit, is my all.

Yesterday, I had a fit of the blues, in consequence of my old Kaffirs, Tanga and Matakitakit, leaving me. The former I have had off and on for eight years, and the latter has been with me the last five years, constantly, in all my long rambles into the interior ; and I am really sorry to lose them, as they knew my

ways, and I placed the utmost confidence in them
both ; the former an excellent cook and driver, and
altogether a strong, useful, handy, most obliging
fellow, and the latter invaluable as a horse-tenter. I
used to call him a second Rarey ; the shyest animal
became perfectly quiet after being a week in his
charge, and he could catch any horse at any time.
They had overheard me say to my head man,
Boccas, that I had made up my mind to go direct to
Mosilikatse, and the mere mention of his dreaded
name quite unnerved them. I had only engaged
them to go as far as Sechele's, being very ill at the
time, and thinking I should not again go into the
interior, but being now so far on my way, and feeling
once more comparatively strong and well, the inducement is too great to resist. They never told me
they were going away until the last minute, and such
a thought never entered my head, and I was much
surprised and vexed. In my haste, I sent them flying away without a shilling, which I regret much
now, as I really had not a complaint to make against
either of them. Another, named Boy, not good for
much, also went with them. Spearman, a Bamangwato, stuck to me, as well as Charley, and I hired
another driver immediately, rejoicing in the name of
Adonis. I promised two Bechuanas some beads to
drive my oxen and horses to Sechele's, and started
within two hours, so that this desertion did not delay
me much. I am only sorry that I did not give the
lads their money, and part on good terms, but any-

thing like regard or gratitude for past presents and kindnesses is not in the nature of any Kaffir. I never heard an instance of one really becoming attached to his master. I had become quite fond of these two, but it was a misplaced attachment, and I find you can only make use of these fellows as you would of a useful, handy machine ; and for the future I will lavish my kindnesses on the two much superior animals, horses and dogs, in spite of the missionaries dunning it into me, that a black man is my brother. I could see yesterday that the good Samaritan was secretly annoyed and displeased that I would not shake hands with a parcel of his baptized, singing heathens.

May 5th.—*Kapong* (*Full moon*).—Midnight is dead : 20*l.* 10*s.* gone to the dogs. This is the last water we shall find for three days, and I had so timed it as to start from this at full moon, but my oxen broke out of the kraal last night, and it is now late in the afternoon, and the Vachters (herd-boys) have not yet returned with them ; therefore I much fear I shall lose the moon, which is of vast import-ance. Game is very scarce. I have been out all the morning and not burnt powder. Yesterday I rode far in quest of giraffes, but have found none as yet. I have been out mostly on foot, and made great havoc amongst guinea-fowls, and had curries till I am tired of them. I found Sechele fat and well, and he helped considerably to lighten one half aum of pontac, and gave me nothing in return. He is sending in with me a wagon full of hunters. I have not seen them, but hear there are some twenty-five, with one horse amongst the lot, which is just now about to expire, if it has not gone off the hooks already. He says he knows that his men will potter about near home, and kill nothing, if they do not go in with me far into the interior, where game is plenty. If they follow me this year I am likely to lead them a pretty dance of it ; as my wagons are heavy with all I require, and my oxen are in splendid order, and for once my people, at present, at any rate, are in the same mind as myself, and are willing to trek into unknown regions. I have been lucky enough to get January once more, whom I mentioned in a former journal. On a spoor he is without an equal, and has a natural instinct in finding his way back to the wagons, which, in a country of such perfect sameness as this is in most parts, is something wonderful. There are no land-marks of any sort to guide the eye ; it is one densely-wooded flat, as far as the human eye can range. In most countries I am myself a pretty good hand, but this land beats me altogether.

9th. — Batlanarmi (a Fountain). — I have been very lucky in finding water in two vleys, and have come over this much-dreaded part of the road in a manner most satisfactory to horses, oxen, and all the party, dogs included. On Monday I fell in with seven bull elands, and had a very long stern chase, in consequence of my gun missing fire both barrels, and owing also to the obesity of my horse Batwing, who went as slow as a coach, labouring frightfully under his load of beef. It was all I could do to come up with them a second time, with an unsparing use of a pair of long military rowels, which did me good service, and will, I hope, do the like again. I eventually killed my eland in the middle of the wagon-road, many miles ahead, however, of the wagons. January, much better mounted, and very light, drove another out to the wagons, where the dogs all baited him in grand style, and Boccas knocked him over, thus laying in a superabundance of delicious meat for both parties. Sechele's party consists of about forty men in all. I have suffered, and am still suffering, so much from rheumatism in my left shoulder, that I cannot raise my gun, and my left hand has sustained a severe bruise, in inspanning an unruly ox. A leaf of tobacco applied wet, and well chewed previously, is our remedy for cases where the skin is broken.

I made this morning a very satisfactory shot at a pallah, a beautiful young ram, of about 100 lbs. weight, little less than 300 yards off. Finding I could not raise my rifle, I made a rest of an old dead tree, and took him beautifully through the shoulder and heart ; he ran about 300 yards in thick bush, but old Wolf, coming up about a quarter of an hour afterwards, hit off his spoor beautifully, and I found him lying dead.

I have this morning rejoiced the heart of old Wildebeest, a Kaffir of Sechele's, who has come

all this way for meat, by giving him the breast of
one of the elands, and he is going to carry it all the
way back to the State, four good days. His load
cannot weigh less than 70 lbs., though when sun-dried
it will of course be considerably less. We have found
two bees' nests. I got a Bakalahari to-day from
Stably, a brother of Sechele's, to go with me the
whole way, and he exhorted me to take care of him,
though they themselves treat them far worse than
dogs. We have been busy patching up Sechele's
wagon; it is in a desperate state; every spoke out
of the nave of one wheel. Still, green hide will
do wonders; it holds like a vice, as it gradually con-
tracts as it becomes sun-dried.

12th.—I write this at Massouey, a fountain, now
full of delicious water, where we arrived last night,
and the roaring of a lion, close at hand, made us
particularly expeditious in getting the oxen kraaled,
and the horses made fast to the wagons. It was too
dark to see to shoot, and we fortunately found a
kraal already made to hand, which only needed a
little repairing to make it all right. The jackals kept
up a concert the whole night, but we heard no more
of his majesty. Three springbucks are all that we
have slain since Batlanarmi. I fell in with an old
gemsbok bull, but my after-rider's horse, Snowdon,
ran right in between us, and so prevented my getting
a shot; he is hot-headed and a bit of a bolter, and
January is a poor hand in the saddle. The sun is
very powerful and the roads heavy. I have just

AN AFRICAN SERENADE

G. Wolf, del.

Hanhart, Imp.

heaved off two eland skins to lighten the wagons, and a starved wretch of a Masara immediately proceeded to make a meal of a part, and cut up the rest in portions that he could carry away for the same purpose.

18th (*Friday*).—*Letloche*.— On Sunday afternoon I left Massouey, and lost my road in consequence of the one I meant to travel being so overgrown with grass as to be invisible. I was sorry on account of the poor oxen, as the sun was roasting, the sand heavy, and the bush thick. I reached Labotani on Monday night, having got over a vast deal of ground; found plenty of water, and rested my oxen on Tuesday, and we killed pallah, blue wildebeest, and springbuck, six in all. I was awakened out of my first sleep by hearing a short husky cough. I started up and never closed my eyes again that night. Alas! I was only too well acquainted with what it portended, and had it been my own summons instead of my poor horse Frenchman's, I could not have been much more concerned. I remained over Wednesday, and I was buoying myself up with the hope that lots of bran mashes and boiled mealies might still bring him round. He came to the wagon and to me, and looked in the most piteous manner for help. I cannot bear to see a dumb animal in suffering, so I shouldered my gun and went after game, and the old nag tumbled over, just as I returned at sunset, dead. Yesterday I inspanned and came on here: this is a wild, pretty out-of-the-way place,

Gordon Cumming's most northerly point — a splendid natural stone fountain, about nine feet deep, but so hidden that a stranger might pass close without the slightest hope or expectation of finding water from the nature of the country around, unless he were guided there by some friendly turtle-dove or Namaqua partridge. I have often been guided to water by these birds, or the croaking of frogs, which can be heard at a long distance in the deathlike quiet of our lovely star-light nights.

I have just enjoyed a delicious swim in this fountain. I feel a little lonely, being without any companion with whom I can converse, with an immense expanse of country all around me, all wood, and not a trace of any human being. To-morrow I am about to strike an entirely new line of country; none of us know anything about it, but there are evident traces of late rains, and a probability of finding rain-water in vleys, which encourage me to proceed.

I intend treking as near due north as the country will allow, capturing a wandering Bushman when occasion offers, and pressing him into my service, until I get a substitute, or he makes his escape. The life is full of anxiety, excitement, hope, disappointment, satisfaction and pleasure, comforts, and the reverse; it has great charms in some respects, but it requires energy, determination, and perseverance. If my health is only spared me I have no fear, but my constitution is very much shaken; I have a very poor appetite, and I live almost entirely on dry toast, cold

roast guinea-fowls, partridges, pheasants, korans, dikkops, and ducks. My youngsters, Meercat and Ngami,
are lively and well, and are very useful and handy,
and beginning to learn to talk Dutch, English, and
Kaffir, or a kind of bastard language of all three
combined.

I can bag any quantity of winged game as long as
I have Juno, and my old favourite gun, made by
Burrow, of Preston, whose guns have a capital name
in the county. I have shot for ten years constantly
with a seven-bore of his make, which for accuracy
and driving qualities could not be surpassed; and in
our first disastrous expedition to St. Lucia Bay,
where eight of my companions died, they had all
previously determined on having similar weapons.
Burrow died during my absence, and his eldest son
now carries on the business.

21st. — Kanye. — I have been detained here two
days trying to get a guide, and have bribed old
Caballa, the captain of a tribe of Bakalahari, considerably, and am now waiting his final answer. I have
bought as much Kaffir corn as I can carry, as many
bucks or goats as I want, and have been busy making
sausages for the road.

On Saturday I shot two tsessebes at one shot,
breaking the leg of one, which the dogs took to the
water and pulled down; and to-day I have been also
successful in bringing to bay a splendid fat eland cow.
Accompanied by January, on old Snowdon, and seven
Bakalahari, we sallied forth, and soon found fresh

spoor, which the Kaffirs followed in the most indefatigable manner; it led us in a regular circle.
Though we maintained a dead silence, the elands
must have got our wind, as we found from the spoor
they were off at full speed. January then took up
the spoor, holding on fast by the pommel with one
hand, and kept it in the most marvellous manner at
a canter, wherever the bush would admit of it, for
three or four miles at least. I followed in his wake,
Ferus (fearless), who is in excellent condition, pulling
hard. I should have called a halt, but the spoor
led homewards. January still kept on at a canter
through the thick bush; at length, I got sight of
three cows; the rest of the party had done their
duty, it was now my turn: I contented myself by
keeping them in sight till we got into a much more
open part, when I let Ferus make play, and he
went at a slashing pace over everything. The elands
led me in among the Kaffir pit-falls, and I steered
my nag wherever the fence was thickest, as being
safest, and he jumped like a stag, and in a very
short brush singled out and ran right into the best
cow, when I fired from the saddle.

25th.—I have got on very slowly since logging up
last. There is no road; we have to cut our way
through the bush, and we have had heavy sand-hills
to contend with. We have had so far an abundance of water, but have come in a very unsatis-
factory zigzag sort of manner. I went out to shoot
a giraffe for food, with two Bushmen as guides, who

knew nothing about the country, and, after waiting in vain for the wagons, were obliged to follow our steps all the way back. Got on the wagon-tracks a little before sunset, and made great play to catch the wagons before it was too dark to see the spoor.

29*th.*—This is a festival of some kind or other in England, it strikes me, but in the centre of South Africa all days are much alike. I have been coming in the right direction, at all events, since my last entry. Early on Sunday we reached by a forced march, on account of water, a pretty little river, which we call Mesa or Nesa—the Kaffirs speak so indistinctly I cannot get at the right pronunciation — clear good water, and some hills in the neighbourhood. The lions had killed two zebras close to where we outspanned, and we made a strong kraal, expecting a visit from them, and I set a stell (a spring gun) for them by the remains of one of the zebras. The oxen rushed pell mell into the large vley here, and seemed to enjoy, not a little, a vigorous pull of good rain water ; the day had been hot, and we had come a long distance.

Adonis has just interrupted me by saying his gun had burst. I expected something serious, but on examination find it is only the stock, and an elephant's ear put on wet, and dried in the sun, will make it all right. One of my Totties has got drunk, and is playing old Harry with the Masaras, chasing them in all directions, and, if I do not at once

interfere, we shall not have a guide left to show us
the next water, which I have every reason to believe
is far off. The game is wild and wary here, and
giraffes shyer than I ever before saw them.

  June 3rd (Full moon).—I am now outspanned at a
vley of rain water, the immense Salt-pan, nine days'
journey long, and two broad, fully in view, and anything more dreary and desolate I never conceived.
I have just returned, with one Masara, from a long
survey of the surrounding country. As far as the
eye can gaze there is nothing but sand, and not a
living thing to be seen but a few wildebeests, an
odd unhappy-looking springbuck or two, and nine
male ostriches, which I saw speeding along in search
of a less barren soil. I have come along the last
five days very satisfactorily, winding about to avoid
occasional hills, but not much out of the right line of
country, and I shall take every advantage of the moon
to cross the pan. I am quite at the east end of it, and
a night and a day will, I hope, see me over it, and then
ere long I may hope to come across a few straggling
elephants. I laid in plenty of flesh yesterday — a
buffalo, quagga, and blue wildebeest — and no less
than twelve Masaras are doing their best to demolish
a good share of it. I leave the Meea river, which
is now dry, a little to the east, and hope to come
to the Qualeba to-morrow night : this part of the
road is dreary and monotonous enough, but I hope
it will lead to something better. At all events, after
coming so far, I will persevere, though I have lots of

impediments to contend with. One front wheel of my wagon is very shaky, but I have rectified it with buffalo-hide as well as I can.

The row I mentioned had nearly had a serious termination. When I went after him, the mad Tottie, after breaking one fellow's head with an iron kettle, had just got his gun and was leisurely buckling on his bandolier to shoot two or three others, who had offended him. They scuttled away like rabbits in the bush, and were hid like magic, and I had great difficulty, at nightfall, in inducing them to return. As soon as I had wrested the gun from the Tottie, he at once packed up all his traps and prepared to start off, but eventually he agreed to wait till next morning, when he re-collected nothing of what had taken place, and all is going on smoothly again, though they are difficult to manage and keep in any sort of order. Two more of Sechele's Kaffirs were ready to decamp, but I induced them to return; still they are dis-satisfied and sulky, and I fully expect desertions from my camp any day, on any pretext. They do not know where they are going, and are getting afraid, and believe implicitly the absurd stories the Bakalahari and other wandering Bushmen tell them, but I am determined to go on, and will succeed. The oxen trek admirably, and the horses are in capital order; but they get little or no work, as I am saving them for the elephants, and do all my hunting on foot. I saw harrisbuck spoor yesterday,

but was not fortunate enough to find any. I found
a vley in the heart of the bush, where immense troops
of buffaloes drank, and at least twenty different paths
of rhinoceros, &c., leading up to it, and should much
have liked to watch the water, but the wagons were
far ahead, and I reluctantly followed on, or else I
might have had great sport.

10*th (Sunday)*.—I missed a day somehow or other ;
at least, I was a day beforehand, as I found out by
the moon. For the last eight days I have come on
well, crossing the Meca, which was dry, as I
mentioned above ; the Qualeba, which had three or
four water-holes at the source, the rest being dry ;
the Chonain, about forty yards wide, also dry ; the
Simvain, the same width, of brackish water on the surface ; and I now write this on the banks of the Shua,
where there is plenty of good water. The country is
very dry. The Masaras say they have had no rain
here. The leaves are all fast falling off the trees, and
everything is dreary and desolate. There is plenty of
rhinoceros spoor, but we have not found them, as
they stand so far off from the water. I have shot a
giraffe and eland, only for food, and last night a
splendid old manikin ostrich, in full feather. A
Bequina, a runaway from one of the Boers, joined
me yesterday, and describes the country in front as
totally without water or game of any description,
and the Boers are all treking home ; but I place no
reliance on his statement, and think it is only a ruse
on his part to induce me to return. The Boers say

that the elephants have all left the country and gone where rain has fallen. I should much like myself to change my route, and hunt to the east of where I now am, in Mosilikatse's country, but that old tyrant is almost sure to forbid me leave; at any rate, I will leave him as my final resource.

I have just lost one of my best oxen (Kaffir by name) at the Simouani; a spiked poison-spear fell on him as he was grazing under the tree, and penetrated through his back, and he swelled up to a great size. Seeing no chance of his recovery, I shot him. The Masaras set these spears (stells) for rhinoceros and other game. They are hung in the branches of a tree, high up, and supported by a line, which comes under a forked stick and across the path, and stuck loosely into the ground with a peg; and any beast running against the line, or pushing it away, brings this great post, four feet long and as thick as a man's thigh, with a poisoned head of a barbed assegai stuck loosely in it, right into the unfortunate beast's back, where the assegai remains, driven, as in this case, right through the body by the weight of the post, and the post falls to the ground.

I hope sincerely my casualties may be few this year, as I can no longer afford very heavy losses. My wagons are getting perceptibly lighter from the consumption of food — ten men feeding daily, besides always a sprinkling of Masaras and six hungry curs; and the carelessness and recklessness of the idle vagabonds, who have already lost and broken the greater part of my cooking utensils. The Kaffirs care for nothing; they carry all their worldly goods on their backs. They eat, drink, snuff, smoke, dance, sing, and sleep, and if they can do all this, they do not seem to have a wish on earth ungratified. I often envy them, I must confess, as I feel very dull and lonely at times. I was amused at one fellow last night, whose only article of clothing was a straw hat, made after the fashion of a bowl. Charlie, my leader, who is a good-hearted boy, compassionated him, and said he would give him an old worn-out cotton blanket of his, worth when new about 2s. 6d., and now about 1½d. ; but, on second thoughts, said he must give him his hat for it, and the exchange was made on the spot. To-morrow at daybreak we leave the river, and our old blear-eyed Masara guide says it is two long days to the next water; after that, we come to the Madinas and Bushmen, and if I can get through the dense forests, which my authority says are impassable in the dry season, I hope yet to reach the Falls of the Zambesi.

13th.—I have been fortunate in getting two good specimens of the rarer sort of antelopes, viz. roan antelope and gemsbok, or oryx; also, a giraffe cow, in prime condition. My horse deserves all the credit of the gemsbok, as he ran with the speed and endurance of a steam-engine. The country was an immense flat, and I had no thoughts of coming up with the herd, and was just pulling up, but seeing them evidently hard-blown, and feeling my horse strong

SHOOT A GEMSBOK.

and fresh, I nursed him for a burst, taking a cool survey of the length of their horns meanwhile, and soon decided on a splendid cow, and when I called on Ferus he was alongside in 1,000 yards. The pace was tremendous, and I rolled the gemsbok over, and narrowly escaped going a header over her myself, as she fell suddenly right under Ferus' nose. I saw the first elephant spoor yesterday, and I may now fall in with them any day, and have all in readiness; it is not, however, my present intention to stay and hunt here, but to get a couple of degrees farther north, where they are three times as thick, and unmolested.

16th.—I have just been paying a visit to some Boers, about twenty miles off, partly from interested motives, and partly from compassion for a sick man, an old acquaintance of mine, to whom I thought I might be of service, from my experience in African fever, and having the usual remedies by me. I found him not so sick, however, but that he knew how to put on a figure of 60l. for his horse, which I at length was glad to buy for 50l. I leave the wagons tomorrow to go forward in search of a route free from that vile scourge the tsetse, which has turned back a party of Boers.

21st.—I have been away only five days from my wagons, as I could not proceed, in consequence of my Kaffirs not being able to keep up. It is terrible hard work to go over the heavy sands on foot; my people were dead beat, and the next stage was two long days on horseback without water, so I was obliged to give it up; but I gained a good deal of information about my journey, in case I make up my mind to go in that direction. I found no elephants, but tsetse in abundance; the country awfully heavy and dry, and drawbacks innumerable, with nothing to encourage one to proceed. I have ridden about seventy miles due north, diverging west and east considerably for water. Makainakanyama is the first water, about five hours on horseback, riding fast; thence to Jurra, a little farther, say six hours; Tamahopa, Tamashaki, the latter about four hours on horseback from Jurra, and my farthest; next Dundallah, too far east; and two days north we come to the En Duiker and Bonga rivers; the latter, my authority says, runs into the Zambesi, four days on foot due north, but I think the information rests on no good foundation. There was little game; only two elands and two quaggas fell to my rifle. Snowdon, seven successive days under the saddle, went marvellously, as also did Ferus. They had nothing but grass, as dry as a chip, to eat. We made the horses fast to a tree every night, on account of the lions. I saw one solitary old harrisbuck and tried to stalk him, but two elands between us gave him warning, unseen by me, and he disappeared in the thick bush, where it was impossible to give chase.

At Tamashaki I first fell in with the striped eland, marked just like a koodoo, but differing

in no other respect from the usual and common
kind. After a very sharp gallop through and over
some very ugly scrub and thorny bush, I ran into
and killed the first I saw of this new variety. Livingstone first discovered them near Sesheke, across the
Zambesi, one of Sekeletu's outposts.

29th.—Ramshua.—I found five bull elephants,
gave chase, and singled and drove out the largest,
and gave him a couple of pills to make him quiet;
he shortly turned and stood at bay, about forty
yards off, and then came on with a terrific charge.
My newly-purchased horse, Kebon, which I was
riding for the first time, stood stock still, and I intended to give the elephant my favourite shot in the
chest, but at every attempt to raise the gun for the
purpose of so doing, my horse commenced tossing his
head up and down, and entirely prevented me from
taking aim. During my attempts to pacify and
steady him, the bull charged, and I fired at
random, and whether the ball whistled uncomfortably
near the horse's ear or not I can't say, but he gave
his head so sudden a jerk as to throw the near
rein over on to the off side; the curb chain came
undone, and the bit turned right round in his mouth.
The huge monster was less than twenty yards off,
ears erected like two enormous fans, and trumpeting
furiously. Having no command whatever of my
horse, I dug the long rowels in most savagely, when
Kebon sprang straight forward for the brute, and I
thought it was all up; I leaned over on the off side

c c

as far as possible, and his trunk was within a few
feet of me as I shot close by him. I plied the rowels,
and was brought again to a sudden stand by three
mapani trees, in a sort of triangle; a vigorous dig,
and he got 'through, my right shoulder coming so
violently in contact with one of the trees as almost
to unhorse me, slewing my right arm behind my back,

over my left hip. I know not how I managed to
stick to my gun, 14 lbs. weight, with my middle
finger only hooked through the trigger-guard, my
left hand right across my chest, holding by the end
of the reins, which, most fortunately, I had in my
hand when I fired, and in this fashion we went

at a tearing gallop through a thick tangled bush, and underwood, mostly hack-thorns, over which my nag jumped like a buck. He was very nearly on his head three or four times, as the soil was very heavy, sandy, and full of holes. The monster was all this time close in my wake; at length, I got clear from him, and he turned and made off in the opposite direction at his best pace. As soon as I could pull up, which I managed after performing three or four circles, I jumped off, righted my bridle, and went after him like the wind, as he had a long start, and I was afraid of losing him in thick bush. After giving him ten shots, and sustaining three more savage charges, the last a long and silent one — far from pleasant, as my horse had all the puff taken out of him, and he could only manage to keep his own before the brute—to my great satisfaction he at length fell, to rise no more. I had long been quite exhausted, and could not even put a cap on the nipple. Boccas, on Batwing, turned up about an hour after; he said he fired all his powder away, giving his elephant sixteen bullets to no purpose; but the horse looked quite fresh, and both barrels were loaded, and every man has a perfect right to form his own opinion as to the reason why and wherefore.

Elephant hunting is the very hardest life a man can chalk out for himself. Two blank days, riding five hours at a foot's pace to a vley, where the Masaras tell you they have drunk; sleeping in the bush, with nothing to eat; a drink of muddy water

in the morning, out of a dirty tortoise-shell, which
serves for breakfast, dinner, and supper; all day in
the saddle, under a broiling sun, following after three
half-starved Masaras in greasy, tattered skins, who
carry a little water in the belly of a quagga, which
is nauseous to a degree, and never seeing life the
whole day. Two days like this, followed by two
successful ones, is about what you may expect.

Nothing more miserable and dirty can be conceived
than a Masara encampment. It consists of temporary
half-thatched sheds, and a few bushes stuck in here and
there to break the wind, with half-putrid dried flesh,
water vessels, and shreds of old skins, hung up in the
surrounding trees. My trusty after-rider brings two
or three armfulls of grass and makes my couch in the
most eligible corner, with my saddle for a pillow, and
here I court sleep till daybreak, lying close to a
greenwood fire, the smoke of which passes over you
when you lie close to the ground, and keeps off the
mosquitoes. There is something quite overpowering
in the death-like stillness of the forest at night — a
brilliant sky, innumerable stars, bright and twinkling,
dusky figures in all possible attitudes lying around,
the munching of our faithful horses, which are tied to
trees all night, and frequently the jackal's cry,
the hyena's howl, the occasional low growl of a
lion, or the heavy tramp and crash in the bush of a
herd of elephants, with a scream which can be heard
at an immense distance. This is the way our nights
are usually passed in the bush, and the most light-

hearted fellow in the world, when all alone for months, must have occasional fits of despondency.

Full of thorns and bruises, and half dead from thirst, I offsaddled Kebon, kneehaltered him, and then lay under the shade of a tree, having not the most remote idea as to my whereabouts, shouting and firing blank powder to bring up the Masaras. To add, if possible, to the many mishaps, my horse had strayed, and I had to follow his spoor, and did not overtake him for nearly a mile, and then I was obliged to retrace my own footsteps, which was not so easy. I had not long returned, when January turned up, and he led the way back at a trot on foot, distancing all the Masaras, and just at sunset got to the wagon, where I first got a drink. Such days as these are rather more than sport. I was much amused by watching the tick birds trying to alarm an old white rhinoceros, that we were approaching from under the wind, quite ignorant of his danger. They ran into his ears, and fluttered about his eyes, keeping up an incessant chirping, but he would not be warned till we got above wind, when he elevated head and tail, snuffed, trotted, and snorted, and went away in grand style at a swinging trot. We had better game in view, but to-night I am going to watch the water, as the moon is high, and then he must be more wary. My fellows have just made a hole at the edge of the water, as game is very scarce, and we are hard up for meat.

July 8th.—Tamashaki.—After much consultation

and deliberation, I have decided, in spite of all the remonstrances of the Boers, to trek due north, and stand my chance of tsetse, kief (poison), with which the bush in many places abounds, thirst, and other impediments. I have a hankering to reach the Zambesi and see the great Falls, which is so strong as to overrule all minor difficulties, though I cannot hide from myself the great risk I incur to horses, dogs, and oxen; still something urges me on, and I will follow my fate, good or evil, and am already three hard days on my route, without accident.

I had a good night's buffalo-shooting by the water; they came in large herds; I was in a hole under the wind, and made very good work, killing five dead on the spot. A sixth had got about a mile away, and no doubt many more subsided in the bush, but as there was a superabundance of delicious flesh, I did not go on the spoor of the wounded. Nothing but buffaloes came, but they in great numbers, and I could have shot many, many more, but my bullets were exhausted. This was not mere butchery, though it looks like it. The crops of the Maccalacas Kaffirs failed this year, and they are more than half starved, and it was only combining sport with charity, as not even a bit of hide was suffered to remain. Poor Gyp, I grieve to say, was taken by a tiger. I had ridden forwards to water, and she came after me on the spoor, before the wagons. It was night, and Adonis heard the scuffle, and poor Gyp's last breath, which left her carcase, not in the shape of a yell, but rather of a fierce angry whine that she could not gripe the brute in return. She was the gamest of the game, and had had numberless escapes, wonderful, lucky, or providential, whatever you like to call them. Except my perfect Juno, I had sooner the fate had happened to any other of the pack.

The country here is frightfully heavy white sand; and the air is so dry, and the sand so sharp, that my wagon-wheel is completely gone. We have driven in no end of wedges, and it is so bound round with buffalo hide as to be almost hidden from sight. An old Boer, however, says he will put new spokes in for me, and the dissel-boom is about to be sacrificed for that purpose.

19th.—Mateste.—I have but little idea of my whereabouts, as I hear such contradictory statements from the Kaffirs. None of us can properly understand the language, which is a great drawback; but I have come to the conclusion the Kaffirs themselves do not know, or at any rate will not tell the way to the Zambesi, or give us any idea of the distance. One man positively affirms that it is only four days, the next that it is a month, the next never heard the name of the river; and they are one and all so stupid and utterly indifferent, that I have given up enquiry, and hold always due north. I have only treked four days since last logging up, two very hard ones without water, and then we came to an entirely different country, bare and thinly wooded, with plenty of small hills in every direction, lots of fountains and running water. I have crossed two rivers, and fancy one must be the Guaka.

My party is now all dispersed.   I have left behind
one wagon and twenty-three oxen, in charge of two
Kaffirs.   Adonis and Isaac are gone into the fly
(tsetse) to shoot on foot three or four days, due east
from where I now write, where elephants are said to
be plenty.

I fell in with an Englishman, Polson by name, who
came in by Walvish Bay, about fourteen or fifteen
months ago, and has not yet got one load—a sorry
prospect for me.   We passed three or four evenings
together very pleasantly, and assisted one another in
the way of exchange.   I got a gun and powder for
ivory and beads ; it was a most agreeable break, and
we were very jolly together, and sorry to part; at
least, I speak for myself.

I wished to leave a heavy lot of flesh for my
Kaffirs during my absence, as they have no means of
providing for themselves, but game was so scarce
that I had two long blank days.   On the third, however, I got four quaggas, one eland, and a black rhinoceros, despatched a wagon and pack oxen, and left
them with abundance until my return.   Somehow or
other, I cannot come across any elephants.   Though
I see lots of spoor, and have had some weary days in
search, they have managed always to elude me as
yet.   This morning, very early, I actually heard one
scream, and, though we sallied out at once, and had
the benefit of January's spooring, we could never
find him, and we were obliged to rest contented with
two fat elands.

24th. — My plans are at present quite undecided. I think I have got nearly as far as it is possible to get. The country now in every direction is rugged, rocky, and very broken, with great hills and numerous rivers, and altogether an effectual barrier to any further attempts with a wagon ; added to which, the tsetse abound in all directions, and I cannot at all make out my whereabouts. The sun is intensely hot, and the nights and mornings bitterly cold. I think the thermometer must vary at least forty degrees in the twenty-four hours, and the country is decidedly most unhealthy at this season. Where on earth the elephants have got to, I cannot imagine.

In my rambles yesterday, I came across another nation, calling themselves Batokas. They are horrid frights : it is their custom to knock out their four front teeth, and to file a small space between each of the under ones, and a more hideous lot of grinning wretches I never saw. I heard, as a reason for their thus disfiguring themselves, that they were anxious to resemble an ox as much as possible, that being, in their estimation, the noblest of animals. All the natives are immensely fond of cattle, but this is carrying their veneration rather far. I have also heard that they have a horror of looking like a quagga or zebra. Remarking on one of my fellows, they said he would be good-looking only for his front teeth. The teeth of a Kaffir are splendid, snow-white, sound and even, and set off the rest of his face to great advantage.

I gleaned from the Batokas that an Englishman, whom from their description I guess to be Dr. Holden, whom I met on my return from the Lake last year, has knocked up a shanty close to their State, but he has no wagons or horses, and they volunteer to take me to him in three days on foot. They tell me he is on the banks of a large river, which must be the Chobè, and I am doubtful whether to look him up or not; if he should have gone, I shall have some tremendously hard work for nothing. My gun, bandolier, and ammunition, without which I never stir, weigh 18 lbs., and trudging under a broiling sun, even without this slight burden, is no easy matter, especially when you consider the bill of fare, which is flesh of some sort or other, salt, and water; I wish I could add bread, but I have no one to carry more than my blanket, as my people are all dispersed.

29th.—After long arguments and reasoning with myself, I at last decided to go on foot to the Chobè, and learn from Dr. Holden my exact whereabouts, and when and where I was likely to reach the great Falls of the Zambesi, as I can gain no intelligence whatever from the natives, and I now believe firmly that none of them know themselves anything about it. I appointed to meet the Batokas on the third day, after in vain trying by bribery to induce them to come with me to the wagon, for I had great doubts in my own mind as to my finding the way back some twenty miles, without a guide, over so rough and broken a country. I reached the wagon in safety, and set off again to meet the Batokas, at break of day, accompanied by January carrying my blanket and a little spare ammunition, and got on well for a long distance, recognising many objects I had before noticed. At less than half the distance I got wrong. Eventually, by great perseverance, I got right again, and kept the direction for miles through thick bush, heaps of tsetse, and heavy sand, and at length reached the Batoka encampment — to find it deserted. Weary and jaded, we made some faint efforts to hit off their spoor, but lost all heart, as they had set the grass on fire in a hundred places, and the whole country looked as dreary and wretched as you can imagine. We retraced our weary steps till dark, when we made a fire and slept, and got back again last night, not a little proud of finding our way.

My hopes of reaching the Zambesi, even on foot, are fled. The only consolation I have had is that I have shot another variety of antelope new to me, the gryse steinbuck. I had often heard of him, but had never seen him before; and now I know of but one single antelope that I have not myself shot, but must content myself with a bought specimen — I mean the nakong.

31st. — I am all alone. Boccas started yesterday into the fly country, and my other driver has been long there. I am off to-day to the Chobè river, two and a half days ahead, and shall endeavour to get through the fly in the night, the moon being now at the full; at all events, I will chance a pair of horses.

After being in the saddle all day, and seeing nothing, just as the sun went down, a giraffe bull stalked out of the bush half a mile from the wagon. I got Batwing saddled forthwith, and had a break-neck chevy after him over regular boulder stones by moonlight for some three miles, as hard as ever I could prevail on my nag to go, but he galloped in fear and trembling. At last, the stones, or rather rocks, became almost impassable even for the giraffe, and he had to slacken his enormous stride, and I, putting on a spurt, was alongside before he could get under weigh again, and rolled him over, to my great glee, as I am most anxious to be off, and I could not leave my wagon without a supply of flesh.

August 4th.—ZAMBESI FALLS at last. I set off resolutely on the 1st, being determined to find the Falls, walked all day and all night, and towards morning I heard the roar of them. I never rested till I threw myself down, just before daybreak, within three hundred yards of the river, and I spent yesterday at the Falls, which far exceeded all I have been led to expect. Rougher travelling I never encountered, but I had the benefit of the full moon.

I struck the river first about two miles above the Falls, and there it is not less than two miles wide, covered with islands of all sizes, one at least ten or twelve miles round, wooded to the water's edge — mowana trees, palmyra and palms, and plenty of wild dates, some of the former measuring twenty yards round the bole. The river is the finest and most beautiful I ever saw. It is rocky and rather shallow, and, just above the Falls, about one mile wide. And now for the Falls. I heard the roar full ten miles off, and you can see the immense volumes of spray ascending like a great white cloud, over which shines an eternal rainbow. · The whole volume of water pours over a huge rock into an enormous chasm below, of immense depth. I counted from sixteen to eighteen, while a heavy stone of about twenty pounds weight was falling. I could not see it to the bottom, but only saw the splash in the water. I stood opposite to the Falls at nearly the same elevation, and could almost throw a stone across. The gorge cannot be more than a hundred yards wide, and at the bottom the river rolls turbulently boiling.

You cannot see the largest falls for more than a few yards down, on account of the spray, and you are drenched with rain for a hundred yards round from the falling mist. It is one perpendicular fall of many hundred feet, and I should think there are no less than thirty or forty different cascades, of all widths. The gorge cannot be less than 2,000 yards long, and the outlet is not certainly more than forty yards wide. This outlet is not at the end of the gorge, though how far off I cannot say; the streams meet, form a wild mad whirlpool, and then rush helter-skelter through the pass. Looking up the gorge from that point is the most magnificent sight I ever beheld. It is as if streams of brimstone fires were ascending high into the clouds. There was a never-ceasing rain for fifty, and in some places a hundred yards, on the high land opposite, and the rocks are very slippery, and the ground where there are no rocks is a regular swamp, where the hippopotamus, buffalo, and elephant come to graze on the green grass. There is one grand fall at the head of the gorge which you can see to the bottom, about eighty yards wide, but not so deep, as the river forms a rapid before it shoots perpendicularly over the rock.

Below the Falls, the river winds about in a deep, narrow, inaccessible gorge — a strong, swift, rocky stream. I followed its windings for some distance, and, after all, was not more than two miles, as the crow flies, from the Falls. It is one succession of kloofs, valleys, mountains, and the worst walking I ever encountered.

The river through this fearful gorge seems not wider than a swollen Highland torrent. The greatest drawback to the otherwise magnificent scene, is that the dense clouds rising from below render the main Falls invisible, and it is only the smaller cascades you can see to the bottom. There are some thirty or forty of these, spreading over a space of at least 1,500 yards. The Makololo are very jealous, and very much alarmed at my having found my way hither, and cannot account for it. I show them the compass, and say that is my guide, and they are sorely perplexed. The baboons here are out of all number.

8th. — I saw the Falls from the opposite side yesterday, and also from above.   No words can express their grandeur.   The view from above is, to my mind, the most magnificent; the water looks like a shower of crystal, and it is one perpendicular fall of immense height.   There is only one outlet, and it is marvellous how such an immense body of water squeezes itself through so small an opening.

I have punted for three days in all directions in the Makololo canoes, and could spend half my life on the waters.   Dr. Livingstone is expected here to-day, and I am waiting to see him.

9th. — I had the honour, yesterday, of cutting my initials on a tree on the island above the Falls, just below Dr. Livingstone's, as being the second European who has reached the Falls, and the first from the East Coast.

Charles Livingstone says they far exceed Niagara in every respect, and the Doctor tells me that it is the only place, from the West Coast to the East, where he had the vanity to cut his initials.

Masipootana, the captain (under Sekeletu) of the Makololo nation, was exceedingly savage that I had seen the Falls without any assistance from him or his people, and sent several messengers to say that I must pay him handsomely.   On the third day I went to see him, and made him a small present, but he was quite on the high horse, and said, that now I had come across he would take care I did not go back again; I must stay there till I had paid him for the water I drank and washed in, the wood that I burned, the grass that my horses ate; and it was a great offence that I had taken a plunge into the river on coming, out of one of his punts; if I had been drowned, or devoured by a crocodile or sea-cow, Sekeletu would have blamed him, and had I lost my footing and fallen down the Falls, my nation would have said the Makololos had killed me; and, altogether, I had given him great uneasiness. As he put the matter in this light, I paid him about 6 lbs. of beads and was released. These beads were sent by Masipootana to Sekeletu, who afterwards returned them to me.

I had some misgivings, at one time, as to our treatment — we were entirely in their power, and January was in such a taking that he could only just manage to drive back floods of tears. He thought it a very hard case indeed that he should be killed as well as I, as it was entirely my doing that he came at all, and very much indeed against his own will; and Masipootana endeavoured, I think, to frighten him, as he told me, when we were left alone at night, that they were going to take us out into the river and throw us overboard, and, in case we swam, pelt us on the heads with stones.

The tsetse, too, spoilt much of my pleasure; and, to crown all, just as I was ready to start back to the wagon, I found both horses in pit-falls, the one coffin-shaped and the other round, narrowing towards the bottom, and about seven feet deep; the ground was clay, baked by the sun till it turned the edge of an American axe, and smoke flew from the blows as if you were striking stones. Towards midnight, with the aid of rheims and a large body of Kaffirs, I extricated them both, very badly bruised, and with horrid, unsightly scars and eyesores on them, but, fortunately, not seriously injured for actual work. Poor Snowdon suffered the most, as he had to sit up like a dog begging for many hours; the hole narrowed at the bottom and was some six inches deep in water, and with the clay he was regularly stuck there as if with plaster and mortar; the only wonder is that we did not pull both head and legs off him. I had buffalo rheims round all his fetlocks, fore and hind, also round his neck, and some eight Kaffirs attached to the ends of each, and so we hauled him bodily out, after we had cut a sort of inclined plane down towards him. We heard several skirmishes with rhinoceros and buffaloes at night, in the thick bush, both going and returning, but ensconced ourselves behind the trees till the fray was over.

I have crossed three rivers between this and the Zambesi — the Manyati, Setabangumpè, and Massouey.

I consider myself very fortunate in meeting Dr. Livingstone and his party. I spent the evening with him, and gained great information about his recent discoveries. He has gone on to Sesheke.

12th.—I returned to the wagon to-day, and found all right.

D D

18*th.*—Just returned from my other wagon, where I had been to get some powder, lead, and caps, to trade with the Makololos. The day I started from this, just towards sun-set, I fell in with a troop of cow elephants, and gave a good account of them; there was scarcely more than half an hour's sun, and consequently no time to lose, as we have hardly any twilight. I chased and shot fiercely at close quarters till quite dark, being well mounted, and bagged five; I let the best, however, escape. Having given her a bullet in the exact spot I wanted, I thought she could not possibly go far and left her, and she is free, though no doubt will die, but without benefiting me. I made up my mind for mischief on my return, but was two whole days in the saddle without coming across any more; they are very scarce, and it behoves a man to do his very best, whenever and wherever he meets with them. A grey jackal, whose brush now adorns my hunting-cap, and a fine old bull roan antelope, completed my best day this year. Poor Snowdon is dead; tsetse, sand-fly, midges, and gnats proved too many for him, together with the frightful struggles he made in the pit-fall, which no doubt hastened his death. Kebon, my fifty-guinea purchase, has turned out badly; he is so flat-footed as to be dead lame, and utterly useless, on stony ground. My hunters in the fly have not done so badly; ten or eleven, in all, I hear, and some big bulls, which help fast to make up a load.

The Maccalacas Kaffirs rile me frightfully; during

my absence they have set the velt on fire in a hundred places; the grass is as dry as old tinder, and with the high wind we have daily it roars away for scores of miles, thus driving the little game there is away. What their object is, except to drive me away, I don't know, as they have no cattle, sheep, or goats.

I shot a waterbuck yesterday, for no reason but just variety, as they are bad eating, but I want to see how many different kinds of antelopes are to be got in the interior of South Central Africa. From what Dr. Livingstone told me, I believe that I am now within a couple of days of the middle between the east and west coast, two days nearer the former.

25th.—My plans are entirely changed, and I intend now to make the best of my way to Mosilikatse's country, as I have quite lost heart of finding elephants here, and the ground is so frightfully stony as to make our unshod horses dead lame in a few days.

I was disappointed in trading any tusks from the Makololos, for some reason or other best known to themselves; but I believe the captain is exceedingly annoyed at a number of his men lent by his father to Dr. Livingstone remaining behind, and he blames the Doctor, who, he says, ought to have made them come back, and he is vexed also at the non-arrival of the cannon and horses which the Doctor was to have brought him — at least, so says my interpreter; but I have not much faith in his veracity.

Sept. 9th. — Tamashaki. — I hardly know what I

have done the last fortnight; I have been five conse-
cutive days in the saddle, without finding elephants.
I am now three days on my road back again — a weary,
long journey, without water so far, and I shall be
obliged to wait for rain before I can get out; besides
which, the velt is now full of a poisonous herb,
which is certain death in a few hours to oxen, so
that we are obliged to be most cautious. Painter
was left behind yesterday for dead; thirst and the intense heat of the sun had, to all appearance, finished
him; but, to my amazement, he turned up again this
morning, having found his way in the night to our
old outspanning place.

The best of my stud, Ferus, yesterday got desperately staked in the breast. A wounded buffalo, which
I was trying to drive towards the wagon-spoor,
charged me most savagely, and none other but Ferus
could have brought me safely out. It was a near
thing for about one hundred yards, and when she was
not two yards from my horse's tail, taking advantage
of an opening in the bush, I wheeled half round in
the saddle, and gave her a bullet through her right
ear and grazed the top of her back, without, however, doing her any harm; but she shortly gave up
the chase, when I reloaded, dismounted, and shot her
through the lungs dead. It was amongst hack-thorns,
and my clothes were completely torn off my body. We
had not a bite of anything at all at the wagon, and
no near probability of getting anything, therefore I
was rash, as a buffalo is a beast you cannot drive.

CHASED BY A BUFFALO.

The nipple of my gun broke short off in the worm the other day, and I tried every means to get it out for some time without effect, only making matters worse by breaking a plug short off that I had been hardening and shaping to fit all day. At last I made a drill bore, and succeeded beyond my most sanguine expectations, and she is now none the worse. I also put 3 lbs. of lead in the stock, as my right cheek and bone are nearly cut to pieces, and the blood at every shot runs into my mouth. We are obliged to load heavily for South African game; six drachms are my smallest dose, and my powder this year is excellent. I only wish my nerves were as good.

14th.—*Jurea.*—I think it hardly possible for the country to be or look worse than now, and my poor oxen and horses have fallen off fearfully. All the vleys are dried up, and we only get a small quantity of water at the fountains after hard digging, and the little grass there is terribly dry. In the early mornings, evenings and night, it is so cold that there is ice in all the water-vessels, while the days are intensely hot; from ten to four it is hardly possible to trek; we sometimes have high, and often hot winds; game of all sorts is as thin as deal boards, and the fare, consequently, very indifferent.

Last night I watched the water, more out of bravado than with any hopes of shooting anything, as Boccas got a fright the previous night that nearly drove him out of his wits. He had made a hole and covered it in with strong branches, and lots of grass and earth over, about 9 feet long by $2\frac{1}{2}$ feet wide, and there lay in wait for elephants coming to drink. One savage cow got his wind, rushed up to the mouth of the hole, thrust her trunk in as far as possible, hammered away at the sides, and felt for him everywhere, but could not reach him, and had not quite sagacity enough to throw off the branches, or she must have got him. He assures me she stayed full five minutes, and he could see nothing to shoot at but her fore feet and trunk. I was more fortunate; I heard a brute in the water, peeped cautiously out of my hiding place, and just as she turned round after quenching her thirst, I gave her my bullet behind the shoulder, at a distance of twelve yards, with such force as to go right through her, and there were two streams of blood from the water to where we found her, about 1,000 yards off, dead this morning. My face is in such a bruised, discoloured state that my dearest friend would scarcely recognise me; and no wonder, the reader will perhaps say; but in this night shooting you have only one chance, and if you don't take advantage of that, you have your long solitary watch for nothing.

Tusks are gradually accumulating, and I shall have one good load at all events, but have let the best of the season go by, in my wild-goose chase after the Zambesi Falls. I shall trek out in about a month at farthest, and hope again to spend Christmasday in Natal.

I am going to sleep to-night at a fountain some

ten miles off, called Zebizenà, where I hear lots of
elephants drink, and take the spoor from the water
at daybreak, but it is hard work following spoor, as
the elephants stand so far from the water; horse and
man are wearied and jaded to death before finding
them, and, if we get above the wind, we have no
chance of ever seeing them.   They have been persecuted this year much more than usual.   All the
stores are coming to an end, and I anticipate another
hard bout of it, unless we get the rains which are
now due, but I do not see the remotest chance of any.
Ostrich eggs are now plentiful, but too rich and
bilious for me to eat many of them ; I greatly prefer
elephant's heart.   We have abundance and variety
enough of animal food, but my people are most
extravagant with the stores, and this year I have
helped so many sick men as to leave myself almost
destitute.

20th. — Still at Jurea, sick and tired.   I know not
why I take up my pen, unless to kill time, as I have
nothing to log up.   We found nothing at Zemizena
but swarms of starved Maccalacas Kaffirs, and I have
been very sick and ill since ; I thought I was in for
the fever.   The elephants came once again while I
was watching the water.   I heard them a very long
way off; at length the branches broke, and they came
at a swinging pace, with a heavy tread, and in single
file, within fourteen yards of where I was ensconced,
and began pouring the water down their throats with
a loud gurgling sound.   I took the biggest behind

the shoulder broadside sharp right and left, and the
whole herd vanished like smoke; then came innumerable hyenas, making the most appalling noise,
fighting, running, and yelling like demons. I cannot
imagine what was the cause, as I never heard them
so before. I heard lions, and hoped they would come,
but they did not ; and, just before the morning star
rose, feeling confident that no more elephants would
come, I shot a hyena, and sent men off on the spoor
of the wounded elephant. As it was Sunday, I would
not go out to hunt myself. They found the herd, and
the wounded one standing alone, some distance off,
but the dogs chased him, and he eventually got clear
away, and we have seen no more since ; we have shot
elands, quaggas, wild boar, harrisbuck, and roan antelopes by the water, but nothing that will help to pay
expenses. It is now too warm in the day to do any
good ; I myself cannot stand it. The hack-thorns
have torn all my clothes to rags ; they are patched
up in twenty places, and I am still hardly decent,
even for the velt, where any mortal covering will
do ; nothing but leather has any chance, and that is
too hot. A little bacon still left, though shaded
as much as possible from the sun in the very middle
of the wagon, has almost all melted away ; my other
wagon and two hunters are still behind, and I am in
hopes they will kill a good number, as among the
tsetse elephants are very numerous, but it is killing
work for a white man on foot. I must go and try
for a guinea-fowl or partridge by way of change, as

I am quite tired of this strong living—buffalo, eland, or elephant day after day; I cannot eat quagga; and the smaller varieties of antelope are awfully dry, and the horses have now too little flesh to catch a giraffe.

30th (*Sunday*). — Malakanyama, a Maccalacas chief, came over to see me at Jurea, and besought me to shoot some game for him and his people, as they had fled from Mosilikatse and were starving. The Matabele had killed great numbers of them, when they at length showed fight — an unheard-of thing—killed two of the principal captains, and are now in daily expectation of a large commando coming in quest of them.

Boccas shot twenty-three head in all, myself seventeen, chiefly rhinoceros and buffalo, and two elephants. He killed three harrisbuck with one bullet, an extraordinary shot by moonlight; and last night, he and I, by the water, killed four rhinoceros and four buffaloes. Every vestige of the meat disappeared at once, but we have left the poor fellows a large lot of dried flesh to go on with. Malakanyama was very grateful, and sent me a present of four tusks, which paid well for powder and lead.

I lost the wagons for seven days, during five of which I had not a bite of anything but flesh. I did not lose myself, but it was owing to a mistake the wagon took the wrong road, and Batwing ran away back to the place from which I started, about forty miles, finding his way in a most miraculous manner. The Kaffirs on his spoor eventually brought him back, to my great joy, as the chances were about three to one in favour of a lion making a meal of him.

By-the-by, I shot a very fine old manikin lion, but having no arsenical soap was unable to preserve the skin, and the claws and skull are all that I have got as a trophy. I was alone watching the water when he came, and I killed him dead within fourteen yards. Three buffaloes, one white rhinoceros bull, one quagga, a lion, and an elephant, fell to my rifle that night, my best night's shooting. My bullets were reduced to five, and, not having an idea when or where I was likely to find my wagon or horse, and being entirely alone, I was in no enviable position, and had some fear of hunger before my eyes ; but I succeeded in bagging two buffaloes and one quagga, and had still two bullets left when the horse made his appearance. The wagon came the following morning, and I enjoyed the luxury of a cup of tea, and a little boiled maccaroni. Polson's wagon accompanied mine, and I took leave of him yesterday, our roads lying in opposite directions : he goes by Walvish Bay to the Cape, and has some desperate hard work before him, as his wagon has not less than 4,000 lbs., and his oxen are young, light, lean, and weak. He will take at least four good months to reach Walvish Bay, if he accomplish it in that time.

A sick ox and horse are waiting to be doctored ; the latter I hope may pull through, but the former I must leave behind, I fear. I shall wait at Nanta,

NIGHT SHOOTING.

J. Wolf, lith.

Hanhart, imp.

three days ahead, for my other wagon, and then, after the first rains, go out together.

Adonis has killed four more large bulls; he runs with the speed and endurance of an ostrich, and is one of the very best shots in all Africa. With these accomplishments of nature, if his heart was only in the right place, he might, in a few years, make a fortune, but even a moderate amount of pluck has not fallen to his share. Nothing would induce him to watch the water at night, even in company, and the roar of a lion at night makes him take himself off at his best pace at once. Still, he is the best man this year of my party, heading me in elephants by two, and he is on foot and I on horseback; but he is in the midst of numbers, while I seldom find one; the tsetse prevent my being able to go into their stronghold.

My plans are now to go on horseback to Mosili-katse, if he will receive me, to ask him what I must pay him to give me a hunting-velt next year, and send him also presents to the amount of about 15l.; but I shall be no loser by doing this, as he is certain to send me in return, if he accepts them, more than an equivalent. It is about seven days from here to his State, I believe; but it is almost impossible to get at the truth from any enquiries amongst the natives here, as he is so much dreaded by one and all, that they are positively afraid to speak of him.

Oct. 8th. — *Nanta.* — I take up my pen to kill time, as it weighs very heavily on my hands just now. I am out of sorts both in body and mind, and anxiously awaiting the arrival of my second wagon, which is overdue, and this is the place I fixed to wait for it, and a more comfortless, barren, desolate spot no human being could conceive. There is neither grass, wood, nor water; the sun is intensely hot, and there is no shade of any sort, and we have had three successive days of hot furnace-like winds. Nevertheless, we have been labouring our utmost to get a supply of fresh water for the oxen, and have dug large holes in different places; but though the water is drinkable at first, after an hour's exposure to the sun it is as salt as brine. To add to our discomfiture, our only spade has broken through the middle; still we contrive to kill enough game for actual necessity, but the meat will not keep many hours, and, worst of all, my oxen are dying daily. I make a post-mortem examination, but am no wiser. I know neither the disease nor the cure. They swell up to an enormous size, drink gallons of this brackish stuff, and, when opened, are full of a nasty yellowish water. I tried bleeding without any good effect, and this morning have tried cutting the skin where most swollen, and letting the water run out.

The Masaras say there is not a drop of water ahead, and what is to be done I do not myself know. I was far down the river this morning and found better water, and have sent the oxen thither. The Kaffirs showed me a white man's grave; I can learn no particulars as to the person buried there, but a more desolate spot to lay one's bones can hardly be conceived : I only hope such a fate may not be mine. I was very nearly losing two of my horses; they went back in search of water at night, and at daylight we started on the spoor. Boccas was first, and saw two lions lie in waiting; he was within fifteen yards when he first perceived them, fired at the head of one and jumped into a tree; fired again out of the tree, wounding one, when they made off, and five minutes after, the lost horses came trotting down to the water. The lions were as thin as planks ; they had not killed anything, and would have pounced on the horses instantly, but it is not their usual practice to kill game in the day-time.

I have no appetite, and trail my limbs after me as if they did not belong to me ; it is a great exertion to get into the wagon, and my system is fearfully enervated. There are wild ducks here, but I have not energy enough in my whole frame to go and shoot them, though they are not 200 yards off. I send my youngsters to stir them up, and take my chance of a dinner as they come past, and, as they keep the river in their flight, I generally intercept one or two as they come past, with the same small eighteen-Burrow.

11th.—Wearied to death : still at Nanta, waiting for my other wagon, and no news, good or bad, of it as yet. No Kaffir can keep an appointment. My oxen are not in a fit state to retrace their steps, and my horses are equally poor ; two of the former are dead, and one of the latter is useless, on account of a sore back. I unsaddled him when hot, the sun blistered him, and then rolling in the sand and fine stones completed the business. Not being able to get two loads of ivory, I am preparing or curing heads, male and female, of all sorts that are to be met with here, but there is no great variety. This salt water has been of inestimable value to my wagon wheels; I have let them all soak for twenty-four hours, and they are now as tight as drum-heads. We had the tail of a passing thunder shower last night, but all appearance of rain has vanished this morning, and the wind still continues in the old quarter from which it invariably blows—due east.

I am considerably better again, and hope I may now altogether escape the fever; I have had two or three twinges, but have thrown it off so far, and now trust I may escape this year. Yesterday the heat was so intense that I could not even bear the palms of my hands on the sand, while I was trying to creep up to some ducks; from hard work, the covering is much more like horn than skin.

16th.—How I have managed to kill the last five days, and how to get rid of the next ten or fifteen, is a perfect puzzle. I can find nothing in the world to do, but very little to eat, and that little by no means tempting; wood next to none; and I have drunk almost enough brackish, nauseous water to share the fate of Lot's wife. Boccas set off two days ago in search of my other wagon, a good 200 miles at least, back again. The weather has been long threatening rain, and this afternoon a very few heavy drops have fallen, but I think it can hardly pass entirely away without a downfall. It is almost as bad as being becalmed on the Line.

To break the sameness of the thing, three Macca-lacas Kaffirs were to show me some fresh elephant spoor, and I shot three springbuck for them, made bullets, and started ; and when I had got about ten miles away, they told me it was old spoor, that I had better turn back, and that they were going to their kraals, and then deliberately set down my blan-ket, &c., to continue their journey. I waited my opportunity quietly ; made a savage onset on one, wrested his assegais and kerry from him, broke one of the former over his head, jumped on Ferus, a hot-headed, hard-mouthed horse, rode right over a second, sending him, salt, kalabash, fells, &c., in all directions, and hurled the broken weapon at the third. Two of them fell on their knees, begging for life, and the third sped like an ostrich over the velt. I gave them a little good advice, not to try and humbug an Englishman again, and left them.

A Masara told me he had seen a lion not far off, and I immediately went in pursuit, inviting Spear-man and January, but they declined, not being ashamed to confess they were afraid. The Masara was afraid, too, but he went eventually, and we took the lion's spoor for about half a mile, when the Masara ran away, making frightful gesticulations.

We were approaching the lion from above the
wind, and the old brute was wide awake. On
first perceiving him, about sixty yards off, he was
half crouched under some thick thorns, facing me,
and intently watching my every movement, but
before I was on the ground to shoot he turned and
made off, and I went after him. He went away only
leisurely, and I might have shot at him from behind
more than once, but I thought, if I headed him and
got below the wind, he would stand. Ferus was
ready to hunt him, but immediately he got the lion's
wind he became very much alarmed, snorting and
very restive. The old manikin, likewise, on heading
him, growled savagely and shot into some very dense
underwood—his stronghold, in fact—where, without
dogs, it would have been insanity to follow him; so
I left him, consoling myself that, even if I had shot
him, he was only a yellow-maned one, and his skin,
from poverty, not worth preserving.

It has hitherto always been my choice to be alone,
but I now feel my solitude so much that I am determined, on any future journey, to take a companion
with me. I have two Masara boys about eight years
old, and January, by the wagon, and that is all. The
two former, though they understand every word, and
are most useful and handy, are mute as mice, though
I never speak cross to them, and they are to all appearance as happy as the day is long, and make row
enough by themselves; but when I try to converse
with them, they hang down their heads like dogs

convicted of sheep-worrying, and January laughs like a born idiot. Spearman, the ox-vachter, sometimes comes, but he has got hold of a Dutch psalm tune, the most horrid concoction on earth, which he is everlastingly humming, and which drives me quite distraught; so I generally greet his appearance with a kick that sends him howling back again.

19th.—I have so persecuted the widgeon here, that the remaining four out of seventeen are uncommonly shy, and whip under the lee-bank of the river with the swiftness of sand martins. And I must not forget to mention some rabbit-shooting I have had, which has reminded me more of England than anything since I left. Rabbits are the same all over the world, and excellent sport; these differ in no respect from those at home, but they have no holes. I found them all lying out, but could make no hand at them the first two days, as I gave them too much law; but I got into it the third, bagging five couple. Some rascal Masara has stuck one of my oxen, Pontac, an especial favourite, which I broke in myself. I have sewn up the wound, and have hopes of him, unless the assegai is poisoned. He and his mate Claret, so named from the resemblance in colour, are about the prettiest pair of Zulus I ever saw, and better were never yoked.

Dull and lonely as it is, I could manage to get over the day, but the nights are dreadful. When the sun goes down, the wind invariably does the same; then come mosquitoes, midges, gnats, and sand-flies, and

E E

the air is as close as a draw-well. I can hardly endure a rag over me, and I lie on my back slapping right and left, here, there, and everywhere, taking hundreds of lives without diminishing the buzz, and praying for morning or a breeze of wind, and getting up occasionally to look at the stars, and see how far the night has advanced. Even if I can, at times, bear a blanket over me, it is not much protection, unless I can manage to raise it an inch or so with my knees and elbows, as the mosquitoes bite through it. I dread a still night above everything, and would give, at times, all I possess for a wind, when the mosquitoes vanish.

'Sar, here come a folstrens on,' was January's intimation to me about an hour and a half ago, and I abandoned my pen for my rifle, and have been creeping under the river-banks in the hopes he would come to drink, keeping parallel with him for about three miles; but he had drunk, I suppose, as he never came nearer than 600 yards.

24th.—No news yet of the wagon. I have been waiting more than three weeks, and can now neither eat, drink, nor sleep, as there is neither food nor drink to be got, and the mosquitoes and midges take care I shall not sleep. I have become wrinkled and haggard; and, if my telescope, which I use as a looking-glass, does not belie my appearance, prematurely aged. My tea and coffee are all but finished, and I must reserve a little of the latter for night-work, to keep us awake when going out, as it is

simply impossible to move in the day-time across
these heavy sands in the hot, parching winds. The
water here gets more and more salt daily, it is
nauseous both to taste and smell ; and the game has
been so persecuted that it has entirely left this part,
and nothing is now to be seen. I have reduced the
ducks to a couple, with a vast amount of perseverance,
and have slain this morning, I verily believe, the last
rabbit within a circle of eight miles ; the Kaffirs
have lately had nothing but these to live on. No
rain comes, and all appearance of rain has vanished.
I started at dawn of day to shoot a giraffe, a weary
way across the desert, to some makolani trees ; found
eight, and shot one, a cow, when Ferus got away from
me, and never let me come within gunshot of him
till he made the wagon. I was never so exhausted
in my life ; the heat was beyond all description, and
I was sore afraid I should be sun-struck, as my
leathern cap was as hot as an oven. I could not rest,
or even stoop down to tie my shoe, which came undone, as the sands were burning hot, and there was
no shade for a good twelve miles of desert. The
dogs remained behind, and did not come back till
near midnight ; and I should have been wise to
follow their example, but I could not bear up so
long against thirst ; it gave me the greatest pain to
swallow, and I suffered much, but after two hours in
the shade I was all right again. To-morrow I fully
expect to hear some tidings of the wagon, and I shall
bless the day I get out of this, though the Kaffirs

say there is neither game nor water ahead. The great
Salt-pan, in which the Zonga river loses itself, is only
a couple of hours west, and there is often a hurricane
blowing across the desert, with clouds of dust and hot
winds. I think my ox Pontac will recover, but
Ringals, the best front ox ever inspanned, is dead.

27th.—I have managed to supply the larder abundantly, with two rhinoceros and two elands ; all lean
as crows, however, and very bad fare. I had to go a
weary way in search of them, and the flesh was gone
bad ere it reached the wagon ; but this morning I
had not much trouble with an old black bull rhinoceros. I was lying half asleep a little after sunrise,
the mosquitoes having at last given me a little peace,
when he came to the water. I gave my rifle fifteen
drachms of coarse powder, as it was an open flat,
and I resolved to make short work of him. I crept
close to him, as he was drinking with his head in a
hole, and shot him through the lungs dead, with the
first barrel, which was just as well, as the cap of the
second barrel sprang off with the recoil, and though
I tried to give him a second pill, as he went away
for 500 or 600 yards, it was a case of snap, of course.

I made bad work of an ostrich yesterday, but the
glare of the sun on the sand of the dry bed of a river
was too much for me ; my eyes smarted, and I was
more than half mazed, and though I succeeded in
stalking within 200 yards, I felt sure I should miss
him, as I was as shaky as if I had got the palsy, and
I accordingly did miss him. The hardships of an

CHASE OF AN OSTRICH.

African hunter are great, that is, if he really follows up his game. I breakfasted yesterday about 2 P.M. on a raw talo, a root somewhat resembling a huge potato, but soft, sweet, and moist. Had a most refreshing drink of water out of the paunch of a quagga, a horrid thing to drink out of, and which requires great skill, but, notwithstanding, it is the very best thing one can carry water in, as evaporation takes place, and though the sun is burning hot, the water is remarkably cool and good. In any other water utensil it would be as hot as charcoal. There is a bonny medley of things lying around my wagon — heads and horns of all descriptions ; lions' and wolves' skulls ; ostrich eggs ; jackal and wild-cat skins ; koodoo, tsessebe, wildebeest, springbuck, rhinoceros horns and ears ; great lumps of salt ; dry flesh hanging up ; rheims, neck-straps, and yokeskeys ; guinea-fowls, ducks and geese, pheasant and partridge feathers in all directions ; rabbit-skins without number ; pots, pans, dog-meat ; ostrich feathers ; buffalo and eland hide. This is what I cast my eyes on from where I now sit; such a chaos I never beheld.

Nov. 4th. — I think it is Sunday, but every-thing is so monotonous, I have nothing to mark the flight of time, and I may just as likely be out of my reckoning as not. No news of the missing wagon. The old saying, ' ill news flies fast,' is rather consoling to me, as I now really begin to think there has been some foul play somewhere. I place every

confidence in Boccas, whom I started three weeks
ago, with the strictest injunctions to let me know the
cause of the delay without a moment's loss of time,
and he had my favourite and best horse, Batwing. If
the Mosilikatse's Kaffirs, or any others, have made
an end of my Kaffirs and men left in charge, my
losses will amount in all to 500*l.* ; wagon, oxen,
stores, guns, horse, and 500 lbs. of ivory that I
know of, besides probably much more, and some of
the finest heads and horns, of different sorts, of the
rarest antelopes I ever saw. We have been particularly fortunate this year, and shot an incredible
number, over 400 head, I think. I left meal, sugar,
and dried fruits, also behind, and am myself totally
without anything of the sort. I am positively in rags,
and my flesh resembles boiled lobster more than
anything else, being literally roasted with the sun.
The pain is very great, and all for want of a needle.
I had four in my hat on leaving the wagon, but they
have all got lost; I might have saved the life of an
ox or two, had I only had a couple of pins. I bled
one, and tried to take up the vein with a thorn in
lieu of a pin, but it broke in the night, the vein
burst open again and the ox bled to death, and I
have been afraid to venture a second time. What
riles me most is, that the other wagon had more
than enough of all these requisites ; but I have not
yet quite lost all hope of its turning up some day
or other.

The days are so intensely hot, that it is impossible

to stir, and the moon is just seven days past the full; therefore, I must now wait fourteen days, so as to have the full benefit of it, and then, if I hear nothing previously, start myself in search, a good 250 miles, without other meat or drink of any sort than what my rifle will provide me with—which is precarious, to say the least of it—and then back again another 250 miles. It has rained about forty or fifty miles ahead at the Qualeba, and I hear that the young grass is fast springing up, and that there is plenty of water. As the residue of my oxen are wretched in appearance, and keep on dying, I shall start to-morrow on the oxen's account, and see if I can come there, but I have great misgivings, as the wagon is very heavy and I am but a poor driver; however, I cannot stay longer here. We have been most providentially sustained with a good supply of meat all along; two more rhinoceros, an eland, springbuck, quagga, tsessebe, roan antelope, pallah, and blue wildebeest having succumbed, and weeks ago I thought the last head had taken itself off to other quarters.

Now for an adventure with a lion, which I have reserved for the last. On Friday the old Masara captain paid me a visit; he had seen a lion on the path, and left a lot of Masaras to watch him. I had been working hard all day in the hot sun with an adze, making a dissel-boom for the wagon, and was tired, lame, and shaky in the arms, and did not feel at all up to the mark for rifle-shooting;

but I ordered Ferus to be saddled, who was also not at all fresh, having had a tremendous burst in the morning across a flat, after a lean eland cow. Just after I caught sight of about twenty-five Masaras sitting down, all armed to the teeth with shields and assegais, my attention was attracted to a Kaffir skull, which struck me as a bad omen, and the thought entered my head, that it might be my fate to lay mine to bleach there. I did not, however, suffer this thought to unnerve me, but proceeded, and found that the lion had decamped. The Masaras followed his spoor about a couple of miles, when he broke cover. I did not see him at first, but gave chase in the direction in which the Masaras pointed, saw him, and followed for about 1,000 yards, as he had a long start, when he stood in a nasty thorn thicket. I dismounted at about sixty or seventy yards, and shot at him; I could only see his outline, and that very indistinctly, and he dropt so instantaneously, that I thought I had shot him dead. I remounted and reloaded, and took a short circle, and stood up in my stirrups to catch a sight of him. His eyes glared so savagely, and he lay crouched in so natural a position, with his ears alone erect, the points black as night, that I saw in a moment I had missed him; I was then about eighty yards from him, and was weighing the chances of getting a shot at him from behind an immense ant-heap, about fifteen yards nearer. I had just put the horse in motion with that intention, when on he came with a

tremendous roar, and Ferus whipt round like a top, and away at full speed. My horse is a fast one, and has run down the gemsbok, one of the fleetest antelopes, but the way the lion ran him in was terrific. In an instant I was at my best pace, leaning forward, rowels deep into my horse's flanks, looking back over my left shoulder, over a hard flat excellent galloping ground. On came the lion, two strides to my one. I never saw anything like it, and never want to do so again ; to turn in the saddle and shoot darted across my mind, when he was within three strides of me, but on second thoughts I gave a violent jerk on the near rein, and a savage dig at the same time with the off heel, armed with a desperate rowel, just in the nick of time, as the old manikin bounded by me, grazing my right shoulder with his, and all but unhorsing me, but I managed to right myself by clinging to the near stirrup-leather. He immediately slackened his speed ; as soon as I could pull up, which was not all at once, as Ferus had his mettle up, I jumped off, and made a very pretty and praise-worthy shot, considering the fierce ordeal I had just passed (though I say it who ought not), breaking his hind leg at 150 yards off, just at the edge of the thicket. Fearful of losing him, as the Masaras were still flying for bare life over the velt, with their shields over their heads, and I knew nothing would prevail on them to take his spoor again, I was in the saddle, and chasing him like mad in an instant. His broken leg gave me great confidence, though he went hard on three legs; and I jumped off forty yards behind him, and gave him the second barrel, a good shot, just above the root of the tail, breaking his spine, when he lay under a bush roaring furiously, and I gave him two in the chest before he cried ' enough.' He was an old manikin, fat and furious, having only four huge yellow blunt fangs left. Then I had to hunt up the Masaras, who, of course, never came near, nor never would have done so, if he had taken a day and a half to eat up my carcase. The gloomy forebodings which the skull gave rise to at starting, were much nearer being fulfilled than I reckoned for ; and why a man risks his life for no earthly gain, is a problem I cannot solve. I only know this, there is a secret feeling of inward satisfaction at having conquered, that is almost worth the risk to be run, though there are no applauding friends or spectators present. I wish my powers of description equalled those of a Masara; I think I never enjoyed a greater treat than to hear one of them describe this adventure. I did not understand a word he said, but his gestures and attitudes were splendid ; his eyes flashed fire, he broke out into a streaming perspiration, and mimicked the lion so perfectly, as to make me feel quite cold. It would be impossible to surpass his imitation of the horse galloping, with myself spurring him, and all the other incidents of the chase. I had the satisfaction of seeing that I held the very first place in his estimation, and ever since the Masaras have paid me great attention, bringing wood and water unasked.

My waking thoughts and midnight dreams are of the missing wagon, and I cannot help thinking that something serious has happened. The Kaffirs have only one punishment — death, for every offence; and Mosilikatse has been jealous of our hunting without his permission, as he claims the country, and there is no law here but that of the stronger.

I shall go in search with a revolver, as well as my rifle, to guard against surprise, and then I should not be much afraid if I were well mounted; but my poor nag is all skin and bone, and I am afraid he will not stand the journey.

9th. — I have got over some sixty miles of the journey. Twenty hours in the yoke without water, three rivers which we crossed being dry; at length we came to some pits, and after working in the broiling sun, clearing them out like galley-slaves, eight only of my unfortunate oxen were able to get any water, and this they drank out of a zinc bucket. In this emergency a Masara told me he had seen a little rain water in a vley a long way off, and after a great deal of wrangling, not having any beads to pay him, he agreed to show me the water, if I, in return, shot him a giraffe. To these terms I at once joyfully acceded, and he set off with the vachter and the poor oxen, and yesterday I fulfilled my share of the compact, but not without great difficulty. After no end of hunting, I at length sighted one giraffe-cow, going at a slapping gallop a long way ahead over a villanous country covered with scrub bush; but Ferus at length managed to get up to her. I was doing all I knew to head the giraffe from a thick forest of makolani trees, and she strained every nerve and sinew to gain her point. Ferus was going splendidly, and fifty yards more must have finished the business, as I was then not more than eighty yards off, when over and over he rolled in a hole, like a rabbit shot at full speed, and I, standing up in my stirrups leaning far forward, was shot a prodigious distance, clear out of all harm's way. I was on my legs in a minute, but my gun barrels were so covered with dust and old dead roots of grass, which we had managed to tear up, that I could not see the sight. I rapidly gave my gun a brush with the cuff of my coat and shouldered her again. The giraffe was at least 200 yards off, and I struck her with both barrels, the first within an inch of the hip-bone, the second through the fleshy part of her off hind leg, but without doing her any injury. I fully calculated on a walk back, but, for a wonder, I managed to recapture my nag. I took up the spoor, and found the giraffe lying dead less than a mile off.

11th (*Sunday*).—*Matibele (a Fountain).* — Got here yesterday, after a journey of three days from Qualeba, smoking hot and dog-tired, and I vowed over and over again that nothing but sheer necessity should ever compel me to come again to this thirst-land. The oxen, hollow and flat-sided, did nothing but low, and when outspanned kept on the track, and would not stand or eat a moment. The ground was so hot that the poor dogs to whom I gave water could not stand still to drink, but had to keep moving their feet ; the velt is, if possible, gradually getting worse and worse, and it is three hard days to the next water. I was never before in such a strait, and the Masaras positively refuse to go with me, as they say there is no water. The fiend assuming the shape of a Masara, who was the cause of my leaving Nanta, by his assurance of green grass and abundance of water, vanished in the night, or I should have crippled him for life at least, and I have been forced into coming thus far to save the lives of my oxen, and people, and self; it has added another hundred miles to my journey back in search of my other wagon, and I must now give up the idea altogether, as I am sure my poor horse will never accomplish it. I place every confidence in the people I left in charge of the wagon ; if they are alive they will bring it out, and if dead I could not bring the wagon out myself, but should most probably share their fate. I shall therefore do all I can to get out with what I have, a bird in the hand being worth two in the bush ; but this is but poor consolation for a loss of at least 500*l.*

12*th*. —I dread more what I am just now about to undertake than I ever dreaded anything before. It is three long days to the next water ; heavy sand most

of the way, the wagon also heavy, the near hind
axle-tree sprung ; and no offer whatever will induce
a Masara to go with me, as they dread sun and
thirst too much.   I must, however, attempt it, as I
am greatly in need of a change of food, and
thoroughly sick of meat, meat, meat, without anything
besides.   No news, good, bad, or indifferent, of the
other wagon. I have long since ceased making conjec-
tures, but must first replenish my stores, and then
go in search.   There is little use in waiting for the
chance of rain, as Dr. Livingstone told me, that when
he was living at Kolobeng, Sechele's country, it never
once rained for five years.   The trees, notwithstanding the drought, are all fast coming into leaf again,
and the bush is getting green and thick, so that
there is no more hunting; besides, the unhealthy
season is just beginning, and it is high time to get
out into a better climate.   Driving my own wagon is
cruel hard work, very different from walking, lying,
riding in the wagon, or on horseback, just as my inclination tended ; now my hands are all scars and
sores from the oxen's horns, and I am quite hoarse
with calling and shouting at them.

   17th. — We are now at the River Mesa, which we
reached two days ago.   I had miscalculated the distance, it being four days instead of three ; but I got a
little water for my oxen half way, in a vley.   That
indefatigable, careless vagabond, January, hit off a
Bushman's spoor and caught him up, and though he
assured him positively that there was no water, that

the vley he drank out of was dry, and that he was just then starting himself in search, yet, when the news reached me, I outspanned at once, saddled up and took my gun, and made the Bushman show us a vley where there was barely sufficient, but it was worth its weight in gold to me. About four miles ere reaching this, my pole pulled out of the iron bolt, and the oxen walked on quite unconcerned, leaving the wagon a fixture. I remedied this temporarily with the rheim-chain, making the pole fast with rheims round the fore tongue just for the two after-oxen to steer by, and got here without further mishap; yesterday I put in a new dissel-boom, and intended to proceed when the sun had sunk a few hours.

Dog-tired, I went fast asleep as soon as I lay down, and never awoke till the morning-star rose, when I heard lions roaring, and immediately jumped up to see if my horses and oxen were all right. I was horrified at seeing no signs of either, sent the Kaffirs off at once, and now came the climax of all my misfortunes. January had never made the oxen fast, though he had seen five lions in the afternoon, and poor Ferus and Kebon lay dead within sixty yards of one another and some 600 from the wagon, the latter, who was in very fair condition, being entirely devoured; Ferus was untouched. They cost me 90l. cash, and I should have got at least 120l. for them, had I wished to sell. At sunset the Kaffirs returned, reporting the deaths of Yambrown and Scotland, two of my middle oxen, devoured by lions. They had followed the oxen's spoor several hours, and eventually brought back all the rest, and we made a strong kraal and kept watch all night, with several large fires round, but, apparently satisfied with what they had already done, the lions did not pay us another visit. It is vexatious to suffer such a loss through the carelessness of the Kaffirs, but I must make some allowance for them ; the poor lads were as dead beaten as myself with our four days and nights forced march.

I have no brass wire, beads, or anything to trade a goat or sheep, or a little Kaffir corn from the Kaffirs, and can shoot nothing now on foot but small dry bucks, or a quagga or other rubbish, hardly eatable, and I shall have a hard bout of it now, ere I once more reach civilisation. When I do reach it, I shall not be in a hurry to leave it again. I am writing with a mixture of coffee and gunpowder.

In about eighteen or twenty-one days, if all goes well, I hope to reach Sechele's, where I may reckon on a few comforts from the German missionaries ; but the wagon runs heavily, squeaking all the way, and the wheels are as dry as tinder, and where now to procure a bit of grease to smear them with, I do not know.

I had not even the satisfaction of shooting one of the lions, as it was mid-day ere I found the horses, and there were then no traces to be seen of them. January had taken himself off, sneaking back in the night.

18*th*. — Rain at last, but only in heavy passing showers. I am now outspanned under the very same tree as three years ago on my return from Mosilikatse's with Martinus Swartz. I little expected then ever to be here again, as I had a very hard bout of it that time. I have led but a vagrant sort of life since then, doing little good for myself or anybody else, except supplying the ungrateful, half-starved Masaras and Maccalacas with abundance of flesh. I have scarcely ever been still, and must have journeyed over some twelve or fifteen thousand miles at least, and that at much less than foot pace, having been through the Transvaal Republic, Free State, and part of the Old Colony, twice down to Natal, and twice round Lake Ngami, and now over the Zambesi into Makololo and Batoka lands; and it is now, I think, nearly time to call a halt.

I have this morning come over some very heavy sand-bolts, with thick trees, and sharp, short turns, entirely to my own satisfaction, with a very heavy wagon and the loss of two of my oxen, and I take a deal of merit to myself. It is rather exciting work, and, if I had only food, I should not mind it at all. I have got once more into a hilly country, which quite gladdens my eye after the immense amount of flat, uninteresting country I have lately passed over.

24*th*. — I have endless difficulties to contend with in the way of writing fluid, having lost my ink-bottle, and have nothing but a little tea and coarse gunpowder in a bullet-mould, which oozes out fast. I got on well for three days, when I lost the way and got under the Bamangwato Hills, the roughest and thickest bush a wagon ever encountered. I was congratulating myself that we should come to Letloche next day, where I should get into a beaten path, and the worst of my difficulties would be over, when at last the tent of my wagon was carried bodily away with a crash, horridly grating to my ears. Guns, telescope, oil-flask, ostrich feathers, and a variety of things made fast thereon, went with it, and the two sails, torn from top to bottom. I could no longer steer the wagon, and the oxen were dead beaten ; that night, when I had no protection, of course it rained in torrents, and we had most violent thunder-storms, the first we have had for ten months. While treking across an extensive open plain by moonlight, I found an ostrich nest with fifteen eggs, which we bagged at once. About twelve the following day I reached Letloche, where I spent two days repairing damages, and I hope to reach the Bamangwato State (Sicomo's) early to-morrow.

Waddington and Aldersley, two Englishmen, joined me here, greatly to my astonishment ; they had chartered a vessel from the Cape to Angra Peguina, on the west coast, in February last, and had worked their way up to the Lake, through Great Namaqua and Damara lands, and are now on their way back to the Cape. A pretty good round they will have had of it. We sat up all last night relating our different adventures, though three hours previously perfect strangers to one another. A chance meeting of this sort is most refreshing and delightful, after being months and months alone, and tongue-tied in the desert.

I had the good fortune to exchange my only blanket, six days back, for a little Kaffir corn, and got an intombi (young girl) to stamp it in a block for me, and have been luxuriating on porridge and salt for breakfast and dinner ever since ; it is about as coarsely ground or crushed as fine gravel, but very wholesome, and a great treat it was for the first three days, after being so long a time living entirely on flesh or fowl, cooked in every conceivable way. I am now beginning to think that a little sugar, milk, or treacle, might be no bad addition ; but in another ten days, if all goes well, I may hope for some Boers' meal from the German missionaries at Sechele's, the most hospitable men in the whole world. My poor oxen are very much used up, but I hope to purchase two or three fresh ones here, which will wonderfully assist me. I have left my friends behind; their oxen are entirely done up, falling in the yoke from sheer poverty and leg weariness.

29th.—Massouey.—I am here again for the seventh time, and last, I hope, as I see no encouragement to return. I spent two days at the Bamangwato State, and bought six oxen, young, thin, and unbroken. I have already had four inspanned, but was obliged to fall back on two of my old ones again in place of

two whom no amount of flagellation would induce
to trek. I got also about 45 lbs. of ivory, but it
was very dear, and I plainly perceive that there is
no more good to be done. We have had a heavy
thunder-storm, and I fully expect to get a little rain-
water ahead, for after leaving Lopèpè, a day and a
half from this, we get no more to Kapong, three
hard days, with a good deal of night work added ;
but I do most of my treking at nights, whenever the
moon is near the full.

I heard of a dreadful accident which happened to
three Englishmen on the velt this year : three wagons
and their contents blown all to rags, from the explo-
sion of 1,600 lbs. of powder; seven horses killed, one
Hottentot and one Englishman.

Four Maccalacas Kaffirs joined me here to go to
Natal, so that I am now quite independent of any
Natal Kaffirs.

I have just potted five ducks, the whole batch, in a
most disgraceful manner. It was too great a windfall
in these times to give them a ghost of a chance, and
I got well under the wind, crawled in upon them on
all fours like a snake in the grass twice successively,
and bagged all but one on the water, when I might
have taken them fairly on the wing, right and left.
I now contemplate them with great satisfaction, as I
have been living villanously since the death of my
nags, and—what makes it, if possible, still more
aggravating—we yesterday saw a troop of giraffes
from the wagon, and made a vain effort to stalk in

upon them on foot, when the best of the herd must
have bitten the dust had my poor Ferus been alive.
Those rascally Mangwatos stole my last spoon and
axe, a box of caps, and my knife also, and very likely
many more things that I have not yet missed.

Dec. 2nd (Sunday).—*Lopèpè.*—This is the last
water for three long days, and there are no signs of
rain, though it is so late in the year. I hear the
Bakwains at Sechele's State are all starving : a comfortable prospect before me. I am getting all in
preparation for a move—cask, water-vats and calabashes full, rheims and neck-straps mended, that we
may have no cause of delay or hindrance of any kind
that a little foresight might have avoided, and I shall
do all I can to get over this much-dreaded part of
the road to Kapong, after which, except the flooded
rivers, it is all plain sailing to Natal. I have rested
here the best part of three days to recruit my poor
oxen, but they have not benefited much, as the
grass is too scarce. I have broken in three young
ones from Bamangwato, but they only help in the
day, as they plague too much yet for night-work,
and are continually getting wrong in the yoke. I
have bagged this time with great difficulty one pallah
and one springbuck, and should be very glad if I had
with me any young ardent sportsman to take this job
off my hands, as it begins now to pall upon me, and, as
soon as ever I have procured sufficient for the day, I
immediately make the best of my way back. It is no
longer sport; the days are now gone by when I

would walk from Leyland or Hoghton to Brinseall
and back, for the chance only of a shot or two at a
snipe, or from Ledard to the port of Monteith and
back, ten long Scotch miles each way, for a day at
rabbits and woodcocks, as I used to do every Saturday
all through the winter.

4th. — Waddington lent me Dr. Livingstone's work
at Letloche, and I have just now for the first time
read his description of the Falls of the Zambesi, and
compared notes with my own ; they differ materially,
but on carefully reperusing mine I cannot alter a
word. He has much underrated their magnitude. I
saw them every successive day for a week from every
accessible point, from opposite, from both sides, and
above. Distance is most deceiving in this country,
and still more so on the water ; when I stepped it off
opposite I was myself surprised to find it so far, and
am confident I have not overrated the river at 2,000
yards wide. I may perhaps have rather overrated the
depth, but the Umgani Falls in Natal are 100 yards
deep, and the Zambesi, as far as the eye can judge,
look as deep ; as to the width, I can throw a stone
ninety yards, and though I had some good ones to
choose from, and threw with force and confidence
from within twenty feet of the edge, having a very
good head and never getting dizzy, yet I never succeeded in many attempts in throwing one across.
It is probably, therefore, as many yards as the
Doctor says feet ; otherwise his description is very
good, and exceedingly well expressed. He has

erred on the right side, being too careful not to
exaggerate; he allows that he has a bad eye and is
not a good judge of distances, as he says himself
that he judged a distance to be 400, which proved
to be 900, yards. The discovery of the Falls was
made in 1855, and from that time to this (1860),
with the exception of Livingstone's party, no European but myself has found his way thither.

To give myself a good idea in rifle-shooting at game,
I have been for years constantly judging and stepping
off distances — for instance, from one ant-heap to
another — and have hardly ever shot any game on the
flat that I have not previously in my own mind
first judged the distance, sighted accordingly, and, if
successful, afterwards stepped it off, so that I can now
form a very good idea. It is astonishing what wide
shots others make who have not been in the habit of
so doing; objects look very much nearer than they
really are, owing to the clearness of the atmosphere.

9th (*Sunday*).—Got to Sechele's three days ago,
and am now the best part of a day on my road
towards Merico. My two Bequina boys left me at
Sechele's, and we had a whole day's quarrelling as
to pay, their captain demanding much more than
had been previously agreed upon, in consequence
of the distance and time that I had been away; he
also demanded as their right one tusk for every
elephant shot by a Bequina, and this matter still
rests in the hands of the German missionary,
Mr. Schroeder, whom I have appointed to act in

my stead, when (if ever) my lost wagon makes its appearance, as the Bequinas will not otherwise allow it to pass.

I am now left almost entirely to my own resources to manage wagon and oxen over a heavy path, and some very ugly drifts and places. My Maccalacas, though willing enough, are surprisingly stupid, and we cannot understand one another a bit, and had all but broken the wagon twice yesterday from short turning and losing the spoor; but they will, it is to be hoped, improve as they go on.

I got a supply of bread, sugar, and coffee from Mr. Schroeder, and a few beads also, and two sheep. He treated me more than hospitably; my difficulties and hardships are now only things to be looked back upon, and I am none the worse, though they thought me very lean and fine-drawn, and stuffed me, during my stay, as they do a Norfolk turkey ten days before Christmas; Germans feed in such an extraordinary manner. I had boiled rice and raisins, cinnamon and nutmeg, boiled dried peaches, a lot of fried very fat mutton swimming in grease, pancakes and sugar, all piled up on my plate at once. I begged and implored them to stop, and when Mr. Schroeder, as a climax, poured some yellow fluid, which I took to be melted butter, but which proved to be vinegar, over all this compound, I need hardly say I had a bilious headache all the following day, as I was ravenously hungry, and saw through most of it, and then drank coffee to an enormous extent. There were all the ingredients for a very good repast, if they would only have allowed me to take it in my own manner, and help myself, but Mr. and Mrs. Schroeder took every opportunity, when my attention was called away, to load up another spoonful or two of anything that came to hand. I had once or twice the satisfaction, by suddenly whipping my plate away, of letting a few compounds fall on the table, to be snapped up by the numerous black progeny, immediately after grace was said.

I reached Merico in due course, where I left my two lads, Meercat and Ngami, in Mr. Zimmerman's charge. I got my fresh oxen there, and made good play once more to Durban, where I arrived all right in about a month, without any occurrence of note, invested in two fresh and fat horses in Mooi River Dorp, and kept the wagon and my Maccalacas supplied with wildebeest, blesbuck, and springbuck, until we crossed the Drakensberg. My Kaffirs turned out active, clever, intelligent fellows in no time, trustworthy and honest in every respect, capital hands with their long needles at sewing, and excellent cattle and horse-herds. Two whom I turned into grooms were wild with joy at the success of the horses in their charge at the Durban Race Meeting, and their consequent reward, and when I left for England immediately after, they returned again to their native homes on the Cashan Mountains, some 700 miles NW.

My missing, and, as I thought, lost wagon, came

down to Natal, about six weeks after my arrival, in
charge of Boccas, with a heavy load of ivory. The
oxen and poor Batwing were in a sad state of poverty,
but I had the pleasure of seeing them marvellously
recruited before I left the colony. Boccas had hung
up all my trophies, many of the finest specimens I
ever saw, in trees, to make room for the ivory, the
more valuable commodity; consequently, I had the
mortification of losing them all, though I was com-
pensated in a great measure by some very fine ivory.
The number of elephants they found in the tsetse
country had been their inducement for remaining so
long behind, and altogether they gave a most satisfactory account of themselves.

'THE END.'

THE following is a List of Game killed by four guns in my last
expedition (1860) to the Zambesi, with the Kaffir names — as
far as I am acquainted with them — attached:

English	Kaffir	English	Kaffir
61 Elephant	Inthlovi	12 Blue Wildebeest	Inconcon
2 Hippopotamus	Imvubu	2 Black ,, . ,,	
11 Rhinoceros, white	Incomba	71 Quagga	Idube
12 ,, black	Borele	Zebra (Burchall's)	
,, blue		Reitbuck	Umsica
,, two-horned		Oribo	Iula
11 Giraffe	Ututla	3 Duiker	Impunzi
21 Eland	Impofu	Klipspringer	Iyoko
30 Buffalo	Inyati	Bush Buck	Inconka (m.)
12 Harrisbuck	Potoquaine		Imbabala (f.)
14 Roan Antelope		Red Bush Buck	
2 Gemsbuck	Kukama	Bluebuck	Umpiti
9 Koodoo	Iganthla	10 Steinbuck	Nkina
4 Waterbuck	Ipifa	1 Gryse Steinbuck	,,
1 Hartebeest	Inthluzela	Pokur	Pokur
12 Tsessebe	Tsessebe	Nakong	Nakong
18 Impala	Impala	1 Fall Rheebuck	
Inyala	Inyala	Roy Bluebuck	
Leche	Leche	Kama	Kama
1 Blesbuck		2 Striped Eland	Impofu
25 Springbuck	Insepe		

English	Kaffir	English	Kaffir
4 Lion	Inconyama, or Imbubi	9 Silver Jackal	
Leopard	Umsila	Grey ,,	
Panther	Ingwe	Lynx	
Hyena, Striped		Rattle	
4 ,, Spotted	Umpisi	Pole Cat	
Wild Dog	Inja	Otter, two kinds	
Small Wild Dog		Porcupine	
Black Wolf		Anteater	
2 Wild Cat		Bush Boar	Inglubi

English	Kaffir		English	Kaffir
2 Velt Boar, or Flac Fare			Baboon	
Crocodile	*Nguana*		Umsemanga . .	*Umsemanga*
Guana			Monkeys, various	
Armadillo			3 Hare	
Ocelot			24 Rabbit	
Meercat			Rock Rabbit	
			1 Tiger Cat . . .	*Nlozi*

LAND BIRDS

2 Ostrich
Large Crested Bustard
Common   „
Koran, or small   „   six varieties
Guinea Fowl, Black
    „   „   Blue or Grey
Pheasants, two kinds
Partridges, three kinds
Quail, two kinds
Snipe, Common and Painted

Dikkop
Namaqua Partridges, three sorts
Plovers, three kinds
Pigeons — Wood, Rock, and Turtle Dove, six of the long-tailed variety
Hadada
Sacred Ibis
Bush Turkey, not eatable

WATER BIRDS

Black Goose
Grey   „
Golden   „
Muscovy Duck
Yellow-billed „
Common   „
Brown   „
Wigeon
Teal
Divers
Coots

Water Hens, and every variety of Water Fowl
Curlew
Pelican
Flamingo
Hammer Kop
Meahem
Herons
Storks
Cranes

INDEX.

INDEX.

ABO

ABOUTI Inyouti, a beer, 77
   African cuisine, 333
— Gum-trees, 84
Amabouche, an African fruit, 62
Amas, 13, 69, 71
Amasi, thick sour milk, 350
Amatonga bread, 84
Amatongas tribe, the, 75, 119, 121;
   their courtesy, 77; their industry, 85
Amobella meal, 13
Antelopes, 199, 382
Ants, 25, 69
Ant-heaps, 283
Armadillo, 146

BALDWIN, William Charles, early life,
   2; land in Natal, 4; first hunting expedition to St. Lucia Bay, 5;
   encounter an elephant, 8; sup on the
   elephant's heart and foot, 9; go out
   duck-shooting, 9; escape from a crocodile, 10; trade with the natives, 11;
   sleep in a Kaffir hut, 12; am charged
   by a buffalo, 14; shoot my first sea-
   cow, 15; construct a house of reeds,
   16; am taken ill, 17; become my
   own doctor, 17; boat attacked by a
   sea-cow, 18; am attacked by ague,
   20; break up of the camp, 21; return to Natal, 22; recover from a
   long illness, 23; two years on the
   Inanda, 24; monotonous life, 24;
   narrow escape from crocodiles, 26, 27;
   go into the Zulu country, 29; fall

BAL

under a wagon, 30; shoot an eland,
32; receive a visit from a panther,
34; chase after buffaloes, 35; enter
King Panda's country, 38; sent back,
39; hard chase after a buffalo, 42;
narrow escape from a lion, 46; wound
a lion, 49; shoot a blue heron, 51;
lose my dog Hopeful, 52; bring back
ample supplies, 53; am conducted by a
honey-bird to a bees' nest, 53; chase an
eland bull, 55; breakfast upon buffalo
tongues, 56; disappointed of food, 60;
kill a bush pig, 61; life in Africa,
62; run down a tiger-cat, 62; finish
a pair of boots, 64; bad weather, 64;
short of food, 66; pursuit of 'Justice,'
66; a wet night, 68; short commons,
69; shoot sea-cows, 70; a good dinner, 70; kill an eagle, 73; shoot for
the Zulus, 75; visit the Amatongas,
75; bag an inyala, 76; come upon
lions, wolves, &c., 78; through the
bush, 79; come upon an elephant,
79; cross the Pongola, 81; chastise
the Kaffir Jack, 81; am swept out
of a canoe, 87; encounter with a sea-
bull, 89; symptoms of fever, 90;
purchase cattle, 93; go into the Zulu
country, 95; dangerous descent, 96;
lose a favourite horse, 98; narrow escape from crocodiles, 100; missions
in the Zulu country, 104; shoot a
rhinoceros, 106; meet a puff adder,
111; third hunt in the Zulu country,

BAL

112; tent invaded by a lion, 117;
am charged by a buffalo, 123; desperate situation, 124; a hurricane,
131; war among the Kaffirs, 133,
frightful state of the country, 136;
enter the Transvaal republic, 142;
am visited by a Coranna chief, 154;
a night in the open, 155; go into the
Merico country, 160; life amongst
the Boers, 164; chase a giraffe, 171;
a timely storm, 176; encounter a
giraffe. 178; feet pierced by thorn,
180; my rifle damaged, 182; pursue
a giraffe, 187; suffer from heat, 188;
suspected by a Kaffir chief, 195;
shoot my first tsessebe and first harrisbuck, 197; chase of an antelope,
199; chase after Bryan, 202; want
of water, 207; narrow escape from an
elephant, 212; lost in the bush, 215;
a Maccateese kraal, 217; a Hottentot
maid, 225; Christmas in Africa, 229;
am arrested under suspicion of smuggling, 232; adopt a Masara boy,
248; deserted by my Kaffirs, 249;
alone in the desert, 251; dangerous
encounter with elephants, 263; see
Lake Ngami, 265; a Kaffir repast,
266; barter with Kaffirs, 268; Kaffir
cruelty, 269; lose a valuable horse,
274; am seized with ague, 276; a
strong stomach, 277; farewell to
Leche, 282; Masara boy deserted,
286; return of fever, 287; hot pursuit of a giraffe, 289; am ungrate-
fully treated by Sechele,. 290; re-
monstrate with Sechele, 292; bush
on fire, 296; great scarcity, 301;
horses, 305; go on another trip, 305;
heavy losses, 308; harvest time, 309;
course of a bullet, 309; get robbed,
312; how we find water, 313; after
elephants, 316; fear of the tsetse,
321; hard pursuit of an elephant,
322; exciting chase, 327; African
cookery, 333; in search of a rhinoceros, 334; a riddle solved, 335; am
deserted by the Kaffirs, 336; am presented with Ngami, a Masara boy, 337;

BOC

have a return of fever, 339; great
heat, 340; visit some English missionaries, 342; suffer from thirst, 343;
from hunger, 345; birds, 349; sell
my ivory, 353; a bad gun, 353; narrow escape from drowning, 354; difficulties of crossing the Tugela, 356;
our wagon upset, 357; a finished
actor, 360; knock David down, 361;
upset with Midnight, 364; a Kaffir
Rarey, 368; African serenade, 372;
lose my horse Frenchman, 373; a
hunter's life, 374; after elands, 376;
view of the Salt-pan, 378; light
pockets, 382; perilous position, 385;
a Masara encampment, 387; trek
due north, 389; my dog seized by a
tiger, 391; meet an Englishman, 392;
shoot a gryse steinbuck, 395; arrive
at the Zambesi Falls, 396; meet Dr.
Livingstone, 399; in the hands of
Masipootana, 401; see Dr. Livingstone
again, 403; savagely charged by a
buffalo, 404; watch the water, 406;
shoot a lion, 410; in difficulties at
Nanta, 412; am deceived by and
punish some Maccalacas, 415; persecuted by mosquitoes, 419; shoot
a rhinoceros, 420; water from the
paunch of a quagga, 421; unenviable plight, 422; adventure with
a lion, 424; am thrown in the pursuit of a giraffe, 428; through the
thirst country, 431; my horses destroyed by lions, 431; retrospect, 433;
accident to my wagon, 434; meet two
Englishmen, 434; dreadful accident,
436; return to Natal, 437; lost
wagon recovered, 442

Baboons, 128, 209, 398
Bamangwatos, a Kaffir tribe, 293, 308
Barbel, 241
Bashoo nuts, 275
Batlanarmi wells, 178, 295
Batokas, a tribe in South Africa, 393
Bees' nests, 372
Blue wildebeests, 204
Boccas, a servant of Mr. Baldwin's,
    409, 413, 427, 442

BOE

Boers, the, 165, 194
Buffaloes, 14, 35, 42, 44, 77, 109, 122, 128, 139, 191, 223, 333, 335, 340, 390, 404
Bush on fire, 296
Bush koran, 332
Bustards, 114, 152. 332

CABALLA, 284
Camelopards, 241
Cattle, price of, in Natal, 24
Chapeau, or Beauclekky, 241
Chase of an eland bull, 55
Clapper, a wild fruit, 198
Crabs, 208
Cranes, 79
Cream of tartar, an African tree, 311
Crest-peau, or bustard, 114
Crocodiles, 10. 15, 26, 86, 100, 110, 130

DEATH of Arbuthnot, Price, and Monies, 22
— — Bessie Bell, 98
Delagoa Bay, 208
Dikkop (thickhead), a bird, 36, 109
Disturbances amongst the Kaffir tribes, 291
Dogs trained to face hyenas, 211
Dog-wolf shot, 46
Dog attacked by a tiger, 40
Drakensberg mountain, 142
Dress of an African hunter, 58
Duikers, 7
Durban, 94, 441

ELANDS, 32, 52, 60, 206, 311, 370, 375
— striped, 384
Elephant, the, 8, 9, 13, 80, 85, 212, 259, 261, 271, 316, 322—28, 385—87, 402, 406

FEROCITY of lions, 151
Fletcher, Mr., killed by cow elephant, 31

IRI

GAME killed, list of, 443
Gemsbok, or oryx, 246, 256, 307, 308, 372, 382
German Missionaries, 298
Giraffes, 171, 178, 185, 187, 188, 223, 224, 279, 289, 342, 396, 428, 437
Goats, 217
Golden-goose, chase of a, 16
Gryse steinbuck, 395
Guia, or Tobacco River, 206
Guinea-fowl, 82

HARRISBUCK, or Potoquaine, 186. 187, 201, 282
Harrysmith, 143
Hartebeest, 210
Heat, effects of, on clay, 401
Heron, a blue, 51
Hippopotamus, or sea-cow, so called in Southern Africa, 5, 15, 69, 89, 121
Holden, Dr., 341
Honey-birds, 53, 300
Horses, 305, 307
Horse in a pit, 320; eaten by lions, 431
Hottentots, beauty of their hands and feet, 31; their extravagance, 312
Hunting expedition into the Zulu country, 29; into the Amatonga country, 59
Hyenas, 116, 118, 125, 127, 145, 211, 319, 329, 350, 408

IA, a Hottentot maid, 225
Impalas, 79, 125, 126, 127, 347
Impangane, the, a small river, 33
Inseline, the, a small river, 11
Inkukus, a river, 67
Instinct of dogs, 312
Inyalas, 76, 92, 117, 282
Inyati, a Kaffir guide, 21
Inyelas, 73
Inyesan, plains of the, 8, 53, 61
Inyoni River, 105
Inyons, a servant of Mr. Baldwin's, 306, et passim
Inyonti porridge, 75
Irish informer, 302

IVO

Ivory, 110, 161, 205, 214, 221, 294, 344, 353, 414

JACKALS, 127, 230, 372, 402
  Jurea, 407
'Justice' in difficulties, 65

KAFFIR appreciation of wealth, 105
  Kaffir church, 103
Kaffir banquet, 266
Kaffirs, the, habits and manners, and traits of character of, 7, 14, 17, 18, 24, 31, 72, 73, 74, 83, 98, 104, 105, 114, 135, 175, 177, 183, 203, 219, 242, 265, 266, 268, 273, 277, 292, 298, 300, 326, 347, 348, 352, 361, 369, 377, 379, 382, 413
Kaffirs, war among the, 133
Kleinboy, 306, 313
Klip River, 142
Koodoos, 34, 41, 74, 129, 131
Koran, 109, 114

LADYSMITH, 142
  Laughing hyenas, 62
Leches, 247, 279
Lechulatebe, 331
Leeches, 208
Letloche, 233
Lindley, Mr., an American Missionary, 25
Lions, 46 — 51, 109, 116, 118, 126, 145, 151, 162, 185, 294, 300, 366, 410, 413, 416, 424, 431
Lion velt, 352
Livingstone, Dr., 173, 278, 385, 399, 401, 403, 430, 439
Lopèpès vley, 181, 294, 346

MACCALACAS, an African tribe, 181, 311, 319, 403, 415, 440
Maccateese tribe, the, 149
Makolani trees, 419, 428
Makololos, the, an African tribe near the Zambesi, 398, 402

PON

Malakanyama, a Maccalaca chief, 409
Mamba, a snake, 99, 222
Mangwatoe tribe, 437
Manyati River, 401
Mapani trees, 246, 296
Masaras tribe, the, 191, 296, 308, 313, 321, 337, 338, 388, 416
Masipootana, a chief, 400
Massouey, a fountain, 372
Massouey River, 401, 435
Matakoola River, the, 31
Matchevi, a fountain, 342
Matibele, a fountain, 428
Meea River, 380
Meercat, a Masara boy, 338
Merico country, 160, 162, 298, 301, 441
Mesa River, 430
Moffat, Rev. Robert, 193, 295
Mooi River Town, 143, 441
Mosilikatse, a Kaffir chief, 195, 205, 214, 219, 273, 290, 309, 329, 411
Mosquitoes, 11, 134, 340, 418
Mowane trees, 268

NAMAQUA partridge, 152
  Nanta, 412
Ngami, Lake, 257, 265
Ngami, a Masara boy, 338
Nights in the Amatonga country, 79; in the Zulu country, 102; near the Zambesi, 418
Norwegian Missionary, 103

OMBOMBO Mountains, 116
  Oryx, or gemsbok, 246, 256, 307
Ostriches, 143, 178, 420
Ostrich eggs, 407

PALLAH, the, 78, 371
  Panda, king, 38, 67
Panthers, 34, 210
Peau, 114
Pet Jacobs, a famous hunter, 343
Pheasants, 328
Poisonous herb, 404
Pongola River, the, 81, 139

POW

Powder, amount of, for African game, 405
Puff adder, 110

QUAGGAS, 74, 143, 156, 278, 421
    Qualeba River, 380

RABBITS, 417
    Raffeta, the Bastard, 338
Rats, 78, 91
Reedbucks, 65, 108, 114
Reitbuck, the, 7
Rhinoceros, 106, 109, 125, 127, 223,
    334, 389, 420
— hump, 190

SALT-PAN, the, 378
    Sangarni, 182
Schroeder, Mr., Norwegian Missionary,
    104, 113
Sechele, 290, 295, 296
— feigns to be religious, 295
Setabangumpè River, 401
Sicomo, 307, 309
Slatakula bush, 40
Snakes, 69, 221
Springbuck, 415
Steinbok, 65
Steinbucks, 7, 109, 114
Stew, a good, 68
St. Lucia Bay, 118
St. Luey River, 74, 108, 116

TALO, a root like a potato, 421
    Tamalakarni River, 323
Tegwan, a mountain, 128
Thirst country, 343, 430
Tiger-cat run to bay, 62
Tigers, 328, 391
Tsessebes, 168, 375

ZUL

Tugela, the river, 5, 31, 59, 98, 112,
    136, 354
Two-legged wolves, 303

UMGOWIE Mountains, 68
    Umkusi River, 78, 108
Umlilas, the, 9, 33, 98
Umpongal, an Amatonga chief, 86, 90
Umsindoosie River, 71, 115, 134
Umslali, the, 30
Umslatoose, the river, 33, 67, 113
Umsutie, or Mapoota River. 86
Umveloose, the black, 12, 21, 36, 40,
    51, 72, 105, 115
Umvoti, the, 6, 30, 31

VAAL River, 353
    Viljoen, John, a famous hunter, 343
Visit to King Panda, 38
Vultures, 127

WATCHING the water, 406
    Waterbuck, 78, 403
Waterrails, 79
Wedding trip, a, 341
White man's grave, a, 413
Widgeon, 79, 417
Wild boars, 159
Wild dogs, 342
Wild ducks, 413
Wild fig-tree, 81
Wolves, 78, 127, 167, 328

ZAMBESI River, 205; falls of the,
    396, 439
Zebizena, fountain, 407
Zonga River, 328
Zulus, the, 35, 74
Zulu feast, 75

LONDON
PRINTED BY SPOTTISWOODE AND CO.
NEW-STREET SQUARE

MR. BENTLEY'S

NEW PUBLICATIONS.

In a Handsome Volume, 8vo. with Fifty beautiful Illustrations by WOLFF (the
eminent animal-painter) and J. B. ZWECKER, with a Map and Portrait
of the Author, price £1 1s. bound,

AFRICAN HUNTING

FROM

NATAL TO THE ZAMBESI, LAKE NGAMI, KALAHARI,

From 1852 to 1860.

By WILLIAM CHARLES BALDWIN, F.G.S.

Specimen of the Illustrations.

In folio, with very numerous Illustrations in Photography, Glythography, Wood
Engraving, and Lithography, price £4 4s. neatly bound,

SINAI PHOTOGRAPHED:

BEING

PHOTOGRAPHS FROM THE INSCRIPTIONS ON THE ROCKS OF
THE PENINSULA OF

MOUNT SINAI,

RECORDING THE EXODUS OF THE ISRAELITES.

WITH

A Narrative and Translations of the Inscriptions.

BY

THE REV. CHARLES FORSTER,

RECTOR OF STISTED, ESSEX.

In 8vo. with a fine Portrait, price 14s.

THE LIFE OF JOSEPH LOCKE,

ENGINEER.

By JOSEPH DEVEY, Esq.

In 2 vols. post 8vo. with a Map, price £1 1s.

FLINDERSLAND

AND

STURTLAND;

OR

THE OUTSIDE AND THE INSIDE OF AUSTRALIA.

BY W. R. H. JESSOP, M.A.

OF ST. JOHN'S, CAMBRIDGE.

In post 8vo. with an Illustration, price 10s. 6d. bound,

THROUGH ALGERIA.

BY THE

AUTHOR of 'LIFE in TUSCANY.'

JOURNALS OF MR. WILLS, THE GREAT
AUSTRALIAN EXPLORER.

—♦—

In 8vo. with fine Engravings and Map.

Dedicated by permission to His Grace the Duke of NEWCASTLE, K.G.

NARRATIVE

OF

A SUCCESSFUL EXPLORATION

THROUGH THE

INTERIOR OF AUSTRALIA,

FROM

𝔐𝔢𝔩𝔟𝔬𝔲𝔯𝔫𝔢 𝔱𝔬 𝔱𝔥𝔢 𝔊𝔲𝔩𝔣 𝔬𝔣 ℭ𝔞𝔯𝔭𝔢𝔫𝔱𝔞𝔯𝔦𝔞,

In 1861.

INCLUDING THE

JOURNALS OF MR. WILLS, AND A BIOGRAPHICAL MEMOIR OF HIM

BY HIS FATHER,

DR. WILLIAM WILLS.

〰〰〰〰〰〰

' Mr. Wills, whose history of the journey is all that is left to us, is deserving of a
nation's tears. His extreme youth, his enduring patience, his evenness of temper,
his cheerful disposition even in extremities, his devotion to his leader, all tend
to stamp him as the real master-mind of the expedition.' — AUSTRALIAN PRESS.

Vols. I. and II. 8vo. neatly bound,

THE

LIVES OF THE ARCHBISHOPS

OF

CANTERBURY,

FROM THE MISSION OF AUGUSTINE TO THE DEATH OF DR. HOWLEY.

BY THE

REV. WALTER FARQUHAR HOOK, D.D., F.R.S.

DEAN OF CHICHESTER.

VOLUME I. price 15s.—AUGUSTINE to STIGAND.

VOLUME II. price 18s. — LANFRANC to STEPHEN LANGTON, including A'BECKET and ANSELM.

'Written with remarkable knowledge and power. . The author has done his work diligently and conscientiously. Throughout, we see a man who has known much of men and of life: the pure Anglican divine, who at every step has been accustomed to make good his cause against Romanism on the one hand and against Puritanism on the other. We must express our high sense of the value of this work. We heartily like the general spirit, and are sure that the author has bestowed upon his work a loving labour, with an earnest desire to find out the truth. To the general reader it will convey much information in a very pleasant form; to the student it will give the means of filling up the outlines of Church history with life and colour.'—QUARTERLY REVIEW, *July* 1862.

' If the grandeur of a drama may be conjectured from the quality of the opening symphony, we should be inclined to anticipate from the introductory volume that English literature is about to receive an imperishable contribution, and that the Church will in after-times rank among the fairest and the ablest of her historians the author of this work.'—ATHENÆUM.

'Dr. Hook is throughout fair, and more than fair. He really understands his characters, and does not praise or condemn from any cut-and-dried nineteenth-century standard. In such a work this is one of the first and rarest of all merits, and we know no ecclesiastical writer who can lay claim to this pre-eminent merit in a higher degree than Dr. Hook.'—SATURDAY REVIEW.

' The work of a powerful mind and of a noble and generous temper. There is in it a freedom from any narrowness of spirit.'—GUARDIAN.

In 2 vols. 8vo. with numerous fine Portraits from Original Paintings and Miniatures of Dr. Whalley by Sir Joshua Reynolds; of Mrs. Siddons and Miss Sage by Cosway; and Mrs. Sage by Romney, price 30s.

THE

LIFE AND CORRESPONDENCE

OF THE REV. DR.

THOS. SEDGEWICK WHALLEY,

LL.D.

INCLUDING

ORIGINAL LETTERS OF MADAME PIOZZI,

MISS SEWARD,

MRS. HANNAH MORE,

MRS. SIDDONS,

ETC. ETC.

BY THE

REV. HILL D. WICKHAM, M.A.

RECTOR OF HORSINGTON, SOMERSETSHIRE.

MIRTH AND MARVELS.

———

In small 8vo. Fiftieth Thousand, 5s. neatly bound,

THE INGOLDSBY LEGENDS

OR,

MIRTH AND MARVELS.

Also, in 2 vols. handsomely printed, the Illustrations by GEORGE CRUIKSHANK
and JOHN LEECH, price 21s.

THE LIBRARY EDITION OF

THE INGOLDSBY LEGENDS.

'Abundant in humour, observation, fancy; in extensive knowledge of books and men; in palpable hits of character, exquisite, grave irony, and the most whimsical indulgence in point and epigram. We doubt if even Butler beats the Author of these legends in the easy drollery of verse. We cannot open a page that is not sparkling with its wit and humour, that is not ringing with its strokes of pleasantry and satire.' — EXAMINER.

COMPANION VOLUME TO 'THE INGOLDSBY LEGENDS.'

———

In small 8vo. Second Edition, price 5s.

THE BENTLEY BALLADS

A SELECTION OF THE GEMS FROM 'BENTLEY'S MISCELLANY.'

Including Ballads and Legends by FATHER PROUT, Dr. MAGINN, LONGFELLOW,
THE IRISH WHISKY DRINKER, GEORGE CANNING, &c.

———

'A capital collection of amusing verse. Stories and merry jests abound.'—EXAMINER.
'In every way a credit to modern literature. Is it not to be bidden to a royal banquet, to be offered nearly five hundred pages of contributions abounding in wit, pathos, learning, and humour?' LONDON REVIEW.
'This volume contains songs of love and humour, wit and sentiment, by a host of kindred spirits, forming a volume of modern lyrical poetry to satisfy readers of all tastes.'
NOTES AND QUERIES.

CUISINE CLASSIQUE.

In 8vo. with Sixty Illustrations, price 12s.

THE MODERN COOK.

By ELMÉ FRANCATELLI,
Pupil of the celebrated Caréme.

'The *magnum opus* on which the author rests his reputation in SÆCULA SÆCULORUM.'
TIMES.

CUISINE BOURGEOIS.

In small 8vo. with Forty Illustrations, price 5s. neatly bound,

. THE COOK'S GUIDE.

'An admirable manual for every household. The whole book has the merit of being exceedingly plain, of containing sufficient cross references to satisfy a Panizzi, and of being so serviceably arranged in all its parts that we defy you to miss any of the consolations intended for your physical infirmities.'—TIMES.

'Mr. Francatelli combines our food into forms endowed with tastes, odours, and virtues that are proudly perfect and defy the curious analyser to do aught but eat them. After reading "The Cook's Guide" a housewife might be driven to despair, and a husband to register a vow never to forgive cold mutton or tough steak.' — ATHENÆUM.

'Intended mainly for the middle class. A cookery-book from Francatelli is an authority. He has such a variety and choice of rare dishes, that a table spread by him would be a nonpareil.'
OBSERVER.

In fcp. 8vo. price 2s. 6d. bound,

EVERYBODY'S PUDDING BOOK.

BY THE
AUTHOR OF 'GOURMET'S GUIDE TO RABBIT COOKING.'

'It will take a twelvemonth to do justice to this book, that is, to taste or rather test its merits. But a fair critic, to whom we have submitted it, reports so favourably of it that we cannot refuse to give Mr. BENTLEY one PUFF in return for so many PUDDINGS.'
NOTES AND QUERIES.

Also, price 2s. 6d. neatly bound,

FOREIGN DESSERTS FOR ENGLISH TABLES.

BY THE
AUTHOR OF 'EVERYBODY'S PUDDING BOOK.'

In neat vols. Foolscap 8vo. price 2s. 6d. and 3s. 6d.

BENTLEY'S
STANDARD NOVELS:

INCLUDING

THE SEMI-ATTACHED COUPLE. 2s. 6d.

ANTHONY TROLLOPE'S THREE CLERKS. 3s. 6d.

RITA. 2s. 6d.

THE LADIES OF BEVER HOLLOW. By the Author of 'Mary Powell.' 2s. 6d.

THE SEASON TICKET. 2s. 6d.

THE SEMI-DETACHED HOUSE. 2s. 6d.

EASTON AND ITS INHABITANTS. 2s. 6d.

QUITS. By the Author of 'The Initials.' 3s. 6d.

VILLAGE BELLES. By the Author of 'Mary Powell.' 2s. 6d.

NELLY ARMSTRONG. By the Author of 'Rose Douglas.' 2s. 6d.

To be followed by

VONVED, THE ROVER OF THE BALTIC. By W. HURTON.

THE INITIALS. By the Author of 'Quits.'

AND OTHER WORKS OF EMINENT WRITERS OF FICTION.

This popular Series is unexceptionable in point of taste. Here are to be found works of brilliant wit and humour, and stories of exciting interest and tragic power. There is not one story to offend the most fastidious. Bentley's Standard Novels will be a welcome guest in every household.

TIMBS' ANECDOTE BIOGRAPHY.

In Four neat volumes, small 8vo. with numerous Portraits, price 24s. bound,

ANECDOTE BIOGRAPHY.

By JOHN TIMBS.

FIRST VOLUME......STATESMEN.
SECOND VOLUME ...PAINTERS.
THIRD VOLUME ...WITS AND HUMOURISTS.
FOURTH VOLUME...WITS AND HUMOURISTS.

☞ ANY VOLUME MAY BE HAD SEPARATELY.   Price 6s.

'The cream of a dozen interesting biographies.'—SATURDAY REVIEW.
' Executed iu Mr. Timbs' best manner.'—DAILY NEWS.

In small 8vo. price 5s.

MOTHERS OF GREAT MEN.

By Mrs. ELLIS.

' This work will be placed by the majority of its readers not only at the head of Mrs. Ellis's works, but in the very first ranks of English literature. It is peculiarly valuable, and ought to be in the hands of every mother in the land.'—ILLUSTRATED NEWS.

In 8vo. with a Portrait, price 14s. bound,

MEMOIR

OF

DR. MARSHALL HALL, M.D.

By his WIDOW.

' Dr. Marshall Hall was not less an amiable man than a scientific enquirer, with an intellect of noble proportions and lofty aim. In the world of physiological science he may fairly be ranked as the companion of Harvey and Bell.'—ATHENÆUM.

' As a narrative this work is more interesting than a novel ; as a memorial of a great English worthy, it will be perused with pride ; as an incentive to honourable toil and the practice of virtue, this story of Marshall Hall deserves to take rank amongst the most favourite tales of the triumphs of genius.'—LANCET.

In small 8vo. with Illustrations, neatly bound, price 6s. with an Introduction by
the Author of 'MARY POWELL,'

JERUSALEM THE GOLDEN

AND

THE WAY TO IT.

By the Rev. HERMAN DOUGLAS, M.A.

Author of ' Londoners Over the Border.'

DR. CUMMING'S WORKS.

In small 8vo. price 7s. 6d. Thirteenth Thousand,

THE GREAT TRIBULATION.

By the Rev. Dr. JOHN CUMMING.

In small 8vo. price 7s. 6d. Sixth Thousand,

REDEMPTION DRAWETH NIGH.

By the Rev. Dr. JOHN CUMMING.

In small 8vo. price 7s. 6d,

THE MILLENNIAL REST.

By the Rev. Dr. JOHN CUMMING.

'Whether Dr. Cumming's interpretations be right or wrong, there is no doubt that the barometer of Europe singularly corresponds with his deductions from prophecy.'—TIMES.

New Edition, in small 8vo. 6s. neatly bound, with Portrait of M. Guizot,

NARRATIVE OF AN EMBASSY

TO THE

COURT OF ST. JAMES

IN 1840.

By FRANÇOIS GUIZOT,

AMBASSADOR FROM HIS MAJESTY LOUIS PHILIPPE.

'The descriptions of character, the reminiscences of men, manners, conversations, dinners, and joyous sayings and doings are here given true, brilliant, eloquent, and sparkling.'
ATHENÆUM.

'This volume will be read with more avidity than any which has lately come from the press. It is one of the most valuable contributions hitherto made to the history of modern times. The author is one of the best read and most correctly judging of French historians.'—MORNING POST.

In small 8vo. price 6s. with fine Portrait of the Protector,

THE

LIFE OF OLIVER CROMWELL

LORD PROTECTOR.

By FRANÇOIS GUIZOT.

' M. GUIZOT has unravelled Cromwell's character with singular skill. No one, in our opinion, has drawn his portrait with equal truth. M. GUIZOT's acquaintance with our annals, language, customs, and politics is altogether extraordinary. He is an earnest and profound writer.'
QUARTERLY REVIEW.

' M. GUIZOT has given us an admirable narrative, far more candid than any from an English pen.'
TIMES.

' We cannot doubt that this important work will meet with a hearty and universal welcome. The position of M. GUIZOT, the circumstances of his country, and the interest of his theme, will combine to attract towards his " History of Cromwell " no ordinary share of public curiosity.'
ATHENÆUM.

LIBRARY EDITION,

IN TWO VOLS. WITH A PORTRAIT, TWENTY-ONE SHILLINGS;

AND A

POPULAR EDITION,

In One Volume, small 8vo. with a Portrait and Four Charts, price 5s. neatly bound,

THE AUTOBIOGRAPHY

OF THE

EARL OF DUNDONALD

(LORD COCHRANE).

'We may safely predict for this work an unbounded popularity. It is worthy of one of the very best places on any shelf of military and naval memoirs, and is full of brilliant adventures, described with a dash that well befits the deeds.' — TIMES.

'We are glad and proud that such a man as Lord Dundonald survives to tell his own story. Everything about his biography is strange and romantic: he was more like Nelson than any officer of his generation. He performed brilliant exploits and acquired celebrity and friends. He has freed Republics, captured frigates, driven a French fleet ashore, been taken and retaken. His career recalls that of the Raleighs, Willoughbys, and the Herberts of Cherbury. This work will take its place with our best naval histories.'—ATHENÆUM.

'The career of Lord Dundonald yields the best illustration of the spirit which in our day can defend England. With a conscious dignity, related in no way to ostentation, Lord Dundonald tells the story of a life of manly daring at the age of eighty-four, and his work proves that neither under age nor injury has his heart sunk or his intellect failed in its vigour.'—EXAMINER.

'A work which, once read, will imprint itself on the memory for ever. It is an admirable work.'—SPECTATOR.

'A compact, inexpensive, yet an elegant and complete edition of a book which every Englishman ought to read.'—DAILY NEWS.

THE GREAT FRENCH REVOLUTION.

In 5 vols. small 8vo. with Forty-five fine Engravings of the Startling Events, and Portraits of all the most Prominent Persons engaged, in the Revolution,

THE HISTORY

OF

THE FRENCH REVOLUTION

From its Commencement in 1789 to the Period of the Establishment of Napoleon Bonaparte as First Consul in 1801.

By M. THIERS.

THE FINE ENGRAVINGS INCLUDE

ATTACK ON THE BASTILLE
PORTRAIT OF THE DUKE OF ORLEANS
PORTRAIT OF MIRABEAU
PORTRAIT OF LAFAYETTE
ORGIES OF THE GARDES DU CORPS
PORTRAIT OF MARIE ANTOINETTE
RETURN OF THE ROYAL FAMILY FROM VARENNES
PORTRAIT OF MARAT
THE MOB AT THE TUILLERIES
ATTACK ON THE TUILLERIES
MURDER OF THE PRINCESS DE LAMBALLE
PORTRAIT OF THE PRINCESS DE LAMBALLE
PORTRAIT OF MADAME ROLAND
LOUIS XVI. AT THE CONVENTION
LAST INTERVIEW OF LOUIS XVI. WITH HIS FAMILY
PORTRAIT OF LOUIS XVI.
PORTRAIT OF DUMOURIEZ.
TRIUMPH OF MARAT
PORTRAIT OF LAROCHEJACQUELEIN
ASSASSINATION OF MARAT
PORTRAIT OF CHARLOTTE CORDAY

PORTRAIT OF CAMILLE DESMOULINS
CONDEMNATION OF MARIE ANTOINETTE
PORTRAIT OF BAILLY (MAYOR OF PARIS)
TRIAL OF DANTON, CAMILLE DESMOULINS, &c.
PORTRAIT OF DANTON
PORTRAIT OF MADAME ELIZABETH
CARRIER AT NANTES
PORTRAIT OF ROBESPIERRE
LAST VICTIMS OF THE REIGN OF TERROR
PORTRAIT OF CHARETTE
DEATH OF THE DEPUTY FERAUD
DEATH OF ROMME, GOUJON, DUQUESNOI, &c.
PORTRAIT OF LOUIS XVII.
THE 13TH VENDEMIAIRE (Oct. 5, 1795)
SUMMONING TO EXECUTION
PORTRAIT OF PICHEGRU
PORTRAIT OF MOREAU
PORTRAIT OF HOCHE
PORTRAIT OF NAPOLEON BONAPARTE
THE 18TH BRUMAIRE (10th November 1799) &c. &c.

'The palm of excellence, after whole libraries have been written on the French Revolution, has been assigned to the dissimilar histories of Thiers and Mignet.'—WILLIAM H. PRESCOTT.
' I am reading "Thiers's French Revolution," which I find it difficult to lay down.'
REV. SYDNEY SMITH.

In Five Volumes small 8vo. with Portrait,

THE HISTORY

OF

THE BRITISH NAVY,

FROM THE COMMENCEMENT OF THE REVOLUTIONARY WAR TO THE BATTLE OF NAVARINO,

BY W. JAMES.

'The best naval history of England. Its impartial statement of facts is so well established that it was constantly referred to by French naval officers visiting my ship in the Mediterranean to decide any question in discussion.'—ADMIRAL SIR PULTENEY MALCOLM.

'This book is one of which it is not too high praise to assert, that it approaches as nearly to perfection, in its own line, as any historical work perhaps ever did. The principal transactions narrated in it, and we trust by this time the narrative itself, are fortunately too well known to require a detailed notice of its contents. But a general sketch of its plan, and the manner of its execution, will we think convince our readers that the high character we have given of it is not exaggerated. Mr. James commences his work with a very useful introduction, in which he briefly and clearly sketches the progress of Naval Architecture in Great Britain, and the origin of the principal improvements in the British Navy before the time of the French Revolution. The history itself opens with the declaration of war in 1793, and closes with the general peace of 1815. [The History has since been brought down to the Battle of Navarino.] Every year between these two periods occupies a separate division of the work; and every such division is subdivided under three heads, detailing respectively the movements of the hostile fleets, the encounters of single ships and boat attacks, and all colonial naval operations. The research necessary to procure materials for twenty-eight such abstracts, and the labour of composing them, must have been so great, that they alone may be considered as a striking monument of industry. With a candour almost as uncommon as his accuracy, he never fails to notice any variation of consequence in the statements of the hostile party; and either to refute it by argument, or fairly to balance it with the opposing testimony. We cannot contemplate without admiration the impartial and unwearied zeal for historical truth which alone could have supported him through his tedious and thankless labours.'—EDINBURGH REVIEW.

'A new and popular edition of one of the most valuable works in the English language.'
UNITED SERVICE GAZETTE.

'A new and well-edited edition of our standard naval history. The interest in our navy never was so active as it is now. The desire to perpetuate that interest by showering upon our young people gift-books relating to the sea is more manifest every year. The book before us is a standard history and not a child's book, but for that reason perhaps it is more worthy to be chosen as a gift-book for the boy who will soon have his manhood to assert.'—EXAMINER.

SIR EDWARD CREASY'S WORKS.

In one handsome volume 8vo. Twelfth Edition, price 10s. 6d.

THE

FIFTEEN DECISIVE BATTLES

OF THE WORLD,

FROM MARATHON TO WATERLOO.

By Professor (now Sir Edward) CREASY, Chief Justice of Ceylon.

'It was a happy idea of Professor Creasy to select for military description those few battles which, in the words of Hallam, "A contrary event would have essentially varied the drama of the world in all its subsequent scenes." The decisive features of the battles are well and clearly brought out; the reader's mind is attracted to the world-wide importance of the event he is considering, while their succession carries him over the whole stream of European history.'
SPECTATOR.

Also, by the same writer, Sixth Edition, post 8vo. price 7s. 6d.

THE RISE AND PROGRESS

OF

THE ENGLISH CONSTITUTION

A POPULAR ACCOUNT OF THE PRIMARY PRINCIPLES;
THE FORMATION AND DEVELOPMENT OF THE ENGLISH
CONSTITUTION, AVOIDING ALL PARTY POLITICS.

'This book is well adapted to answer its purpose as a summary of constitutional history or an introduction to more elaborate works. Mr. Creasy exhibits originality of view, and presents his facts and opinions with clearness and in an attractive manner.'—SPECTATOR.

'We are not aware of any book on the subject which could be so safely put into the hands of a student.'—MORNING CHRONICLE.

Fourth Edition, in 8vo. price 10s. 6d.

THE AMERICAN UNION.

By JAMES SPENCE.

'This work is the best that has appeared on the American crisis.'—TIMES.

'We can hardly speak too highly of it. It is the most able statement of the whole case, written with remarkable knowledge and power, and we strongly recommend it to our readers if they wish to make themselves acquainted with the facts of the great American controversy, which are so often obscured by passion and distorted by interest.'   QUARTERLY REVIEW.

BY THE SAME AUTHOR.

In 8vo. price 1s.

ON THE RECOGNITION OF THE SOUTHERN STATES.

In small 8vo. in Two Series, price 12s.

CURIOSITIES OF NATURAL HISTORY

PART I. Containing RATS, SERPENTS, FISHES, MONKEYS, &c. 6s.

PART II. Containing WILD CATS, EAGLES, WORMS, DOGS, &c. 6s.

By FRANCIS BUCKLAND, Esq.

'These are some of the most fascinating works on Natural History.'—MORNING POST.

' Full of interest, and well worth reading.'—MORNING HERALD.

' It is quite impossible to do justice to the merits of this book. Nothing short of its own clearly defined originality, cleverness, and detail can lead to a proper appreciation of its intrinsic excellencies.'   BELL'S WEEKLY MESSENGER.

' So pleasant and gossiping, and written in so popular a tone and on so popular a subject, that it is fair to contemplate for it as large a share of favour as the first series so deservedly attained.'   NOTES AND QUERIES.

EDITION AUTHORIZED BY THE FAMILY.

In 3 vols. post 8vo.

Volumes I. and II. now ready, price 15s.

THE

LIFE AND LETTERS

OF

WASHINGTON IRVING

AUTHOR of 'The SKETCH-BOOK,' &c.

'The most interesting portion of the first volume relates to Washington Irving's sojourn in London ; then follows the account of his love-making affair with young Matilda Hoffman. Washington Irving sojourned in England seventeen years.'

ATHENÆUM.

'A life-like portrait of Washington Irving. Here he is his own biographer. In this second volume we have some of the best descriptions of men and manners which Washington Irving ever traced. We find him in friendly communication with Campbell, Scott, Leslie, Alison, Jeffrey, and others noble in literature ; and with Siddons, Young, Kean, Cooke, and the aristocracy of the stage. This is a book to be read and re-read. We have derived much pleasure from its perusal.'

MONDAY REVIEW.

'Washington Irving has been most universally admired ; he has the reputation of being the most refined of American writers. A wide circle of eager readers will doubtless be found for this interesting biography.'   DIAL.

'When thought flowed from Irving's brain through his pen, he was most attractive, most brilliant, most full of pleasant sayings and playful suggestions.'

ATHENÆUM, *in review of Second Volume.*

In small 8vo. price 18s. boards,

THE HISTORY OF ROME

FROM THE EARLIEST TIME TO THE PERIOD OF ITS DECLINE.

By DR. THEODOR MOMMSEN.

TRANSLATED WITH THE AUTHOR'S SANCTION, AND ADDITIONS,

By the Rev. W. PITT DICKSON,

AND WITH AN INTRODUCTION BY DR. SCHMITZ.

'Since the days of Niebuhr, no work on Roman History has appeared that combines so much to attract, instruct, and charm the reader. Its style — a rare quality in a German author — is vigorous, spirited, and animated. Professor Mommsen's work can stand a comparison with the noblest productions of modern history.' DR. SCHMITZ.

'This is the best history of the Roman Republic, taking the work on the whole — the author's complete mastery of his subject, the variety of his gifts and acquirements, his graphic power in the delineation of natural and individual character, and the vivid interest which he inspires in every portion of his book. He is without an equal in his own sphere. The work may be read in the translation (executed with the sanction of the author) not only with instruction, but with great pleasure.' EDINBURGH REVIEW.

'A book of deepest interest, and which ought to be translated.' DEAN TRENCH.

'Beyond all doubt to be ranked among those really great historical works which do so much honour to our own day. We can have little hesitation in pronouncing this work to be the best complete Roman History in existence. In short, we have now for the first time the complete history of the Roman Republic really written in a way worthy of the greatness of the subject. M. Mommsen is a real historian ; his powers of research and judgment are of a very high order; he is skilful in the grasp of his whole subject, and vigorous and independent in his way of dealing with particular questions. And an English critic may be allowed to add, that his book is far easier and more pleasant to read than many of the productions of his fellow countrymen.' NATIONAL REVIEW.

'An original work, from the pen of a master. The style is nervous and lively, and its vigour fully sustained. This English translation fills up a gap in our literature. It will give the schoolboy and the older student of antiquity a history of Rome up to the mark of present German scholarship, and at the same time serve as a sample of historical enquiry for all ages and all lands.' WESTMINSTER REVIEW.

DR. McCAUSLAND'S WORKS.

Ninth Edition, in fcp. 8vo. 4s. neatly bound,

SERMONS IN STONES;
OR,
SCRIPTURE CONFIRMED BY GEOLOGY.

By Dr. DOMINICK McCAUSLAND, LL.D., Q.C.

The object of the author in this work is to prove that the Mosaic narrative of the Creation is reconcilable with the established facts of geology; and that geology not only establishes the truth of the first page of the Bible, but that it furnishes the most direct and sensible evidence of the fact of Divine inspiration, and thereby authenticates the whole canon of Scripture. The word of God is thus authenticated by His works.

'The object of this work is to reconcile the discoveries in geology with the Mosaic account of the Creation. The case is clearly made, and the argument cleverly managed.'—SPECTATOR.

Also, by the same Author, in 8vo. price 10s. 6d.

THE FALL OF JERUSALEM.

'The book of a reverent student of Scripture.'—GUARDIAN.

'More conclusive than any work we have yet met with on the difficult subject of which it treats, and possesses all the merit which ought to obtain for it a standard reputation.'
MESSENGER.

'The general argument of this work respecting the part which the Jewish nation are yet intended to play in development of God's purpose, and the position which Rome occupies in relation to the Christian Church, is well worthy of attention — more particularly in watching the process of the remarkable events which are now taking place.'—PRESS.

New Edition, in small 8vo. price 5s.

RAMBLES BEYOND RAILWAYS.

By W. WILKIE COLLINS,
AUTHOR OF 'THE WOMAN IN WHITE,' ETC.

'An attractive and interesting work.'—OBSERVER.

'Any publication, especially of the lively, truthful character of Mr. Collins's impressions of his rambles and explorations, we heartily welcome.'—GLOBE.

With fine Steel Engravings and many Woodcuts. 8vo. 14s.

HOW WE GOT TO PEKIN;

A Narrative of the Campaign in China in 1860.

By the Rev. R. L. M'GHEE, Chaplain to the Forces and to His Excellency the Earl of Carlisle.

'There is a spice of broad hilarity in this narrative. Mr. M'Ghee was as fond of campaigning as of travel, and his visit to the Summer Palace is well and amply described, and the whole narrative entertaining.'—ATHENÆUM.
'A very entertaining book.'—JOHN BULL.

In crown 8vo. with Illustrations.

ON THE MOUNTAIN:

Being the Welsh Experiences of Abraham Black and Jonas White, Esqrs., Moralists, Photographers, Fishermen, and Botanists, &c.

By the Rev. GEORGE TUGWELL, M.A.

THE NOVELS OF MISS AUSTEN.

A LIBRARY EDITION. 5 vols.

Vol. I. SENSE and SENSIBILITY	Vol. IV. NORTHANGER ABBEY, and PERSUASION
Vol. II. EMMA	
Vol. III. MANSFIELD PARK	Vol. V. PRIDE and PREJUDICE

With Ten Illustrations, 15s.

'Miss Austen has a talent for describing the feelings and characters of ordinary life, which is to me the most wonderful I ever met with. Her exquisite touch, which renders ordinary commonplace things and characters interesting from the truth of the description and the sentiment, is denied to me.'—SIR WALTER SCOTT.

In 4 vols. 8vo. with fine Portrait, £3.

DIARY AND CORRESPONDENCE OF LORD AUCKLAND.

With a Preface and Introduction by the Right Hon. and Right Rev. the Bishop of Bath and Wells.

'In the midst of all these we have samples of the 18th century social life. Mr. Storer is the Sydney Smith of the circle, Lord Sheffield sarcastic, Lord Loughborough keen and shrewd. Mr. Pitt's letters are full of interest. We have Lord North's irresoluteness and wit, and Louis XVI. speaking and reading English well. We have a peep into life at Court, and find the Duchess of Marlborough and Lord Harcourt as tired as poor Madame D'Arblay of waiting on Her Majesty. Some sketches also of Parliamentary skirmishes are drawn to the life. Entertaining anecdotes abound throughout the whole work.'—UNION.
'For all those who love to be amused, and who delight in anecdote, sketches of character, and traits of social life, this work will have great attractions.'—ATHENÆUM.

In post 8vo. gilt edges, 5s.

ANECDOTES OF ANIMALS.

With Eight spirited Illustrations by Wolf.

'An agreeably compiled and well selected miscellaneous collection of anecdotes, containing much fascinating matter in the way of personal adventures, and in all respects admirably suited to popular reading.'—LIVERPOOL ALBION.

———◦———

In 8vo.   12s. boards.

HISTORY OF ROMAN CLASSICAL LITERATURE.

By R. W. BROWNE, M.A., Ph. D., Prebendary of St. Paul's, and Professor of Classical Literature in King's College, London.

'Professor Browne is not only a classical scholar, but one of the most graceful of English modern writers. In clearness, purity, and elegance of style, his compositions are unsurpassed ; and his sketches of the lives and works of the great authors of antiquity are models of refined taste and sound criticism. This is a work which, for utility of design and excellence of execution, may challenge comparison with any which the present century has produced : nor can we hesitate to regard it as a very valuable instrument for the instruction of the national mind, and the elevation of the national taste.'—MORNING POST.

———◦———

In post 8vo. 7s. 6d.

GEMS AND JEWELS:

Their History, Geography, Chemistry, and Ana, from the earliest Ages down to the Present Time. By Madame BARRERA.

'A really charming volume, as amusing as it is instructive, and in its graceful "getting up" worthy of a place in every locality where useful books are as highly valued as carcanet or ruby. We cheerfully recommend her pretty volume to the general public.'—ATHENÆUM.

———◦———

Crown 8vo. 5s.

STORIES FROM THE SANDHILLS OF JUTLAND.

By HANS CHRISTIAN ANDERSEN. Translated by Mrs. Bushby.

'These stories are not exceeded by any of the same hand. His fancy, humour, tenderness, are in no respect dimmed or deadened. He is, as of old, a king and ruler in his own world without a peer. Few tales have been more touching than the first. "The Mail King's Daughter" is also a capital tale ; but, for one reason or other, every one of these stories could be commended. It is long since we have dealt with a book so fresh, so individual, so full to over-flowing with gamesome fantasies, right feelings, and pure morals as this.'—ATHENÆUM.

'Andersen's tales are welcome to every household and every age. They stand unrivalled for delicate humour and gentle wisdom.'—SATURDAY REVIEW.

———◦———

TALES FROM BENTLEY'S MISCELLANY.

4 vols. 1s. 6d. each, sold separately ; or in 2 vols. 6s.

———◦———

In 8vo. 7s. 6d. boards.

THE LETTERS OF JAMES BOSWELL TO THE REV. WM. TEMPLE.

'Equally with the famous biography of Dr. Johnson, these Letters have the charm of sincerity—a charm which, as long as the world lasts, will be the greatest which the writings of one man can have for another. Boswell never disappoints us. He is an unfailing joke. Whether he writes about love, or riches, or literature, he is always the same, inimitable and inexhaustible. It is rarely that we come across a volume with so much to entertain us and make us laugh.'—SATURDAY REVIEW.

Third Thousand. In 3 vols. post 8vo. 31s. 6d.

THE CHANNINGS.

By the Author of 'East Lynne.'

In fcp. 8vo. 4s. boards.

SELECTIONS FROM THE WRITINGS OF PLATO.

By Lady CHATTERTON.

' An elegant volume of selections, in which Lady Chatterton has brought together some of the most impressive passages of Plato.'—QUARTERLY REVIEW.

In 8vo. price 4s.

MILITARY OPINIONS.

By General the Hon. Sir JOHN BURGOYNE, K.C.B.

In 8vo. price 12s.

THE LIFE OF THE GREATEST OF THE PLANTAGENETS.

By EDMUND CLIFFORD.

In 3 large vols. 8vo. with Thirteen fine Portraits. FIRST SERIES, £2 10s.; Second Series, in 3 vols. 8vo. with Nine Portraits, and a copious Index to the whole work, £2 10s.

THE AUTOBIOGRAPHY AND CORRESPONDENCE OF MARY GRANVILLE (MRS. DELANY),

With Interesting Reminiscences of King George the Third and Queen Charlotte.

Edited by the Right Hon. Lady LLANOVER.

. *Only a few copies remain unsold of this elegant work.*

' The reader wends his way as amused and bewildered and dazzled as if at a masquerade. Here is the abiding charm of these volumes. They abound in the illustrations of the period, and still more in sketches and portraits. There a sweep by us a whole bevy of ladies, with hoops and head-dresses that come in collision now and then with the chandeliers. In details of their love-making, and their marriages, these volumes are more than ordinarily rich. The Royal characters (George III. Queen Charlotte, and their jubilant family) which figure in them are even more interesting than the noble and gentle men and dames who flock, bow, and cringe before them. A book that may speedily be in so many hands needs no further illustration.'—ATHENÆUM.

Seventh Edition. In crown 8vo. price 6s.

EAST LYNNE.

By Mrs. HENRY WOOD, Author of 'The Channings.'

In 2 vols. post 8vo. 15s.

LIVES OF THE QUEENS OF ENGLAND OF THE HOUSE OF HANOVER.

By Dr. DORAN.

'These "Lives" indicate afresh the wealth and variety of Dr. Doran's collections.'—ATHENÆUM.
'An extraordinary repertory of facts and anecdotes.'—SPECTATOR.

Used at Eton and other Public Schools.

THE ANDROMACHE OF EURIPIDES;

With Suggestions and Questions at the foot of each page; together with Copious Grammatical and Critical Notes; also with a Brief Introductory Account of the Greek Drama, Dialects, and Principal Tragic Metres.

By the Rev. J. EDWARDS, M.A., and Rev. C. HAWKINS, B.C.L.

A Greek Play, prepared for Schools.

Price 1s.

THE AUTOBIOGRAPHY OF A WORKING MAN.

By the Hon. Miss E. EDEN.

In crown 8vo. price 5s.

CHAPTERS ON WIVES.

By Mrs. ELLIS, Author of 'The Mothers of Great Men,' &c.

In 8vo. with three beautiful Portraits, 5s.

NARRATIVE OF HER LIFE DURING THE GREAT FRENCH REVOLUTION.

By Mrs. DALRYMPLE ELLIOTT.

'When Mrs. Elliott returned to this country, and the gossip of what she had heard, seen, and suffered reached George the Third, it cannot be matter of surprise that he should wish to have her own statement in writing. He must have read it with no little interest, which may be shared by everybody who takes up the volume.'
NOTES AND QUERIES.

In post 8vo. With numerous Illustrations. 10s. 6d.

JAPAN, AND RESIDENCE AT NAGASAKI IN 1859-60.

By C. PEMBERTON HODGSON, H.M. Consul.

Post 8vo. 7s. 6d.

LIFE OF DR. JOHN JEBB,
Bishop of Limerick.

By the Rev. CHARLES FORSTER.

Vols. 1, 2, 3, 4. 8vo. 14s. each. Sold separately.

PERSONAL MEMOIRS OF HIS OWN TIME.

By FRANÇOIS GUIZOT.

'Will be devoured as a history of our own times by one of the most conspicuous men now alive, and will be referred to hereafter when much popular literature will have been devoured by the worms. Guizot is a man of genius—and genius is immortality. This is one of the few books that will mark the generation that gives it birth.'—ATHENÆUM.

Bentley's Edition, the only unabridged Edition. Post 8vo. 2s. 6d.

LECTURES ON COMPARATIVE PHYSICAL GEOGRAPHY
In its relation to the History of Mankind.

By PROFESSOR GUYOT.

'We have never seen the science of physical geography explained with greater clearness and elegance.'
ATHENÆUM.

8vo. 1s.

AN ADDRESS TO THE UNIVERSITY OF EDINBURGH.

By the Right Hon. W. E. GLADSTONE.

With numerous Illustrations, Map, &c. 8vo. 9s.

THE HISTORY OF THE MUTINIES IN OUDH.

By MARTIN GUBBINS.

'The second edition is enriched by two notable narratives—a lady's escape from Sultanpore, and Major Eyre's account of the famous Arrah expedition. This is the most important book on the siege of Lucknow yet published, or ever likely to be published.'—EXAMINER.

THE LIFE OF RICHARD III.

AND MEMOIRS OF SOME OF HIS CONTEMPORARIES.

With an Historical Drama of the Battle of Bosworth.

By JOHN HENEAGE JESSE, Esq., Author of 'The Court of England under the Stuarts,' &c.

'Mr. Jesse is a very honest writer, and deals fairly with evidence, and is no sophist. He brings out in a most salient manner the good points of Richard's character. He has here given us an interesting book.'—SATURDAY REVIEW.

AN ARCTIC BOAT VOYAGE IN THE AUTUMN OF 1854.

By ISAAC T. HAYES.

Edited, with an Introduction and Notes, by Dr. NORTON SHAW.

KING CHARLES THE FIRST IN THE ISLE OF WIGHT;

WITH ORIGINAL LETTERS FROM THE KING.

By W. HILLIER.

HINTS TO CHRISTIANS ON THE USE OF THE TONGUE.

By the Rev. G. W. HERVEY.

Edited, with an Introduction, by the Rev. STEPHEN JENNER.

ESSAYS ON ART AND LITERATURE.

By Mrs. JAMESON.

MADELINE: A TALE OF AUVERGNE.

By JULIA KAVANAGH.

New Edition, in 2 vols. 8vo. 21s.

THE HISTORY OF CHRISTIAN CHURCHES AND SECTS,

FROM THE EARLIEST AGES OF CHRISTIANITY.

CONTENTS:

Church of Abyssinia—The Albigenses—Episcopal Church of America—Anglo-Catholics—Arians—Armenian Church—Armenians—Baptists — United Brethren, &c. &c.—United Brethren—The Brownists—The Calvinists—The Covenanters—The Donatists—The Church of England— The Church of Scotland—Free Church of Scotland—The French Protestant Church—The Society of Friends—The Greek Church—Gnostics—Lady Huntingdon's Connexion—Independents—Church of Ireland—Irvingites—Lutherans—Mormonites—Nestorians—Presbyterians—Puritans—Church of Rome—Church of Russia—Scottish Episcopal Church—Shakers—Swedenborgians—Unitarians—Universalists—Wesleyans—Wesleyan Methodist New Connexion.

By the Rev. J. B. MARSDEN.

'Probably the best book on the subject current in our literature.'—ATHENÆUM.
'Mr. Marsden's information is well digested, his judgment sound and impartial, his manner of statement not only clear, but with a sustained vividness. The work has somewhat the appearance of an Encyclopædia, but it is only in appearance. The exposition has the freshness of an original work. The philosophic impartiality of the author should not be passed over. He has, of course, opinions, but he indulges in no violence or harshness of censure. The arrangement is well adapted for the important point of conveying complete and full information.'—SPECTATOR.
'Possesses the essential quality of accuracy, and the style is smooth and clear. It is a most useful book of reference on all subjects connected with ecclesiastical history.'—MORNING CHRONICLE.
'Full, accurate, and impartial.'—LITERARY GAZETTE.
'Supplies a want long felt by the clerical student.'—MORNING POST
'Mr. Marsden's History has a fair chance of becoming widely known in England, and also in Scotland. The work exhibits high literary power and a thorough appreciation of the elements requisite for popularising a theme which all the dulness of the many who have written on it can never render wholly uninteresting.'—EDINBURGH GUARDIAN.

1 vol. post 8vo. 5s.

MEMOIRS OF REMARKABLE CHARACTERS:

Nelson, Bossuet, Milton, Oliver Cromwell, &c.

By M. LAMARTINE.

'This work will materially raise the reputation of Lamartine. Along with the brilliancy of style and warmth of imagination which characterise all his writings, we find here gravity of thought and earnestness of purpose. The subject also is well suited to his peculiar genius and talents. As a sketcher of historical scenes and of historical characters, choosing his own subjects, suggested by his own tastes or sympathies, no living author is capable of greater or more successful efforts. In this work we have a gallery of illustrious portraits, drawn in bold, striking style, and glowing with life-like feeling and expression.'—LITERARY GAZETTE.

In 8vo. 6s. With numerous fine Plans and Plates.

THE DEFENCE OF KARS:

A Military Work,

By General ATWELL LAKE.

Small 8vo. 3s. 6d.

LAST DAYS OF ALEXANDER OF RUSSIA AND FIRST DAYS OF NICHOLAS.

By Dr. JOHN LEE.

With Illustrations. 8vo. lithographs, 21s.

SHOOTING IN THE HIMALAYAS:

A Journal of Sporting Adventures and Travel in Chinese Tartary, India, Thibet, Cashmere, &c.

By General MARKHAM.

Crown 8vo. 5s.

ESSAYS ON SOME OF SHAKESPEARE'S CHARACTERS:

Sir John Falstaff, Jacques, Romeo, Bottom the Weaver, Lady Macbeth, Timon of Athens, Polonius, Iago, Hamlet.

By Dr. MAGINN.

New Edition. Crown 8vo. 6s. With two beautiful Portraits of the unfortunate Queen.

THE LIFE OF MARY QUEEN OF SCOTS.

Two Portraits. By M. MIGNET.

'The standard authority on the subject.'— DAILY NEWS.
'An impartial history of Mary Queen of Scots.'— LITERARY GAZETTE.
'A valuable and admirable model of thorough research and impartial statement.'— MANCHESTER REVIEW.
'Good service has been done to historical accuracy by the graphic work of M. Mignet. It will be in all our libraries, and re-read, as it deserves to be.'— MORNING POST.

Crown 8vo. Portrait. 5s.

SELECTIONS FROM HER CHOICE POETS AND PROSE WRITERS,

And Memoirs of her Literary Life.

By MARY RUSSELL MITFORD.

2 vols. post 8vo.

RAISING THE VEIL.

By JOHN POMEROY.

Fcp. 8vo. 2s. 6d.

NOTES ON NOSES.

By EDEN WARWICK.

Small 8vo. 5s.

THE LIFE OF THE REV. H. POLEHAMPTON,

The Chaplain of Lucknow.

Post 8vo. Vignettes, 7s. 6d.

KANGAROO LAND;

Or, Life in the Bush.

By the Rev. ARTHUR POLEHAMPTON.

'There is a moral in this book very opportune at the time when another gold fever is seizing the nation. We recommend this interesting narrative to all young men desirous of bettering their lot by emigration to the gold countries, the perusal of which we recommend to all weary of snug quarters at home, and think of trying their lot at the gold fields.'—ATHENÆUM.

Vols. 1 and 2, crown 8vo. 21s.

EARL RUSSELL'S
LIFE OF CHARLES JAMES FOX.

2 vols. 8vo. 9s.

THE DIARIES AND CORRESPONDENCE OF
THE RIGHT HON. GEORGE ROSE.

WORKS BY THE AUTHOR OF 'MARY POWELL.'

Crown, 3s. 6d.

THE STORY OF ITALY.

Post 8vo. 4s. 6d.

TOWN AND FOREST:

A Story of Hainault Forest.

———

Fcp. 8vo. 2s. 6d.

SALAD FOR THE SOCIAL.

CONTENTS:

Bookcraft — Money — The Toilette — Pulpit Peculiarities — Mysteries of Medicine — The Humours of Law — Larcenies of Literature, &c. &c.

———

Fcp. 8vo. 2s. 6d.

BYE-LANES AND DOWNS OF ENGLAND;

With Turf Scenes and Characters.

With a Portrait of Lord George Bentinck. By SYLVANUS.

———

2s. 6d.; rose cloth, 3s. 6d.

SAY AND SEAL.

By AUTHOR of 'WIDE, WIDE WORLD.'

———

Fcp. 8vo. 3s.

A BOOK FOR A RAINY DAY;

Or, Recollections of the Events of the Years 1766—1833.

By J. S. SMITH, Author of 'The Life of Nollekens.'

———

Crown, 5s.

RAMBLES THROUGH THE STREETS OF LONDON;

With Anecdotes of their more Celebrated Residents.

In post 8vo. 5s.

THE STORY OF CAWNPORE.

By Capt. MOWBRAY THOMSON.

In post 8vo. 5s.

TYPES AND ANTITYPES OF THE OLD AND NEW TESTAMENT.

By Lady SCOTT.

In fcp. 8vo. 1s. 6d.

TRUTH ANSWERS BEST;

Or, Jean and Nicolette.

By the Rev. C. B. TAYLER.

Fcp. bound as a present, 4s.

NOT OF THE WORLD;

Or, Lady Mary.

By the Rev. C. B. TAYLER.

In 2 vols. post 8vo. 7s. 6d.

VONVED THE DANE, THE ROVER OF THE BALTIC.

Fcp. 8vo. 5s.

SELECTIONS FROM THE WRITINGS OF ARCHBISHOP WHATELY.

Bound as a present, 5s.

THE MARTYRS OF CARTHAGE:
A Tale of the Times of Old.

By Mrs. WEBB.

A NEW PHRASEOLOGICAL LATIN DICTIONARY,

For the use of Eton, Winchester, Harrow, and Rugby Schools, and King's College, London.

By C. D. YONGE, Author of the 'English-Greek Lexicon,' 'The New Latin Gradus,' for Eton, Winchester, Harrow, Rugby, &c.

Part   I.—ENGLISH-LATIN, in post 8vo. 9s. 6d.
Part II.—LATIN-ENGLISH, in post 8vo. 7s. 6d.

The Two Parts bound together in One Volume, 15s.

It was suggested to Mr. Yonge, some years ago, to undertake this work. It has been submitted to the most eminent scholars and Masters of Schools in the kingdom (Dr. Goodford, Head Master of Eton; Dr. Maberly, of Winchester; Dr. Vaughan, of Harrow; Dr. Goulburn, of Rugby; and Dr. Jelf, of King's College, London), who all agree that a careful examination of Mr. Yonge's Dictionary has convinced them that it would *fully* supply the want so greatly felt.

They have, in consequence, authorised the book to be described as published 'For the use of Eton, Winchester, Harrow, and Rugby Schools, and King's College, London ;' and ordered that it shall be, for the future, the only English-Latin Dictionary used in those, the principal places of education in the kingdom.

' A very capital book, either for the somewhat advanced pupil, the student who aims at acquiring an idiomatic Latin style, or the adult with a knowledge of the language, who wishes to examine the differences between the structure and expressions of the English and Latin tongues by a short and ready mode. It is the best—we were going to say the only really useful—Anglo-Latin Dictionary we ever met with.'—SPECTATOR.

Post 8vo. 7s. 6d.

A NEW VIRGIL,
With the Notes of Hawtrey, Key, and Munro.

Edited by C. D. YONGE.

SPOTTISWOODE AND CO., PRINTERS, NEW-STREET SQUARE, LONDON

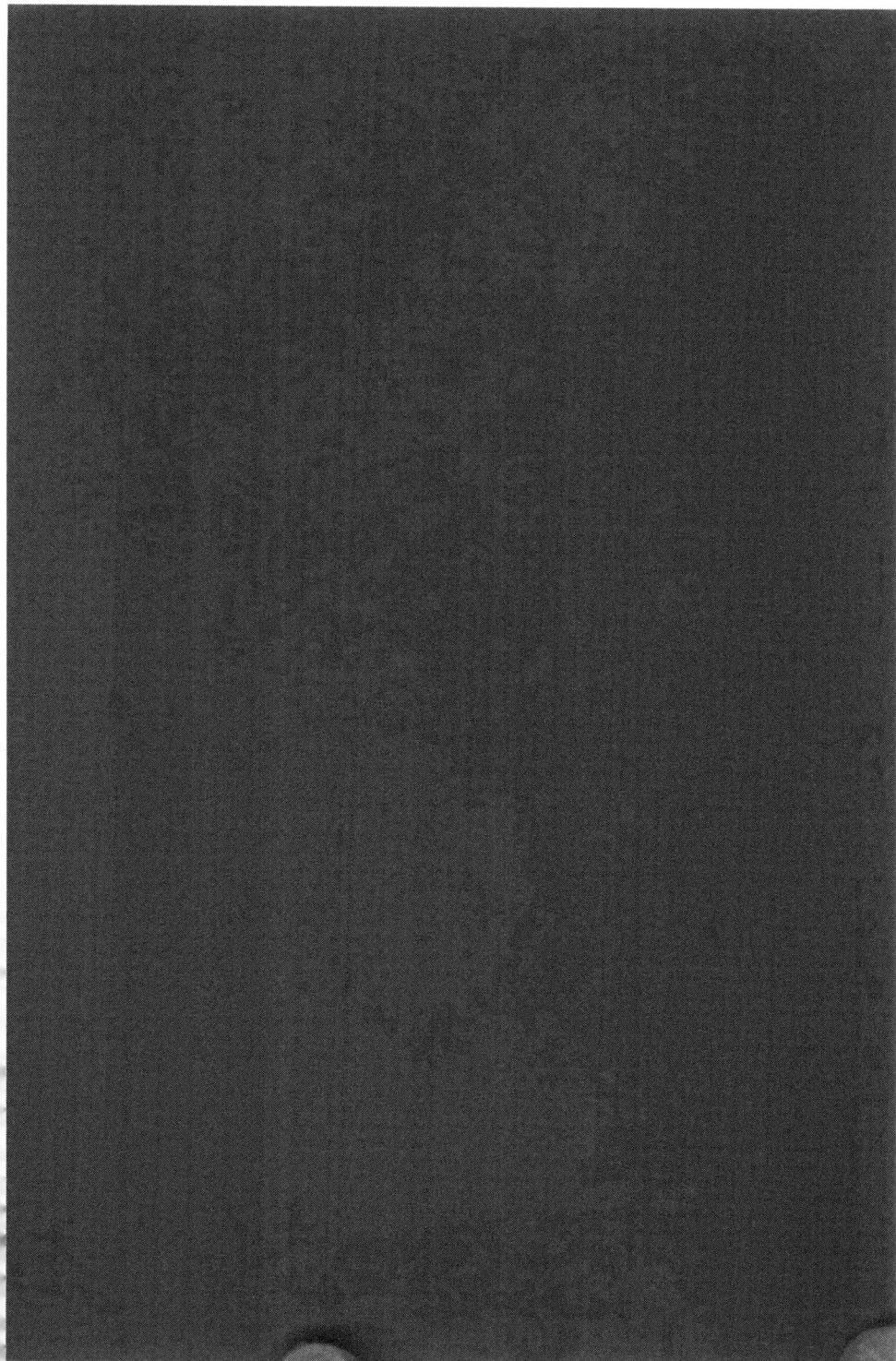

Lightning Source UK Ltd.
Milton Keynes UK
UKHW021110101219
355076UK00008B/275/P

9 780343 222840